T0272641

Origin Uncertain

Origin Uncertain

Unraveling the Mysteries of Etymology

ANATOLY LIBERMAN

OXFORD
UNIVERSITY PRESS

Oxford University Press is a department of the University of Oxford. It furthers
the University's objective of excellence in research, scholarship, and education
by publishing worldwide. Oxford is a registered trade mark of Oxford University
Press in the UK and certain other countries.

Published in the United States of America by Oxford University Press
198 Madison Avenue, New York, NY 10016, United States of America.

© Oxford University Press 2024

Library of Congress Cataloging-in-Publication Data
Names: Liberman, Anatoly, author.
Title: Origin uncertain : unraveling the mysteries of etymology / Anatoly Liberman.
Description: New York, NY : Oxford University Press, 2024. |
Includes bibliographical references and index.
Identifiers: LCCN 2023046751 | ISBN 9780197664919 (hardback) |
ISBN 9780197664933 (epub) | ISBN 9780197664940 (ebook)
Subjects: LCSH: English language—Etymology. | English language—History.
Classification: LCC PE1571 .L54 2024 | DDC 422—dc23/eng/20231204
LC record available at https://lccn.loc.gov/2023046751

DOI: 10.1093/oso/9780197664919.001.0001

Printed by Sheridan Books, Inc., United States of America

Contents

Introduction

The Ways of Words and Word Hunters

> But the dictionary-maker must expect, on the one hand, to be snubbed when he makes a mistake, and on the other, to be neglected when he is right.
>
> —*Notes and Queries* 7/X, 1890, 253

This book is not a dictionary, but since it is about words, the epigraph—borrowed from an old and venerable periodical and to which multiple references will grace the pages that follow—may not be out of place. Therefore, I'll begin with a few remarks about why and how I put together this volume and what the reader will find in it.

More than thirty years ago, I began working on a new dictionary of English word origins. The project resulted in a hefty "Introduction" to that dictionary, a stream of papers, a voluminous bibliography, and, most recently, an explanatory and etymological dictionary of English idioms (*Take My Word for It*). In 2005, Oxford University Press, after it brought out my book *Word Origins . . . and How We Know Them*, invited me to take over its incipient blog "Oxford Etymologist." I was happy to accept the offer, and, on March 1, 2006, the blog was born. Since that day, my posts on the history of English words have been appearing almost every Wednesday. Seventeen years later, on March 1, 2023, I submitted to the Press the book you have now opened. On Oxford University Press's invitation, I had reread my close to eight hundred posts, selected the most interesting ones, edited or rewritten them from scratch, and organized the stories into a semi-coherent whole.

Libraries are swamped with books on English words. We may wonder: Does the world need one more? This question is not for me to answer (obviously, I cannot be objective in assessing my own contribution), but I can say something about why I agreed to embark on this project. *Every short essay in the book is the result of my research.* I did not succeed in solving all or even most riddles that had bedeviled my numerous predecessors, sometimes for centuries (to expect such a result would be unrealistic), but, in dealing with etymological riddles, I said something that I had learned from reading and assessing the achievements of countless language historians from the sixteen hundreds on. In most cases, I also ventured to offer an approach to what I considered to be a reasonable solution. Yet in the chapters that follow, references to the scholarly literature have been reduced to the barest minimum. Those who are interested in following and evaluating my sources will find them in twenty or so languages in *A Bibliography of English Etymology* (University of Minnesota, 2010).

Strange as some people may think, it often takes a greater effort to write a good "popular" book than a scholarly one. In a work addressed to specialists, the reader's knowledge of the main facts and special terminology is taken for granted. Not so in the popular genre! In 1906, Joseph Dent founded Everyman's Library, which became an immensely popular book series (it still exists and brings out excellent works). Its motto was borrowed from an anonymous medieval morality play: "Everyman, I will go with thee and be thy guide, / In thy most need to go by thy side." Dent meant that he would be publishing first-rate books in all areas, not that he would cater to the needs of the nonexistent average reader. But a book like the present one[1] should, ideally, be accessible *and interesting* to a high school student and a professional linguist. The same holds for my blog. Walking such a tightrope has not been easy. To most of today's college students, to say nothing of the general population, even terms like *voiced consonant* and *superlative degree* are new. (Ernest Weekley, my role model in the popular genre, faced a better-prepared readership.) Though, luckily, this volume is about neither phonetics nor grammar, some initial information about word history should be given a short introduction.

---

[1] This may be a proper place to express my sincere gratitude to Mr. David A. Coats for his help in editing the book.

Some English words are late, while others are old and even very old. Their origins are often equally hard to penetrate or reconstruct. This book opens with a chapter titled, mockingly, "Words Whose Origin Has Bothered You for Years." As a matter of fact, most people have never heard, let alone used, any one of them. But once you have read that chapter, you will realize what it takes to dig through the dust of many centuries in search of the impulse that resulted in the coining of an adjective, a noun, or a verb.

One does not have to be a linguist to notice that languages are related. Think of French and Italian, German and Dutch, Swedish and Norwegian, Lithuanian and Latvian, Russian and Ukrainian. But it is far from obvious that English is related to Lithuanian or Russian. The great linguist Roman Jakobson (1896–1982), who was born and educated in Moscow and came to the United States at the beginning of World War II, sometimes taught advanced courses on Slavic subjects in Russian. When other graduate students at Harvard complained that this practice prevented them from joining such classes (everybody wanted to listen to Jakobson, regardless of the subject matter), reportedly, he used to answer: "Try to understand. Russian is easy." Perhaps it is a joke, one of those often invented about luminaries, but an etymologist must indeed "try to understand" all kinds of languages.

Be that as it may, in the remote past, English and, for instance, Norwegian, were much closer to each other than they are today, though even some time around 890, the English King Alfred almost certainly could not understand the Norwegian Ottar (Ohthere) without the help of an interpreter. (Ohthere's report of his travels has been preserved only in English.) Likewise, in the fourth century, no German would have been able to understand a Goth, whose language (Gothic) we happen to know rather well. And yet, some old language, called Common Germanic or Proto-Germanic, seems to have existed, though even then it, of course, consisted of various dialects.

The same holds for Proto-Slavic, Proto-Celtic, and Proto-Romance. The existence of Proto-Romance is easy to accept because we know that Italian, Spanish, Portuguese, and French, along with some other languages, indeed developed from Latin, even though an overlay of indigenous dialects did not go anywhere. By contrast, Proto-Germanic, Proto-Celtic, and Proto-Slavic are the products of reconstruction.

Finally, most languages spoken in Eurasia from Norway to Ceylon form a family that is now called "Indo-European."

How, then, is it possible to learn the origin of a word? Let us look at an easy case. *Dude* and *dandy* are nineteenth-century creations. *Dude* was coined in American English, while *dandy* is a British invention. The great *Oxford English Dictionary* (the *OED*) gives the date of every word's first occurrence in texts, handwritten for the pre-Gutenberg times and printed for the post-1450 epoch. Obviously, if some author mentioned a word in, say, 1730, unless it is his or her coinage, it must have turned up in the language at least a bit earlier, but the time interval between the word's "day of birth" and its first occurrence in a text need not have been too long. Antedating the *OED* is a favorite occupation of countless word lovers, but dramatically earlier dates than those given there are found very rarely.

Strange as it may seem, the origin of even *dandy* and *dude* (don't they sound alike, with their *d-d* roots?) still remains a matter of intelligent guessing. Nonspecialists do not always realize that every word must have been launched into existence by a creative individual and that such is the history of every innovation and every discovery. If the novelty (in our case, the word) finds approval by the community, it survives, and the inventor's name is soon forgotten. Sometimes we remember who coined the words we use: *gas, robot, serendipity, chortle,* and a few others are among them. Does that mean that, as far as origins are concerned, *ax(e)* and *brain*, to cite two random examples from the book, have the same humble origins as *dude* and *dandy*? No doubt, unless you believe that, throughout history, there have been countless committees responsible for creating words. Jacob Grimm, whom most people associate only with fairy tales but who was, first and foremost, a great historical linguist, once said, "People create" (the German phrase was: "*Das Volk dichtet*"). They sure do, but not "collectively." Hiccoughs and coughs are natural phenomena, while the words designating them were produced by individuals.

Even when we know something about the documented early stages of a word, we may not be able to find the sought-for etymology. It is no longer a secret who used *dude* for the first time. But did that man coin the word, and, if he did, how did he arrive at his creation? Unfortunately, there is no one to ask. *Dude* is a lucky case; *dandy* much less so. But what about *brain* (another random example)? The word goes back to the earliest period. Consequently, we cannot even hope to find out who called the gray matter this.

The history of recorded English is traditionally divided into three periods. The name of "Old English" has been given to the period from the oldest written texts in the language—that is, roughly from 650 to the Battle of Hastings (1066) or, according to a more generous estimation, to 1150. Thus, King Alfred, who died in 899, spoke Old English. By the same token, *Beowulf* was also composed and written in Old English. Printing came to England in 1477, and the Reformation began there in 1534. Those are roughly the dates associated with the next period, known as "Middle English." Consequently, Chaucer (1342/1343–1400) composed in Middle English, while Shakespeare (1564–1616) belongs with early Modern English.

How can we discover the origin of a word like *brain*? In such cases, language historians try to find out whether similar-sounding words have been recorded in Frisian, Dutch, German, Scandinavian, and Gothic, all of which are Germanic and related to English. Perhaps in one of them, its lookalike is less opaque and (an ideal case) can be interpreted as "the inside of the skull" or "a sustaining dish," or anything along such lines. To us, *brain* is an arbitrary combination of three consonants and two vowels. If a sought-for word turns up, we will say that it probably once existed in English but changed its form beyond recognition. Think of a word like *bo's'n*. Unless you have been told that *bo's'n* is a so-called allegro form of *boatswain*, its etymology will remain as puzzling as the etymology of *brain*.

Unfortunately, our search will yield no promising results because *brain* is rather isolated in Germanic, and its lookalike also means "brain" and nothing else. Faced with this result, the etymologist begins to examine the words for "brain" in as many languages as possible. Does at least one of them exist that is transparent? If so, does it provide a clue to our problem? The words to be examined need not sound alike even if they are related. English *two* is reminiscent of German *zwei*, Latin *duo*, and Russian *dva*. But English *four* hardly resembles Latin *quatuor*. Yet they are related, though in a rather obscure way. Apparently, a language historian should know how to compare words across language borders, and, indeed, books are full of such rules.

Related words are called *cognates*. The word we are investigating may have cognates or be completely isolated. If no help comes from anywhere, intelligent guessing begins.

"Anywhere" can also mean "from another language." One thing is to say that the numeral *two* has a cognate in Latin (*duo*), and something quite different is the statement that *duet* is an eighteenth-century "loan" from Italian. A single example from this book will suffice. The word *awning* is hopelessly opaque, but since such a word exists, someone must have coined it. This someone may have heard it from a foreigner or come across it in a book in a language other than English, liked it, but perhaps remembered it with a mistake, and introduced it to a group of friends. Now everybody knows this word and tries to guess where it came from. Native? Or from Hindi, Persian, or French? All those sources have been suggested, quite often by serious and well-informed researchers. "Origin uncertain," as our dictionaries tell us. And *awning* is an eighteenth-century noun, rather than a mysterious noun of two thousand years ago!

All this goes a long way toward explaining why the literature on etymology is so huge. Some of the hardest words have been attacked multiple times and yet retain the label "origin uncertain"! This verdict rarely means that no one has ever said anything about the word's etymology. Usually the opposite is true: many astute scholars have dealt with the problem but failed to achieve persuasive results. *Awning* has just been mentioned. Another example of this situation is the history of attempts to "decipher" the Middle English word *henchman*, to which a long essay is devoted in Chapter 3. That essay reads like a thriller, with villains and casualties at every step. All the elements of a good detective story are present, except that the "criminal" has left the investigators partly at bay.

The readers of this book are of course never dispatched without some information. Everything they need to know is explained along the way. However, mention of two things will not be out of place here. We have no way of discovering when and how language originated (though, predictably, several good theories exist on this score), but it may not be too adventurous to suggest that the impulses behind word creation have not changed too radically over the millennia. English speakers believe that pigs "say" *oink-oink*, while dogs go *bow-wow, woof-woof,* or *ruff-ruff*. Though fifteen hundred years ago, the Germanic invaders who settled in Britain heard the same sounds and probably invented similar words, we miss the record of those creations. The possibilities are not too few. For example, the Japanese hear *boo-boo*, Russians prefer *khriu-khriu*, while Swedes render the grunt with the help of the combination *nöff-nöff*. To be honest, I am not sure how good pigs are at producing umlauted vowels. Though, of course, pigs "say" nothing like it, I have a partiality for the Swedish version because, in the picture book of my childhood, the three little pigs were called Niff-Niff, Noof-Noof, and Nuff-Nuff. Be that as it may, *oink-oink* and the rest of them are also words, and each has an etymology.

Such words are sound-imitative, and that's all there is to it, except that *sound imitation* has a learned synonym: *onomatopoeia*. Not only the likes of *bow-wow* are sound-imitative. English *cough* probably began its existence in the form *cohhian*, and *laugh* goes back to *hlahhian*. Apparently, those who coined *laugh* did not refer to merriment but treated it like *cough* (a deep guttural sound). It is tempting to explain *splash*, *screech*, *thud*, *bump*, and many other words as onomatopoeias. As usual in such cases, one seldom knows where to stop. Does *sneeze* also belong here? Once we leave the most obvious words (i.e., *woof-woof* and its likes), we are seldom sure. Is *plump* sound-imitative? The Latin for "lead," the name of a metal, is *plumbum* (hence English *plumber*). Otto Jespersen, a famous linguist, thought that the word was onomatopoeic: Roman speakers, he asserted, would drop a piece of this heavy metal into water, hear *plumb!*, and call lead accordingly. Is such a hypothesis credible? The existence of the English verb *to plump* "to sink heavily" perhaps bears out Jespersen's suggestion. This book has numerous references to words like *sneeze* and *plump* (see *sound imitation* in the subject index).

Snot seems to have something to do with *snout* and reminds one of *sneeze*. Snotty people are often snobs. Sneaking is sometimes uncomfortable, regardless of whether, a few days ago, you sneaked or snuck out from an important but dull meeting. One begins to react to the initial group *sn-* as having a life of its own. *Snip, snap, sniff, snuff, snub, snort, snivel, sneer*. . . . The list goes on for quite some time. Then we encounter *snow* and realize that there is no law or rule here, but a strong aftertaste remains.

The group *sl-* behaves in a similar way. So many things are slovenly, sloppy, slippery, and slimy, and so many people are sly that when we encounter the adjective *sleazy* and discover what it means, we feel vindicated. What else could *sleazy* refer to? Initial *sn-* and *sl-* are, to use the term invented for such cases, *sound-symbolic*. Sound symbolism is not always easy to distinguish from sound imitation. Both may be evasive, but both phenomena must have played a decisive role in the word creation of old, and they are equally virile today. Sound-imitative and sound-symbolic words are born, die, and are created again. Friedrich Nietzsche's idea of an eternal return fits such creations with amazing accuracy.

Studying word origins is like participating in an eternal carnival. Masks beckon to you, invite, tease, give a kiss, or bamboozle by unrealistic promises. All is about *snipp*, *snapp*, *snorrum*, an incantation Hans Christian Andersen liked, or, to use Hemingway's phrase, a moveable feast.

1

Words Whose Origin Has Bothered You for Years

One, Two, Three, Alairy . . .

Girls, in many parts of the English-speaking world, say, or rather recite, while bouncing a ball: "One, two, three, alairy, four, five, six, alairy," and so on. According to an "eyewitness report," they say so while bouncing a ball on the ground, catching it with one hand, keeping the score, and accompanying each *alairy* with a circular swing of the leg to describe a loop around but not obstruct the rising ball. Each time *alairy* is said, another author explains, the player lifts her right foot over the ball, crossing the right leg over the left, but where I wrote *alairy*, she heard *aleary*, changed by folk etymology to *O'Leary*. Other people knowledgeable in such matters report that the nonsensical word sometimes rhymes with *airy* and sometimes with *eerie*. (However, see the last note below!) *O'Leary ~ O'Laery* may be left to his (her?) ghostly fate, but where did girls learn the word *alairy/aleary*?

Counting out rhymes and children's verbal folklore is astoundingly conservative. Empires collapse, rulers come and go with promises of the kingdom of heaven on earth, but Russian girls keep saying: "Éniki, béniki, sikolisá/ Éniki, béniki, bá" (*á* has the value of *ah* in English *bah*). It may seem that only a hopeless dullard or a bookworm who has never seen the light of day or a playing child will ponder the etymology of such gibberish. Look before you leap and don't jump to conclusions. (Isn't it odd that English has at least five synonymous verbs: *jump*, *leap*, *spring*, *bound*, and *hop*, and each suggests a slightly different movement?) Those who have as much as looked at the *Annotated Mother Goose* or ever wondered why the counting-out rhyme *eeny-meeny-miny-moe* has spread over almost the whole world know how deep the roots of such gibberish may be. Children's games are sometimes the last resort of ancient customs that have lost their cultic significance. Therefore, their wording deserves the attention of linguists, anthropologists, and specialists in comparative religion. However, *alairy* won't take us to such depths of history or human psyche.

Several researchers have tried to explain the origin of *alairy/aleary* and offered the same explanation, unaware of the attempts of their predecessors. (This is a common case in etymological studies. Indeed, how do you find out publications on any word, especially on such an exotic one? I have the advantage of having the voluminous *Bibliography of English Etymology* that my team compiled over the years. It was published by the University of Minnesota Press in 2010, and it is being constantly updated.)

There once lived a poet named William Langland (ca. 1332–1400), a contemporary of Chaucer from the West Midlands. As follows from the dates, he wrote in a language we now call "Middle English." In his long and once popular poem titled *Piers Plowman*, among many other things, a gang of impostors is described. They are beggars feigning bodily defects. *Some leide here leggis a-lery, as suche losellis cunne*, that is, "some laid their legs *a-lery*, as such abandoned wretches (louts, scoundrels) know how to do."

Some disagreement exists about *how* they "laid" their legs, but, apparently, the beggars looked as though they had only one leg or no legs at all. They pretended to be cripples in order to arouse compassion and extort alms. The trick is no secret to actors who have to impersonate a one-legged character, for example, Long John Silver in *Treasure Island* or an invalid with one limb amputated. It must have been practiced by mountebanks since the beginning of creation. *Alery* never occurs in other Middle English texts, and even contemporary scribes seemed to have trouble with it, for they wrote *a leery, a liry, a lyrye, a liri*, and *alery*, or substituted another word for it. According to a plausible suggestion, Langland used a cant term badly understood outside the circle of professional mendicants.

The meager information we have about Langland has been culled from his poem. He was born in Shropshire but later moved to London. According to one of the histories of English literature, he was a kind of clerical vagabond and earned his bread by singing *Paternoster, Placebo, Dirige*, the Psalter, and the Psalms for the souls of those who contributed to his support. He must have spent days and months on the road and acquired firsthand knowledge of the ragtag and bobtail he described.

The prefix a- in a-lery and its variants goes back to on (as in Modern English atop, aboard, and so forth). The Old English noun lira has also been attested, and the Oxford English Dictionary (OED) has the entry lire "flesh, muscle, brawn" (obsolete except Scottish and northern dialectal). Whatever the status of alery in Middle English might be, Old English lira was not a chance word. It turned up several times and had unquestionable Scandinavian cognates. But "on the flesh" is hard to interpret, and the line from Piers Plowman has been tentatively translated "made their legs lame, acted as if paralyzed" and "crossed their legs or thighs." The second translation, suggested by Walter W. Skeat, the author of the poem's earliest academic edition and a great etymologist, fits the modern girls' chant (he offered his translation without referring to the chant, which he may or may not have heard from his daughter), but it takes the edge off the beggars' trick, for what is so pathetic about crossing one's legs? Though Skeat seems to have interpreted the line correctly, we still do not quite understand the implication of being cross-legged.

Is it possible that an obscure, extremely rare word should have come down to us in a children's game? To begin with, lire, as we have seen, is not obsolete in the northern part of Great Britain. Second (and here I can add something to what I have found in the works of my predecessors), while reading Charles Mackay's 1877 book The Gaelic Etymology of the Languages of Western Europe and More Especially of the English and Lowland Scotch, and of their Slang, Cant, and Colloquial Dialects, I ran into the curious low slang word chickaleary "aged pedestrians on winter mornings" (evidently, a collective noun). The book, as one can conclude from its incredible title, is useless (a ludicrous tribute to Celtomania in etymology), but Mackay knew both branches of Gaelic and northern English very well, and, as I can testify from long experience, the forms he cites are always reliable. I was struck by the amusing specificity of the word chickaleary, a word that Mackay, predictably, derived from a Gaelic compound.

In light of what has been said above, the origin of chickaleary is almost obvious. It designates elderly people unsteady on their feet because they are perhaps drowsy and because, on a frosty morning, roads are slippery (I assume that *chickaleary* is a collective noun). Criminals' wicked sense of humor is famous. Those potential victims of robbery were "chicks." Their legs were often "aleary," they stumbled and fell down. While helping them rise from the ground, one could pick their pockets. The *a* in the middle of the word is the same as in *jack-a-napes, rag-a-muffin*, and *cock-a doodle-doo*. It may be a relic of *on* or *of*, but sometimes it is inserted for rhythmic purposes.

If my idea has merit, Middle English *alery* has survived as a "cant word" (it has been vulgar throughout its history) and (!) in an innocent girls' game. Let us note that the researcher who suggested that Langland's word must have been cant did not know Mackay's book, while Mackay was, most probably, ignorant of the occurrence of *alery* in *Piers Plowman*. It remains to be said that *leer* "malicious look," *leery* "distrustful" (derived from *leer*), and German *leer* "empty" have nothing to do with the word discussed above.

Note

I am aware of three publications on the history of the word *alairy*: G. Legman, "One, Two, Three, A-Lairy." *American Notes and Queries*, 5, 1945, 72; Eric Colledge, "Aliri." *Medium Ævum* 27, 1958, 111–13; and Sister Mary Jeremy " 'Leggis a-lery,'" *Piers Plowman* A VII, 114." *English Language Notes* 1, 1964, 250–51.

The essay on *alairy* was posted on April 4, 2007 (search for "Oxford Etymologist" and either add that date or the title as above). Never in the history of this blog have I received so many comments. The most recent one appeared in March 2020! Those comments are a valuable resource for anyone interested in children's games and children's folklore. Readers from all over the English-speaking world shared their memories of the bouncing game and offered numerous variants of the words accompanying it. Predictably, they did not comment on the etymology of *alairy*, but the explanation given above is, most probably, correct.

Aroint Thee

Dozens of words have not been forgotten only because Shakespeare used them. *Scotch* (as in *scotch the snake*), *bare bodkin*, and dozens of others would have taken their quietus and slept peacefully in the majestic graveyard of the *OED* but for their appearance in Shakespeare's plays. *Aroint* would certainly have been unknown but for its appearance in *Macbeth* and *King Lear*. This is a passage from the speech of the first witch (*Macbeth* III, opening scene): "A sailor's wife had chestnuts in her lap, / And munch'd and munch'd and munch'd.—'Give me,' quoth I: / 'Aroint thee, witch!' the rump-fed ronyon cries." And in *King Lear*, Edgar, pretending to be mad (III. 4, 129), also says "Aroint thee."

The origin of *aroint* has been the object of an intense search. In 1874, Horace H. Furness, the editor of the variorum edition of Shakespeare, knew almost everything said about the word but confined himself to a dispassionate survey of opinions without comment. Very long ago, in Cheshire, *rynt*, *roynt*, and *runt* were recorded. Milkmaids in those quarters would say "*rynt thee* to a cow, when she is milked, to bid her get out of the way." The phrase meant "stand off." "To this the cow is so well used that even the word is sufficient." *Rynt you, witch* as part of the proverbial saying *rynt you, witch, said Besse Locket to her mother* turned up in a provincial dictionary published in 1674, approximately sixty years after *Macbeth* and *King Lear* were written. The lady whom Robert Nares, the author of an 1822 glossary of obscure words, consulted, added: "the cow being in this instance more learned than the commentators on Shakespeare." The taunt missed its target: philologists are not cows, and neither the lady nor the milch cows elucidated the word's origin. (In my experience, no one understands the word *milch*, and that is why I have used it here.)

The derivation of *aroint* as a compound from some verb for "go" and a cognate of *(be)hind* hardly merits attention. The familiar dialectal pronunciation of *jint* for *joint* suggests that the original vowel in the verb *rynt* was *oi*, not *i*. Old English had the verb *rȳman* "to make room" (read long ȳ as German ü in über), and Walter W. Skeat derived *aroint* from the phrase *rime ta* (*ta* = *thee*), imperative, "which must necessarily become *rine ta* (if the *i* be long)." I am not sure why the change was necessary, but Skeat sometimes struck with excessive force. Anyway, he reasoned along the same lines as most of his predecessors and followers who thought that *aroint* meant "begone." A similar idea underlies several attempts to find a Romance etymon of *aroint*.

Horne Tooke, famous, among other things, for a two-volume book *Epea Pteroenta, Or, The Diversions of Purley* (1798–1805), traced Shakespeare's word to "*ronger, rogner, royner*; whence also *aroynt* . . . is a separation or discontinuity of the skin or flesh by a gnawing, eating forward, malady" (compare Italian *rogna* "scabies, mange" and *ronyon* in *Macbeth*, above). He obviously glossed *aroint* as "to be separated" and found several supporters. Other early candidates for the etymon known to me (for nearly all of which I am indebted to Furness's notes on *Macbeth* and *King Lear*) are French *arry-avant* "away there, ho!", *éreinte-toi* "break thy back or reins" (used as an imprecation), Latin *dii te averruncent* "may the devils take thee," and Italian *arranca*, the imperative of *arrancare* "plod along, trudge." A strong case has been made for *aroint* being a phonetic variant of *anoint* or acquiring in some contexts the figurative sense "thrash" (a defender of the latter derivation was George Hempl, a distinguished American philologist), or because it "conveys a sense very consistent with the common account of witches, who are related to perform many supernatural acts by means of unguents." Finally, Thomas Hearne's *Ectypa Varia ad Historiam Britannicam* . . . (1737) contains a print in which "a devil, who is driving the damned before him, is blowing a horn with a label issuing from his mouth and the words: 'Out, out Arongt.'" *Arongt* resembles *aroint*, but its existence does not clarify the etymology of either.

The opinions are many, but only one conclusion is almost certain. Shakespeare, a Stratford man, knew a local word, expected his audience to understand it even in London, and used it in his plays dated to the beginning of the seventeenth century. Thus, he did not invent *aroint*, and the suggestion that it is his adaptation of *around* cannot be entertained, for how would it then have passed into popular speech in that form? We have also seen that, in addition to witches, cows in Cheshire understood *aroint thee* and that the phrase became proverbial in some parts of England. The milkmaids' experience notwithstanding, it will probably not be too risky to propose that *aroint thee* was coined to ward off witches, damned souls, and their ilk (*arongt* does look identical with *aroint*) and that only later it spread to less ominous situations.

Perhaps the origin of *aroint thee* has not been discovered because nearly everybody glossed it as "begone, disappear, stand off." But (and this is my main point) *aroint thee* may have meant something like *beshrew thee, fie on you*. Louis Marder, in updating Furness's *Macbeth* (1963), said: "The local nature, the meaning, and form of the phrase, seem all opposed to its identity with Shakespeare's Aroint," because *ryndta!* in Cheshire and Lancashire is "merely a local pronunciation of 'round thee'= move around." Except for having doubts about the currency of *ryndta* in Lancashire, the *OED* endorsed this verdict. In my opinion, the *OED*'s *ryndta* does not necessarily have to go back to *round thee*, while the local character of the phrase cannot be used as an argument for or against its identity with what we find in *Macbeth* and *King Lear*.

At least as early as 1784, it was suggested that *aroint* has something to do with *rauntree*, one of several variants of the tree name *rowan*. This tree, perhaps better known as mountain ash, is famous in myth and folklore from Ancient Greece to Scandinavia. One of its alleged qualities is the ability to deter witches and protect people and cattle from evil. The great Scandinavian god Thor was once almost drowned in a river because of the wiles of a mighty giantess but threw a great stone at her, was carried ashore, caught hold of a rowan tree, and waded out of the water; hence the tree's name "Thor's rescue." It would be quite natural to shout *rauntree* or *rointree* in order to chase away a witch: on hearing the terrible word, she would be scared and flee.

Rowan is a noun of Scandinavian origin (Icelandic *reynir*, Norwegian *raun*; the first citation in the *OED* goes back to 1548), so that various diphthongs, including *oi*, developed in it. An imprecation like *a raun ~ reyn to thee* seems to have existed and become *aroint thee*. The only lexicographer who entertained a similar idea was Ernest Weekley. He wrote: "Exact meaning and origin unknown.? Connected with dialectal *rointree*, rowan-tree, mountain-ash, efficacy of which against witches is often referred to in early folklore." I take it to be the most promising hypothesis of all. The word (*rowan*), pronounced differently in different dialects, reached England from Scandinavia, but the curse is probably local. In any case, its Scandinavian analogs have not been found.

Galoot

I have written about this strange word, which means "a clumsy, oafish man," twice, and my solution seems to have been noticed and even cited without reference to the source. This is a common occurrence. Etymologies in dictionaries are expected to be anonymous, and hardly anyone wonders who discovered the origin of *man*, *bird*, or *dog*, or why the verdict "origin unknown" crops up so often in the most dependable reference works. Has anyone tried to unearth the source and, if so, have they all failed? Why then did they succeed in other cases? Therefore, if I was successful in my search for the etymology of *galoot*, and if dictionaries eventually accept it, I cannot wish for a greater reward. I would only like to thank the readers of my post in the blog "Oxford Etymologist" for July 23, 2008. The most recent comments go back to 2020 (compare what is said about the comments on *alairy*). English speakers from many countries recount how they use *galoot* or how they have heard it used by others and sometimes suggest their ideas on the word's origin. My small discovery shows that serendipity and luck play a noticeable role in a historian's work. I was once asked about the etymology of *galoot* but did not find a single citation in my huge database, and the information in the best dictionaries took me nowhere. Yet the question made me aware of the problem, and I began to take notice.

The *OED*, naturally, features *galoot* (of which, surprisingly, no example in a printed text predates 1812), marks it as nautical, registers the spelling variants *galloot* and *geeloot*, and quotes several sentences from which it follows that the earlier references were to an awkward soldier and an inexperienced mariner. In American English, *galoot* vacillates between a term of abuse and a fairly inoffensive synonym of *nincompoop*. Elsewhere, it is or was used as a term of ironic endearment. The word seems to be still understood and, on occasion, even used in the entire English-speaking world.

All we find in the *OED*, in the etymological section in the entry on *galoot*, is *slang*. The dictionaries that are derivative of the *OED*, naturally, write "origin unknown." The few lexicographers who dared a hypothesis suggested fanciful sources: possibly from Dutch *gelubt* "castrated" or Dutch *genoot* "companion," or Gaelic *gille* "servant." Those look-alikes lead nowhere because none of them begins with *ga-* or ends with *-loot*, and none has anything to do with the sea. *Galoot* lacks obvious cognates. It is indeed slang—presumably, sailors' slang (which means that it may be a borrowing from one of a dozen languages)—and, as I already said, it has never been discussed in any detail.

Although everything is grist that comes to my etymological mill, I try to read only such articles as hold out some promise of containing material useful to me, and my subject is the origin of English words and of their immediate cognates. But a reference to a 1940 publication on the influence of Italian on German caught my fancy (mainly because of my respect for the author, whose publications I had known and valued), and I decided to look it through. This is what I found there. As early as the thirteenth century, the Italian word *galeot(t) o* "sailor; steersman on a galley" became current in French, German, and Dutch and acquired an additional sense, namely "pirate." *Galeotto* continued into Modern Italian, and has, among others, a derogatory sense, though not coinciding with that of English *galoot*. It is glossed as "galley slave; convict" and "pimp." The sense "galley slave" may have been old; the path from it to a term of abuse would be short. The form closest to English *galoot* is Middle Dutch *galioot*, and this is, most probably, the immediate source of the English word. The phonetic match is not absolute but good. The main hitch is the chronology: we have no evidence of *galoot* before the beginning of the nineteenth century, and, if my reconstruction is right, it follows that the word existed in oral form for hundreds of years but managed to escape notice. However, such gaps in attestation, especially in the history of "low words," are not uncommon.

An unexpected parallel may perhaps reinforce my conjecture. There is a German word *Moses* "ship's boy," and it has been suggested that *Moses*, far from going back to the Biblical name, is a folk etymological alteration of Italian *mozzo* (the same meaning as in German). This looks like a promising suggestion. The role of Italian vocabulary in the development of European seafaring terminology needs no proof, but German *Moses* (assuming that it traces to *mozzo*) is slang, like English *galoot*, so that a certain parallelism between them can be detected.

Though answers to etymological puzzles are sometimes up for grabs, the dust heap one has to go through is so huge that finding them becomes a matter of luck. Also, no linguist knows all the words of all languages. The most important clue may be hidden in Greek, Lithuanian, or Russian, but even a well-informed student of English or German may have no command of any of the three. Emil Öhmann (1894–1984), the author of the article about the influence of Italian on German, would, of course, have pointed out that English *galoot* belonged with the words he listed if he had been aware of it, but he most probably was not. A Finnish linguist, he was a first-rate specialist in the Germanic and Romance languages, but he could not be expected to know English slang. I have encountered similar situations more than once. For example, English etymologists never heard the German word *Pimpf* "a small boy," while German scholars had no chance to come across the English word *pimp*. Therefore, no one connected *Pimpf* and *pimp*, though the similarity is almost too obvious to miss. As a result, the etymology of *pimp* was supposed to be unknown.

By the way, *galiot* ~ *galliot* "a small galley" is also an English word from Dutch (from French, and ultimately, from Middle Greek). It has no direct ties with *galoot* (though the root is the same), but I may recall the episode told in the preface to the second (1929) edition of the *Concise Oxford Dictionary*. After the dictionary appeared in 1911, a man bought it to find out whether *galliot* should be spelled with one *l* or two. The word was not there, and he returned the book. Lexicographers and etymologists cannot expect laurels. They should be happy if no one pours abuse on them. See the epigraph to the introduction of this book.

Wayzgoose

Wayzgoose is an odd compound many people still understand because the ritual connected with it (a printers' annual banquet) was revived in the twentieth century. The word turned up in our texts only in 1683, that is, in early Modern English. For some reason, great dictionaries, beginning with Samuel Johnson's, preferred not to include *wayzgoose* (the one important exception will be discussed later). In Webster, to give one example, it appeared in 1880 (i.e., a few decades after the great man's death), was expunged from the next edition by the editors, and reinstated only in 1934. Yet *wayzgoose* does not resemble any old vulgarity, and I have no explanations for this example of lexicographical ostracism.

The *OED* of course features *waysgoose*, and, at the end of the nineteenth century, the word's origin was often, and not always unprofitably, discussed in the popular press. Joseph Moxon, the author of *Mechanick Exercises* (1683–1684), wrote: "It is customary for the Journey-men every year to make new paper windows, whether the old will serve or no; Because that day they make them the Master Printer gives them a *Way-goose*, that is, he makes them a good Feast, and not only entertains them at his own house, but besides, gives them Money to spend at the Ale-house or Tavern at Night. . . . These *Waygooses* are always kept at *Bartholomew-tide* [August 24]; and till the Master-Printer have [sic] given this *Way-goose* the Journey-men do not use to Work by Candle Light." The *OED* reproduced the passage (discovered long ago) in full because no pre-1683 mention of *waygoose* seems to exist.

It will be seen that the earliest citation at our disposal speaks of *waygoose*. *Wayzgoose* surfaced for the first time in Nathaniel Bailey's immensely popular dictionary (1731; countless reprints), and we still do not know why he added *z* to this word or whether *wayzgoose* lost *z* in Moxon's dialect. *Waygoose* is now believed to be the original form. Lexicographers have suggested that Bailey, not being able to explain *waygoose*, changed it to *wayzgoose* to get the meaning "stubble goose" or "a goose fed on stubble" because he presumably understood *wayz* as "stubble." This conclusion, even if not wrong, is not entirely satisfactory. Bailey's etymologies are typical of the beginning of the eighteenth century, but it would have been silly to distort the name of a feast still celebrated or at least remembered in 1731. Consider publishing a modern dictionary with *Thank-giving* as a recommended variant! No one has done printers' work more famous than Charles Henry Timperley. One of his books is titled *Songs of the Press and Other Poems, Relative to the Art of Printing . . .* (1833; the *OED* refers to it, too). In it, we find an anonymous, undated "Song, Composed for a Printers' Way Goose" (p. 23; it is a drinking song); so again *waygoose*, not *wayzgoose*. The word occurs too rarely to justify generalizations.

In 1866, W. Carew Hazlitt published a poem *The Schole House of Women* (1572), in which the following lines occur (with reference to the rib taken from Adam): "A Dog vp caught, and a way gose/ Eat it clene." To this place he added a note on the origin of *waygoose* (p. 124; I will return to it later). As ill luck would have it, Hazlitt was an unreliable editor. What he misread as *gose* "goose" was *goes*. Those with a taste for watching other people's humiliation are invited to read James Russell Lowell's review of Hazlitt's endeavor in his book *My Study Windows*. His comment on this place runs as follows "a goose that could eat up a man's rib could only be matched by one that could swallow such a note,—or write it!" (p. 373 of the 1899 reprint). Thus, we do not have a 1572 example of *way-* or *wayzgoose*.

Much later, *wayzgoose* gained some currency, but, by the nineteenth century, the custom referred to by Moxon had fallen into desuetude, and the word had acquired an antiquarian ring. It is a mystery why it has reemerged or survived in Bailey's form. The *OED* remarks that even the alleged custom of eating a goose at the feast called *waygoose* is not supported by any evidence, even though Timperley said: "The derivation of this term is not generally known. It is from the old English word *wayz*, stubble. A wayz Goose was the head dish at the annual feast of the forefathers of our fraternity." He never participated in that feast and imprudently copied Bailey's entry. If, as the *OED* suggests, *waygoose* is an alteration of some word unknown to us, our chance of finding its etymology is zero. Yet, as always, it is instructive to see what different people have said about *waygoose ~ wayzgoose*.

According to one hypothesis, *wayz*, with its exotic spelling, should be understood as *ways*, *way's*, or *wase*. The dialectal noun *wase* "bundle of straw" exists. Even if some geese became fattened on stubble (an unlikely proposition), no one has seen a goose gaining weight on "bundles of straw." Also, geese are still lean at the end of August. The suggestions that the geese allegedly consumed by printers were stolen from the common or that they were fen-geese because *wayz-* is the continuation of a Middle English word for "mud," are fanciful. Equally improbable is the connection between *wayz-* and some cognates of the verb *wax* "to grow." In the periodical *Verbatim* for 2005 (30/3), Dorothy E. Zermach mentions Brett Rutherford's suggestion that *waygoose* is French *oie* (pronounced as [wa]) "goose," combined with English *goose*.

Tautological compounds like Middle English *love-amour* were plentiful (mainly in legal texts), but *goose-goose* as the name of a printers' feast makes little sense.

Other etymologies trace *wayz-* to some place name. I am returning to the hapless Hazlitt. He believed that *waygoose* was a corruption (a common term in his days) of Dutch *Waes-goose*: "In Le *Calendrier Belge*, 1862, ii. 270, an account is given of the solemnity and enthusiasm with which the people of Waes, in Brabant, celebrated in former times the festival of Saint Martin, when it was usual to kill a large number of geese, the Saint's peculiar bird." He added that "*wayz-goose* is the designation applied to certain annual banquets (though at no fixed period of the year)." However, the banquet, as we remember, "was always kept at Bartholomew-tide," while St. Martin's day falls on November 11. Nothing points to the Dutch origin of the English custom. Other attempts to derive *way(z)goose* from names have been equally ingenious and equally fruitless, though, in principle, a word like *waygoose* ~ *wayzgoose* may have owed its origin to the place where it was held for the first time. Stephen Goranson unearthed the sixteenth-century phrase (or compound) *wake goose*. Yet no bridge connects this mysterious goose with the one in which we are interested.

If it indeed happened only in the middle of the seventeenth century that British printers began to celebrate the coming of autumn and coined the word for the feast, the question about the etymological obscurity of the term they invented receives no answer. If, however, the word sprang up long before that time, we have no explanation for its absence from earlier texts. It is probably safer to assume that the word and its first occurrence are roughly contemporaneous. The *OED* must be right in suggesting that *waygoose* was an alternation of some other word and that etymologists bothering about its initial meaning need not look for geese. Most probably, we are dealing with printers' slang or some joke. New paper windows may have been made to the shouts of "Away goes!"; hence a way-goose. The joke or the slang must have been local and forgotten early, with the result that some people began to insert s ~ z in the middle of the word. Whatever the connection between *waygoose* and *goose*, it did not prevent Moxon from treating the compound as not depending on *goose*, as is evidenced by his plural *waygooses*.

Pilgarlick

Will anyone recognize the word *pilgarlic* (or *pilgarlik*, or *pilgarlick*)? The chance is not great. Yet about a hundred and fifty years ago and even some time later, people knew and discussed it in newspapers and periodicals. *Pilgarlik* (often with the epithet *poor* appended to it) means "wretch." Also, *pilgarlic* was a facetious, half-contemptuous designation of a bald-headed man, with reference to peeled (!) garlic because, in regional speech, words for *pill ~ peel*, *ship ~ sheep*, and their likes have been confused for centuries, as evidenced, among other things, by Shakespeare's puns. Joseph Wright's great *English Dialect Dictionary* contains multiple examples of the word's use, and, in the not too remote past, *pilgarlic* also referred to someone on whom some unfortunate responsibility had fallen, in which the victim was likely to be the scapegoat.

In the earliest sources, *pilgarlic* was associated with syphilis, though one finds only an obscure reference to "a venereal disease." Later, when even such hints could not be mentioned in print, those who wrote about *pilgarlic* stressed the connections between isolation (or being forsaken) and leprosy, as the disease was treated in the Middle Ages and beyond. However, baldness is not one of the symptoms of leprosy. By contrast, syphilis is indeed often accompanied by hair loss, though among the many visible marks of syphilis, baldness is certainly not the most prominent one. The path from either disease to baldness remains unclear.

Garlic, as we read in mid-nineteenth-century publications, isolates people who consume it. The Greeks forbade those who had recently consumed it to enter their temples. The reasoning in older periodicals sounds rather weak: a bald head resembles a head of peeled garlic, garlic isolates, and so do leprosy and syphilis. Consequently (!), a bald-headed man, an outcast, is called a "pilgarlic." The whole does not sound like a syllogism. Other explanations of the words are not better. A pilgarlic, we are told, is someone who peels garlic for others to eat and endures the hardships of ill-usage while others are enjoying themselves.

Some light on the mysterious word may perhaps come from the old allusion to pulling, not peeling, garlic. In the old discussion about the origin of *pilgarlic*, Chaucer's Pardoner was of course noticed. In Canterbury, the Pardoner made an appointment with the Tapster. He gave her money to buy a good supper, but, on his return, he found that his place was occupied by another man who ate his goose, drank his wine, and beat him with his own staff while he spent the night under the stairs in fear of the dog. "And ye shall hear the tapster made the Pardoner/pull Garlick all the long night till it was near end day." A Chaucer specialist pointed out to me that the lines had been added after Chaucer's death, but the text goes back to approximately 1400. I would like to propose an explanation of the enigmatic word and hope that it is new. In etymology, one can never guarantee being the first to suggest a solution. Be that as it may, in no annotated edition of Chaucer have I found anything similar.

How did the unfortunate man spend the night? Surely, he did not find a heap of garlic in need of pulling. Humiliated, hungry, and possibly driven almost crazy by listening to the love games of the happy couple above him, he, I am afraid, masturbated. *Pullgarlic* (such was probably the noun's original form) must have referred to a forsaken lover or someone vainly trying to attract a woman of his choice. Erotic slang is extremely rich and hard to interpret. Today's phrases reminiscent of *to pull garlic* (as I understand it) are equally bizarre and equally obscure to an outsider: *spank the monkey*, *flog the dolphin*, and *choke the chicken*, among others. I'd rather not comment on which part of the Pardoner's anatomy looked like a clove of garlic and a bald head (modern wits call it a bulb or mushroom, among dozens of others). And, to be sure, pulling and peeling garlic was never thought to be a dignified or pleasant occupation. Eric Partridge, a great specialist in the area of English slang, wrote a book with the title *Bawdy Shakespeare*. Later, other more detailed books dealing with Shakespeare's sexual allusions and innuendos went much farther. It is almost incredible how "bawdy" Shakespeare was. Yet those who have read Boccaccio's *Decameron*, let alone an uncensored, unbowdlerized version of *One Thousand and One Nights*, will be neither surprised nor shocked.

To be sure, pulling and peeling garlic could never be anyone's favorite occupation. The rest of my reconstruction is less secure. Perhaps the phrase *pull garlic* varied with *pill ~ peel garlic*, and a hapless lover ousted by a rival or someone who contracted a venereal disease and forfeited all sexual pleasures was called *pullgarlic* and *pi(l)garlic(k)*, but only the second word has survived. Later, baldness came to the forefront, though becoming an outcast did not go away. References to leprosy have no support in the evidence, while only one short step separates "a man who contracted the pox" from "an unsuccessful lover" and "a solitary person in misery."

The phrase and the word were of course low slang. Discovering the origin of even modern slang is extremely hard. Some wit launches a word. The "street" makes it popular, and the coinage either stays or dies a few years after. A look at our *Urban Dictionary* suffices to make the picture clear. Above, I attempted to reconstruct a piece of fourteenth-century slang. It is no wonder that the result cannot be final.

2

Words Bizarre, Misbegotten, and Born by Mistake

Bizarre

Unexpectedly, the story of the word *bizarre* returns us to the vegetation on men's faces. According to an often-repeated etymology, the root of this adjective should be sought in Basque *bizar* "beard": a mustached man is supposedly a man of spirit. (Note that the word we need is *bizar*; the form *bizzarra*, cited in many sources, is this noun with an article.) The Basque etymology of *bizarre* is wrong but far from stupid. Hirsute males are familiar figures in literature and myth. Numerous examples occur in the Bible. Among the better-known ones is the Old Testament judge Samson, whose strength was in his hair. Also, men were sent to Jericho (in the literal sense of the phrase!) to wait for their beards to reach respectable length before they could be seen in public. Nowadays, *to go to Jericho* means "to go to the Devil," but the original Jericho was a temporary place of banishment, not hell. The red-bearded Barbarossa, we may assume, did not get his name for nothing. The Icelandic word *skeggi* "bearded" (related to English *shaggy*) became a male proper name. The great god Thor, as we know from excavated figurines, was depicted with a gigantic beard.

The word *bizarre* reached English from French in the seventeenth century. In Modern French, *bizarre* has the same meaning as in English ("peculiar, eccentric, strange"; the sense "brave" is now extinct). In French texts, it first turned up in 1533, that is, earlier than in English, but still comparatively late (i.e., not in Old French). A usual caveat about such dates is in order: a popular, perhaps even slangy word, may have existed for a long time before some author risked using it in a book. Also, the French adjective, like the English one, might be a borrowing from a third language, and this might be the reason it made its way into a manuscript when it did.

The cognates (related forms) of the French adjective have been recorded all over the Romance-speaking world, but their senses match only partially. Only Italian *bizzarro* (with voiced *zz*, as in English *adze*) yields the same familiar glosses in our dictionaries ("strange, odd, whimsical, eccentric"). By contrast, Spanish and Portuguese *bizarro* (in Spanish texts, since 1569) means "gallant, courageous; grand, splendid"). In Italy, the word was known to Dante. It meant "fiery, furious, impetuous." Around the same time, its lookalike *Pizzaro* turned up as a proper name or nickname.

Whether *Pizzaro* is a regional form of *bizarre* cannot be decided. Some words not too seldom first emerge in texts as names and only later as regular nouns or adjectives. The Italian verb *sbizzarire* (approximately "to push, thrust") occurred around the same time. We should note the astounding chronological gap in our texts: in Italy, the word was known at least two and a half centuries before it reached Spanish, Portuguese, and French. For this reason, the renowned Spanish etymologist Joan Corominas concluded that the homeland of the Romance adjective was Italy, from which it spread to other languages.

If Corominas was right, the Basque etymology falls to the ground, and indeed, at present, hardly anyone derives *bizarre* from Basque. Another casualty of Corominas's etymology is *-arro*: outside Basque and Catalonian, such a (pejorative) suffix has not been recorded. The multitude of partly incompatible senses is also odd, whatever the origin of the adjective. If the initial meaning was "fiery, impetuous, unrestrained," "brave" sounds natural, but "peculiar, eccentric, whimsical"? In French, *bizarre* crossed the path of *bigarré* "variegated, motley," another adjective of unknown origin (also slang?). Dante's word sounds like an epithet typical of a warlike, aggressive attitude, and "brave" is close. But the derivation of Modern Italian "strange, eccentric" from "fiery, impetuous" needs special pleading.

After the Basque etymology of *bizarre* was rejected on chronological grounds, this adjective (in all the languages in which it occurs) joined the sad crowd of words of unknown etymology. However, several scholars have tried to penetrate the darkness surrounding it. Each offered his own solution, a situation that does not bode well.

Obviously, if *bizarre* was not borrowed from Basque, it does not follow that it could not be taken over from some other language. And the ghost of Gothic, a dead Germanic language, was conjured up. Gothic, it will be remembered, has not always been dead. Two kingdoms of the Goths flourished in what is today part of the Romance world: in Italy and in Spain. Modern Italian and Modern Spanish have preserved relics of many Gothic words, some of which do not occur in Bishop Wulfila's translation of the New Testament. Some such words have been reconstructed from the dialects spoken today. They exist as thoroughly assimilated inserts of Old Germanic in the modern regional speech. Theoretically, *bizarre* could be one of such words.

In the oldest texts, recorded in German, the verb *bâgen* "to fight" occurs (*â* designates a long vowel, as in English *spa*), and one of its cognates exists in modern Norwegian dialects (*båg* "resistant, unwilling, etc."). The idea that *bizarre* is a relic of a Germanic (in this case, Gothic) adjective, related to *bâgen*, occurred to the founders of Romance historical linguistics, but to trace the way from that unattested word to the Romance form, one must posit several unlikely phonetic changes. As far as I can judge, though the most recent author of this etymology was one of the greatest specialists in the field, the Gothic etymology of *bizarre* looks too complicated.

A seemingly more promising attempt to penetrate the past of *bizarre* takes us to Latin *vitiosus*, which meant "vile, depraved." Yet, most probably, this approach is another blind valley. *Vitium, vitiosus*, and *vitiare* referred to vice and damage, rather than to fervor and eccentricity, and it would be a minor miracle if all the recorded senses of the Romance adjective were secondary and late. Also, we run into the familiar problem of *v* becoming *b*. It won't do to say that this alternation is common in the languages of the world. Each case needs proof, and, *bizarre* has never been attested with initial *v*.

Finally, here is one more desperate attempt to find a Romance root for the word *bizarre*. Latin *invidia* means "envy, jealousy, ill will" (compare English *invidious*). Allegedly, it changed to *imbibia* (again *v-* to *b-*, but here through assimilation after *m*), with *in-* ~ *im-* being understood as a prefix or a preposition. The suggested end result was *bizarre* (the troublesome suffix *-arre* will remain a problem in any reconstruction). This old etymology was rejected quite early by two outstanding

Romance historical linguists and resurrected about sixty years ago. In the meantime, it has not gained recognition, but scholarly problems are not solved by voting. For example, it does not matter how many people believe that the sun orbits around a stable earth. Yet the derivation of *bizarre* from *invidia*, though ingenious, is not particularly attractive. I may add that the more ingenious and complicated an etymology is, the smaller the chance that it will prove to be correct. Correct etymologies are usually simple: it is difficult to find, rather than understand, them. Yet the derivation of *bizarre* from *invidia* has one redeeming quality: next to *bizarro*, we find Italian *bizza* "whim, caprice; freak; outburst of anger." As if to mock us, the origin of *bizza* is also unknown, but it would be a minor miracle if the two words were not in some way related, and the researchers who traced *bizarre* to *invidia* took that relation for granted.

Against this background, there is still a way to penetrate the past of this invidious word. The word seems to have emerged as a sound-imitating adjective. Sound imitation (onomatopoeia) and sound symbolism are mentioned more than once in this book, but since I am writing a collection of short detective stories rather than a novel, I cannot expect the readers to remember the intricacies of all the plots at every turn of the events described and am sometimes obliged to repeat familiar things.

Sound imitation is an obvious concept: words like *bow-wow* and *oink-oink* attempt to reproduce the cries of dogs and pigs. *Crack, crush, croak, crunch, creak*, and to a certain extent *crumble* also belong here. The existence of sound symbolism cannot be proved, but its existence is beyond doubt. Thus, to many speakers of the European languages *fl-* seems to be the right initial group for words like *flutter, flitter, flicker, fly, flow, flee*, and *flip-flop*, while *gl-* fits *gleam, glory, glow*, and *glamor*. There is nothing absolute in those connections. For instance, *glow, glitter, glamor*, and *glory* coexist with *glum* and *gloom*. *Slime, sloven, slum, slut, slattern*, and the rest endowed *sl-* with a certain meaning. Yet *slice, sleep*, and *slender* arouse no unpleasant associations. Sound imitation, whether in *bow-wow* or *glug-glug*, is obvious. Acceptance of sound symbolism is a matter of conviction.

It may pay off to look at some words resembling *bizarre*, or rather the syllable *bizz-*. English *busy* is one of them. Dictionaries are unanimous in their verdict: "of unknown origin." German *böse* "evil, wicked; angry" and *erbost* "furious" are also close by. Many words sound like *böse*, and their etymology has not been discovered. Unlike *böse*, *busy* is not isolated in Germanic. The Dutch for "busy" is *bezig*. Close to it are Dutch *biestert*, which at one time seems to have meant "running wildly, etc.," *verbazen* "to amaze" (*ver-* is a prefix), German dialectal *baseln* "run madly around," and Swiss dialectal (German) *bausen* "to do useless work in the kitchen; rummage," among quite a few others. If Old Catalonian *basarda* "fear" and fifteenth-century French slang word *basir* "to kill" belong here, we may conclude that either some similar-sounding Germanic words once reached the Romance territory or that the same sound-imitative and sound-symbolic impulse was at work in Germanic and Romance.

As early as 1912, Wilhelm Braune, one of the greatest Germanic philologists of his time, cited numerous French words of this type and suggested their Germanic origin (see the entry *Gibberish*). He passed by English *busy*, but Leo Spitzer, another distinguished scholar, in 1935, did cite *busy* in connection with two French verbs meaning "to stun, bewilder." The problem with such fugitive remarks is that they are like needles in a haystack, and it is no wonder that English etymologists did not notice them. To the words mentioned above, I may add Icelandic *bisa* "to work hard; drag an object along." *Bisa* is a late word (no records before the seventeenth century), but Norwegian *bisa* "to talk nonsense" seems to be related. In this almost endless list of *b-s/b-z* words, we find such senses as "carouse" (hence English *bouse* ~ *booze*), "swell," "twaddle," "exert oneself," "do harm," "run along," and "puff up." The idea of puffing up, that is, swelling, is said to underlie *boast*. German *Bise* "the wind from the Northeast" and English *beestings* may or may not belong here. I'll skip the *b-s* ~ *b-z* words for "kiss" and "female genitals" and the names Bisinus ~ Basina from Medieval Germanic tales because their ties to the group being discussed here are doubtful. In wading through such swampy ground, one never knows where to stop. Yet English *busy* seems to belong here.

We have a "buzzword" (as it were) and its progeny spreads all over Germanic. Perhaps in the Middle Ages it reached the Romance-speaking world; yet parallel development supplementing borrowing cannot be ruled out. I believe that *bizarre* is one of many *b-s* ~ *b-z* words. A bizarre person may swell himself and be furious, valiant, and prone to heroic deeds. Or this person's behavior may be odd and therefore "peculiar, eccentric."

Russian borrowed from Polish the word *bzik* "whim, caprice." It earlier referred to the behavior of the cattle running away from hornets, horseflies, gadflies, and their likes. This is exactly what French dialectal *beser* and several German dialectal verbs (*biesen ~ biessen* and *busseln*) mean! Russian *bystryi* "quick, fast" looks like their kin, but, in dealing with such words, a good deal of danger lurks in casting the net too wide. These words are not related as is, for instance, English *father* to German *Vater* and Latin *pater*. Therefore, I treat without much enthusiasm the idea that, in the remote past, some root *b-z* existed and that all the words mentioned above and many words I left out of this story are its offspring. It seems that they are more like mushrooms growing on a stump: they resemble one another, they even look like having the same root, but this is an illusion. See the entry *Booze*, where the same is said almost verbatim.

Most often, the root *bhou* has been reconstructed in this context. Another candidate is *bhēs* "active" (*ē* denotes a long vowel as in German *leben*, *heben*, and so forth) or "feverish." Pierre Guiraud, the author of a provocative dictionary of words of unknown origin (*Dictionnaire des etymologies obscures*, 1982), reconstructed the root *big-* "bent, crooked" and combined *bizarre* and *bigot*. This looks like a move in a wrong direction. I may rather visualize a picture of a herd of cows fleeing wildly from pestiferous insects, with our remote ancestors describing the scene with the help of a sound-imitating and sound-symbolic word. As time went on, similar pictures of superactive beasts and busy, boisterous, bizarre people engendered similar, sometimes even identical, sound complexes again and again.

Bamboozle

The origin of *bamboozle* is almost beyond reconstruction. The Internet is awash in hypotheses, while responsible dictionaries prefer to remain close-lipped, and the only reason for my attack on this impenetrable verb is that I also have a suggestion. The story of *bamboozle* is not unlike that of *dandy*: the word appeared in English printed texts around 1700 and may or may not be much older. Scottish *bombaze* ~ *bumbaze* "to confound, perplex" are, apparently, variants of the same verb.

In a search for the etymology of *bamboozle*, some insecure roads lead to Rome, others to Paris (i.e., to Italian and French). However, the syllables *bam*, *bum*, and *bom* are so obviously sound-imitative (compare *boom*) and expressive that words containing them can be found in most languages. Dickens's Mr. Bumble and Italian *bambino* "boy" did not get their names for nothing. Such nouns usually denote noises, little children, someone who can be duped like a baby, puppets, and so forth. *Bamboozle* may be an alteration of some such word, for instance, of French **bambocher** "to play pranks" or Italian **imbambolare** "to make a fool of one." Close enough is German **Bambus** "a good-for-nothing; idler" (with several other related senses, as in *Bambusen* "bad sailors"), possibly of Slavic origin.

The idea of borrowing is persuasive only when we succeed in showing how a foreign word reached its new home (through what intermediaries and in what milieu). Reference to common European slang (mentioned in the essay on *Dandy*) makes sense, but provides no details. *Bamboozle* surfaced among many other words at an epoch when London was swamped with such neologisms, and the only support we have for reconstructing its past is that, at approximately the same time, its synonym *bam* came into use. If *bam* is the source of *bamboozle*, Italian or French etymons should be ruled out, but if *bamboozle* was "abbreviated" into *bam*, all the questions remain. However, as a general rule, nouns, not verbs, are curtailed in English (*lab* for *laboratory*, *prom* for *promenade*, *trig* for *trigonometry*, and so forth).

Contrary to some of the most eminent etymologists, I tend to think that the story began with *bam*, a word suggesting silliness or some sort of undignified activity (no one respects bums). The second *b* hints at reduplication (as in **bonbon**, literally *good-good*, *goodie-goodie*). The vowel sound *oo* has the ability of giving a word an amusing appearance. Whoever hears *snooze*, *canoodle*, and *nincompoop* begins to smile; add *boondoggle* to this list. Hence the idea of the "ooglification of American slang," formulated in this form by American linguist Roger Wescott: if you want a word to sound slangy, substitute *oo* for its stressed vowel. An association with *booze* may also have helped, and *-le* is a typical suffix of frequentative verbs, such as *scuttle*, *paddle*, and their likes. To put it differently, *bamboozle* looks like a fanciful extension of *bam*. Even from a phonetic point of view, it seems hard to believe that *bamboozle*, a funny and colorful word with stress on the second syllable, could have been reduced to *bam*.

In British dialects, *bamfoozle* "deceive" has been recorded (with *f* from *fool*?). The starting point in the history of *bamboozle* may have been *bam* and *bamfoozle*, which later yielded *bamboozle*. *Bamboze*, *bumbaze*, *bamboze*, and *bambosh*, all referring to abuse and deceit, also exist. Against this background, there is probably no need to posit a Romance etymon. Ernest Weekley began his entry on *bamboozle* most reasonably: "Perh[aps] connected with the onomat[apoeic] *bab-* (*babble*, *baby*, *baboon*, etc.)," but then cited a French and a Catalan verb. A first-rate specialist in Romance linguistics, he had a soft spot for French etymons of English words. In the first edition of his dictionary, Walter W. Skeat traced *bamboozle* to thieves' cant, namely, to the phrase *a bene bouse* "a good drink." Salutations used when presenting a drink to a guest do sometimes merge into compounds. Such is *wassail*, ultimately from Old Norse *ves heil* "be in good health!" (in Old English, the same phrase existed but in a slightly different form). Drinking songs have also been looked upon as the source of some words. Thus, *lampoon*, from French *lampon*, presumably goes back to French *lampons* "let us drink!" (this looks like a folk etymology; however, the only other etymology I know is not much better), but the idea that *bamboozle* originated in such a context lacks plausibility, and later, Skeat gave it up. In the last (concise) edition of his etymological dictionary he said curtly: "Unknown," an uncharacteristic formulation, for he seldom left his readers without some hypothesis, however tentative. Reference to Romany ("Gypsy language") has no foundation either. Eighteenth-century lexicographers called the verb very low, but slang is "low" by nature.

Also at the beginning of the eighteenth century, the verb *banter* appeared in the speech of the people whom Swift despised heartily. It is even more opaque than *bamboozle*. In my database, I have only one note on it. A distinguished German etymologist believed that *banter* is a "nasalized" variant of *batter* and listed several verbs whose meaning developed from "beat, strike" to "tease." This is a far-fetched idea. Here, too, a French origin was sought (from *badiner*, familiar to those English speakers who remember the noun *badinage* "raillery"). British dialectal *bant* "vigor; to conquer; haggle," another putative etymon of *banter*, has such a limited geographical distribution that it could not claim success in London. Nor is its meaning close enough to "friendly teasing." In Skeat's concise version, referred to above, we again read: "Unknown." It is curious that two hundred years ago, London wits reveled in new words whose descent is enveloped in almost complete darkness. But to repeat, slang is destined to remain obscure: *bamboozle, banter, balderdash*, and their likes rarely reveal their origins to the eager etymologist.

Note
Wescott, Roger W. "Ooglification in American English slang." *Verbatim* III/l4, 1977, 5. Apparently, the "ooglification" of slang is not limited to American English.

Chicanery and Shenanigans

English borrowed *chicanery* from French in the late seventeenth century. Romance linguists argue endlessly over its origin. Since Romance linguistics is not my area, in dealing with a French loan in English, I can at best summarize the opinions of specialists and risk sharing the one that seems more reasonable than the others. I probably would not have dared touch on *chicanery* if what I have read about it had not convinced me that the case is not entirely hopeless and if a possible clue had not led me to *shenanigans*, a word that seems to have perplexed even the boldest inventors of folk etymologies. My database contains zero citations on it (i.e., in the more than thirty thousand articles, published between 1592 and 2022, I have amassed while working on my etymological dictionary of English, no mention of it occurred even in passing)—an extremely rare case, when the origin of a universally known word is at stake. In this desert, perhaps even an unacceptable suggestion may provoke at least a rebuttal (still better than nothing). Dictionaries of course mention *chicanery* but do not go beyond pointing to the French source. The original *Oxford English Dictionary*

(*OED*) says: "Probably fanciful." This verdict seems to mean: "An individual coinage; a piece of slang without any discoverable root." But slang, however "fanciful," does have roots! Think of English *boondoggle* and *bamboozle*!

The sound complexes *shick* and *chick* (I spell them as they would be pronounced in English) are easy prey for onomatopoeia. For example, verbs designating sharp noises and quick motions have been derived from them. Once such words come into being, they often develop figurative meanings, and their ties with sounds become harder to reconstruct. In French, the verb *chicaner* was first recorded in a poem of François Villon, one of the greatest medieval poets (born in 1431). It occurs in a mock description of a dialogue between him and his prosecutor, who advised him "to chicane." Knowing Villon's adventurous biography and the company he kept, we may be almost certain that *chicaner* belonged to the contemporary cant rather than to the established vocabulary of the legal profession.

The verb emerged from the depths of French low slang but proved to be surprisingly long-lived and attractive. As time went on, not only English but also German, Dutch, Swedish, and Norwegian borrowed it with the sense "harass," and, of course, it continued into Modern French. It is less clear what it means in Villon's poem. Since, in the Romance languages, many words with the root pronounced as *shick* denote smallness (for instance, Old French *chic* "small"; and compare Spanish *chico ~ chica* "little"), it has been suggested that the poet was advised to indulge in trickery and caviling or, to put it differently, in pettifogging, and thus confuse the judge(s). The same root is used in naming small things, that is, in nouns. Such is French *chique* "a small ball," and the connection with balls may be significant.

An old conjecture traced *chicanery* to the game of mall, from there to a dispute in that or other games, and further, as the *Century Dictionary* puts it, to sharp practice in lawsuits. (From *mall* we have *pall-mall*, the game, the alley where it was played in London, and, presumably, our pedestrian and shopping malls; *mall* is related to *mallet*.) The root of *chicane* was believed to go back to the Medieval Latin unattested noun *zicannum* "a club or bat used in polo," from Middle Greek, ultimately from Persian. A moment in a match of *chugan* has been preserved in a fine old Persian drawing: the game looks like pall-mall or hockey on horseback. However, we probably need not go so far for the etymology of *chicanery*. Pall-mall presupposed a good deal of trickery and wrangling. Both were its essential components. Words borrowed from the language of cards, dice, racing, and so forth have always been numerous. Our speech is also full of metaphorical expressions that originated as literal (nonfigurative) phrases current in sports (*to drop the ball, the ball is now in your court*, and the like). The hypothesis that *chicanery* arose in the environment of a game seems reasonable. The root is then sound symbolic or onomatopoeic and has nothing to do with Persian or Greek.

In looking through an extremely long entry on the roots mentioned above in Walther von Wartburg's great French etymological dictionary, I stumbled upon the form *sikanadenn*, a Breton word for "a kind of whip or rod" (Breton is a Celtic language spoken in Brittany, France). It was borrowed from French. Even if French *chicaner* does not refer to smallness, we are confronted by several homonymous sound-imitative roots. The Breton word resembles *shenanigan*, which surfaced in American English in the middle of the nineteenth century. The resemblance is not striking but not insignificant. A hundred years ago, dictionaries cited only the singular (*shenanigan*, not *shenanigans*).

Is it possible, I wonder, that some word like Breton *sikanadenn*, Celtic or not, is an alteration of *chicane*, turned into *shenanigan*? *Chicanery* was first defined as "nonsense; humbug," rather than "the use of trickery." Today *shenanigans* means "dishonest maneuvering; mischief." The two words are near-synonyms. American English is a repository of odd local words of undiscovered origin. I don't set high store by my suggestion. There are enough absurd etymologies in the world, and I could have abstained from increasing their number but for the fact that no one seems to have dealt with *shenanigans*.

I first mentioned this etymology in January 2009, and am not aware of any response. It will be seen that I compared *shenanigans* and *chicanery* almost by chance, but serendipity plays an important role in many searches. What if I guessed well? The two words do resemble each other!

Pun

The author of a book on etymology is supposed to explain the origin of the words included in its pages. But if the sought-for origin is known and can be found in a dictionary or on the Internet, what is the point of writing such a book? And if the answer has never been found, why bother? Those who have read the introductory chapter realize that they face two situations. Perhaps the author knows the solution to the riddle while most people don't. *Alairy* (see Chapter 1) provides a good example. I have read some articles few people have read and, though I was not the first to "decipher" the word, the answer will be new to most readers. But, as a rule, if a word has until now remained a riddle, the chance that I will solve the problem is relatively small. (Small, but not improbable: in my life, I have been able to explain the derivation of a few hopelessly opaque words.) However, sometimes, I can offer a reasonable hypothesis. The etymology of *pun* is a case in point.

The date of the earliest citation of *pun* given in the first edition of the *OED* is 1669. Now, a 1644 example is known. The word seems to have emerged some time around the sixteen-forties. This date tallies with the fact that Abraham Cowley's comedy *The Guardian* (acted in 1641) has a character Mr. Puny, described as "a young Gallant, a pretender to Wit." In the revised version of the play (1661), the adjective *Punish* occurs, with reference to that gentleman's kind of wit. Cowley does not use the word *pun*, and we cannot decide how the name and the adjective were pronounced. On paper, *Puny* and *Punish* look like *puny* "tiny" and the verb *punish*, respectively. Both must have had punning connotations.

Names of this type were popular in Cowley's days. For instance, Goldsmith and Sheridan have Mr. Slang (unfortunately, no lines are assigned to him) and Mr. Fag (*fag* "servant"). So-called telling names like Fielding's Squire Allworthy and Dickens's Mr. Bumble had a long life. Eighteenth-century dictionaries feature *pun*, which they define as *quibble, witty conceit, fancy,* and *clench*. "Play on words" was also mentioned regularly, but the original connotation of *pun* seems to have been "an over-subtle distinction" (this is what *clench*, a side-form of *clinch*, means), rather than what we today understand by it.

From the outset, two forms have competed in attempts to etymologize *pun*: French *pointe* and English *pun* "to pound," the latter from Old English *punian* (none of my references antedates 1730, the year Nathaniel Bailey's unimaginably popular and now forgotten dictionary was published). But alongside those two, numerous wild conjectures abounded. Among the suggested sources of pun, words beginning with *f-* show up (e.g., English *fun* and a made-up Icelandic adjective related to *funi* "fire, flame"), Irish Gaelic *bun* "root, foundation, etc." and its Welsh cognate, Latin *punica* (or English *Punic*), as in *fides punica* "Punic faith" (i.e., "treachery"), a segment of the phrase *play upon (words)*, and even the blend of *puzzle* and *conundrum*. One sometimes wishes for a punitive expedition against the people who offer such hypotheses, but since they are all dead and therefore invulnerable to my slings and arrows, the raid has to be called off.

Joseph Wright's *English Dialect Dictionary* (a great multivolume work) lists two homonyms of *pun*: *pun* "a slow inactive person," usually applied to female servants (I have no clue to its origin, but the meaning is as far removed from that of *pun* "play on words" as can be), and obsolete Scots *pun* "sham," of which one example is given ("A flattern' title's but a pun"), a word not listed in either of the two great dictionaries of the Scottish tongue. Skeat was a stubborn defender of the *punian* etymology. In a pun, he said, one pounds words, bends them into new senses, and hammers at forced similes. Skeat's reputation lent respectability to this idea, and it is still mentioned in modern books.

The verb *pun*, a "rustic" variant of *pound*, is the least probable source of a word that must have been coined by the wits intent on word play, and the path from beating (pounding) to punning is hard to detect. Yet Skeat clung to this derivation even in the revised (1910) edition of his dictionary. Therefore, it comes as a surprise that, in the last concise version, published almost at the same time, he switched to a variant of the French etymology. What caused this sudden change of heart? Apparently, no solution known at that time satisfied him.

French *pointe* could not become English *pun* for phonetic reasons, and the net was cast for the Romance words beginning with the syllable *pun*. The catch contained Latin *punctilio* and Italian *puntiglio* derived from it. The *OED* records the short-lived synonyms of *pun*, namely *punnet* and *pundigrion*; yet *pun* cannot be a clipped form of either. Rather, *punnet* is a mildly amusing diminutive of *pun*. *Pundigrion* is baffling. An illiterate spelling of *punctilio* (Ernest Weekley's unconvincing suggestion)? But isn't *pudigrion* a facetious formation, like our *rumbustious, rambunctious, scrumptious*, and the rest? Given a word that those playful wits understood as *pointe d'esprit*, why shouldn't they have enjoyed altering it out of mischief?

The incomprehensible *-degrion* resembles the second half of a nobleman's title (Manon's Le Chevalier des Grieux comes to mind at once) or *-drion* of *synedrion*, the Greek for *Sanhedrin* "the supreme counsel of the Jews" (the more remote the association, the better?). Or Rabelais's Pantagruel could have inspired the punsters. Besides, in the sixteenth and seventeenth centuries, there were rather numerous words like *tatterdemalion*, with *-de-* in the middle, a wild and meaningless addendum. In any case, it is more likely that *pundigrion* is an extension of *pun* than that *pun* is a clipped form of it. The unrecorded dialectal French words that could have become English *pundigrion* (Leo Spitzer gives several of them) are of little interest, just because they are unrecorded.

Eighteenth-century literati loved clipping long words: *mobile (vulgus)* became *mob*, *citizen* became *cit*, and so forth (the entry on *pun* in the original *OED* ends with a list of such words, including *snob*, but, in my opinion, *snob* should be expunged from it). Jonathan Swift detested trendy monosyllables of whatever origin, and one can easily imagine what he would have said if flooded with our *bus, cab, math, prof, lab, doc, prom*, and dozens of others. The etymology of *pun* will remain unresolved, but it is rather probably a clipped form. A Latin etymon (*punctilio*) appears to be more plausible than Italian *puntiglio*.

Special words for "pun" are not too common. As a rule, people say simply "play on words." However, French has *calembour*, whose origin is as problematic as that of *pun*. It found acceptance in all the Slavic languages and German. In German, folk etymology changed *calembour* beyond recognition (*Kalauer*). A feeble attempt was made in the nineteenth century to introduce *calembre* into English (the *OED* lists two insignificant examples), but English stayed with *pun*. Nothing can be said against this choice, but regrettably, we have lost *clench*.

Conundrum

It is rather amusing that the pompous coinage *conundrum* lives up to its reputation so well. People keep repeating that no one knows the origin of this word. The whole nine yards of the Internet space have been devoted to the question about the plural of *conundrum*: Should it be *conundra* or *conundrums*? But the question is moot: though *conundrum* ends in *-um* and looks like a Latin word, no such word has been found. Even if it could be shown that we are dealing with a bona fide Latin noun of the second declension, why should we pretend that we are Romans? What is the plural of *presidium* and *momentum*? I hope not *presidia* and *momenta*.

For centuries, students have played with words to make them look like fruits of classical derivation, and some native Greek-Latin puns resulted in brilliant hybrids. English *-um* should be treated with great caution. For example, *tantrum* has no Latin ancestor. It rather looks like *dander* (in *to get one's dander up*), but *dander* is equally obscure, and there may be no connection between the two. Samuel Foote (1720–1777), a playwright and disturber of the peace, mocked Charles Macklin, his erstwhile fellow actor, who boasted that he could memorize any text after hearing it only once. He invented a string of rigmarole about cabbages and bears (as a matter of fact, there is only one she-bear in the piece) to test the man's memory. In the story, a character called the great Panjandrum (a parody of Macklin) appears. If *pan-*, as is usually assumed, means "all," *-jandrum* is a nonsense pseudo-scholarly word, coined for fun.

Panjandrum stayed in the language and means "a pompous ass." *Cockalorum* "a young whippersnapper" surfaced in the first half of the eighteenth century. Its humorous effect depended on the contrast between the domestic word *cock*, with its obscene connotations, and a Latin ending (just what is needed for naming a pretentious fool). In other cases, unconnected with *-um*, reminiscences of Latin grammar may also lead us astray. *Quibble* begins with *qui-*, and several Latin words immediately spring to mind. They may spring and jump as much as they wish, for *quibble* refuses to reveal its Latin past (is it related to *quip*, *squabble*, or *cavil*?). *Gazebo* looks like *gaze* with a Latin ending of the future but has nothing to do with it.

Although the seemingly rootless neologism *conundrum* appeared in English only at the end of the sixteenth century, it may have had a longer history. At that time, rather many words made it to the Standard from dialects (first to London slang and then to the language of the educated class). Walter W. Skeat's predecessor and rival Hensleigh Wedgwood pointed to the Pembrokeshire word *condrim* "perplexity, confusion of mind; trouble" (Pembrokeshire is a county in the southwest of Wales) and compared it with Middle English *wandreme* "tribulation" (it occurs only once in a poem, and its form and origin are dubious). The distance between *condrim* and *conundrum* may be hard to cover, but *conundrum* had so many variants (*conimbrum, quinombrum, quonundrum,* and *quadundrum*) that we cannot be sure which one was the oldest.

Condrim and *conimbrum* sound similar. However, a regional noun with minimal currency is hardly a promising etymon of *conundrum,* a word authors like Thomas Nashe (1567–c. 1601) and Ben Jonson (1572–1637; both excellent playwrights and wits) did not disdain. The proliferation of variants can also be interpreted in many ways. Perhaps the witty neologism took London by storm. People laughed and repeated the word, and it changed its shape from mouth to mouth. Or *conundrum* reached English from abroad, and Londoners were uncertain of its exact form. Or a dialectal word suddenly became fashionable in the capital, and no one knew its "correct" pronunciation. *Conundrum* "whim" precedes in texts the meanings "pun," "puzzle, riddle." It was sometimes used in the tautological alliterative phrase *crochets and conundrums* (*crochet* "whim, fancy").

Thus, both the form and the signification of *conundrum* were unstable. The circumstances in which it arose and gained popularity are said to be lost. We only know that it was later used at Oxford, which may indicate scholarly influence. *A word's earliest recorded sense* and *a word's initial sense* are not synonyms because, in our documentation, a great deal depends on chance. *Conundrum* "whim" and "pun, puzzle, quibble" may have coexisted from the start. Words with such meanings tend to emerge from "the lower depths" and baffle etymologists. For example, *quibble, whim, puzzle,* and *pun,* all of which have been mentioned above, are of obscure origin.

Let us look at what has been suggested about the etymology of *conundrum* during a century and a half of speculation.

1. Since *conundrum* means "pun" and presupposes an imaginary or fanciful agreement between some two objects, the etymon

may be Greek *koinon duoin* (Latin *commune duorum*); substitute Latin *duorum* for Greek *duoin*, and you will get a good approximation of *conundrum*.

2. Perhaps *conundrum* is a modified and disguised form of Latin *conventum* "agreement." For *v* the letter *u* often turns up in books. *Conuentum* could have been misunderstood and mispronounced as *conundrum*. (Both of these anonymous hypotheses were offered in 1859.)

3. See Wedgwood's etymology above (1873).

4. In Ben Jonson's days, *conundrum* could occasionally mean "false information, canard." Skeat (in 1880 and never again) suggested that the sought-for source was perhaps Dutch *kond rondom* "known round about." (This phrase is made up, but, in any case, *conundrum* is not a kind of word English would have borrowed from late Middle Dutch.)

5. In South India, according to a correspondent to *American Notes and Queries*, names like *Trivandrum* and *Chellumbrum* occur. Could *conundrum* be of Tamil or Telugu origin? (Certainly not in sixteenth-century England.)

6. One of the citations in the *OED* runs as follows: "These conimbrums, whether Reall or Nominall, went down with Erasmus like chopt hay" (1651; the first citation of *conundrum* is dated 1586). Here is the etymology, published in *The Nation* 57, 1893, No. 1481, p. 370 and signed by the initials C. S. P.: "There surely can be no doubt what this word [that is, *conimbrums*] is. The reference to realists and nominalists shows that something in the scholastic philosophy is referred to; and 'conimbrum' is easily recognized as meaning *argumentum Conimbrienum*. The doctors of Coimbra, in their celebrated commentaries published in the sixteenth century, have in all cases a great deal to say of the 'multiplex significatio' of one word and another. Indeed, such remarks are their great weapon. They used it for all it was worth, and a little more. Accordingly, a dealer in verbal quibbles might naturally have been called by Oxford students a *Conimbricus*, and his quillet *Conimbrienum argumentum*. The original *c*, which this hypothesis requires, is preserved in another old form of the word '*conuncrum*.' *Conimbrica* was in the sixteenth century the most

usual Latin form of the name Coimbra, though Conimbria is also common. Colimbria was obsolete." (This etymology would have been fully persuasive but for two snags: the fact that the earliest recorded and still remembered form is *conundrum* and the existence of so many variants of the word. But no theory will explain away that variety; it can only mention the circumstance that slang words often exist in multiple forms.)

7. *Conundrum* (with all its variants) and *quandary* belong to the family that goes back to French *calembredaine* "nonsense talk" and *calembour* "pun," both allegedly traceable to Old French *bourde* "twaddle" (Leo Spitzer, 1943 and several times later). The trouble is that the French words Spitzer cited appeared in texts only at the end of the eighteenth century, and their etymology also remains a matter of debate. A word of questionable origin cannot shed light on another opaque word, but note that Coimbra was at one time Latinized as Colimbra, and this form bears some resemblance to French *calembour* and German *Kalauer*, evidently, a borrowing of it.)

8. An Italian manuscript mentions a Medieval Latin name *conandrum* for a simple (i.e., a medicinal herb) used against a headache. This word was presumably changed to *conundrum* and came to mean a riddle that causes headaches (Johann Knobloch, 1984; far-fetched).

The progress of etymology is hampered (and hampered fatally) by the absence of comprehensive bibliographies. Researchers either display unpardonable naiveté and start from scratch or pretend that they had no predecessors. Did Knobloch, a serious historical linguist, know Spitzer's articles? If he did, he chose not to mention them. But who can expect anyone's familiarity with a note in *The Nation* for 1893? I was fortunate. While working on a new etymological dictionary of English, I sent my volunteers to comb through all the popular magazines of which I was aware. This is how C. S. P.'s letter to the editor ended up in my database. But it could have been missed, or *The Nation* may have fallen between the cracks (I got interested in it only because of the scholarly reviews it published and realized that the entire set required my attention).

Do we know the origin of *conundrum*? I decided that Mr. C. S. P. had come closer to solving the riddle (puzzle) than anybody else. He may also, even though unwittingly, have said an important thing about French *calembour*. I published my musings on *conundrum* in the blog "Oxford Etymologist" on December 3, 2008, and Dr. Stephen Goranson suggested that C. S. P. were the initials of Charles Sanders Peirce (1839–1914), one of the greatest modern scholars in the Humanities. The opinion of such a man cannot be dismissed as a chance conjecture by some resourceful outsider. Stephen Goranson also pointed out that the Italian manuscript *conundrum* might be a copy error of *coriandrum* or *coriander*, sometimes prescribed for headache.

When all is said and done, I'll risk suggesting that Peirce's etymology of *conundrum* is correct despite some doubts that still remain in some people's minds. And yes: the plural of *conundrum* is *conundrums*.

Punk, Spunk, and Funk

Pippi Longstocking, the heroine of Astrid Lindgren's famous book, and her friend once went on an expedition in search of something called *spunk*. Unfortunately, they had no idea what *spunk* means so that finding the coveted thingy became a formidable task. They searched high and low. The object never turned up: whatever they happened to spot did not look good enough to bear the mysterious name. But in the end, tired and frustrated, they came across a glowworm and realized at once that this was indeed a true spunk! We are very pleased for the children, but have to remember that *spunk* was Pippi's coinage: such a word does not exist in Swedish.

Yet, though it has existed in English since at least the sixteenth century, next to nothing is known about its etymology, except that it is surrounded by a host of equally obscure look-alikes. I occasionally refer to the capricious, unpredictable *s-mobile*. Hence the question: "Can *spunk* be related to *punk*?" And if *punk* has something to do with *spunk*, where do *funk* and *fungus* come in? Etymologists flounder in this net of homonyms and near-synonyms and have never succeeded in extricating themselves.

Spunk has several senses. Two of them are "spark" and "touchwood." Touchwood is what becomes of wood when certain fungi convert it into a soft mass; once ignited, it can burn for hours like tinder. The word is defined in dictionaries through its synonym *tinder*. "Spark" and "flammable substance" are compatible senses. *Spunk* "spirit, mettle" can be understood as a figurative extension of "tinder." The slang sense "semen" is an obvious extension of "spirit, virility," though one can say, "You are a spunk," without overt sexual connotations (the verb *to spunk* is more explicit).

Next comes *punk*, again "touchwood." In Shakespeare's days, *punk* meant "prostitute." The word seems to have gone underground and resurfaced in the memory of the people still living: no longer "prostitute" but still a derogatory term. Despite the opinion that *punk* "strumpet; ruffian" is a coinage of unknown origin, it is probably not as opaque as most researchers believe. Multiple words like *Puck* and *buck* go back to primitive formations denoting "something swollen." They often have *n* in the middle. In Scandinavian languages and dialects, *punk* refers to all kinds of trash and occasionally stands for "thingy." Its twin is *bunk(e)*. Whether English *punk* traces to Scandinavian is immaterial in the present context. Since touchwood is porous and looks swollen, perhaps all the senses of *punk* belong together ("something bloated, a big fat thing").

It is harder to tell whether *punk* and *spunk* are related. *Spunk* may of course be *punk* with *s-mobile* added. If so, the development was from "swollen thing" to "touchwood" and "spark; fiery temperament, mettle; virility." The riddle might have had a satisfactory solution if alongside *punk* and *spunk*, *funk* did not exist. The noun *funk* has been recorded with the following senses: "spark; touchwood (the same as *spunk*)," "strong smoky smell, especially tobacco smell," "kick, stroke; anger," and "fear, panic" (e.g., *to be in a blue funk*). The etymology of each of these senses is problematic, and there can be no certainty that any one of them is connected with any other. How is it possible that in some contexts *punk*, *spunk*, and *funk* mean the same? We are especially interested in *funk* "spark; touchwood." To be sure, burning spunk might have aroused associations with an offensive smell. While inhaling it, people would become angry, panicky, and, if one is allowed to mention the somewhat overused modern slangy adjective, funky. Such steps are easy to reconstruct for, in semantics, no river is so broad that it cannot be crossed by an ingeniously built bridge. The bridges look safe, but one should think twice before crossing them.

Walter W. Skeat believed that *spunk* "tinder" and *fungus* are related to *sponge* (because fungus is spongy). From a phonetic point of view, nothing can be said against his conclusion. Greek had the form *sphóggos* (*gg* designated *ng*) "sponge," and *spunk* would be an acceptable adaptation of Latin *spongia*. However, only the *fungus-sponge* equation is irrefutable, for none of three English words—*punk*, *spunk*, and *funk*—looks like a learned borrowing from Latin. *Funk* "panic" seems to have originated in eighteenth-century university slang, and, although a close analog of the phrase *to be in a funk* has been found in older Flemish, one wonders how it got there and how it made its way to Oxford, where no one would be fluent in Flemish. A play on some Latin noun suggests itself, but no such noun exists. To give an example of puns and verbal games in this area, I will retell the entry on the slang word *fug* from the *Oxford Dictionary of English Etymology*. *Fug* means "stuffy atmosphere"; it turned up in printed texts only in the nineteenth century and may be a blending of *funk* and *fogo*, both meaning "offensive smell" and recorded also in the nineteenth century. Compare *fogus* "tobacco," a seventeenth-century word, perhaps a jocular Latinization of *fog*, but *fug* exists as a variant of *fog* in Scots. We are in a maze with no thread to show us the way.

A good etymology is like a jigsaw puzzle: *all* the pieces must find their places. Skeat was a great master of linguistic reconstruction, but he left his problem in the middle. *Spunk* and *sponge* form a natural union only if we forget about *funk*. Yet we are not allowed to forget it. Perhaps *punk*, *spunk*, and *funk* interacted at one time. Some senses of all three words were "low," and their figurative senses were probably better known than their reference to tinder. They rhyme, a factor that plays an important role in the history of words, for words do not live in isolation: they fight, fall prey to fatal attraction, and tend to behave like spiders in a jar.

Although I am unable to disentangle the knot of *punk*, *spunk*, and *funk* to my or anyone's satisfaction, my tentative conclusion may not be entirely fanciful. *Punk*, an almost generic name of a swollen object with analogs outside English, was evidently the "progenitor" of this group. *Spunk* looks like *punk* with *s-mobile* added to it; a later word, despite the fact that some inconclusive evidence points to its earlier attestation. *Funk* may have a prehistory independent of those two (but it hardly goes back to an Indo-European word like *sponge*). Yet when it arose, it began to play lobster quadrille with them. Today, they are inseparable, even though some senses are obsolete and little remembered. Too bad there is no *spunk* "a funky glowworm" in some Swedish dialect to help us out.

Quiz and Gig

The following dialogue takes place in the play *The Heir at Law* by George Colman the younger: "*Dick.* But what a confounded Gig you look like. *Pangloss.* A Gig! umph! That's an Eton phrase; the Westminsters call it Quiz" (Act IV, Scene 2). The play was first performed at the Haymarket in 1797. The *OED* quotes Pangloss's reply at *gig*, but it is the exchange that will interest us. The earliest known citation for *quiz* "odd-looking figure" goes back to 1782. By the end of the century the word must have spread far and wide and could be recognized by theater-goers. Its synonym *gig*, along with *fag* (another piece of fashionable school slang: "a junior performing certain duties for a senior boy," perhaps scurrilous, but devoid of sexual overtones), came into vogue around the same time. The senses of *quiz*, recorded in the *OED*, are as follows: "odd or eccentric person," "odd-looking thing," "bandalore" (i.e., "whirligig," a kind of yo-yo; note *gig* at the end of *whirligig*), "someone who likes to make fun of others," "hoax," and finally, "oral examination." The latest meaning, the only one remembered today, originated in the United States and was attested in the eighteen-nineties. Dr. Stephen Goranson sent me a passage from *The Microcosm . . .* by Gregory Griffin: "There's a quiz! There is a good one! My God! What a Gig! What a tough one!"

The origin of *quiz* is supposed to be unknown, but its recorded history is before us, and we can draw some tentative conclusions. Wherever the word arose, its success must have stemmed from its use by the young elite. *Quiz* has always referred to something droll and whimsically comical, be it a ludicrous figure, a funny object, or a toy. Most probably, it was coined shortly before the time of its first attestation, that is, a few years before 1780. If those conclusions are right, the idea that *quiz* is in some way connected with the dialectal bird name *quist* need not be considered.

School slang can occasionally be traced to Latin and Greek. Both languages constituted the core of boys' education for centuries and gave rise to many pseudo-classical words and phrases. The old conjecture that *quiz* is the middle syllable of *inquisitive* (it had even Skeat's tepid support) is not bad. The quizzes of old were mostly given to banter, but the 1864 edition of Hotten's *Slang Dictionary* states that, at Oxford, *quiz* designated a prying person and not only an odd fellow. Still, it seems that prying was not a conspicuous feature of the earliest quizzes. (To anticipate an obvious suggestion: the adjective *quizzical*, 1800, was derived from the noun; therefore, *quiz* is not a back formation from it. The short-lived neologisms *quizzish*, *quizzity*, *quizzy*, and *quizzify* also existed. All of them were near contemporaries of *quiz* and testify to the popularity of the word from which they were derived.) Another (unattractive) hypothesis traces *quiz* to "a corruption" of Latin *quid is't* (= *quid is est* "what this is").

Some folklore has grown around the circumstances in which *quiz* came into being. According to one story, the inventor of *quiz* was a certain Daly, the manager of a Dublin theater, who, in 1791, wagered that a word of no meaning would become the common talk and puzzle of the city in twenty-four hours. In the course of that time, the letters *q*, *u*, *i*, *z* were chalked or posted on all the walls of Dublin with an effect that Daly won the wager. Thus, we are again in Ireland. Some such episode is not unthinkable. However, two more people have been named as the winners of the same wager. Besides, as the citations in the *OED* show, by 1791, *quiz* was at least nine years old, so that Daly's writing on the wall comes too late.

I doubt that many people are in the habit of reading *The Eclectic Magazine of Foreign Literature, Science, and Art*, once published in New York, and will therefore quote a passage from its volume for 1865, with the sole purpose of providing entertainment. In an article entitled "Eccentric etymologies" and meant for "leisure hours," an anonymous author wrote: "There is the phrase *to quiz* a person; concerning which we have seen this explanation: 'A certain great personage is said to have exhibited the exercise of a child's plaything called the quiz, in consequence of which the citizens of Dublin and London were for some time ridiculously employed in the same puerile sport whenever they appeared in the streets; whence to quiz a man came to signify to dupe him sportively with a ludicrous mistake.'"

This story is silly, but a few details may be worthy of consideration: reference to "a certain great personage" seems to hearken back to an oft-repeated anecdote about the Duke of Wellington, then Captain Wesley, who allegedly "amused himself with a quiz, the toy, when serving on a committee of the Irish House of Commons; it is assumed that *quiz* emerged as the name of a toy" (not an unreasonable assumption) and was only later applied to people; finally, Dublin is, characteristically, mentioned in the story before London. Despite the obscurity surrounding the history of *quiz*, at some time the Irish may have occupied themselves with that toy more than the British.

Quiz has always been a "funny word." This fact needs no additional proof, but a specific circumstance underscores its comic effect. *Quiz* had the doublet *quoz*. The change of short *i* and *e* to short *o* seems to affect only playful words or such as are made to sound playful. Thus, *wedge* has the variants *wodge* and *wadge*; both designate a particularly big or bulky lump. In similar fashion, *freshman* yielded *frosh*, and *umbrella* degenerated into *brolly*.

Regardless of whether *quiz* began its life as a coinage by a university wit or as a street name of a popular toy, we may ask how the sound complex *q-u-i-z* occurred to its inventor. English words ending in *z* (*buzz, razzmatazz, showbiz, fizz*, and so forth) usually lack dignity. Likewise, *sizzle, puzzle, dazzle, razzle-dazzle*, and their ilk, though not vulgar, are showy. By contrast, the influence of *squeeze* or *question* on *quiz* (a hypothesis by a serious scholar) seems unlikely. If *quiz* reminds us of any other word, it is, first and foremost, *whiz*. This is what Skeat thought. Though the *Century Dictionary* followed Skeat, it went further. It assumed that the first quiz was a toy but considered *quiz* to be a dialectal variant of *whiz*. There is probably no need to refer to regional speech here. *Whiz* is an excellent name for a toy and for anything that makes one feel giddy. Consider how quickly our computer wizzes (*wiz* was an abbreviation of *wizard*) turned into whizzes. *Quiz* may have been a sound-symbolic formation of the same order as *whiz* or a deliberate alteration of *whiz*: new merchandise needed a new but evocative name. We would be better off if we knew who made and sold quizzes, and where. Perhaps the history of *gig* may shed additional light on the origin of *quiz*.

The main meanings of the noun *gig* are as follows: "something that whirls," for example "top" (known since approximately the middle of the fifteenth century), "flighty girl" (attested as early as 1225), "odd-looking figure" (chiefly Eaton slang; the earliest citation is dated 1777), "joke, whim" (1590), "fun, merriment" (again 1777), "light two-wheeled one-horse carriage" (1791), "a kind of boat" (1790), and "live performance of popular music" (1926); hence "a job for a musician." Today, only the last-named meaning is alive in everyday speech. The verb *gig* "move back and forth" has also been recorded. It is believed to be either sound-imitative or sound-symbolic: supposedly, it renders the sound of a whirling object or suggests quick rotation by its form. Even though the earliest sense that turned up in texts is "giddy girl," the direct meaning ("whirling object") must have preceded the figurative one. Wherever we find a verb meaning "to move back and forth," obscene connotations should be expected. *Sheela na gig* is the name given to carvings of naked women displaying an exaggerated vulva. The origin of this *gig* is not far to seek.

Perhaps the most surprising thing about the history of *gig* is the chronology. The word existed at the beginning of the thirteenth century. "Joke, whim" made its way into literature in Shakespeare's lifetime. Two hundred years later, a boat and a vehicle called *gig* surfaced, and, at the peak of the jazz generation, musicians appropriated the word. Are we witnessing an uninterrupted, even if imperfectly recorded, history of the same word, or does the palindromic sound complex *gig* possess an inherent force that makes speakers endow it with ever new but related meanings? We do not have the means for an adequate answer to this question, but a bird's-eye view of *gig* and its extended family may clarify the picture a little.

The sound complex *g-g ~ g-k* can easily be found in sound-imitative words. One of them is *giggle*, which resembles verbs of the same meaning in various languages. *Gak, gok, gek, gik,* and their likes are often used to render the impression made by inarticulate speech. In the past, speakers of the Germanic languages heard *cuckoo* as *gauk*. Geese "say" *ga-ga* nearly everywhere; a byproduct of *ga-ga* is *gaggle*.

A whirling top hardly makes a sound resembling *gig-gig*, but *g-g* ~ *g-k* words can also denote movement away from the right or straight course. Such are German *gaukeln* "flit, flutter" and *geigen* "move back and forth" and especially Icelandic *geiga* "take a wrong direction." Any geek will be able to cite more such words.

It is hard to tell what those sound combinations have to do with deviation from the straight line, but words beginning and ending with the same consonant *(bib, gag, dud,* etc.) do not command respect and tend to denote objects and actions lacking dignity. Their etymology is usually undeterminable, and their look-alikes turn up in a variety of languages. They can be borrowed or native, and they can be coined many times with a similar effect. Dictionaries are not sure where *jig* came from. It may be English, but Old French *giguer* "gambol" is close enough (this verb is perhaps of Germanic origin). German *Geige* "fiddle, violin" resembles Old French *gigue* (the same meaning). One can imagine that the German fiddle is called *Geige* because the bow moves back and forth, but it is equally probable that the instrument's name derives from the sound it makes. I would prefer to trace English *gig* and German *Geige* to the *g-g* verbs of movement. However, the question remains open; the sound-imitative origin of *Geige* is not excluded.

Gig, in the role of a "sound gesture," seems to have lingered in the collective memory of English-speakers for nearly a millennium. It engendered words pertaining to spasmodic and guttural sounds, such as *giggle* and *gaggle* (was Old English *geagl* "throat, gullet" one of them?) and to erratic movement. Giddy human beings (flirtatious young women among them), as well as things inconstant and "weightless," from precarious carriages to (temporary) jobs, were doomed to be called gigs. A top and a yo-yo qualify for the name *whirl-gig*. At the end of the eighteenth century, *gig* became part of Eaton slang. The circumstances in which this momentous event took place are now beyond recovery, but the motivation behind the coinage is obvious.

A gig is a toy, an oddity, a lightweight. So is a quiz. If we are allowed to combine the evidence from the history of both words, the following picture will emerge. People called gigs are eccentric; their moods are unpredictable. This quality endeared them to English-speakers and ensured the longevity of the word *gig*. Flighty girls were referred to as gigs in one of the most polished books of the English Middle Ages (instructions to nuns how to conduct themselves and how to avoid reprehensible behavior); even then *gig* must have had unmistakable slangy coloring. Five hundred and fifty years later, it was reinvented with a similar meaning in the most prestigious public (i.e., private) school of England.

The etymology of *quiz* is less transparent. Most likely, the earliest quiz was a toy. It matters little that *quiz* "toy" was found in texts eight years later than *quiz* "odd person." The recorded history of such words tells us when they were first used by authors, not when they were coined. Antedatings by the team of the *OED* and by other readers teach us caution. In dealing with slang, special caution is required, for racy, informal speech and belles-lettres are at cross-purposes even today. Finally, what is eight years in the life of a word? All the other meanings of *quiz* appear to be derivative of "toy." If so, the paths of *quiz* and *gig* to British public schools were not dissimilar. Today, they are worlds apart: one is a test in a classroom; the other, a job. With the scanty information at our disposal, we should tread gingerly while offering etymologies, but it may not be too daring to suggest that *quiz* is an alteration of *whiz*. To placate those who are not satisfied with the tentative nature of my solution, I may add that the etymology of *top* (the toy) has also been discussed many times and also with astonishingly meager results ("origin unknown").

Oof

There is an almost incomprehensible number of English words for money and various coins. Some of them, like *shilling*, are very old. We know (or we think we know) where they came from. Other words (the majority) surfaced as slang, and our record of them seldom goes beyond the early modern period. They belonged to thieves and counterfeiters' vocabulary; outsiders were not supposed to make sense of all those boodles, crocards, firks, prindles ~ pringles, and wengs. Words are like people, and it is no wonder that some upstarts make their way into high society and become respectable. Among them are, for instance, *buck* "dollar," along with the now fairly obsolete *quid* "pound" (such a strange Latinism!), *bob* "shilling," and *stiver* "a small coin." Coins have always circulated far outside their countries of origin (Dutch *stiver* is one of them). Cant words, along with money in general, discovered the joys of globalization long before our time. The international community of criminals accepted them, and that is why so much "monetary slang" is "foreign-born" and why its etymology puzzles historical linguists.

A word lover can enjoy names without knowing their origin: they are like pets (mongrels are often much friendlier than purebreds). Who can resist the charm of *scittick* ~ *scuttick* ~ *scuddick* ~ *scurrick* and their cousins (or perhaps look-alikes) *scat* and *squiddish*? *Boar*, *grunter*, *hog*, and the aforementioned *buck*—aren't they impressive-looking beasts? Money, as Kipling's Mowgli said, are things that change hands and don't become warmer in the process. Very true, but we are word hunters, not merchants, and this story is about the word *oof*, British slang for "money." Its origin has been guessed, and there is every reason to be proud of the result.

It was amateurs who initiated the guessing game about the etymology of *oof*. They were inspired by the famous Osborne trial (1892; of course, its fame faded long ago), at which the word *oof* was used more than once; this circumstance explains the date of the first letters on this subject sent to *Notes and Queries* (1893). By that time, *oof* had been around for several decades but needed a push from outside to become public property. Some people fell into a trap. They knew the phrase *oof bird* "an imaginary provider of wealth." Most likely, the phrase emerged as a joke and was coined under the influence of French *oef* "egg," with reference to the bird that lays golden eggs. Quite naturally, they concluded that *oof* is the English pronunciation of *oef*. It did not bother them that no English speaker, however atrocious his or her accent might be, would turn *oef* into *oof*.

On the other hand, there was a man called William Hoof, a "wealthy railway contractor, who died in 1855, leaving upward of half a million sterling." *Hoof*, with its *h* dropped, would have yielded *oof*. In the middle of the nineteenth century and much later, such wild conjectures filled the pages of many popular journals. But there were others whose ideas were not only sensible but also correct. A correspondent to *Notes and Queries*, who identified himself by his four initials (S. J. A. F.; many readers must have known who hid under those letters), remarked that in Low German there was the slang word *ofti[s]ch* "money." "It has descended to its present low estate from certain semi-Bohemian circles." He also cited the word *oofless* "penniless." Soon after him, Willoughby Maycock pointed out that the word in question was of Jewish origin and had its roots in London. Its etymon, he repeated, was the phrase *ooftisch* "on the table": the stakes had to be put on the table before the game began. The word "was introduced . . . by the facetious columns of the *Sporting Times*, but not invented by that organ." *Money on the table* would be an approximate analog of English *cash on the nail* and especially of Russian *den'gi na bochku* "money on the barrel" (*money on the barrel* or *cash on the barrelhead* has some currency in English, especially, as it seems, in American English).

Walter W. Skeat found the noun *spinuffen* "money" (plural) in a Westphalian dictionary and derived *oof* from *uffen* (1899). Strangely, he disregarded (more probably, missed) the explanation offered six years earlier. His note made James Platt, Junior, a versatile student of word origins, to write in his rejoinder that it was as certainly courting failure to explain *oof* without reference to its full form *ooftisch* as it would be to attempt the derivation of *bus* and *cab* without taking into account *omnibus* and *cabriolet*. Skeat rarely conceded defeat gracefully and wrote to *Notes and Queries* again. No, he was not at all sure that *spinuffen* and *ooftisch* are unrelated, "for the latter, whether it represents *ooft-isch* or *ooft-ich*, may be suspected to be formed upon the base *ooft*." He was wrong and never tried to defend his etymology again. The first edition of the *OED* recognized the Jewish derivation of *ooftisch*, though without absolute certainty. All the later dictionaries followed the *OED*. Be that as it may, *oof* does seem to go back to *ooftisch*.

A small triumph! One insignificant "slangism" has emerged from its obscurity, but this is how, nowadays, the science of etymology progresses: by infinitesimal steps. Unlike "regular" words, slang comes from popular culture and the underworld; it is a product of the ludic spirit. In that area, researchers can seldom base their conclusions on precedent. Phonetic correspondences play little or no role in the development of slang. Words of allegedly Jewish origin are particularly dangerous, for, time and again, Hebrew and Yiddish are conjured up to account for the coinages (particularly when it comes to crime and swindling) that have nothing to do with the life and language of the Jews. British English slang depends on Yiddish to a much smaller extent than does German. But *ooftisch* lost its second element in England; so *oof* can be called English, especially because it rhymes with *hoof* (the *oo* in its source sounded like English *awe*). Dictionaries mark *oof* as British slang. However, the word was not unknown in the United States, and the *Century Dictionary* has a good American citation.

Tip

Tit for tat is a well-known phrase. At one time, English *tip for tap* also existed. Words like *tip, tap, top, tick, tack, tock, tit, tat,* and *tot*, as well as those with voiced endings like *tid-* (compare *tidbit*, the American version of *titbit*), *tad*, and *tod* ("bush; fox"), are ideal candidates for sound imitative coinages. One of the Swedish calls to hens is *tup-tup-tuppa* (*tup* "rooster"). The Russian for "knock-knock" is *took-took-took*, whereas *top-top* means "thump-thump."

The symbolic value of such words is equally obvious. *Tip* and *tit* designate small objects, while the things called *tap* and *tat* must be big. But the devil is in the details, and those are many and diverse. For example, *tup* is "rooster" in Swedish but "uncastrated ram" in English (whence the verb *tup* "to copulate," memorable from *Othello*: "an old ram is tupping your white ewe"). Are we dealing with an ancient, undifferentiated name for a male animal that acquired one meaning in Swedish and another in English, or with a sound complex applied to the rooster and the ram arbitrarily, by chance? Was the idea of copulation foremost in the minds of those animal breeders who dealt with mammals and fowl? Words for "having sex" are often short and energetic. The list of nouns and verbs like *tip, top,* and so forth is long and has vague contours. They multiply like maggots, have partly overlapping meanings, pretend to be related, but refuse to divulge their pedigree.

Another aggravating factor an etymologist faces is the rampant homonymy among such words. First comes *tip* "a pointed end" (alongside the verb *to tip*, as in Chaucer's *tipped with horn*). It is supposed to have reached England from Scandinavia, for its ancestor did not turn up in Old English (not a conclusive argument because such words may exist in popular speech for centuries without making their way into a book). Anyway, the Old Icelandic form was *typpi*, evidently from *tuppi* "top." It is rather disconcerting to know that, if you look at *tip* long enough, you may discover *top*. Northern (i.e., Low) German also had *tip*, but this form, like its English equivalent, was recorded late, so that we cannot decide to what extent (if at all) it enjoyed popularity in England and interacted with the Scandinavian form. Thus, *tip* is *top*.

Next we notice the verb *tip*, whose earliest recorded meaning was "to pat," and realize that *tip* is also *tap* (and we cannot help noticing that *tap* is simply *pat* read from right to left). The verb *tip* had a strange history. It was used in a most respectable thirteenth-century book, then disappeared for four hundred years, reemerged in thieves' cant, and stayed in honest people's usage with the sense "to strike lightly," as in the following sentence from Swift (cited in the *Century Dictionary*; Swift detested the newfangled monosyllabic slang of his time): "A third rogue tips me by the elbow." Perhaps it is the same verb as in Chaucer's *tipped with horn*, but there is no knowing. Such words are often coined, stay for a while, die, and reemerge again with the same or a similar meaning.

Tip also means "overturn" (a tip-cart in British English corresponds to the American dump truck), and it, too, may or may not be of Scandinavian descent. But it emerged in texts so late (in the seventeenth century) that its "prehistory" is beyond reconstruction. In close proximity to *tip* we find *tipple* and *tipsy*. *Tippler* seems to have preceded *tipple*. If such is indeed the order of these words' appearance in language and not only in our texts, then the verb is a back formation from the noun (like *beg* from *beggar* and *sculpt* from *sculptor*). Presumably, tipsy people are unsteady on their legs. The suffix -*sy* is not productive, even though it occurs in a few adjectives, such as *topsy-turvy*, and deceptively in *clumsy*, *flimsy*, and a few others.

The circumstances in which *tipsy* sprang up remain unclear, especially because a tipsy person, unlike somebody who is three sheets to the wind, cannot serve as the embodiment of unsteadiness. Regional Norwegian has *tippa* "drink in small quantities" and *tipla* "drink slowly." Verbs with the suffix -*le* (they tend to refer to recurring action) are called *frequentative*. In English, *babble*, *cackle*, and the like are usually of northern German or Dutch origin. In the Scandinavian languages, such formations exist, too; however, some frequentative verbs are probably native English (thus, *gobble* seems to be from *gob*). Be that as it may, *tipla* is a frequentative extension of *tippa*. A tippler sips liquor, that is, indulges in what is called *tippa*. The idea of small-ness is unmistakable in *tippa*, but the connection with tipping and tapping is not. *Tap* "faucet" provides no help, for its basic meaning is "plug."

The most interesting part of the story concerns the origin of *tip* "to give advice" and *tip* "to give a gratuity." In principle, it is not too difficult to derive *tip* "advise in a small way" from *tip* "touch," and *tip* "gratuity" from "thing 'tipped' into a hand." For Samuel Johnson, whose great dictionary appeared in 1755, *tip* "give" was "a low word." Colloquial and slangy phrases with the verb *tip* were frequent, and some of them are still or were not long ago current in slang or in a fully unbuttoned variant of colloquial English: "tip me your daddle *or* flipper" (hand), "tip me a hog" (shilling), "tip him a wink" (advice), "tip the traveler" (humbug a guest at an inn with travelers' yarns), "tip the double" (de-camp), "tip the grampus" (an old seafaring phrase, meaning: "duck a skulker for being asleep on his watch"), "tip a stave" (sing), and "tip one's rags a gallop" (run away; thieves' slang), to mention a few.

It is the predominantly "low" sphere in which this meaning of the verb *tip* has always flourished and a sudden explosion of its use in the second half of the sixteenth century that make the idea of a straight line from *tip* "touch, tap; turn over" to *tip* "give" suspect. One wonders whether we have to look for a missing link in northern German slang. German etymological dictionaries are cautious. In the entries on the cognates of *tip*, *tap*, and *top*, we read that the origin of those words is unknown or known insufficiently.

Given the verb *tip* "provide" (almost anything from money to in-formation), *tip* "gratuity" constitutes no problem. More often, verbs are formed from nouns, but occasionally the process goes in the op-posite direction. Two other etymologies of the noun sound improb-able. One connects *tip* with *stipend*, that is, *stip* or *stips*, minus initial *s*. The other goes back to the following story (I quote from Leo Pap's 1982 article): "One day at the Cheshire Cheese tavern in London's Fleet Street—that famous hangout of Dr. Samuel Johnson, of Boswell, Goldsmith, Reynolds, and some other men of letters who had constituted themselves into a Literary Club—a waiter hung a small wooden money box onto the wall near the dining room entrance. On this box, which evidently was in imitation of the receptacles customarily displayed in private houses at Christmas and on visiting days during the year, for donations which the servant staff expected from guests or from the master's own family—on the box the waiter painted the words TO INSURE PROMPTNESS. The idea, of course, was that entering guests who wanted to be assured of speedy service might do well to drop a tinkling little penny or halfpenny in the box, so as to shoot some joyful energy into the servitor's tired legs. Similar collection boxes went up in other coffeehouses and hostelries in town; and soon the motto on the box could safely be reduced to the mere initials, T. I. P. Before long, *the T. I. P box* was commonly referred to as the *tip box*, whence *tip*." Although Pap doubts that the story was "fabricated out of whole cloth," he does not believe that this is how the word *tip* "gratuity" came into being. It is indeed a cock-and-bull story, good enough only to "tip a traveler." In my experience, all etymologies that refer to common words as acronyms (F. U. C. K., P. O. S. H., and their ilk) are wrong. (*OK* is a special case.) Apparently, the verb *tip* everybody understood in the days of Johnson, Goldsmith, and Reynolds, was "decoded" into T. I. P. and "glossed" as *to insure promptness.*

There is one more hitch in the etymology of *tip*. In several European languages, a gratuity of this sort goes under the name of "drink money" (German *Trinkgeld*, French *pourboire*, etc.), with the intimation that the servitor will drink it up. English *tip* "a draught of liquor" has been recorded (and let us not forget *tippler* and *tipsy*). It is possible but not very probable that two factors contributed to the rise of *tip* "gratuity": the money could have been "tipped" into the waiter's hand, and he could have been expected to drink the giver's health. Ever since the word struck root in the language, waiters have been tapping their patrons' pockets, and patrons have been tipping waiters. We have perfected the system: add 10%, add 15%, or eat free but give (tip) a "donation."

Note
The article by Leo Pap was published in *Forum Linguisticorum* 6, 1982, 259–64.

Helpmeet and Syllabus

In the Authorized Version of the Bible, we read: "And the Lord God said, it is not good that the man should be alone; I will make him an help meet for him." The phrase *meet for him* is supplied with the following marginal note: "Heb. *As before him.*" The Hebrew word for *help* (its old-fashioned pronunciation is approximately *a-z-er*) has a meaning slightly different from the one that the context of Gen. II:18 suggests to the modern reader because it is regularly used in addressing God in the Psalms (in which "help" is also the gloss). Psalm 27: 9, "Hide not thy face far from me; . . . thou hast been my help." Perhaps the most colorful example occurs in Psalm 70:5, "O God: thou art my help and my deliverer; O Lord, make no tarrying." Obviously, *help* in the story of how Eve was created does not mean "servant" or "assistant," as in the advertisement: "Help wanted."

Meet "fit, suitable" is an obsolete adjective. It has nothing to do with the verb *meet* "encounter," but shares the root with *mete* in the equally archaic collocation *mete out* and the noun *meat*. Both refer to measuring: *mete (out)* does so directly (compare German *messen* "to measure"), and *meat* indirectly (the noun designated "portion of food"; the ancient sense of *meat* "food" has been retained in the idiom *meat and drink* and in compounds like *mincemeat* and *sweetmeats*). Thus, with the emergence of Eve, Adam acquired someone on whose love and help he could depend, a companion, a partner "measured out" and thus fit for him. The Authorized Version gives a marginal note to this place because the Hebrew phrase corresponding to the conjunction *like* is hard to render in English, but "help" does not seem to have caused the translators any problems. The Vulgate text (in Latin) has *adiutorium similem sibi* (*adiutorium* "help, assistance; support").

As time went on, but as early as in the seventeenth century, printers began to hyphenate *help-meet* in the Biblical verse, though the reason for this practice is not clear: no one could have been in doubt about the meaning of the adjective *meet*. The result was that *help-meet* and *helpmeet* (without a hyphen) was understood as a single unit and *for him* appeared redundant. When the compound *helpmeet* came into being, Wordsworth and Tennyson used it, and the newcomer became a competitor of its synonym *helpmate*. This part of the story can be found in the *Oxford English Dictionary* and in every book that deals with the origin of *helpmeet*. James Murray, the first editor of the *OED*, did not conceal his contempt for the fools who coined a useless word. The *Century Dictionary* echoes Murray: "An absurd compound, taken as equivalent to *helpmate*."

We have enjoyed the *OED* so long that we cannot imagine our education without it. A chance remark in a correspondence to the immensely popular periodical *Notes and Queries* brought forth a lively—tinged with acerbity, though invariably polite—exchange that would hardly be possible in today's newspapers and magazines. Our word columns, to the extent that they still exist, devote some space to slang and usage, but, at the end of the nineteenth century, educated Britons found it worth their while to argue endlessly over whether *helpmate* had been derived from *helpmeet* or whether the process had gone in the opposite direction.

The polemic started in 1898, and opinions, as always, were divided. The phrase *meet help* (i.e., "appropriate help") was cited, Wordsworth and Tennyson were quoted to prove the legitimacy of *helpmeet* (it is astounding how well people remembered their favorite authors), the question about whether *helpmeet* is applicable only to the wife or also to the husband produced several noble statements about the high status of the first woman in Paradise, the meaning of *mate* (as in *playmate* vs. *helpmate*) was pondered, and the experience of great authors was declared to have greater weight than the evidence of dictionaries. But the basic question, which word appeared in English first (*helpmate* or *helpmeet*), remained unanswered. Once again, sides were taken and arguments put forward in defense of each view. None of it would have been worth recalling but for the dramatic denouement. In the middle of the polemic, the section *Heel—Hod* of the *OED* was published, and anyone could see that *help-meet* first occurred in Dryden (1673) and *helpmate* in 1715. Moreover, it became clear that *helpmeet* achieved full recognition only in the nineteenth century. The *OED* suggested that *helpmate* might have experienced the influence of *helpmeet*. Now nothing was left to talk about, and one of the proponents of the wrong opinion withdrew his considerations in a footnote.

Today, neither *helpmate* nor *helpmeet*, let alone the short-lived *helpfellow*, seems to be current, but, as noted, the best poets used *helpmeet*. Should we pity their inadequate mastery of English? We'd rather not. Language constantly delivers freaks, and if they are accepted by the speaking community, they begin to look like well-formed creatures. In usage, everything is right that the majority considers right, which does not mean that every novelty is beautiful.

By way of conclusion, I would like to recapitulate the story of another monster that has prospered beyond the wildest expectation of its chance inventors. In one of his letters, Cicero used the word *sittybas* (which is the accusative plural of Latin, actually Greek, *sittýba* "label, title slip"). In an English fifteenth-century edition of Cicero, *sittybas* appeared as *syllabos*, with three misprints. To ennoble the misbegotten noun, it was respelled in Greek with the spurious ending *-os* and returned to Latin. This is how *syllabus* was born, and, once surrounded by other venerable *-us* words, it had to join the Latin second declension. Hence the plural *syllabi*, which our manuals and spellcheckers treat with disapproval, as though the form *syllabuses* can make restitution for a misprint going back to 1470. Such is the way of a good deal of linguistic flesh. People "corrupt" and "pervert" words, shed endings, merge declensions and conjugations. The entire history of language is an epic of "corruption" and "decay" if every older stage is believed to be loftier than the next one, more or less by definition. Some scholars call change in grammar and the vitality of ill-conceived words progress, others bewail it. The cultured class is always conservative when it comes to usage, but the rest of the world does not care.

3
It Takes All Sorts to Make the World Go Round

Bigots, Bugger, and Beggars

An epic poem the size of the *Iliad* can be written about English *b-g* words. Look up the etymology of *bag, bog, bug, beg, bogey, buggy* "a light horse vehicle," and even *big*, and you will see the same disconcerting answer: "Of unknown/uncertain origin." Many such words have lookalikes or perhaps even cognates in related and unrelated languages. Russian *buka* (pronounced as *booka*, stress on the first syllable) means the same as English *boogey(man)*; the Finnish for *boy* is *pojke*; *bag* has "twins" in Scandinavian and French, and no one knows for sure which came first. Quite a few *b-g* words refer to things and creatures that expand, make a lot of noise, burst, and fill people with fright. But if you want to know where *boogie* came from, reference to some vague general principle will hardly satisfy you. Are most of those words sound-imitating, like *bang* or like *boo*, that some people won't say to a goose? The verbs *boost* and *boast* also begin with *b* and refer to inflating and noise. Perhaps some of them are so much alike across language borders because they are baby words, and language acquisition by children passes through the same stages all over the world.

Be that as it may, below we'll concentrate on the origin of only three (mainly two) *b-g* nouns. At the end of the exploration, their origin will remain partly obscure, but the journey may still be worth undertaking. It appears that the complex *b-g* contributed to the words' staying power: in some mysterious way, their sound shape suggested their negative meaning and ensured their popularity. To put it differently, some *b-g* words seem to be sound-symbolic: you pronounce them and predict that the reference will be to objects low, mean, and reprehensible. What made *b-g* acquire such a reputation is a question for psychologists, and a branch of scholarship called "psycholinguistics" does exist, but we won't risk trespassing on its domains.

Even if we recognize the sound-imitating and sound-symbolic nature of *bug*, *bogey*, and *boogie*, we are still none the wiser with regard to *bigot*, *bugger*, and *beggar*. Only *bugger* seems to have been traced to its root in a convincing way. The origin of *bigot* and *beggar* remains a matter of discussion.

As always, we'll have to wade through both fanciful and clever conjectures, sift them, and try to tease out the grain of truth from numerous conflicting hypotheses. Sadly, the best-known one is not necessarily correct, and, quite often, we wonder where the authors of popular articles get their information. For example, in October 1997, the *Catholic Digest* informed its readers that *bigot* derives from Nathaniel Bigot (1575–1660), an English Puritan preacher. I have not been able to find any information about Nathaniel Bigot (the omniscient Internet does not feature him), but even if that gentleman existed, there can be little doubt that the *Digest* misled its readers, who were also introduced—and in the same cavalier spirit—to Mr. Botch, Mr. Comma, Mr. Fiasco, and even Mr. Doldrum (all in dead earnest).

According to a legend, preserved in an old chronicle, the story of *bigot* begins with Rollo of Normandy. Rollo, a wildly successful tenth-century Viking, a Dane, whose Scandinavian name was Hrólfr, in 918 received his dukedom, later known as Normandy, from King Charles the Simple in return for the promise to stop attacking and ravaging France. Normandy remained part of France, the Vikings soon forgot their Scandinavian heritage and tongue, and when William the Conqueror attacked England in 1066, he spoke the northern dialect of French (Old French, as we call it, the predecessor of Anglo-Norman), and, for all intents and purposes, he was a typical French baron. The legend has it that when the time came for Rollo to kiss Charles's foot, as a sign of his allegiance to the king, he said (in English!): "Nese bi god," that is, "It may not (or 'won't') be so, by God," and this is, the story continues, how *bigod*, later *bigot*, became an opprobrious moniker of the duke and then of the Normans.

The legend is too good to be true. Neither Rollo nor Charles spoke Old English, and if Rollo did say something at the ceremony, he said it in Old Norse or Old French, or (ideally) in Latin, though he may not have known any foreign languages. It is also hard to believe that at the elaborate (agreed on and rehearsed) ritual, Rollo would have violated the protocol. Some taunting name of the Normans, who did have a reputation for bad manners (sea robbers and pirates are seldom admired by their victims or held up as models of courtesy), apparently, existed because Old French (!) *bigot* did turn up in a poem by the once famous and influential twelfth-century Anglo-Norman poet Robert Wace as a term of abuse for the Normans by the French. But Wace was born in Jersey and probably remembered or even knew some English. We cannot decide whether the insult had any currency. Curses and swear words travel freely in isolation, as the worldwide popularity of our ignominious *F*-word shows. By the way, contrary to German, neither Old Norse nor Old French (nor Old English, for that matter) devoiced final consonants, so that it is not clear why we have *bigot*, rather than *bigod*.

To make matters worse, *bigot* emerged in English texts only at the end of the sixteenth century and meant "superstitious religious hypocrite." In French, too, *bigot* resurfaced in the sixteenth century, and its history in the interim period (if such a history existed) is unknown. Most probably, late Middle English *bigot* and Wace's *bigot* are not related, and their similarity is a coincidence. The Norman story has too strong a taste of a folk etymological guess invented in retrospect to explain an obscure word. French *bigot* still means "excessively pious, superstitious."

One of the twentieth-century hypotheses on the origin of *bigot* connects it with Yiddish *begotish* "pious." (Yiddish *bagotish* "godly" also exists, a popular alternation of *begotish*.) Otto F. Best attempted to connect *bigot* with *God* and a word for "moustache," because Spanish *hombre de bigotes*, literally "a man with a moustache," means a steadfast man, a man with a strong character. (However, *los bigotes* also refers to people of irrational authority, prone to pass arbitrary judgment—thus, erring on the side of fanaticism.) Otto F. Best reconstructed a situation in which anti-Semites heaped abuse on the Jews clinging to their religion and refusing to shave off beards. By contrast, he continued, the Jews reviled the beard-shaving apostates. We cannot help wondering why and where the Romance languages borrowed the word *bigot* from Yiddish.

The suggestions about the origin of the word *bigot* are many, but here I will confine myself only to the ones that made their way into accessible reference works and at first sight look plausible. Among them is the derivation of *bigot* from *Visigothi*, the Latin plural of the Visigoths' name. The powerful Germanic tribe of Goths had two branches: Ostrogoths and Visigoths, usually understood as Eastern and Western Goths, though this is not what the names meant when they were coined. In the fourth century, the Visigoths embraced Arian Christianity and were consequently looked upon by Rome as heretics. (The conversion of the Goths is an event of great cultural importance because their bishop Wulfila undertook the translation of the Bible into the language of his flock. Though only part of the Gothic New Testament has survived, it is the earliest long consecutive written text in a Germanic language.) Nothing is gained by finding a similar-sounding ancient word and declaring it to be the etymon of *bigot*. Even if we agree that initial *v* and *b* often alternate in languages, we wonder what to do with the syllable *-si-* in the middle and what happened to the word between roughly the fourth and the sixteenth centuries. The Gothic source of *bigot* inspires little confidence.

A convincing etymology of *bigot* should, most probably, be sought in the religious sphere. Words referring to intolerance and fanaticism often develop from the names of unorthodox groups, viewed as apostates and "enemies of the people." Even *heresy/heretic* derive, via Latin and Old French, from an innocuous word meaning "choice." Hensleigh Wedgwood, a prominent etymologist of the third quarter of the nineteenth century, noted that several religious groups had names sounding like *bigot* and cited *Beghardi*, *Beguines*, and *Beguttæ*. Dean Richard C. Trench, to whom we owe the idea of a collection that later became The *Oxford English Dictionary* (*OED*), believed that *bigot* goes back to *Beguttæ*, and Wedgwood shared his opinion. All such groups, he wrote, "professed a religious life, and wore a distinctive dress, without . . . binding themselves by permanent vows." "We don't gather from the quotations," he continued, "that there was originally anything offensive in the names themselves. . . . But the pretension to superior strictness of life easily falls under the suspicion of insincerity, and thus these names soon began to imply a charge of exaggeration and even hypocrisy." This is true, but in all such etymologies we notice the absence of an important link: Why should just *Beguttæ* have developed into *bigot*?

Both Trench and Wedgwood may have read the book *De Beghardis et Beguinabus Commentarius* by the famous church historian Johannes Laurentius Mosheim (Leipzig: Weidmann, 1790; this is a posthumous edition and the only one I have consulted). The first chapter (a hundred pages) is devoted to the names Beguina, Beguinus, Begutta, and Beghardus. Mosheim did not deal with *bigot*, but Trench certainly had full command of Latin, probably knew the book, and, I assume, was influenced by it.

Trench and Wedgwood seem to have been on the right track. A telling parallel example is the history of the word *bugger*. Its ultimate source is Medieval Latin *bulgarus* "Bulgarian," with reference to the Orthodox Church (thus, heretics from the point of view of Rome). This sense of *Bulgarian* surfaced in the fourteenth century. It reached England two hundred years later. All "heretics" have been invariably accused of sexual perversion, and this is how *bugger* acquired the sense of "sodomite." *Bugger* has never been a popular word in the United States, but it is very well-known in Canada. In British English, the word "ameliorated" has its meaning. *You little bugger* is almost as innocuous as *you little rascal*. Thus, from "Bulgarian" to "heretic" and "pervert" and to the appellation of someone who is perhaps a bit too cute, rather than cocky or obstreperous.

So much for buggers, and back to bigots. In the scholarly literature I have found references that seem more promising than any of those cited above. *Bigot*, it has been proposed, is a shortening of *Albigot*. Albigensian heresy was not a minor event in the religious history of Europe. It flourished at the end of the twelfth and the beginning of the thirteenth century in southern France—that is, exactly where and when the word *bigot* seems to have turned up for the first time. To accept this derivation, we probably have to ignore the evidence of Italian verbs *sbigottire* "to dismay" and *sbigottirsi* "to be dismayed or amazed, dumfounded." Perhaps they are not related to *bigot*, and the coincidence is fortuitous. The derivation of *bigot* from *Albigot* was suggested, among other sources, in a review of an excellent etymological dictionary of French, and it must have been noticed by the authors, but I have not found any response to it anywhere.

Though *bigot* is perhaps no longer a word of unknown origin (the derivations from *Albigot* look promising), we can only say with certainty that some of the older proposed derivations are undoubtedly wrong, while the seemingly correct one is destined to remain an object of dispute. But such is the leitmotif of this whole book. The words it treats have come in from the murk, and my hope is to throw some light on their obscurity, rather than dispel it once and for all. In any case, a disquisition on a highly problematic word is probably more rewarding than the verdict we find in all dictionaries: *bigot* "of unknown origin."

We can now turn to the history of *beg* and *beggar*. This history is full of dramatic moments. Both words turned up in English texts in the early thirteenth century, and we cannot know which came first. If it was the verb, we wonder why *beggar* was not spelled *begger*. The variant *begger* appeared much later and must have arisen because of the belief that *beggar* had originated as an agent noun (like *writer* from *write*, *reader* from *read*, and so forth). If *beggar* preceded *beg*, the verb will end up among other examples of so-called *back formation* (like *peddle* from *peddler* and *sculpt* from *sculptor*).

The attempt to trace *beg* to German *begehren* "to desire, covet" was given up quite early because *be-* in *begehren* is and has always been an unstressed prefix. No one would have clipped *be´gehren* to *beg*, just as today no one would clip English *belittle* to *bel* or *befuddle* to *bef*. The first volume of the *OED* with the letters A and B was published in 1884. By that time, James A. H. Murray, the *OED*'s editor, had known all the hypotheses that reference books occasionally recycle to this day. And so did Walter W. Skeat, whose dictionary of English etymology was completed in 1882.

Skeat and Murray had many predecessors. One of the earliest English dictionaries of word origins, by Stephen Skinner, came out in 1671. In dealing with words *come*, *go*, *get*, *do*, and their likes, the early etymologists were at a great disadvantage because they seldom went beyond looking for similar-sounding words in Hebrew, Greek, and Latin, but *beg* seems to have been medieval slang, so that a writer living in the seventeenth century could offer as reasonable a suggestion about its source as anyone three hundred years later. Skinner proposed that beggars got their names from carrying bags. Two knowledgeable nineteenth-century scholars shared Skinner's opinion.

Hensleigh Wedgwood wrote in 1872: "It must be borne in mind that the bag was a universal characteristic of the beggar, at a time when all his alms were given in kind, and a beggar is hardly ever introduced in our older writers without mention being made of his bag." Eduard Mueller (or Müller), a reliable but almost forgotten German etymologist of English, followed Wedgwood. Yet theirs is a hopeless hypothesis because beggars were never called baggers, and the change of *a* to *e* cannot be explained away. Skeat and Murray had every right to dismiss the *bag ~ beg* etymology as untenable.

An important event in the search for the origin of *beg* occurred in 1871, when Henry Sweet, one of the greatest English philologists ever, brought out his edition of King Alfred's *Pastoral Care*. Pope Gregory's book *Cura Pastoralis* on the duties of the clergy enjoyed tremendous popularity all over the medieval world. Written around 590, it was translated into English under the guidance of or by King Alfred at the end of the ninth century. Sweet's edition appeared in two volumes and contained the Latin and the Old English text supplemented by a translation into Modern English and notes. Once, and only once, the word *bedecige* "I beg" turns up there (Chapter 285, line 120). The jubilant Sweet wrote: "I do not doubt . . . that we have in *bedecian* [the infinitive] a simple derivative of *biddan*, which is itself used to express the idea of 'begging.' . . . Such a derivative exists in the Gothic *bidagwa* 'beggar.' The Old English verb is no doubt the original of our 'beg,' whose etymology has always been a subject of dispute" (I have left out some technical phonetic details). He also mentioned *bedecian* in the preface, and, indeed, he had no reason to fake humility: in etymological studies, discovering the origin of a common but opaque word is a major feat.

Sweet was a man of extraordinary talent, and, as concerns Old Germanic and every aspect of linguistics, he had few rivals, but even he should not have said *I do not doubt* and *no doubt*. Those words usually, if not always, retaliate. As mentioned above, Wulfila translated the Bible into Gothic in the fourth century, and this very early monument of an old Germanic language is of prime importance in understanding and reconstructing all things Germanic. The Gothic noun *bidagwa* "beggar," as though to mock researchers, also occurs only once (John IX: 8) and seems to be a scribal error for *bidaga*. Assuming that *bidaga* is the correct form, it cannot be anything but a cognate of Old English *bed-eci-an* (*-eci-* is a suffix), in which, contrary to German *be-gehren*, *be-* (stressed) is part of the root *bed-*, rather than a prefix. Both seem to be related to English *bid*, as Sweet suggested. Close to *bidaga* is German *Bettler* "beggar."

All this is fine, but it does not follow that *bedecian* is related to *beg* because the consonants given above in bold do not match. Murray treated Sweet's idea with utmost respect. The rare *d ~ g* difference does not seem to have bothered him, but he wondered why, between Alfred's time and the 1240s, the verb in question never turned up in texts. Later, it was shown that *bedecian* did occur in post-Alfredian Old English. Nevertheless, a rather wide chronological gap remained. Skeat also initially accepted Sweet's derivation. Yet it hardly looks convincing. Middle English absorbed countless borrowed words, and it is counterproductive to assume that a rare Old English verb for "beg" lay dormant for at least two centuries to reemerge in a slightly different form in the thirteenth century and become universally known. Mendicancy was such a widespread phenomenon that the verb for "beg" and the noun for "beggar" must have been common. Also, the postulated phonetic change from *d* to *g*, though not unique, has very few analogs. Finally, in the European languages, the story of *beg* versus *beggar* usually starts with the noun; the verb is derived from it later. Even German *Bettler* may have preceded the verb *betteln*.

We should now return to what was said earlier about *bigot*. Several religious groups had names such as *Beghardi*, *Beguines*, and *Beguttæ*. Outsiders may not have always known or cared who belonged to which group: all of them were "heretics" and despised outsiders. Some (only some!) of them were vagrants and mendicants. Accusing "heretics" of sexual perversities and of being idlers who sponged on those who worked ("beggars") did not require any confirmation in fact. *Beggar* was probably clipped from *Beghardi* or some other similar name. *Bigot* seems to have had a different origin, but *beggar*, most likely, arose as an insult, akin to an ethnic slur. It remains for me to add that in dealing with *beggar*, the Internet sticks to Sweet's etymology, unless it makes do with the safe but uninspiring verdict "of uncertain (unknown) origin." If I say that in matters of etymological interest, the Internet should be treated with caution because it is deficient in producing safeguards, this statement, I fear, will be an example of begging the question. So, I'd rather not say anything.

Note

Very little has been written about the word *bigot* in English. Those interested in the older attempts to find the etymology of this word will find some remarks in the periodical *Notes and Queries* 1/I, 1850: 204–5; 1/V, 1852: 277; 1/9, 1854: 560–61; 3/IV, 1863: 39, 137, 171, and in *The Academy* 16, 1879: 104–5. *In French*: Albert Dauzat, in *Festschrift für Ernst Tappolet* . . . (1936): 66–70 and Maurice Grammont in *Revue des langues romanes* 67, 1933: 227–28 (an important piece). In German: Gottfried Baist in *Romanische Forschungen* 7, 1893: 407–13, Leo Spitzer in *Zeitschrift für romanische Philologie* 44, 1924: 188–200 (see pp. 188–92), and Otto F. Best in *Die neueren Sprachen* 18 (n.s.), 1969, 497–502.

The only journal articles (rather, very short notes) devoted entirely to *beggar* are again in *Notes and Queries* 6/I, 1880: 173–74 and 460. In German: Josef Brüch, in *Zeitschrift für romanische Philologie* 40, 1920: 690–91 and Leo Spitzer, also in *Zeitschrift für romanische Philologie* 41, 1921: 351–52. *Beggar* has nothing to do with the beguine movement. See Walter Simons, *Cities of the Ladies: Beguine Communities in the Medieval Low Countries 1200–1565*. Philadelphia: University of Pennsylvania Press, 2001, 32, 120–23, and the notes on pp. 214–15.

Henchman

Nowadays, *henchman* denotes "mercenary adherent, venal follower." This meaning originated in the United States but is known all over the English-speaking world. Yet the word has seen better days. It surfaced in texts in 1360, that is, at the peak of the period known as Middle English (for comparison: Chaucer died in 1400, which means that at some point the word might have been new to him). As usual, several forms of what is now spelled *henchman* competed in medieval manuscripts. The first extant texts with this word were written in Latin, but scribes had no good Latin equivalent for this English noun, which apparently meant "squire, attendant, groom." As was common at that time, they Latinized the form somewhat. *Henchman* appeared as *hengestmannus*. Later, the first component turned up in the forms *henxt-*, *hanks-*, *hanse-*, *heynce-*, and *hensh-*. Only in 1500 do we at last encounter *henchemen* (plural). As far as the pronunciation is concerned, the fluctuation is not unusual. Other words with *s* and *n* in the middle also had comparable variants: for instance, *lynchpin* goes back to *lynspin*.

As far as the origin of *henchman* is concerned, the root of only one form mentioned above makes sense to a scholar: *heng(e)st-* is immediately recognizable as the Old Germanic word for "stallion." It is the same in the Scandinavian languages, and it existed in Old English. For example, the legendary leaders of the invasion of England by Germanic tribes in the fifth century were called Hengest and Horsa, that is, Stallion and Horse. At first sight, the origin of *henchman* poses no problems: if it goes back to *heng(e)stman*, the word meant "horseman." But this etymology does not do justice to the official's duties and hits a chronological snag: by 1360, the English word *hengst* had become hopelessly obsolete. It occurred for the last time in a long poem about old days at the very beginning of the thirteenth century, and even then, it was probably an archaism.

In 1360, *hengst* must have been as little known to English speakers as it is to us, and the spelling *heng(e)stman* never occurred again. Why then did that scribe use it? The term and the office were, apparently, new, so that the scribe may have pronounced the word approximately as *hengestman*. Or perhaps he was an antiquarian, a lover of old poetry, someone who remembered *hengst* and enjoyed showing off. Be that as it may, the form *hengestman* played a decisive role in the attempts by modern researchers to trace the word's origin. Though everybody is aware of the chronological gap, the difficulty does not appear fatal to most lexicographers (contrary to the *OED*, some dictionaries don't even mention its existence). Yet fatal it probably is.

Did *henchman* ever mean "horseman"? And what is a horseman? An officer in charge of stables, a groom, an expert rider? Some light on this word might be expected to come from the 1440 English-Latin dictionary titled *Promptorium Parvulorum* ("*Storehouse for Children*"), compiled in Norfolk. *Hengstman* appears there and is glossed (i.e., translated into Latin) as *gerolocista* or *gerelocista*. One may expect that, in 1440, *hengstman* meant the same or approximately the same as it did in 1360. But the Medieval Latin gloss is almost as obscure as the English word it was supposed to elucidate. Latin *gero* means "to carry," and *gerulus* is "bearer, carrier." If *-ista* is a suffix, the letter *c* in the middle of *gerolocista* remains unexplained. Though the mystery of this word has never been solved to everybody's satisfaction, the gloss in *Promptorium Parvulorum* looks like a genuine (even if garbled) Latin word, so that *ger-* has nothing to do with English *gear*, understood as "harness." If this conclusion is correct, the word in *Promptorium* does not refer to horses and furnishes no clue to the origin of *henchman*.

Characteristically, some older researchers did not associate *henchman* with horses. For example, in the seventeenth century, Thomas Blount, the author of *Glossographia, a dictionary interpreting all such hard words of whatever language now used in our refined English language* (1656; such long titles were typical of that epoch), defined *henchman* simply as "domestic, or one of a family." He copied this definition from an earlier source (he may not have known any better!) and called the word German, unfortunately, without giving reasons for this attribution. Blount, we are surprised to note, considered the word *henchman* hard (i.e., recognized by few of his contemporaries). But it was not "hard": it was becoming or had become obsolete! For some reason, those who used it widely between 1360 and 1600 no longer needed it.

Henchman is still a living word only because Walter Scott revived it. He found *hanchman* (*sic*) in Edmund Burt's *Letters from a Gentleman in the North Scotland*, explained as one who is always at his master's haunch, which, as Ernest Weekley pointed out in his *An Etymological Dictionary of Modern English*, is either a blunder or an invention. There may be no real connection, he added, with the Middle English word! But we are of course interested in the origin of that old word, regardless of Walter Scott's idea, and we realize that without him *henchman* would have become even "harder" to us than it was to Blount (to put it differently, it would have been dead).

Perhaps an association between *henchman* and *haunch* goes back to Burt and Scott. In any case, at one time, it was considered certain. This is what one could read in the *Quarterly Review* (1846–1847,

p. 344) note: "There is a curious etymological indication of an intermediate state of servitude in our olden time, when personal attendants,
in public, were called henchmen, men at the haunch or side; in the
Scotch dialect lackeys are still called flunkies . . ., which is from French
flancier." The comparison between *henchman* and *flunkey* was commonplace; *henchman* designated "a personal attendant or chief gillie of
a Highland chief" as early as the eighteenth century (*gillie* "attendant
on a Highland chief"). A still older etymology derived *henchman* from
Latin *anculus* "servant" (compare English *ancillary* "subordinate").
Neither *haunch* nor *anculus* has anything to do with *henchman.* That
much we know for sure.

If, from a historical point of view, *henchman* is not a horseman, what
did the word mean when it was coined? Here we are approaching one
of the most dramatic episodes in the history of English etymological
research. In the second half of the nineteenth century, word origins
were discussed widely not only in learned journals but also in popular periodicals. Among the contributors, many were amateurs who
knew several languages, studied Latin and Greek at school, and often
suggested the solutions that still stand. One of the main outlets for such
letters to the editor was the London biweekly *Notes and Queries*, established in 1849. In its pages, subscribers from all over the English-
speaking world asked questions and received quick answers about
practically anything: history, economy, politics, archeology, geography, numismatics, literature, genealogy, and language, to name
a few popular areas. The greatest lexicographers constantly asked
questions and received answers from the pages of that journal. As far
as etymology is concerned, an extremely active contributor was Frank
Chance, a medical doctor, who almost never sought other outlets for
his contributions. He died in 1897, and, as the popularity of *Notes and
Queries* waned, his name also fell into desuetude. Today only a few
specialists remember him, but while he was active, as an etymologist
he was equal to the best.

It was he who ignited a long controversy about the etymology of
henchman. His points were two: the word *hengst* "horse" could not be
used in 1360 as part of a compound (because no one knew it), and the
gloss in *Promptorium* does not refer to horses either ("carrier" is too
vague a term). He also noted that no English name for "groom, squire,

attendant" ever had the element *horse* in it. He was right. (I may add that even *equerry* "squire," a late word, acquired its form under the influence of folk etymology: people thought that a person bearing such a name had to do something with horses!)

Frank Chance's main opponent was the celebrated English etymologist Walter W. Skeat, who as a polemicist was no less fiery than Chance, but in that controversy, his defense looks unusually restrained. He reluctantly admitted that *hengstman* could not be a fourteenth-century English word and suggested that it had come to England "from the continent." Later, he replaced "the continent" with "Low German or Dutch." But *hengst* was not the main Middle Dutch for "horse." Besides, Skeat and some of his allies kept digging up examples in which henchmen were said to deal with horses, and Chance countered that, in the Middle Ages, almost everybody rode a horse or tended to a horse. James A. H. Murray, the first editor of the *OED*, followed the discussion but interfered only once in a noncommittal note and refrained from voicing an opinion. Skeat refused to admit defeat, and his dictionary reproduced the old etymology. Eventually, Murray supported Skeat but, as already mentioned, did not conceal the difficulty of the traditional interpretation. Chance's attack has never been repealed. It has been forgotten, which is a pity.

If *henchman* is not "horseman," what is it? According to Chance, *hengest*, *henxt*, etc. are English versions of some German proper name. He referred to such German family names as *Hansmann*, *Hanschmann*, *Hentzelmann*, *Heintzelmann*, and their likes. Later, he paid special attention to *Heinz* "household spirit" and mentioned the diminutive sprite *Hängstemännekenn*, whom a noted German folklorist connected with *Heinzelmann* (*Heinzelmännchen*) and ultimately with *Hendrik ~ Heinrich*. Indeed, at some time, Heinrich became a synonym for "faithful servant," as follows from the Grimms' tale "The Frog Prince." When an enchanted frog turned into a beautiful young man, his long-suffering faithful servant called Heinrich appeared. According to Chance's reconstruction of events, *henchman* began his career as the German name of a friendly attendant. Perhaps Blount was right in calling *henchman* a German word.

Did Frank Chance solve the riddle? That we cannot know. Why was it necessary in the fourteenth century to borrow a garbled German word meaning "attendant" if in Germany it has never turned up in exactly this form? (But let us not forget that at one time Skeat also agreed that *henchman* had been borrowed from "the continent"!) Etymologies can seldom be proved the way mathematical theorems are, but sometimes enough arguments exist to disprove an unsustainable solution. Even if Chance guessed well, his derivation is bound to remain a clever hypothesis. In any case, *henchman*, most probably, never designated "horseman," and it won't harm language historians to return to the controversy that long ago raged for nine years in *Notes and Queries* and to look at the old problem with fresh eyes.

Note

In *Notes and Queries*, Series 8, Vol. 9, 1896, p. 251, Frank Chance published a list of his contributions and Skeat's rejoinders to them. The rest of the polemic is rarely worth rereading.

Scoundrel

Words designating rogues, swindlers, and other members of this "family" tend to originate among rogues and swindlers, that is, in low slang and the so-called cant. In the past, mendicants, thieves, and other "artful dodgers" often had close ties with their "colleagues" abroad, and in seeking the origin of the names designating such professionals, we should always be on the lookout for a possible foreign source of an English word. That being said, two warnings are in order. Many people (usually nonspecialists) believe that slang for "thief" or "criminal" must have either Jewish or Romany roots and offer fanciful derivations, taken on trust by the gullible public. Yet the etymology of such words is usually obscure and not less complicated than that of more "respectable" nouns and verbs.

Quite naturally, the earliest citations of *rogue, scoundrels*, and so forth in our dictionaries do not go back to Old or even Middle English. Not that there was a paucity of riffraff in King Alfred's or Chaucer's days, or that people had no names for the dregs of their communities. The reason is simpler: we do not know ancient slang unless it was recorded in extant texts. *Scoundrel* surfaced in English books and was probably coined in the modern period. The *OED* has no citations of it prior to 1589.

Given that date, an etymologist faces familiar questions. A borrowing from Scandinavian or Old French should theoretically have turned up in texts long before the end of the sixteenth century (for example, *rascal*, from French, was already current in 1330), while if the word in question is not an import, one might expect some ties between it and other native words. Yet such ties are often dubious, to say the least. All in all, *scoundrel*, in which only the suffix is or seems to be transparent (compare *mongrel* and *wastrel*), will probably defy our efforts and remain a word of "uncertain origin." I am offering the discussion that follows for the sake of the conclusion: an idea occurred to me that may perhaps shed additional dim light on the origin of the otherwise almost impenetrable word *scoundrel*.

The first to risk a conjecture about the derivation of *scoundrel* was Stephen Skinner, the author of a 1671 English etymological dictionary; it appeared posthumously. John Minsheu, the author of the first such dictionary (1617), did not feature *scoundrel*: he may not have known the word. Though Skinner's scholarship reflected the state of the art reached by roughly 1650, he made numerous interesting suggestions. Thus, he cited Italian *scondaruolo* "blindman's buff" (misprinted as *scondamolo*); hence "a hider." The connection is not good: a scoundrel's most conspicuous feature would not have been his hiding from the law. However, the root of *scondaruolo* is the same as in *abscond*, from Old French, from Latin (*abs-* is a variant of *ab* "away," and *condere* means "to put together, stow"). The *OED* would have agreed to trace *scoundrel* to Anglo-French *escondre* "abscond," but for the late date of its first occurrence. Even if we dismiss *scondaruolo* as not related directly to *scoundrel*, we should admire Skinner for coming close to what may have been the right solution.

With minor amusing variations, Skinner's etymology occupied a place of honor until the appearance of Walter W. Skeat's dictionary (1882). Yet there was no lack of other proposals: from Old English *sconde* "disgrace" (and *scondlic* "base, ignominious, disgraceful"), from *scummer* (*scoundrel* = *scum*), from German *Schandkerl* "villain" (i.e., *Schand-kerl*; *Schande* means "disgrace, shame," and *Kerl* means "fellow"), and even from two Scottish Gaelic roots: *sgon* "bad, vile, worthless" and *droil* (or *droll*) "idler." Those were shots in the dark. But one etymology should be quoted almost in full: "I rather take it [*scoundrel*] to come from the A.-S. [Anglo-Saxon] *onscunian* or *scunian*, to shun . . . , and to be connected with the Scotch *to scouner* or *scunner*, and the substantive *scunner*, one of the meanings of which given by Jamieson is an object of loathing, any person or thing which excites disgust. *Scoundrel* will then be *scunnerel*, a diminutive of *scunner*." F. J. V., the author of this derivation, refers to other examples of inserted *d* (compare English *thunder* and German *Donner*, without *d*). This correspondence was published in *Notes and Queries* (Series 5, vol. 6, for July 15, 1876, p. 306). I am sorry that I don't know who hid behind the initials F. J. V.

Skeat's dictionary put an end to the amateurish stage of English etymology. His entry on *scoundrel* in the first (1882) edition of his dictionary was long. It contained a polemical section in which he rejected the proposals of his predecessors, including Carl F. Mahn (the German etymologist for Webster's 1864 dictionary), whom he accused of inventing the word *Schandkerl*. Skeat, who never lived in Germany, must have had a great fighting spirit to impute to a native speaker of German the fabrication of a word in that person's native language. Moreover, German compounds easily, and many such words are quite natural coinages "for the nonce." *Schandkerl* is indeed a rare compound (in the Grimms' multivolume dictionary, a single citation from Kleist is given), but Mahn did not produce it to bolster his derivation. Old English *sconde*, mentioned above, is a cognate of German *Schande* "shame, disgrace," so that Mahn's idea was not even wholly original. But Skeat correctly disassociated *Schandkerl* from *scoundrel*: the German word had minimal currency and does not resemble *scoundrel* enough to equate them.

This is Skeat's proposal. I'll quote from his last (1910) edition because he never changed his mind about this word; he only expunged the attack on his predecessors because, thirty years later, their opinions no longer bothered him or anybody else. "Lit[erally] 'a loathsome fellow.' Aberdeensh. *scoonrel*; for **scun-ner-el*, where *-el* is an agential suffix. From Lowl[and] Scotch *scunner*, *sconner*, to loathe, also (formerly) to shrink through fear, act as a coward; so that a *scoonrel* is one who shrinks, a coward. . . . The verb *scunner* is the frequentative of the

North[ern]. form of A.-S. [Anglo-Saxon] *scun-ian*, to shun; see **Shun**."
The asterisk before *scun-ner-el* means that this is a reconstructed rather
than recorded form.

In 1882, Skeat wrote: "I have no doubt that this solution, here first
proposed, is the right one." The great man allowed his temperament to
get the better of his judgment. No one should say that the new solution
is right. Etymology is a morass, and those who do not tread gingerly
there sink. Besides, scholars say "no doubt," "undoubtedly," and so
forth only when the doubts are real. A dictionary of word origins is not
a book of homilies, and nothing is gained by heated rhetoric. Finally,
considerable danger lurks in the statement "here first proposed."
Etymological proposals tend to appear in the most unlikely places, a
bibliography of etymology is a bottomless pit, so that one should always reckon with the existence of a predecessor.

Even Skeat did not know everything, and I wonder how he managed to miss F. J. V.'s correspondence, considering that he used to read
Notes and Queries with great attention and sent countless letters to it.
In any case, he repeated F. J. V. almost verbatim. It is the meaning that
makes Skeat's etymology less than fully convincing: a scoundrel is not
a coward, not a person who shrinks through fear. By contrast, "a loathsome fellow" is fine. The original *OED* declared "derivation from Sc.
scunner. . . inadmissible on phonological [that is, phonetic] grounds
and although *scoundrel* is now vernacular in Scotland, . . . all the early
examples of the word are English." The reference to phonetics means
that the vowel in *scoundrel* is long (the diphthong, spelled *ou*), while
all the suggested etymons have short *u*. For whatever reason, this difficulty did not bother Skeat, and indeed, we find *scouner* and *scoonrel*,
cited above. More important is the consideration that *scoundrel* does
not seem to be a Scottish word.

The distinguished Romance scholar Leo Spitzer returned to Old
French as the putative source of *scoundrel*, though not to *escondre*
"to abscond" but to *escondre* "to refuse," with the result that the original scoundrel turned out to be "a piece of refuse, trash." A similar semantic idea occurred to Hensleigh Wedgwood, Skeat's predecessor
in nineteenth-century etymology. It was he who derived *scoundrel*
from *scum*; he also cited Danish *skarn* "filth, trash" and "a bad person."
Spitzer pointed out that *rascal* "had the very same meaning 'refuse,

scrapings.'" However, his etymology presupposes that an Old French verb was current in French dialects until the sixteenth century and influenced the English noun. This reconstruction is rather implausible. We observe that Wedgwood's and Spitzer's putative sources of *scoundrel* have short vowels. They, too, ignored the fact made much of by the *OED*.

Here comes the promise made at the outset of this section. I wonder whether Molière's *Sganarelle*, the name of his favorite character, may help us in approaching the origin of *scoundrel*. This name is Italian, which is not surprising, considering the role of the Italian theater in Molière's life. Did he base it on the verb *sganare* "to disillusion, undeceive," that is, "to free (a person) from deception or mistake" or from the diminutive of Zanni? Wasn't there in his days a slang word (of the type Rabelais used with such relish) that meant something like "a shrewd person" or, conversely, "a victim of self-deception" that crossed the channel and perhaps merged with *scunner* to produce *scoundrel* from **sgan(d)rel* or **sgun(d)rel*? (Alas, the vowel in the forms that attracted my attention is short!) The name *Sganarelle*, despite its Italian ring, must have sounded funny to a French audience. How did the French understand it? If someone either confirms or rejects my connection between *scoundrel* and *Sganarelle*, my timid conjecture will have served a worthy purpose.

Note

Leo Spitzer's note appeared in *American Speech* 19/5, 1944, 16–27.

Bullyragging and Lovable Bullies

We are entering the territory of post-medieval English and Dutch/ Low (i.e., northern) German, and the ground is most unsafe. Our first target is *bullyrag*, noun and verb, both said to be of obscure origin. The verb has been attested in several forms, but, among them, only the synonymous *ballarag* is of some interest. From an etymological point of view, it is probably *ball-a-rag* (a compound with an inserted *a*, like *chick-a-biddy*, *cock-a-doodle-doo*, and quite a few others). The attested form *ballywrag* is a fanciful spelling of *ballarag*, while *bullyrag* contains

the familiar elements without the connecting vowel *a*. The first citation of *bullyrag* in the *OED* is late (1790), but slang may circulate for a
long time before, more or less by chance, it makes its way into a printed
text. In 1758, a freshman at Harvard College remembered that some
students had been examined for *bulraging* (*sic*) a certain man. His rec-
ollection pushes *bullyrag* and its closest analogs to the middle of the
eighteenth century.

The later a word of unknown origin surfaces, the more uncomfortable one feels about its derivation. Lexicographer Joseph E. Worcester,
a one-time formidable American competitor of Noah Webster, called
bullyrag local and low. The *Century Dictionary* echoed Worcester
("provincial and low"). I wonder how they came to their conclusions
("local, provincial"). Joseph Wright's *English Dialect Dictionary* says
"in general dialectal and slang use in Scotland, Ireland and America."
Anyway, dialectal use does not mean "of dialectal descent": people
living far away from the capital and large towns are as prone to assim-
ilate common slang as anyone else. The verb's popularity at Harvard
and Oxford (for Oxford, see the *OED*) might even suggest that it arose
in those quarters and spread everywhere, as happened, for example, to
chum and *crony*.

Bally (mainly British) is believed to be a euphemistic alteration of
bloody, but perhaps once it was a word in its own right and became a
milder (less blasphemous) substitute for *bloody*, suggested by the sequence *bl—y*. In any case, the original form of the verb that interests
us seems to have been *bullyrag*, not *ballyrag*. The earliest guess about
its origin I have found belongs to Edward Lye, the posthumous editor of Junius's etymological dictionary (1743; i.e., half a century before 1790 and much closer to 1753). He traced the verb to Icelandic
ból "house, dwelling" and *rægja* "to slander, libel" (I have modernized
Lye's spelling). Did Lye take his cue from *ransack*, a borrowing from
Scandinavian (*rann* "house" and *sækja* "attack; search")? His etymology takes us nowhere. Eric Partridge's tentative derivation "to
make a bully's rag of" should join Lye's. As long as we are dealing with
rags, we may recollect that a rag is used to annoy a bull, but a piece of
"low" British slang would have hardly originated in the custom of bull-
fighting (*corrida*), the more so as the form *bullyrag* occurs more often
than *bullrag*.

The problem is *-rag* rather than *bully*. *To rag* means "banter, annoy; scold"; it is a rather close synonym of *bully*. The *Century Dictionary* quotes a passage from *Notes and Queries*, which I, too, have in my database, but I found it a hundred years later: "To *rag* a man is good Lincolnshire for chaff or tease. At school, to get a boy into a rage was called getting his rag out." The most natural conjecture would be to treat *bullyrag* as a tautological compound: "annoy-annoy." Such words are rather numerous. The simplest way of emphasizing an idea is to repeat it; hence words like *tum-tum* and *do-do*. Going a step further produces tautologies like *courtyard* ("court-court" or "yard-yard") and *pathway* ("way-way"). Bullying people is bad, ragging them is also bad, but bullyragging is truly awful.

If one casts the net for look-alikes widely, the catch will not be too meager: English *rag* "shred of cloth," Dutch *raggen* "to run around in a state of wild excitement," Swedish *ragla ~ raggla* "to wobble," and *rag-a-muffin*, along with *rag-a-bash* "disreputable person" (chiefly Scottish). The Swedish subculture of *raggare* is close by. One of those words may shed light on the etymology of English *rag* "annoy, banter, rail at" (which is, most likely, of Scandinavian descent), but our concern is not with the origin of this verb because, in dealing with *bullyrag*, we take its existence for granted.

We might stop here, but for a word Shakespeare knew and liked. Scene 3 of Act 1 of *The Merry Wives of Windsor* opens so: "FALSTAFF: Mine host of the Garter— HOST: What says my bully rook? Speak scholarly and wisely." One wonders whether the phrase *bully rook* has anything to do with *bullyrag*. In Shakespeare's days, *rook* meant "simpleton" (a usual reference to a bird, any bird being proverbially stupid: compare *gull*, *goose*, and so forth); the senses "sharper, cheat" turned up later. Assuming that *bully* here was part of a friendly welcome, we should agree that the host did not call Falstaff a simpleton, let alone cheat, and that no offence was meant. In all probability, *bully rook* meant "boon companion; honored frequenter" or something similar. In the comedy, mine host addresses other people in the same way. The spelling of *bully rook* poses a minor problem. I followed the *Oxford Shakespeare*, but the variants *bullyrook* and *bully-rook* cannot be dismissed out of hand. Also, *bullyrook* sometimes alternated with *bullyrock*.

The *Century Dictionary* says that *bully-rook* is equivalent to Low German *buller-brook* (pronounce *oo* as *aw* in English *raw*) and *buller-bäck* and is apparently a variant of *bullyrag*. This information seems to have been lifted from Barrère and Leland's 1897 *Dictionary of Slang* (*bullyrag* is said there to be **certainly** of Dutch origin), with the substitution of *Low German* for *Dutch*. Low (= northern) German is a vague term; without an exact reference to the dialect and the source the form cannot be verified. In Middle Low German, for which a splendid dictionary exists, no such word seems to occur. The Dutch counterpart of the *OED* lists only *buller-bäck* "boisterous man" and compares it with German *Poltergeist* and others.

Buller-brook sounds somewhat like English *bully rook ~ bully rock*. One might suggest that the slang Shakespeare used was borrowed from the Low Countries, but, to do so, *bully-brook* must first lose its status of a ghost word. With the scarce evidence at our disposal, we can only say that *bullyrag* and *bullyrook ~ bullyrock* are indeed so similar that the coining of the tautological compound verb *bullyrag* may have been prompted by the existence of a noun meaning "habitué of pubs." However, in *bullyrook* and especially *bully rook*, *bully* meant "good, dear, excellent," with *rook* weakened to "fellow, guy," while English *bully*, as will be shown below, is probably a different word.

English *bully* surfaced in texts around the middle of the sixteenth century and meant "sweetheart, darling," originally applied to either sex but later only to men (the sense was "good friend; fine fellow"). Shakespeare treasured this word and used it regularly, beginning with 1600. Judging by phrases like *lovely bully* and "What saiest thou, bully, Bottom," we can perhaps suspect that, at that time, it was jocular slang, not unlike American *dude* or British *chum*.

Since the word *bully* is late, its supposed derivation from Dutch (and such is the verdict of the best authorities) should not encounter any objections. *Bully* might be an adaptation of Middle Dutch *boele* "lover." Its Modern Dutch continuation is *boel* "mistress, concubine." Compare German *Buhle* "lover" and *Nebenbuhler* "rival" (*neben* "next to"). *Boele*, it seems, crossed the channel with hundreds of other Dutch words, now perfectly domesticated in English. The puzzling thing is that *bully* "lover; friend; fine fellow" disappeared about two hundred years after it had its heyday in English. *Bully* "excellent" is hardly a relic of *bully* "lover." More likely, it is an analog of **damned** *good* and **awfully** *funny*, in which the words suggesting horror and perdition are emphatic variants of *extremely*. The modern senses of *bully* were preceded by "hired ruffian" and "protector of prostitutes," that is, "pimp."

The main question is whether *bully* "sweetheart" and *bully* "ruffian" are, from a historical point of view, the same word. The *OED* thought so (I say *thought*, rather than *thinks* because Oxford's etymological team has not yet revised the first letters of the dictionary). According to James A. H. Murray, "[t]here does not appear to be sufficient reason for supposing that the senses under branch II. [that is, *bully* "ruffian"] are of distinct etymology: the sense of 'hired ruffian' may be a development of 'fine fellow, gallant' (compare *bravo*); or the notion of 'lover' may have given rise to that of 'protector of a prostitute,' and this to the more general sense. In the popular etymological consciousness the word is perhaps now associated with *bull* [animal name]; compare *bullock*." (The reference is to the dialectal verb *bullock* "to bully.")

Meaning can deteriorate or be ameliorated. German *Recke* "knight errant; hero" is a cognate of English *wretch*; English *mad* is a cognate of a Gothic adjective meaning "crippled" and of a Middle High German adjective meaning "beautiful." At one time, English *fond* meant "stupid." Linguistic textbooks are full of such examples. Therefore, "sweetheart" might become "pimp" and still later "someone who tyrannizes the weak." The *Oxford Dictionary of English Etymology* does not disagree with the *OED*. It only mentions the fact that Middle Dutch *boele* could be used as a term of endearment or reproach. However, early Modern English *bully* burdened with mild negative connotations did not turn up: it referred to either lovers or scoundrels. Perhaps "pimp" is an ironic extension of "sweetheart," but "ruffian" and "browbeater" do not fit in with the word's earliest attested sense. Later dictionaries, to the extent that they say anything beyond "of obscure origin," followed the *OED*. Only Henry Cecil Wyld called the suggested connection between *bully* "sweetheart" and *bully* "ruffian" unconvincing.

Stephen Skinner, whose posthumous etymological dictionary came out in 1671, must have known both senses of *bully* (the *OED*'s earliest citation for "ruffian" goes back to 1688), for, otherwise, he would not have vacillated among three etymons: *burly*, *bulky*, and *bulla* (the latter because, in their bullas, Popes threaten and bluster!). None of the three words alludes to love or even friendliness, though Middle English *burly* often meant "noble."

For a long time, it was believed that *bully* was akin to Dutch *bulderen* "boom, roar," German *Poltergeist* "a noisy spirit," and other words designating ruckus and disturbance (so, for example, Skeat, in the first edition of his dictionary, and before him, Wedgwood). This derivation points to a common flaw of many old and, deplorably, new conjectures: the researcher would discover a synonym with a root that matches the item under discussion and not bother about the type of word formation. Assuming that *bully* is related to *bulderen*, how was it coined? Did the speakers isolate the root *bul-* and add a suffix to it? By comparison, Murray's etymology has every advantage, and it is no wonder that, later, both Wedgwood and Skeat gave up their ideas and followed the *OED*.

We can now return to the Middle Dutch form *boele*. As noted, its origin is disputable. Most scholars believe that it is a pet name for *brother* (Dutch *broer*). Yet I suspect that those who separate *broer* from *boele* have a point, mainly because I have seen convincing evidence for separating English *brother* from *buddy* and learned to treat such etymologies with suspicion. Anyway, a case has been made that the Old English personal names *Bola ~ Bolla* and *Bula ~ Bulla* also originally meant "dear brother; lover." Even if this were right, we might come closer to solving the etymology of *bully* "sweetheart" and of its Dutch counterpart but would still be unable to cross the bridge from "sweetheart" to "ruffian."

The usually helpful *Century Dictionary* ignored the etymology given in the *OED*, made no changes between the first and the second edition (despite one reviewer's criticism), and took the unity of *bully*[1] and *bully*[2] for granted. It did not explain how the second sense arose. Wedgwood, partly like Murray, wondered whether the bad sense of *bully* had come "from the conduct of a boon companion or from the special application to the bully of a courtesan, the mate or lover with whom she lives, and calls in to intimidate her customers." Ernest Weekley attempted to connect various hypotheses and wrote that the initial sense "brother" had been affected by the animal name *bull* and Dutch *bulderen*. Weekley might have a point: in the animal world, bulls are notorious bullies, and a connection between them is too obvious to miss.

With due respect to Murray's idea, the speedy development from "sweetheart" to "ruffian" seems improbable, and references to bravos, gallants, and aggressive pimps do not go a long way (I emphasize *speedy* because no evidence supports Weekley's suggestions that *bully* "lover" may have existed in Middle English). An inner development from "lover; gallant" to "blustering tyrant" is possible, but the alleged unprovoked change occurred too quickly to look credible. A bully good man suddenly became a bully.

Perhaps we are dealing with two different words. A dim light comes from English *bulkin*, now obsolete, except in Jamaica. It is derived from a Dutch word for a bull calf (a noun with a diminutive suffix) and is used as a term of endearment and as an expression of contempt. Perhaps *bully*, understood as a cognate of *bull*, merged with *bully* "lover." A timid suggestion along these lines, traceable to Murray's initial etymology, can be found in several modern dictionaries indebted to the *OED*. *Bully* "lover" was probably not "affected" by *bull* but fell prey to the accidental similarity between them. If so, noisy boon companions and chivalrous pimps, along with their frightened "courtesans," need not bother us any longer.

Curmudgeon and Catawampus

The titular heroes of this story have nothing in common except the somewhat similar "prefixes": *cur-* and *cata-*. Who is a curmudgeon? The word has been around in English books since the last quarter of the sixteenth century. Samuel Johnson, the author of a famous dictionary (1755), defined the gentleman in question as an "avaricious churlish fellow." In British usage, a curmudgeon's first quality (love of money) is more prominent than the second (lack of social mores); a British curmudgeon is preeminently a miser. Nearly all lexicographers agree on that point. Only Henry Cecil Wyld, in his *A Universal English Dictionary*, says "a churlish, cross-grained, surly, ill-tempered, cantankerous fellow." He uses five synonyms for "contentious, querulous, grouchy" and not a single one for "greedy."

The British definition of *curmudgeon* prevailed in American dictionaries until roughly the 1950s. Although contemporary dictionaries write: "1. A cantankerous person. 2. *Rare* a miser" or "A bad-tempered, difficult, cantankerous person," it took lexicographers in the United States a long time to notice the difference between British and American usage. As noted, the prevalent definition was "an avaricious, churlish, grasping fellow; a miser; niggard; churl." Only *Webster's Third* (1961) reversed the order and stated that a curmudgeon is 1. *archaic*: a grasping, avaricious man: Miser. 2. a crusty, ill-tempered, or difficult and often elderly person." In the American Upper Midwest, where I live, all those whom I asked what kind of a person a curmudgeon is said without hesitation "an ill-tempered man," and no one had heard about this person's being a scrooge. The American meaning may be as old, if not older, than "miser" because, as is well-known, American English, like any other colonial language, retains many archaic features lost in the metropolis. Or this usage may have been dialectal, regional.

Walter W. Skeat compared *curmudgeon* with Lowland Scots *murgeon* "mock, grumble" and *mudgeon* "grimace." Both words fit the idea of a peevish, disgruntled man well. Not improbably, *curmudgeon* was first applied to an unpleasant, unsociable person and by extension to someone who stays away from jovial company for fear of being robbed or asked to help the less fortunate. Some light on the origin of *mudgeon* falls from the history of the verb *mooch*, which has been attested in numerous variants, including *mouch*, *motch*, and *modge*. *Modge* is closest to *mudgeon*. (The voicing of *-ch* is the same as in *hotchpotch* vs. *hodge-podge* and in *Greenwich*, when pronounced as *grenidge*.)

The root of *mooch* and its variants occurs in words of several languages, for instance, in German *meucheln* "murder (treacherously)" and French *muchier* "conceal, lurk" (still known in some modern dialects). Cognates have been found in Old Irish and Latin. Similar Italian words (mostly regional) appear to have been borrowed from Germanic, and the same may be true of French *mouche* "to spy" and *mouchard* "police informer, stoolie." In English, Hamlet's *miching*, the first part of the cryptic phrase *miching malicho* "sneaking mischief," belongs with *mooch* and *mouch*, and so do, possibly, *mug* "waylay and rob" and *mugger* in *hugger-mugger*. Wherever one of those nouns, adjectives, and verbs turns up, it refers to secret, under-handed dealings. There seems to have been a large group of words, part of international slang or underworld cant, designating actions that shunned the light of day.

Cur- in *curmudgeon* is a reinforcing prefix, widely known in sound-imitative words (*kerbang, kerbunk, kerplank, kerwallop*) and in words like *kerfuffle* "disorder, flurry." They occur with numerous spelling variants, the most common of them being *ca-*, as in *kit and caboodle*. The original curmudgeon was, it appears, a big "mudgeon," whatever the exact meaning of *mudgeon* might be ("someone with an ugly mug"? "a grumbler sitting on his wealth, a penny-pincher"?).

Enter *catawampus*, also recorded in at least a half-dozen spelling variants. As slang, this word must have existed for quite some time be-fore it was first attested in books in the middle of the nineteenth cen-tury. Originally a noun, it was taken early on for an adjective (as though *catawampous*) and applied to things fierce, eager, and in a state of dis-array. The original *OED* suggested a connection with Greek *kata-* (as in *catastrophe, cataclysm*, and the like) and said: "A high-sounding word with no very definite meaning." This is a wonderful definition, appli-cable to many public figures. The *Century Dictionary* (an American product), whose etymologies are detailed and often original, mentions only *catawampous* "fierce; voracious; devouring; destructive"; it was added in the supplement to Volume 1, and its etymology is un-inspiring: "A made word, from *cata-* + *wamp-*, vaguely imitative (cf. *wap, whop*) + *-ous*." "A made word" is probably what some modern dictionaries call "coinage," that is, a word invented by a known indi-vidual (like *blurb*) or a blend. In the past, the *OED* often called such formations fanciful. The problem is that all words were "made" by someone long ago or in recent memory, and, in the beginning, quite a few of them were probably "fanciful."

Today, we have incomparably better databases than those at the dis-posal of our most learned predecessors. *Catawampus ~ catawampous* (and the related adverb) were first recorded in the United States but soon reached England as part of "colonial" usage. A correspondent to the British biweekly *Notes and Queries* wrote in 1880: "We all [!] know the beautiful phrase, imported from America, 'I am catawampusly [sic] chawed up.'" *Chaw* means "chew," as in *chaw tobacco*, and *to be chawed up* means "to be done for." (According to another correspondent, who found the adverb in his German [!] dictionary, one should say "*catawamptiously* chawed up.") It is anybody's guess how this American southernism became known to "them all" in England and even in Germany, and I very much hope that 150 years ago, German students of English did not try to impress their interlocutors in the English-speaking world by flaunting this novelty. Such cases are known. I have read about an innocent foreigner sending his condolences to a woman in England whose husband had recently "kicked the bucket."

Wampus, a noun with sufficient currency, means "monster, hobgoblin," a circumstance that came to the attention of lexicographers relatively late. This explains the senses in the *Century Dictionary* and the following passage (dated 1872): "They are like the catawampuses you see about harvest time; they fly quite pretty in the air, but, O my gracious, don't they sting!" (quoted by the first aforementioned correspondent to *Notes and Queries*; that citation made its way into the Supplement to the *OED*.) Apparently, catawampuses were like "bugs" (a bug is, among other things, a hobgoblin).

A few suggestions about the origin of *wampus* are inconclusive, and I will turn to *cata-*. It cannot be from Greek, for, judging by the way the noun and the adjective were used, *catawampus* ~ *catawampous* did not arise among university students, for who else would have thought of adding a Greek prefix to an obscure regional name of a monster? *Cata-*, also spelled *cater-, kitty-, kiddy-*, and so forth, is a prefix occurring in numerous words that mean "awry, askew, slanting," as in *cater-corner* "diagonally across," altered by folk etymology to *kitty-corner* ~ *kiddy corner* (this *kata-* is from Danish, not from French *quatre* "four," as said in some sources). About eighty years ago, dictionaries began to write that *cata-* in *catawampus* is the familiar prefix meaning "askew." The Internet offers the same explanation. Yet this idea has little merit. What is a slanting, diagonal hobgoblin? The great and beautiful *Dictionary of American Regional English* (*DARE*) lists the following senses of *catawampus* (noun, adjective, adverb, and verb, respectively): "hobgoblin, imaginary monster; utterly, completely; askew, awry, wrong; move diagonally; put out of proper shape."

Add to it *catawampus* as an exclamation (something like *good gravy!*) and the senses from the *Century Dictionary*. I believe that we have reflexes of two words here. At a certain stage, *cata-* in *catawampus* was taken for *cata-* ~ *cater-* "askew," but it could hardly be its first sense. The original fierce, bloodthirsty catawampus was probably a truly humongous wampus, a ca-, ker-, or cur-wampus. There is a convention in historical linguistics to supply reconstructed (not attested) forms with an asterisk. Clearly, my ca- and kerwampuses are asterisked, but some facts seem to support my attitude toward this word. Thus, the *DARE* has recorded the form *catty-ker-wampus!* With time, *cata-* supplanted *ca-*, and, the word, not unexpectedly, acquired the meaning "awry." But "utterly, completely" and "askew" are an ill-fitting pair cast as the coexistent senses of one and the same word. A catawampus, I propose, is, from an etymological point of view, a big wampus, just as a curmudgeon is a big "mudgeon." For this reason, I see no allure in the conjecture that *catawampus* is an alteration of the animal name *catamount* (a lynx or a mountain lion), regardless of whether *catamount* is indeed *cat-a-mount* or a variant of some other word. Perhaps *cata-* in it also refers to the beast's ferocity. And I wonder: Can *wampus* be a garbled version of *vampire*? Mere guessing, as Skeat used to say.

Pettifogger

Pettifogger is a term expressing contempt for the person who deserves being called this, whether the reference is to a lawyer of dubious repute or a quibbler of details. Today, few people use this word casually, but *pettifoggery* seems to be recognizable and even not too rare. It has been known from written sources since 1564 (Shakespeare's time) and, most likely, preceded *pettifogger*. If this sequence of events is true, English *pettifogger* is a so-called back formation of *pettifoggery*, but in the lending language (assuming that the English word is a borrowing), the story of course began with *pettifogger*. As regards the origin of *pettifogger*, *petti-*, that is, *petty*, poses no problems. But *-fogger* has not been explained to everybody's satisfaction. It resembles *f***er*, formerly (alas, formerly) unpronounceable and unprintable in polite company

or writing, and, if my suggestion (see it below) has potential, the resemblance is not accidental.

The Low, that is, Northern, German or Dutch origin of *fogger* is almost certain. The early Modern Dutch form *focker* was Latinized as
foggerus, with *-gg-* in the middle. German has *Focker*, *Fogger*, and
Fucker: local words, none of which has any currency outside their re-
gions. The *OED* cites them from the Grimms's multivolume dictionary
of German. As is known, the *OED* had to bow to the conventions of
its time and excluded "unprintable" words as headwords, but in the
entries, where no one would look for them, offensive forms sometimes appeared: such is a mention of German *fucker*, with lower-case
f, under *fogger*, and of the bird name *windfucker* "kestrel." Although
today, Dutch *fokken* means "to breed cattle," its predecessor had a
much broader semantic spectrum: "cheat; flee; adapt, adjust; beseem;
push; collect things secretly"—an odd array of outwardly incompatible
senses. Most likely, "push" was the starting point; hence "adjust," then
"adjust properly" ("beseem"). But despite doing things as it beseems
or behooves, "pushing" suggested underhand dealings: "collect things
secretly; cheat" and even "flee," possibly from acting in a hurry and
clandestinely.

Despite the lack of consensus, there seems to be little doubt that
the infamous English *F*-word is also a borrowing from Low German.
However, the verb's basic meaning was, "move back and forth," rather
than "push." In various languages, "deceive" and "copulate" often appear as senses of one and the same verb. *Fokken* is a member of a large
family. All over the Germanic-speaking world, we find *ficken*, *ficka*,
fikla (compare English *fickle*), *fackeln*, *fickfacken*, *fucken*, *fuckeln*,
and so forth, meaning approximately the same: "make quick, short
movements; hurry up; run aimlessly back and forth; shilly-shally;
cheat (especially in games)."

English also has and had a few words of this structure: such are
Old English *fācen* "deceit; blemish" and *ficol* "cunning" (the ancestor of Modern English *fickle*). Perhaps British English *firk* belongs
here, too. It means or meant "jerk; copulate" and (!) "cheat." English
words of this group never had *g* in the middle (*fidget* is a borrowing
from Scandinavian). Therefore, one may safely assume that *fogger* is
not native. (For completeness sake, I may add that several Romance

words like Italian *ficcare* "copulate" are, very probably, loans from Germanic, though in the latest dictionaries, it is said to be unrelated to its Germanic counterpart. A few Germanic words of this structure and meaning made their way even into Slavic.) As already noted, the basic meaning of nearly all those words was "move back and forth," "copulate," and, by extension, "deceive." Regrettably, the idea that selling is inseparable from swindling is also almost universal. A pettifogger was indeed a petty fogger. Some successful foggers became respectable merchants. Others remained at the bottom of the social scale; hence *pettifogger*.

It is often hard to explain why certain words are borrowed. Every sizable community has enough swindlers (and names for them), and every human group has at least one verb of copulation. Yet *fogger* has come from either German or Dutch, and the borrowed *F*-word ousted several well-established native English synonyms. (Perhaps *fik* ~ *fak* ~ *fok* ~ *fuk* are expressive, sound-symbolic sound complexes, ideally suited for expressing the idea of moving back and forth, pushing, and jerking.) Apparently, *pettifogger* meant "small pusher" or "swindler on a small scale," or "small (shady) dealer." The problem would have been solved once and for all but for the suggestion in the first edition of the *OED* that *fogger* is "probably derived from *Fugger*, the surname of a renowned family of merchants and financiers of Augsburg in the 15th and 16th centuries." Additionally, the *OED* referred to *fooker*, for which a single 1607 citation was found and which the dictionary traced tentatively to German *fucker* (*sic*). The meaning of *fooker* might be "capitalist."

The later adaptations and digests of the *OED* do not present a united front. The *Oxford Dictionary of English Etymology* makes no mention of the German merchants and bankers and says that *fogger* is a word of unknown origin, perhaps a back formation from *pettifogger*, but the latest *Shorter Oxford* returns us to Augsburg, and so do all the websites I have consulted. One should not assume that every suggestion we find in printed sources and on the Internet is backed up by a long and serious consideration of the problem. Whoever supplies the required information for a new edition or website (with the only exception being the *OED*, where every opinion is backed up by careful research) has to edit multiple entries and tries to choose the safest version. Erring on the side of the *OED* is usually safe.

Absolute proof cannot reward a search like ours, but a few suggestions may not sound too risky. Judging by the facts at our disposal, *fogger*, far from being a word of unknown origin, is a continuation of German/Middle Dutch *focker ~ fogger*. *Pettifogger* is a *petty fogger* ("small dealer in suspicious transactions"), the more so as the English compound has been recorded in the form of two separate words (*petty fogger*). My most important point is that connection with the Fugger family was hardly direct. The origin of the family name Fugger does not seem to present serious difficulties: *Fogger* is *fogger* spelled with capital *f*. In Germany, surnames became common relatively late, and it must have taken the Augsburg Fuggers quite a few years before they reached the position in which we find them. At first, they were mere "foggers." Later, the nickname turned into their surname. We seem to be dealing with a professional name reminiscent of *Smith*, *Goldsmith*, *Cooper*, *Plummer*, and dozens of others.

Simpleton

Simpleton is a deceptively simple word. At first sight, its origin contains no secrets: *simple + ton*. And that may be all there is to it despite the obscurity of *-ton*. We find this explanation in the *OED* and in the dictionaries dependent on it. The word surfaced in the middle of the seventeenth century and must have been a facetious coinage (like our modern Skellington), but we are not sure in what milieu it turned up, and quite often etymologists' biggest trouble is their ignorance of the initial environment of a new term. Who were the wits responsible for launching *simpleton*, and why did it catch on? Samuel Johnson (1755) offered a piece of relevant information in that he called *simpleton* a low word. He often used this label and apparently knew what he was saying. We can assume that in his days *simpleton* was slang or a regional word not fit for polite conversation.

The *Oxford Dictionary of English Etymology*, while expanding the entry in the original edition of the *OED*, states that *-ton* in *simpleton* is the same *-ton* we have in family names derived from place names and cites a few parallels. The names present no trouble. *Newton*, *Hilton*, *Dayton*, *Washington*, *Clinton*, and many others immediately spring to mind. Some of them are transparent (e.g., *Newton* = *new* + *town*), and *Hilton* needs only another *l* to clarify it (the family name *Hillton*, from *hill* + *town*, also exists). The oldest sense of *town* was "enclosure," as in German *Zaun*, and "the space enclosed," as in Icelandic *tún*. A person from Newtown was Mr. Newtown. By contrast, *Clinton* is opaque, for *Clin-* requires an explanation. The little-known word *idleton* "idle person" and the obsolete *sillyton*, along with words ending in *by* (*idleby*, *sneaksby*, and so forth; *by*, from Scandinavian, also signifies "town"), are supposed to bolster the explanation in the *OED*. However, *idleton* and *sillyton* arose later than *simpleton* and may have been modeled on it.

Of special interest is the word *skimmington*, which predates *simpleton* in the *OED* by forty-one years. Its best-known meaning refers to a frontispiece of 1639: "A burlesque procession formerly held in ridicule of a henpecked husband; a cavalcade headed by a person on horseback representing the wife, with another representing the husband seated behind her, facing the horse's tail and holding a distaff, while the woman belabored him with a ladle" (the *Century Dictionary*; "supposed to have originated in the name of some forgotten scold" [!]). The *OED*, with reference to the ladle in the picture, tentatively derived the word from *skimmer* + *ton*. Ernest Weekley also cited *lushington* "drunkard," but this word was a jocular nineteenth-century creation, this time indeed from a family name, containing an allusion to *lush*. It sheds no light on *simpleton*.

In connection with the 1639 frontispiece, I might add that the otherwise incomprehensible proverb (known from printed records since 1755) *the grey mare is the better horse* also refers to a henpecked husband. There may have been an old puppet show (a popular genre in Shakespeare's days and later) that featured a husband riding behind his wife, with his face toward the tail of a gray mare. The horse's color was probably accidental, but *Skimmington* told its story, most probably, along the lines suggested by the *OED*.

In 1882, the first edition of Skeat's English etymological dictionary came out. Skeat's opinion on *simpleton*, as it appeared there, never changed. According to him, *simpleton* is *simple-t-on*, with a double

French suffix, from Old French *simplet* "a simple person" (*-on*, without the preceding diminutive suffix *t*, can be seen in Spanish *simplón* "simpleton," and another word with a double suffix is *musketoon*, i.e., *musket-oon*; *-oon*, as in *spittoon*, *saloon*, etc.). Our "thick" dictionaries are divided in their judgment: most follow the *OED*, while a few side with Skeat. Other derivations of *simpleton* do not explain *-ton* and are often fanciful and not worth mentioning—except perhaps one.

Abram Smythe Palmer, the author of a popular book on folk etymology, quoted the following lines from a satirical 1772 poem: "This fashion, who does e'er pursue, / I think a simple-tony; / For he's a fool, say what you will, / Who is a macaroni." *Tony*, it appears, was not a rare name for "any person." *Simpleton*, Smythe Palmer suggested, was short for *Simple-tony*, as *babe* is short for *baby*. It did not occur to him that *simple-tony* might be a witty alternation of *simpleton*. Skeat did not comment on this idea, but he disliked complex etymologies when an easy one solved the riddle (though his etymology is not particularly easy).

Smythe Palmer's conjecture is ingenious. Yet it can hardly be upheld despite phrases like *any tony* and *to be pointed at any tony* that he unearthed. *Any tony* probably belongs with *Tom*, *Dick, and Harry* (incidentally, also a seventeenth-century creation), and, even if *simpleton* could go back to some such collocation, it would still be desirable to find a common origin for all the *-ton* words, especially for *skimmington*, and assuming (just assuming) that *skimmington* predates *simpleton*, the *tony* idea falls to the ground. As far as we can judge, in the seventeenth century, which was a great age for slang, words ending in *-ton* spread among "the lower orders," and this pseudo-suffix attached itself to a small number of nouns, of which today most speakers of English still remember only *simpleton*. When that happened, the *-ton* words merged with place and family names ending in *-ton*, and the origin of the "first formation" was lost.

Mr. John Cowan pointed out to me that Simpleton makes one think of the many towns of fools known from folklore. Such towns are indeed numerous. From England, we know Gotham ("Goat-town"). In Denmark, Ebeltoft in Mols has a flourishing tourist industry: its memorabilia is centered around the numerous stories of the fools inhabiting the town. As a general case, the connection between this folklore and the place has no historical foundation. It would be nice to find a town called Simpleton, but oral tradition knows nothing about it.

We should now return to the question of the word's milieu. If the -*ton* words sprang up in the streets, the French etymology that Skeat favored has little to recommend it. But it could be a word coined in a dialect with a strong admixture of the Romance element. Frank Chance, an astute etymologist who offered numerous good solutions, discussed French *singleton* in 1883, a year after the publication of Skeat's dictionary. He pointed out that, according to the best authorities, *singleton* "a single card in a suit" or at least its root, had come to French from English, and ended his article thus: "If the word *singleton* arose in French, it is odd that the French should have added a French termination to an English word; but if the word was originally English, it is equally odd that the English should have added on the French termination *(e)ton*. They seem, however, to have done this in *simpleton*; at least, no record is before us of the word's ever having existed in French." Whatever the peregrinations of *singleton* may have been, the French provenance of -*ton* in *simpleton* cannot be considered proven.

Also in 1883, F. C. Birkbeck Terry, another active contributor to the British popular periodical *Notes and Queries*, expressed his hope that "[t]he compilers to the great English dictionary, of which we shall soon have the first instalment [sic], will no doubt be able to supply examples of the use of the word antecedent to 1720." He was right. The first installment appeared in 1884, and a citation with an earlier date was supplied. But the word's origin proved to be less simple than one could expect or wish for.

By way of postscript, we may remember Simple Simon, that proto-simpleton of English folklore and a close relative of Simple Tony, though the poem about him and the pieman goes back to the seventeenth century. A close relative of Simple Simon is German Simplicissimus, the superlative of *simpleton* (as it were) and the hero of a famous seventeenth-century German book by Hans Jakob Chr. von Grimmelshausen.

Snob

In 1875, a man asked a boy in the industrial school at Castle End, Cambridge, whether he had learned tailoring. "No, sir," he answered, "I'm a snob." He meant that he was a cobbler. (Here and below, I am using the words *shoemaker* and *cobbler* as interchangeable synonyms, but originally, cobblers claimed control over the soles of boots and shoemakers over the upper leather.) To most of us a snob is a pretentious person or someone who snubs his inferiors but grovels to a superior. However, the word *snob* has a checkered history. Here are its senses, culled from texts since its appearance in print in 1750: a term of contempt for "tailor," "cobbler," "an inferior," "townsman" (thus, "townie," as opposed to "gownsman," especially at Cambridge and Oxford, but also in a general sense; for example, in the 1830s, "Snobs on!" was a Winchester School war cry, meaning "the town champions are come out to meet us near St. Catherine's Hill"); "a vulgar and ostentatious person"(to use an old definition in the *OED*); "strikebreaker, scab, blackleg" (mainly in the United States). The verb *to snob* has turned up with the senses "to bungle one's work" and "to sob violently" (the latter because it rhymes with *sob*?). In British regional English, the verb *snob*, in addition to the aforementioned "sob violently," can mean "to bite each other gently" (said about horses) and "to catch." The obviously related verb *snobble* has been recorded in dialects with the senses "to entangle" and "to devour greedily." In some such words, the overtones of a strong effort are unmistakable. The syllable *snob* is so expressive that almost any reference to vigor fits it. For instance, in Nottinghamshire (a northern county), a game played with small stones or marbles was once (or perhaps still is) called snobs. Indeed, isn't *snob* a perfect name for a piece of stone? In the *English Dialect Dictionary*, Joseph Wright gives a detailed description of the game.

In 1935, a correspondent to the British biweekly *Notes and Queries* wrote: "Among certain people . . . a snob was anyone who worked for his living, i.e., a banker, brewer, stockbroker, etc. That he was a snob had nothing to do with his character, merely with his occupation. Similarly, the word *cad* had not the meaning it has now [i.e., "scoundrel; reprobate"]. To be a cad simply meant a man who got his living by the work of his hands. . . . Perhaps the most extraordinary thing of all was that in this jargon a solicitor would be called a snob but not the barrister." (Not at all extraordinary: solicitors prepared the case for the barrister, an advocate, especially in higher courts, and thus occupied a lower rung in the hierarchy.)

The American periodical *The Nation* explained in 1913: "An English snob is a man who falls short of the perfect aristocrat through a taint of democratic vulgarity, whereas an American snob is a man who falls short of the perfect democrat through a taint of aristocratic exclusiveness." Very neat, but a century and a decade later, this explanation sounds a bit strained. Also, I found the following statement (with reference to an unnamed 1852 book about Australia) in the *Aberdeen Journal Notes and Queries*: "The majority of the colonists are essentially snobs, and they are justly proud of the distinction," that is, I assume the definition refers to the laborers working for their living, as opposed to "nobs."

Long ago, an annual called *The Keepsake*, a predecessor of later Christmas books, was published in the United States. In the annual for 1831, the following verse appeared: "Sir Samuel Snob—that was his name—/ Three times to Mrs. Brown / had ventured just to hint his flame, / And twice received a frown." I assume that the third time was successful, but more important in this context is why that importunate wooer was given such a name. *Snob* does not rhyme with any word in the poem. Its protagonist was hardly a cobbler. Nor was he a vulgar, smug, or supercilious person, guilty of snobbery, for this sense became universal after the publication of Thackeray's *Book of Snobs* (1848). Most likely, he was a man of low breeding, for otherwise he would not have accosted a married woman (and gained success?) in such an ungentlemanly way.

Let us listen to how nineteenth-century British authors explained what they meant by *snob*: "A tuft [an undergraduate fawning on his instructor] is a snob, a parasite is a snob, the man who allows the manhood within him to be awed by a coronet is a snob. The man who worships mere wealth is a snob." "A vulgar man in England . . . displays his character of snob by assuming as much as he can for himself, swaggering, and showing off in his dull coarse way." "An individual who would enjoy living in a dirty hole providing it had a fine frontage, and who is absolutely incapable of valuing moral or mutual greatness unless it is first admired by big people." On my part, I may advise those who want to know more about the subject to read or reread Dickens's novel *Dombey and Son*. It contains an unforgettable gallery of snobs, from the haughty Mr. Dombey, a rich and arrogant merchant who stands in awe at the sight of a scoundrel if he is an aristocrat and wants to know whether the school for his little son is expensive enough, to Major Bagstock, who never misses the chance of mentioning his Royal Highness, the late Duke of York (allegedly, someone who knew him), to the kind and forgiving Miss Tox, who is almost starving herself to death in order to live in a place wildly beyond her means, and, when asked why she does so, invariably answers: "Yes, but what a situation!"

Such then is the history of the concept *snob*. However, most people want to know two things: (1) What is the connection between *snob* "cobbler" and a societal snob? (After all, the words *snobbery* and *snobbish* have nothing to do with shoe making or St. Crispin, the patron of shoemakers.) And (2) What is the origin (etymology) of the noun *snob*? It is perhaps easier to answer the first question. Snobs and cads, as we have seen, belonged to the lower strata of society. The upper crust, contrary to those who worked, always had nice names to describe their character and status. People who were "urban" (today, "suburban"?) were, by definition, urbane, while villages bred "villains." *Snob* "tailor" occurred rarely, but it did. For centuries, tailors were itinerant laborers, traveling from home to home, staying in one place as long as they were needed and then leaving for another destination. As a reward, they got the mocking saying: "Nine tailors make a man." A few other idioms also have disparaging allusions to tailors. Apparently, *snob* was a generic term for "an inferior" and could be applied to any handyman, a person who was uneducated or lacked gentility, or simply a lout. It probably happened more or less by chance that it stuck to cobblers rather than to some other artisans.

Snob may have remained a universally understood synonym for "cobbler" if Thackeray had not used this word as a generic term for a person obtrusively devoid of refinement. Originally, his essays on multifarious snobs appeared in *Punch*. He presented a whole gallery of them. The world he observed appeared to be infected by snobbery from top to bottom. Surely, he did not invent or coin the word, but he diagnosed a societal disease and suggested a name for it. People abroad looked into a mirror and observed that snobs inhabited all countries, and that is why the English word entered so many languages. In *snobbery*, *-ery* is a suffix designating quality or condition. The Germans and the French say *Snobismus* and *snobisme*. The adjective *snobbish* needs no explanation.

To repeat the warning given above, the origin of the word *snob* will give us more trouble. At one time, it was customary to juxtapose nobs and snobs: nobs were the offspring of the *nob*ility, while their opponents were called honest snobs. This spirit informs the 1831 phrase, quoted in the *OED*: "The nobs have lost their dirty seats—the honest snobs have got 'em." Monosyllabic words like *nob*, *nib*, *nab*, *dab*, *dub*, *big*, *bug*, *bog*, and dozens of others are usually expressive. Their form evokes certain emotions, and when we find out what they mean, we tend to say: "This sense does not come as a surprise." The predictability of meaning is of course an illusion (what is, for example, *tig*, *tag*, *tug*, *tick*?), but a certain impulse does stand behind the coining of such words. Also expressive, but for a different reason, are many words beginning with *sn-*: *snot*, *sneak*, *snip*, *sniff*, *snivel*, *snitch*, *snap*, *snub*, *sneeze*, *snooze*, *snoop*, and so forth. The Modern English word *nob* "head" alternates and is often confused with *knob*. This *knob* ~ *nob* could easily have produced the doublet *snob*: *snob* would then become a twin of British *nob* "a person of wealth and distinction." After that, nobs and snobs would form a natural union.

The etymology I suggest (and its elements have occurred to several people before me) is of course guesswork (or to give it more status, "putative"), but my guessing game may not be groundless. A famous nineteenth-century dictionary of Old Icelandic suggested that English *snob* is an import of Icelandic *snápr* "fool, dolt." This word has cognates in the Modern Scandinavian languages. Scandinavian words flooded English in the Middle Ages, and if *snob* is a loan from Old Danish (the Vikings who conquered two-thirds of England were mainly of Danish extraction), it must have lain dormant in some northern dialect and turned up in London and in the south many centuries later. This is not an improbable scenario. For example, *slang* almost certainly reached the capital from the north. It seems to have ascertainable Scandinavian roots, and, by a weird coincidence, it surfaced in English books at exactly the same time as *snob* (i.e., in the middle of the eighteenth century). Yet I would prefer to list *snob* among native expressive coinages. After all, if a native source of a word is available or at least thinkable, there is no pressing need to go abroad for it. In the north of England, an alliterating phrase was current: "Snip the tailor and snob the cobbler." *Snip* was a mocking name for a tailor. Once again, cobblers and tailors seemed to be sharing company.

In 1850, in the first volume of *Notes and Queries*, the aforementioned British periodical whose popularity and influence are today hard to imagine, Dr. Alfred Gatty suggested that perhaps *snob* had originated at Cambridge and Oxford, where incoming students who were not of aristocratic origin had the Latin abbreviation *sine nobilitate* (*sine* "without," and *nobilitate* is the ablative of the noun meaning "nobility") written in their documents. This suggestion, clever but lacking merit, took on a life of its own, and, since 1850, has been repeated in countless publications. As noted, townsmen were indeed called snobs at Cambridge and seemingly a bit later at Oxford, but by that time the word *snob* ("an inferior; working man; townie; cobbler") had already become well-known.

In 1880, Walter W. Skeat called this etymology a poor joke, but, unfortunately, he did not explain why he thought so. The real work has been done much later by Dr. Paul Horstrup. He first contacted several writers who in their publications referred to the *sine nobilitate* theory. All of them responded that they had simply cited the familiar idea without any research into the subject. Later, he examined the personal files of Cambridge and Oxford students for many years. The authorities, it appeared, were never interested in the students' heritage. The fateful abbreviation did not appear a single time. I am not sure that the "poor joke" has been laid to rest. In popular sources, correspondents keep asking questions about the role of the phrase *sine nobilitate* in the coining of the word *snob*. This is not surprising. Dr. Horstrup published his results twice, both times in scholarly sources and in German. It should also be added that blends of the type suggested by Gatty were probably nonexistent in the eighteenth century. In those days, no one would have given the name *blog* to a we*b log* or coined words like *smog* (*smoke + fog*) and *motel*. Also, abbreviations, allegedly underlying *posh* (as if from *port out starboard home*), and the infamous *F*-word (as if from *fornication under the command of the* *king*) did not exist in the past. Lewis Carroll enjoyed inventing "portmanteau words," but that happened much later (*Alice in Wonderland* appeared in 1865).

Such then is the "putative" short history of *snob*. It is probably an expressive word of northern provenance, but not necessarily a borrowing from any Scandinavian language. Perhaps it goes back to *nob* with initial *s* added for emphasis However, in suggesting this etymology, we enter the area of attractive but unverifiable hypotheses. Even though of all the older senses of *snob* "cobbler" is the best-known one, it does not follow that the word arose among shoemakers. Most likely, it did not. *Snob* denoted all kinds of people having an inferior social status anywhere and not only at the two most prestigious universities. William Makepeace Thackeray invested the word *snob* with a broad meaning, and today the world knows it only as designating mean, despicable people who obsequiously bow forward but kick backward.

Note
This is the reference to Paul Horstrup's journal publication: "Snob." *Zeitschrift für deutsche Wortforschung* 19, 1963, pp. 64–74. Highly recommended is also the work by Margaret Moore Goodell, *The Snob in Literature. Part 1. Three Satirists of Snobbery: Thackeray, Meredith, Proust. With an Introductory Chapter on the History of the Word Snob in England, France and Germany*. Britannica 17. Hamburg: Friederichsen, de Gruyter, 1939. Part 1 contains 51 pages, and it does not seem that Part 2 has ever been published.

Codger and His Evil Brother Cadger

Old codger is a phrase most speakers of American English still understand (in British English, it has much greater currency), but *cadger* is either obsolete or dead. Yet the two words are often discussed in concert. A cadger was a traveling vendor, whose duties may have differed from that of a hawker, a peddler (the British spelling is *pedlar*), or a badger, but all those people were street dealers of sorts. The *OED* defines *cadger* so: "a carrier; *esp.* a species of itinerant dealer who travels with a horse and cart (or formerly with a pack-horse), collecting butter, eggs, poultry, etc., from remote country farms for disposal in the town, and at the same time supplying the rural districts with small wares from the shops." This meaning was recorded as early as the middle of the fifteenth century. Derogatory senses like "a person prone to mooching" surfaced in books much later. Also late is the verb *cadge* "beg," believed to be a back formation from the noun (like *beg* from *beggar*). The origin of *cadger* is unknown, and I have nothing to say on this subject, except for guessing that it must have been influenced by *badger* and citing a very old opinion, according to which, in the days of falconry, the man who bore the "cadge" or cage (a perch for the hawk) was called *cadger*. This etymology has probably little to recommend it.

More interesting is *codger* "stingy (old) man," "grumpy elderly man," or simply "man" (like *chap*, *fellow*, or *guy*). It appeared in books only in the middle of the eighteenth century (Dr. Stephen Goranson found a 1750 sentence with *Old Codger*). Mr. Anthon Cheke informed me of the existence of Codger's Island excavated in East Oxford, but it is unclear whether Codger was a name or a cant term for a swindler. Dictionaries say that *codger* may be a dialectal variant of *cadger*. This is possible but, to my mind, unlikely. Other etymologies are not even worth considering: allegedly, from English *cottager*, English *cogitate*, German *kotzen* "to vomit," Spanish, Turkish, Irish Gaelic, or (particularly silly) from the phrase *coffee dodger*. I am surprised no one derived *codger* from *kosher*.

On January 18, 1890, the periodical *Notes and Queries* published the following letter by the *OED*'s editor James A. H. Murray, who was at that time working on the letter *C*: "Todd explains this [the word *codger*] as 'contemptuously used for a miser, one who rakes together all he can,' in accordance with his own conjectural derivation from Sp[anish] *coger*, 'to gather, get as he can.' Later dictionaries all take this sense from him (Webster with wise expression of doubt), but none of them gave any evidence. I have not heard it so used, nor does any suspicion of such a sense appear in any of the thirty quotations sent in for the word by our readers. Has Todd's explanation any basis? A schoolboy to whom I have spoken seems to have heard it so used; but he may have confused it with *cadger*, which many take as the same." The Reverend H. J. Todd was the editor of Samuel Johnson's famous English dictionary (1818). Doesn't the semantic history of *curmudgeon* provide a weak analogy?

Several people responded to Murray's query. The luckless schoolboy was derided for his incompetence, and almost everybody insisted that *codger*, unlike *cadger*, is a term of endearment, but one letter writer pointed out that, in the fifties of the nineteenth century in Derbyshire (the East Midlands), "*codger* or *rummy codger* had been constantly used when alluding to persons of peculiar and eccentric ways, as well of others of doubtful character, or of whom mistrust was felt. A bungler of work was termed a codger, and it was the fate of every little lass who did sewing at school to cadge her work, that is, make an unsightly mess of the stitching. A piece of bad sewing was called a *codge-bodge*" (clearly, an analogy of *hodge-podge*). Either this letter or the suspicion that, however ludicrous Todd's Spanish etymology may have been, such a reliable lexicographer would not have concocted a sense only to fit a fanciful derivation, made Murray look for more citations, and his printed entry begins with a pre-1818 dialectal example of *codger* synonymous with *cadger*. Todd's definition also ended up in the rubric "dialectal" and was followed by several others from various parts of England. Joseph Wright's *English Dialect Dictionary* has *codge* "to botch, mend clumsily, bungle, patch" and *codger* "a slovenly worker."

Cadger and *codger* certainly overlapped. Yet originally they seem to have been different words. It also seems that *codger* was coined as a term of abuse (if so, dialects that refer to codgers as persons inviting distrust preserved the earliest meaning) and, with time, shed its most prominent negative characteristics. Historical semantics knows two processes: the deterioration of meaning (when a word acquires negative connotations, as, for example, happened to *whore*: the ancient root of this word can be seen in Latin *cara* "dear") and the amelioration of meaning (when the opposite happens, as witnessed by *fond*: several centuries ago, it meant "foolish"). Perhaps *codger* can serve as an illustration of the second process.

To offer an etymology, I have to return to the ideas developed in the story of *nudge* and *dodge*. English words beginning with and ending in *-j ~ -dge* tend to have an expressive character. This does not hold for words of French origin like *large*, *courage*, and *scourge* or for the native words that at one time had *-gg* (*bridge*, *sedge*, *forge*, and so forth). But *jig, jog, jag, job, fudge, budge, grudge*, and their likes are usually words of questionable etymology and are indeed expressive. Variation of the *slush ~ sludge* type can be disregarded here, though it will appear below in the denouement. No phonetic regularity allows us to derive *-dge* from *-g* if the word does not go back to Old English. However, contrary to this rule, *nudge*, a late verb, seems to be related to a sizable group of words whose root did end in *-g*; all of them referring to "petty movements" (*niggardly* is one of them). And this is where my conjecture comes in.

As noted, *codge* "botch, mend clumsily" looks like a back formation of *codger*, but we know so little about this word that there is no certainty. The verb *cog* "cheat at cards or dice" turned up in printed sources early in the sixteenth century. It is a typical cant word of forgotten origin, and I would like to suggest that it may have had an expressive variant *codge* "deceive, play dirty tricks," from which *codger* was formed and of which the recorded verb *codge* may be a relic. (However, the last point is not crucial: *codge* "botch" may have been coined regardless of its putative homonym.) Since peddlers command little respect in society, *codger*, from *codge*, would have crossed the paths of *cadger*. According to the reconstruction I propose, *codger* all but ousted *cadger*. But the victory came at a cost: instead of meaning "swindler," *codger* began to mean "bungler" (already a weakened sense), "stingy man; curmudgeon," and simply "an eccentric old man." If somebody says that since *codge*, from *cog*, is a ghost word, my derivation lacks merit, I'll be the first to agree but will argue that cant words made their way into print unsystematically. A verb like *codge* "cheat" may have escaped the attention of the few writers who reproduced the language of the underworld, especially if it was mostly current in dialects. Although *botch* has the variant *bodge*, and *grudge* has the variant *grutch*, how often do we see *bodge* and *grutch* in print? Finally, if in refuting my etymology, somebody happens to come up with a better idea, I will be more than compensated for my botched effort.

Two Gifts from Our Dutch Uncle: Plug-Ugly and Play Hookey

Even those who know little about the history of English may realize what a debt English owes to French and Latin. On some pages of a comprehensive English dictionary, most words go back to Romance languages. Further exposure to the subject makes people aware of the Scandinavian element in the vocabulary of English. If we keep reading the dictionary, we will soon notice the ever-recurring phrase: "Perhaps from Low German or (Middle) Dutch." The bulk of words featured in such entries appeared in English between the fourteenth and seventeenth centuries. Some are now domesticated, while others are obsolete or rare. There was no Dutch military invasion of England, but, at the close of the Middle English period and the beginning of what we today call modern history, contacts (friendly and hostile) between Great Britain and the continental north were so intense that hundreds of Dutch words flooded English.

Northern Germany speaks dialects subsumed under the name *Low German*. They are sometimes close to and sometimes quite different from the dialects of Dutch, but the proximity between them makes it hard to tell whether the word that penetrated English is a tribute from the speakers of the Hanseatic League or the Dutch. Sometimes the generic term *Low Dutch* is used to cover Dutch, Low German, and Frisian. Although common in our books, this term has little to recommend it, for once we start from **Netherlands**, how can we go any lower? Be that as it may, a combined Low German-Dutch linguistic invasion of English is a fact.

Rather unexpectedly, one of its traces can be detected in children's slang. In England, irresponsible schoolchildren used to play the wag, play the jolly, leg it, and play hook(e)y (with the variant *play hookey walker*), but only *play truant* was dignified enough for official use: the others, the "vulgar" ones, could be repeated in a whisper. Children also *miked* and did a *mickey*. American students bagged school (and of course cut it); one of the New England phrases was *Hook Jack*. This school slang showed surprising tenacity. A common synonym for "miss school without permission" was *mooch*. From "play truant" it developed into "play truant in order to pick blackberries," so that the berries themselves eventually got the name *moochies*. Considering how many variants and related forms *mooch* has (e.g., *mouch*, *modge*, and *miche*, the latter as in Hamlet's *miching malicho* "sneaking mischief"; Shakespeare also knew *micher* "truant"), I wonder whether *mike* ~

mickey belong with it. *Mug* (the verb) and *-mudge-* in *curmudgeon* most probably do.

Dictionaries hedge when it comes to the origin of *play hookey* (and its forgotten lookalike *Hook Jack*). The verb *hook* "steal" and the idiom *hook it* "escape, make off" are often cited in this context. The value of other clues is questionable. For example, in Essex (and perhaps not only there) *Hookey* meant "devil"; hence the expression *as black as Hookey*. Then there is the card game *blind hookey*. Yet *play hookey* is pure Dutch, where its counterpart is *hoekje spelen* (*spelen* "play"), and this fact is not a secret. In my opinion, an informative article by John R. Sinnema (*American Speech* 45, 1969, 205–210) partly settles the question so that dictionaries need not repeat the safe formula "of unknown origin." The root of Dutch *hoekje* (a diminutive) is *hoek* "corner." The original meaning of English *hook*, a cognate of *hoek*, was "curve, bend," which explains the idiom *by hook or by crook*.

There is only one hitch here: as Sinnema explained, *hoekje spelen* means "play hide-and-(go)-seek," not "cut school." The origin of the idiom is clear: someone hides round the corner, and "It" must find that person. But why "play truant" in American English (later, as we have seen, the phrase crossed the ocean and became popular in Britain)? Sinnema devoted some space to the possible reasons for the change of meaning, but a satisfactory explanation may perhaps hide round the corner. In Volume 3 of the Dutch *Archief voor Nederlandsche Taalkunde* (1851–1853, pp. 339–400), A. de Jager wrote a few lines on *schoolverzuim* ("missing school") and mentioned the dialectal expressions *hooikes ketsen* and *hooikes kuiteren* "play truant." I assume that *hooikes* is a variant of *hoekje*. *Ketsen* means "to misfire," and *kuiteren* is probably "to spawn." In the speech of some speakers, *hoekje spelen* and *hooikes ketsen* (*kuiteren*) must have merged, unless all three could always mean both things. The hybrid reached the New World, and *hoekje spelen*, later Anglicized as *play hook(e)y*, triumphed with the sense "cut school." However vague the picture may be, lexicographers would be justified in saying: "*Play hook(e)y*. From Dutch." Jager also mentions Dutch dialectal *plenken* "play truant"; this word made its way to Scotland and stayed there in the form *plunk* with the same meaning.

The original editors of the *OED* knew the early Dutch verb *plencken* but not its modern dialectal reflex.

And now an addendum on *plug-ugly*, another Americanism and another word "of unknown origin." According to the extant evidence, plug-uglies began their activities in Baltimore. The most interesting quotation from the *OED* (reproduced here in part) runs as follows: "derived from a short spike fastened in the toes of their boots, with which they kicked their opponents in a dense crowd, or, as they elegantly expressed it, 'plugged them ugly.'" We have no way of knowing whether this is a true derivation of *plug-ugly* or a folk etymology produced in retrospect to justify the name. In any case, *plug* is a borrowing from Dutch. A word for "plug" can easily develop a figurative meaning ("something unimportant"), and *plug* "subordinate, servant" is indeed current in the dialect of Groningen. *Plug-ugly* surfaced in printed texts only in the middle of the nineteenth century. Yet slang is hard to date, and the earliest "ugly plugs" may have been wicked underlings in the eyes of their victims. Even if Groningen *plug* is not related to *plug-ugly*, here, in the capacity as its Dutch uncle, it will do no one any harm. In American colloquial English, *plug-ugly* sometimes deteriorates into *pug-ugly*.

As usual, most etymological solutions concerning slang remain hypothetical. We can only avow that plug-uglies are not the greatest fans of education and tend to play hooky.

4

Crabbed Age Looks Back at Youth and Feels Amused

Dandy

Dandy first made its appearance on the Scottish border, and, in the 1780s, the word became current in British slang. Its origin (most probably, dialectal) remains a mystery—a common thing with such words. Etymologists have grudgingly resigned themselves to the idea that *dandy* goes back to the pet name of *Andrew*, though how *Andrew* became *Dandy* is unclear (by attracting *d* from the middle?). But this may not be our greatest problem because *Dandy* is indeed a recorded short name for *Andrew* (and incidentally, for *Alexander*). Trying to discover why Andrew was chosen to represent London's overdressed young men (assuming that such an event happened several hundred years ago) would be a waste of time. This mythic character is a member of the club to which Smart Aleck and Jack Sprat (a.k.a. Jack Prat) belong.

Then there are *merry-andrew* "buffoon" and *jack-a-dandy* "a merry foppish fellow" (the latter predates *dandy* by about a century). The *Oxford English Dictionary* (*OED*) is noncommittal with regard to the etymology of *dandy* but admits a possible connection between it and *jack-a-dandy*. Here are two quotations in addition to what the *OED* gives (the second obviously echoes the first or is rather part of a formulaic pattern): "Smart she is and handy, O, / Sweet as sugar candy, O, / Fresh and gay / As flow'rs in May, / And I'm her Jack-a-dandy, O" (no date given); "My love is blithe and bucksome [sic] / And sweet and fine as can be; / fresh and gay as the flowers in May, / And looks like Jack-a-dandy" (1671). In the 1780s, many songs having almost the same refrain were in vogue, with *Dandy, O* substituting for *Jack-a-dandy, O*.

We will ignore a few fanciful suggestions (such as the attempt to trace *dandy* to the name of an ancient tribe and several others, equally imaginative and groundless) and turn to two reasonable derivations proposed in the past. One centers on *dandiprat* "dwarf; urchin; a small coin" (an early sixteenth-century word). Since its origin is also unknown, no help can be expected from those quarters. But it may be observed that the time gap is significant: if *dandy* had been "abstracted" from *dandiprat*, it would probably have surfaced much earlier. Also, *dandy* does not seem to have been used to mock the ostentatious (and indeed often ridiculously dressed) "swells." When dandies attracted public notice, they became an object of good-humored, even if vulgar, curiosity and were more often gaped at than vilified. They resembled the later dudes of American fame. Later, whatever opprobrium associated with them disappeared. Byron, to give a classical example, was a "dandy." Around 1830, people spoke about "Winchester gentlemen, Harrow dandies, and Eton bucks" (*bucks* must have had more than one meaning). Pushkin's aristocratic Evgeny Onegin was "dressed like a London dandy" (1825). By contrast, *dandiprat* never had positive connotations.

Another school of thought looks for the homeland of *dandy* in France, even though French lexicographers unanimously state that *dandy* is an import from England. French *dandin* means "ninny"; hence Molière's immortal cuckold George Dandin. The verb *dandiner* has been glossed variously as "to twist one's body about; have a rolling gait, waddle; occupy oneself with trifles." Even the earliest dandies were not ninnies, though they did comport themselves in a way that aroused amusement. Apparently, *dandy* cannot be traced to French *dandin*.

An etymologist should always explore the surroundings of the word under investigation. *Dandy* "fop" is not an isolated word in English. We find *a dandy of punch* (i.e., a small glass; predominantly Irish), *dandy* "a vessel rigged as a sloop and having also a jigger mast," and *dandy*, a term used as the first element in the names of various contrivances. In a local book, the devil's hounds were called "dandy dogs" (!). A regional dictionary gives *dandy* "hand." And then, whatever the origin of *dandiprat*, its "prat" must have been "dandy." Traveling along the dictionary page with *dandy*, we come across *dander* "an outburst of anger," as in *get one's dander up*; *dander* "stroll, saunter," *dander* "the ferment (of molasses)," and one more *dander* "a piece of slag"; *dandruff*; and *dandle* "to rock a child" (with which we may, if we wish, compare *dangle*). In our texts, none of those words predated 1500 (while some were attested much later), and, surprisingly, the origin of all of them is unknown (in *dandruff* only -*ruff* admits of a convincing explanation). French *dandin* is also obscure.

A word historian often runs into what may be called "common European slang." Perhaps a case in point is the *dand-* words. Middle High German lyric poetry made *tandaradei*, an exclamation of joy, famous. It has been explained as a shout imitating a bird's song. Do birds sing *tandaradei*? English *dandle* resembles Italian *dandolare* "swing; toss; dally; loiter." The *OED* observes about a possible cognate of a similar sounding German verb that "no word of this family is known in Old or Mid. Eng., and the sense is not so close to the English as in the Italian word." Yet German *tandeln* means "dawdle, play, etc."

We will probably never know the origin of *dandy* for sure, but if we venture into the prehistory of slang, we may risk the conjecture that when *dand-* words first invaded some West European languages around 1500, they meant "active, mobile" or "quick, nimble" (Is this where *dandy* "hand" came from? And are dandy dogs quick dogs?). "Swing, shake" would be a natural extension of quickness, and the exclamation *tandaredei* would emerge as a natural expression of animal spirits. *Fine and dandy* looks like a tautological binomial of the *safe and sound* type: all that is quick and nimble is fine by definition. Jack-a-dandy certainly knew how to win a girl's heart. At some time, *dandy* "fop" may have had amorous overtones. French *dandiner* "to twist one's body" fits the picture well (compare "swing, toss"). Twisting in coils found no favor with the French: it must have struck them as idiotic. Hence *dandin*, a back formation from the verb? If this is how *dandy* acquired its meaning, it has nothing to do with *Andrew* so that the association between them is late. The origin of *dander*, in all its manifestations, deserves a special look.

Can my reconstruction of the origin of *dandy* be taken seriously? Slang travels light from land to land. An expressive word can conquer half of Europe in a matter of a few years; consider our modern *cool*. In the past, the process was not so quick. Anyway, if we accept the etymology proposed here as a working hypothesis, we won't be poorer than before, for at the outset we had nothing.

Masher

It is amazing how short-lived some slang is, while other slangy words stay with us almost forever. *Masher* is a perfect example of the first tendency. It enjoyed tremendous popularity at the end of the nine-teenth and the beginning of the twentieth century, before it more or less faded from people's memory. However, those who read old books will have no trouble recognizing the word: it crops up in the literature of the late Victorian era, in American novels written before World War I, and in such popular British publications as *Punch's Almanac*, the *Sporting Times*, and the *Illustrated London News*, among many others. The *Piccadilly Masher* was the title of a popular music hall song of the day. While comparing *swell*, *dandy*, *beau*, and such nice synonyms for "a flamboyant man about town" as *Corinthian* and *mac-aroni*, all designating approximately the same type of person, knowl-edgeable correspondents to magazines said the following in 1882: "A masher is usually a 'swell,' but every swell is not a masher. To be 'awfully mashed on' a young woman is equivalent . . . to being 'terrible spoons' [i.e., nearly losing one's mind, becoming spoony?] or 'very hard hit.' The masher proper is a young gentleman . . . who, having become a devout adorer of some fair actress, nightly frequents the house where she is engaged, that he may feast his eyes upon her beauty." The adoring youth, we are told, becomes the actress's mash, "like the favorite food of a highly-fed horse." Thus, *to be mashed* means "to be dead nuts on" or "hotly in love with" a girl. This is the passive. In the active voice, *to mash* is "to make a girl dead nuts on oneself." *Nuts* deserves special dis-cussion: see the section on *nerd*.

The condemnation of highbrows was loud and unanimous: *this bar-barous addition to our slang, this precious contribution to our vocabu-lary, a detestable cant word, this horrible word in common and certainly vulgar use*, and so forth, but, in retrospect (in 1943, when one would have thought there were more pressing things to discuss), with respect to *mash, masher*, and *mashing*, the admission came that "ugly as [they] were, [they] expressed shades of meaning hard to replace exactly by more elegant equivalents [this is of course why slang exists!] . . . the masher was thought of as well dressed, and offensive, but extreme villainy was not imputed to him" (an American or someone who lived in the United States for a long time must have written those lines).

It is surprising how often people call certain words ugly and detestable. No one chokes on mashed potatoes, while horses are fed mash and enjoy it. What then can be offensive in the innocuous combination of the sounds *m-a-(sh)*? The person (for example a masher) may arouse contempt, but the word? Words can be funny (*geek*, for instance, or *nincompoop*; I sometimes speak about nincompoops in my course on folklore, and the audience always begins to laugh, probably because of the association with *poop*), stupid (such as *irregardless*), stodgy and unnecessary (*orientated*, to give a random example of bureaucratese), confusing (as when *flammable* happens to mean the same as *inflammable*), trampled to death (buzzwords), maimed by ignorance, this great motor of language history, and so forth, but barbarous? Why? One reason may be that words tend to be confused with the things they designate (e.g., a prim and proper person despises mashers and detests the word *masher*). Also, even in the 1920s, *slang* might still signify the same as *argot*, *flash*, and *cant*. Its use was deplored and castigated. The literati would study Catullus, enjoy Rabelais, and explain Shakespeare's obscenities but wince at *masher*. Fortunately, we live in an enlightened age and may say whatever we want in public and in private.

Now back to the origin of *masher*. Some etymologies should be safely disregarded. It has been repeated several times that *masher* is "a gypsy word" (the suggested etymon either does not exist or means nothing even remotely useful for the occasion), an alteration of French *ma chère* (this is out of the question: though a woman could occasionally be called a masher, being a masher was predominantly a male occupation), or an adaptation of Irish *meas* (pronounced as *mash*) "elegant." Ernest Weekley, the author of the only original etymological dictionary of English written since Skeat's days, proposed a derivation that looks rather fanciful: "Can it be a far-fetched elaboration of *to be spoony on*, mash being regarded as spoon-diet? Cf. *to confiscate the macaroon* for *to take the cake*." In 1888, someone stated that *masher* goes back to a Scotch mining term: "*Mash* is a double-edged hammer for breaking coals. *Mash* as a verb means 'to pound small.' From it a curious metaphor has given us a name for that product of this enlightened age known as 'masher.'" There could not have been a less probable environment for coining *masher* than a mine in Scotland, but we will see that the underlying idea of this etymology is sound.

I would like to quote a passage that appeared in *Walford's Antiqurian* (vol. 12, 1887, p. 93). "Mash, to. To impress women. From *mash* as mixture, thus: 1) 'Let's go and have a mash,' that is, a drink. 2) 'Who serves you mash?' 3) 'Who's your mash? (favorite barmaid)?' Soon any girl who officiated in public, as dancer, singer, or actress, was called a mash, and admirers (young fellows that, at this time, always 'got up' in white vest, high white collar, white satin tie, box hat, and bangle on wrist) were termed mashers...." The description of the scene is more exciting than the suggested etymology. It does not seem that mashers first appeared in bars. Most early quotations point to the theater and young bucks doting on actresses. Besides, it has often been suggested that *masher* was imported to England from the United States. The country of origin remains undiscovered, and I failed to find any confirmation of the statement that *masher* was a word used by black "minstrels" (a single reference to this effect in a British magazine does not go far).

Some of our best dictionaries say that the origin of *masher* is unknown. However, if we disregard a few insupportable conjectures, the conclusion at which we will arrive won't surprise anyone: *masher* is *mash* plus *-er*. Only *mash* poses problems. Apparently, something is right about the idea that a masher conquered or tried to conquer women and "struck them all of a heap" or that he "mashed, or softened ladies' hearts" (compare the double-edged hammer, above). It has also been noted that having a mash on a person is "rather like" having a crush on someone. *To have a crush on* is, by all appearances, an American coinage (a fact that gives some credence to the idea that mashers also originated in the United States), and, judging by printed documents, it postdated *to have a mash on* by a few decades.

Since *mash* means "crush," the two phrases are close. When one is in love, one is overpowered by the romantic feeling ("mashed, crushed"). This is probably how both idioms came about. Also, being mashed is the same as being smashed, especially by a smashing beauty. (I am of course not the first to compare *mash* and *smash*.) Then there is *mushy* "cloyingly, treacly sentimental; wishy-washy" ("mushy-mashy," as it were). *Smash* and *mush* may have influenced and reinforced *mash* "to be infatuated." Thus, first *to be mashed* and *to mash* and then *masher*. It is tempting to suggest that once *to have a mash on* lost its popularity, its synonym *to have a crush on*, with *crush* substituted for *mash*, took over and stayed. A similar idea has occurred to several word lovers.

Dude

Dude is a member of a small but close-knit family: *dod* "cut off, lop, shear," *dud* "a coarse cloak" (now obsolete), *duds* "clothes," and *dad* (*did* belongs elsewhere). The original *OED* called *dude* a factitious slang term. *Factitious* means "produced artificially." James A. H. Murray, the first editor and etymologist of the great dictionary, must have meant that *dude* is "a coinage" (a word invented by some individual), and his instinct pointed in the right direction. *Dude* surfaced in the United States in 1883, spread like the proverbial wildfire, and never disappeared, though it has lost its derogatory meaning and become a colorless synonym for "guy, fellow; bloke, chap," applicable to men and women, though 150 years ago and some time later, only men could be called dudes. (It is even more amusing that, with time, *guy* stuck to women, particularly in the plural: after all, Guy is the name of a famous male.)

It may be useful to read what Charles P. G. Scott, the etymologist for the *Century Dictionary* (an American reference work), wrote about *dude*. The word was still relatively new: "A slang term which has been the subject of much discussion. It first became known in colloquial and newspaper use at the time of the so-called 'esthetic' movement in dress and manners in 1882–83. The term has no antecedent record, and is prob[ably] merely one of the spontaneous products of popular slang. There is no known way, even in slang etymology, of 'deriving' the term, in the sense used, from *duds* (formerly sometimes spelled *dudes* . . .), clothes, in the sense of 'fine clothes'; and the connection, though apparently natural, is highly improbable." It will be seen that Scott and the *OED* had a similar attitude toward *dude*. The *Century Dictionary* quoted the journal called *The American*: "The social dude who affects English dress and the English drawl." Later research corroborated both the "factitious" origin of *dude* and the definition given by *The American*.

Oscar Wilde visited the United States in 1883 and was looked upon as the quintessential dude. However, his trip was a success: despite his mannerisms, he swam like the best and drank like the best.

The hypotheses on the origin of *dude* are not particularly interesting. Some of them are remembered only because Skeat took part in the discussion. As early as 1900, Skeat wrote the following (I have expanded the abbreviations): "The origin of *dude* is unrecorded. Perhaps it is short for Low German *duden-dop*, *duden-kop*, a drowsy fellow, a cuckold; a term of reproach. Or it may have been suggested by the verb *dudden*, to be drowsy, or the adjective *duddig*, drowsy. . . . Cf. Old Frisian [Skeat said *Friesic*] *dudslek*, a stunning blow, Icelandic *doði* [ð has the value of *th* in English *this*], *doðna*, to become insensible; which seems to be ultimately related . . . to Gothic *dauth-us*, death. And cf. further provincial English *doddle*, English *dawdle*; Low German *döden*, to dawdle, and [Swedish dialectal] *dödolga*, a dawdler." The fact that, in 1900, Skeat, an Englishman, discussed *dude* in such detail, is remarkable because, as late as 1932, Henry Cecil Wyld, also an Englishman, wrote in the *Universal Dictionary of the English Language*: "Origin unknown (American slang, not used in England)."

Apparently, Skeat did not share Murray's view that *dude* was a word of factitious origin. Modern dictionaries, unless they say "origin unknown," usually cite a severely abridged version of Skeat's entry. One finds reference to Portuguese *doudo*, a dialectal form of *doido* "simpleton, fool." As a parallel to *dude*, English *fop* has been mentioned because the word combines the senses "fool" (the predominant early sense) and "one wearing flashy clothes." A fanciful etymology connected *dude* with *dyde*, the Old English past tense of *do*. Another bizarre guess had it that at one time New York dandies greeted one another with "How *dew* you *dew*?" A few correspondents to *Notes and Queries* believed that *dude* has ties with the name of the now extinct bird dodo. A serious scholar wondered whether *dude* might be a borrowing (via American Spanish) of Arabic *dud* "worm, caterpillar." Early attempts to derive *dude* from *doodle* are also on record. *Dude* appears to be an Americanism coined in New York City, and that is why it may have been brought to the New World by British immigrants. The existence of *dude* in some English dialects cannot be ruled out. Thomas Hardy's novel *Jude the Obscure* appeared in 1895. Since the British pronunciation of *du-* is very often *ju-* (so that *duel* and *jewel* become homophones), the dudes who affected the British accent (see what is said above about *how dew you dew?*) might perhaps associate *Jude* with *dude*, though Jude in no way resembled a dude: he was modest and unassuming, a simple-hearted stonemason, obedient to Hardy's cruel agenda. I don't think for a moment that Hardy, while writing his novel, ever thought of dudes. (He may never have heard the word: see Wyld's statement, above!) Yet in the earlier versions of the book, the protagonist's name was Jack. The idea seems to have been to give the "obscure" character a neutral, almost generic name.

For the fun of it, I will reproduce a passage ascribing the invention of *dude* to the famous American businessman Hermann Oelrichs: "The simple fact is that Mr. Oelrichs, who is distinguished by a deep contempt for effeminacy in either dress or manner, sat one day at a window gazing out on Fifth Avenue. Along came a very much overdressed youth, with so mincing a gait, that involuntarily one of the clubmen with Mr. Oelrichs [the Union Club is meant] began humming an accompaniment to the step, thus: 'du, da, de, du-du, du, de du.' 'That's good!' said Mr. Oelrichs; 'it ought to be called a dude.' And dude it has been called ever since." This was printed in 1889, in Oelrich's lifetime. If this story is true, *dude* again emerges as a "factitious" slang term, but such anecdotes almost never unlock an etymology.

The history and origin of *dude* has been explored in great detail by three American researchers: Gerald L. Cohen, Barry A. Popik, and Peter J. Reitan. At the end of 2022, their monograph of VIII + 261 pages, titled "Origin of the term 'dude,'" came out, self-published by Professor Gerald Cohen, at Missouri University of Science and Technology. The appearance of this book was prepared for by numerous occasional publications in the monthly *Comments on Etymology*, also edited and published by Professor Cohen. The book tells a detailed story of the craze that spread in New York and Washington, DC, in the early 1880s, and we now seem to know under what circumstances the word *dude* conquered America.

On January 14, 1883, Robert Sale Hill (1850–1922) published a poem titled "The Dude." It appeared in the New York newspaper *The World*. The dictionaries refer to three pre-1883 occurrences of *dude*, but, in the opinion of Cohen, Popik, and Reitan, the dating of both texts is open to serious doubt. The *dude* craze certainly began with Hill, who wrote: "Long years ago, / Before there was a mode, oh! / There lived a bird they called a 'Dude,' / Resembling much the 'Dodo.'" The poem is long, and even contains a reference to Oscar Wilde's visit to America. If Hill invented the word *dude*, we would still like to know how he came by it. The formidable epithet *factitious* again stares us in the face. The many cognates Skeat cited lose their value as sources because Hill was not a specialist in German dialects, Frisian, or Old Norse. The only clue he provided for his coinage is the mention of *Dodo* in the first stanza. We remember that an association with *Dodo* also occurred to some of the correspondents to the periodical *Notes and Queries*. But this clue opens no doors.

Cohen and his collaborators derived Hill's *dude* from two sources: *Yankee Doodle* (a phrase that also existed as a term of ridicule) and the British adjective *flapdoodle* "a silly-looking fop," a slang adjective Hill possibly knew. This reconstruction may or may not be correct. Monosyllables beginning and ending with *b, g, d* or *p, t*, and *k* are easy to coin, and many of them are expressive. Compare *bob, bib, babe, gig, dud* (see it above), *pap, pup, poop, boob, kick, cock*, and their likes. Though references to being *in big doo-doo* surfaced in print only in the twentieth century, the childish word *doo-doo* and the phrase *to go doody* are probably very much older. *Dude* "dung" (remembered for the western dude farms) belongs here, too. I would not be surprised if *dude* (assuming that Hill coined this word) meant to him something like "a piece of shit." Snobs, dandies, swells, and mashers, regardless of our attitude toward them, have some substance, while a dude was mere form, a nutshell without a nut, a striving for ostentation, a display of silliness and bad taste.

Therefore, I am not quite sure that *dude* goes back directly to *-doodle* in *Yankee Doodle* or *flapdoodle*. I also wonder why Hill did not spell the word *dood*. The many words Skeat cited as possible cognates or sources of *dude* show how easy it is to coin a derogatory term of the *d-d* type in any language. Obviously, English *dude* owes nothing to Old English, German, Frisian, or Scandinavian, but the impulse that made people at different times and in different countries come up with almost the same sound complex is characteristic. Viewed in this light, the factitious *dude* is a sound-symbolic word: we hear it and more or less know what meaning it conveys.

On Nuts and Nerds

The semantic range of many slang words is often broad, but the multitude of senses attested for English *nut* (see the *OED*) is amazing. Here are some of them, both obsolete and current: "a source of pleasure or delight" ("To see me here would be simply nuts to her"), *nuts* in the phrases *to be (dead) nuts on* "to be in love of, fond of, or delighted with," *to be nuts about*, as in "I was still nuts about Rex," and *to be nuts* "go mad" (hence *nutjob ~ nut job ~ nut-job* "madman; idiot" and *nutsy* "crazy"), *not to be able to do things for nuts* (1895) "to be incompetent" (*bean* shared a similar fate). Apparently, this usage has been known for centuries, even though the citations in the *OED* going back to 1625 are isolated: *old nuts* "a source of pleasure" and *for nuts* "for amusement and, for fun." On the other hand, this slang could be "reborn" two and a half centuries later.

It so happened that, at one time, all kinds of round, especially small round, objects began to be called nuts (as evidenced, among others, by *nuts and bolts*). The exclamation *nuts!* has no obvious point of reference (compare *gee!* or *gosh!*), and it therefore does not come as a surprise that in addition to "pleasure," it can mean "nonsense," or be an expression of frustration, even though *the nuts* signifies an excellent person. Here are two more examples with positive references from my reading: "An English country gentleman might express himself concerning an agreeable incident: 'It was nuts'" and "To edge his way along the crowded paths of life, warning all human sympathy to keep its distance, was what the knowing ones call 'nuts' to Scrooge". The negative senses are "madness" and "stupidity." Since *nuts!* means what the speaker wants it to mean, tracing this word to German *von Nutzen* "of use" (this origin of *nuts* has been proposed in a serious paper) would be a false move.

From *nutty* we may perhaps move to *nut* "fop, masher." In England, the word enjoyed great popularity in the decades before the First World

War, and, at that time, a correspondent to *Notes and Queries* quoted Lafaeu's (or Lafew's) remark on Parolles in Shakespeare's *All's Well That Ends Well*: "There can be no kernel in this light nut; the soul of this man is his clothes" (II: 54, 44). Also, the adjective *natty* and its possible source *neat* were close by to interact with *nuts* and *nutty*. In those days, a nut was someone who made a fool of himself in the eyes of non-nuts but was also an analog of today's cool dude. Since the nut of a century ago, like his sibling masher, was keen on impressing women, he obviously needed "nuts."

I suspect (and, most probably, I am not the first to do so) that the story begins with *nuts* "testicles," even though the earliest recorded examples of this sense are late (however, it must have been so well-known in the United States more than a hundred years ago that the *Century Dictionary* included it). Nuts and genitalia have been compared for centuries. Thus, *nut* occurred with the sense of "the glans penis" (a similar idea occurred to German speakers: they referred to an acorn). In any case, the adjective *nutty* means (or meant) not only "fond, enthusiastic" but also "amorous." The way from "fond" to "amorous" is short, whichever venue we may choose. Not unlikely, *nuts* emerged as a loose word for expressing a strong feeling: *nuts!* "nonsense," *nuts!* "wonderful," *nuts!* "crazy," and so forth. *Nut* "head" sounds like an independent coinage (the head has been likened to all kinds of oblong and round objects in many languages); hence *off one's nut*, though *nuts* "mad" may have reinforced that phrase.

Naturally, since *nuts* existed, the singular *nut* was soon derived from it (so from the plural to the singular, not the other way around, if my reconstruction is right). This is how *nut* "fop" arose. A correspondent to *Notes and Queries* wrote that a few years before 1913 it had been usual in cabmen's slang to describe a keen, sharp-witted person as a nut. "Then came the epidemic of young men with 'doggy' socks, of pink and green and heliotrope, and they were promptly labeled 'the nuts.' The word by this time meant not so much keenness as dressiness, up-to-dateness—the lineal successors of the 'mashers' of the earlier day." Incidentally, *doggy* means "dashing, stylish," from *dog* "style," as in the idiom *to put on (the) dog* "make a vulgar display of wealth."

For decades, the English-speaking world has been wondering where the ubiquitous word *nerd* came from. The Internet is full of excellent essays on the subject: the documentation is complete, and multiple hypotheses have been considered, refuted, or cautiously endorsed. I believe one of the proposed etymologies to be convincing, and my only goal is to defend it. (To give an idea of what nonsense one can find in popular etymological literature, let me give one example. More than a century ago, some wits—they were called wags and cards then— spelled *nuts* as *knuts*, pronounced the first consonant, and joked that King Knut/Canute had been the first nut. One of the "etymologies" of *nerd* traces this word to *knurd*—that is, *drunk*—spelled backward.)

Nut has been an expressive word for a long time, and, as such, it could and probably did have additional forms. For example, the American coinage *nertz ~ nerts* "nonsense," recorded only in 1929, is indeed an emphatic variant of *nuts*. In this function, the syllable *er* is not uncommon (at least so in American English). Dr. Ari Hoptman called my attention to the pronunciation *lurve* for *love* in one of Woody Allen's old movies. If *nuts* can be the etymon of *nerts*, I would assert that there is no reason why *nerd* could not have the same source. This idea has occurred to many people, and one wonders why it has not been accepted, why people keep pounding on an open door and saying "etymology dubious, disputed, uncertain, unknown." The etymology of such a word can never be "known," but a feasible hypothesis need not be treated with extreme caution and listed, for the sake of good manners, along with all kinds of fanciful suggestions. Also, the hapless Dr. Seuss, who by chance coined his own *nerd*, should be left in peace amid his zoo, even if, thanks to his invention, this word got a second lease on/of life. *Nerd*, like *geek*, *wimp*, and *square* "old-fashioned; dull," was launched as a derogatory term. With time, it acquired some endearing overtones. After all, not every intellectual is an old fogey or a social moron. But it is the origin, rather than the word's later development, that interested us here.

Dr. Stephen Goranson alerted me to the following quotation from Thackeray's *Vanity Fair* (1847): "I have a wonderful idea for a humorous publication. . . . Our first issue will have a full page burlesque of Beach Nut. I am going to call it Beech Nerts." (In British English, *r* is not sounded in *nert*, so that *nert* or *nerd* is closer to *nut* than it would be in the pronunciation of an American.) Only the step from *nert* to *nerd* remains undocumented.

As a final flourish, this may be a proper place to cite the simile *as black as the Devil's nutting bag*, which was discussed at great length in the aforementioned periodical *Notes and Queries* between 1854 and 1940. One also finds some references to it on the Internet. According to a reasonable suggestion, the saying may have roots in one of the old harvest festivals that was held when hazel nuts are ripe. The festival of nutting day was celebrated "with a great disturbance of peace." On the other hand, on St. Matthew's day (September 14), no one, we are told, would go out nutting, or indeed, if possible, pass along the lanes of the village in East Sussex, "fearing to meet his satanic majesty." The simile has been recorded in many parts of England beyond Sussex. Why was the festival of nutting celebrated with a great disturbance of peace, and whence the association with devilry? Didn't the harvesting of nuts suggest being nutty and going nuts? Just a thought.

5

Marital Bliss and a Few Diversions

Kiss

Like every other custom, kissing has been studied from the historical, cultural, anthropological, and linguistic points of view. Did the ancient Indo-Europeans (among all the other people of the world) kiss? And if they did, whom, when, and why did they kiss, and what was their method of performing this "gesture"?

In 1897, Kristoffer Nyrop (1858–1931), a distinguished student of Romance linguistics and semantic change, wrote a book called *Kysset og dets historie* (*The Kiss and Its History*). The 190-page book was translated into English almost immediately and is still available. A week after its publication, all the copies were sold out, and Nyrop was asked to prepare a second edition and do so in a wild hurry, to be ready for Christmas sales. As could be expected, he complied. Somewhat un-expectedly, he said nothing about the origin of the word *kiss*. Yet the literature on the etymology of *kiss* is huge.

Below, I'll limit myself mainly to Germanic. The ancestors of today's English, Frisians, Dutch, Germans, and Scandinavians had almost the same word for "kiss," approximately *koss* (*coss*). Part of the New Testament in Gothic has come down to us. Gothic is a Germanic lan-guage, recorded in the fourth century, and the word for the verb *kiss* in it is *kukjan* (the Greek verb Bishop Wulfila saw was a form of *philéō*, which meant both "to love" and "to kiss"). As early as 1861, Dutch di-alectal *kukken* surfaced in a scholarly work, and somewhat later an almost identical East Frisian form was set in linguistic circulation. It became clear that, at one time, Germanic speakers had two forms: one with -*ss*- and the other with -*kk*-.

Most of my survey goes back to an article by Nyrop's contemporary, the distinguished German philologist Theodor Siebs (1862–1941). It was published in the journal of the society for the promotion of Silesian popular lore (*Mitteilungen der Schlesischen Gesellschaft für Volkskunde*) for 1903. Surprisingly, Siebs became aware of Nyrop's book only after his own work had been almost completed and succeeded in obtaining a copy of it only because Nyrop sent him one. He soon realized that his predecessor had covered a good deal of the material he had been collecting, but Nyrop's book did not make Siebs's nineteen-page article redundant because Nyrop's focus was on the situations in which people kiss (a friendly kiss, a kiss of peace, an erotic kiss, etc.), while Siebs dealt with the linguistic aspect of his data.

It appears that the verb and the noun for "kiss" may go back to the words for the mouth and lips; for something sweet (German *gib mir 'nen Süssen* "give me a sweet [thing]"); for love (so in Greek, Slavic, and in Old Icelandic), and for embracing (as in French *embrasser*). As we will see, some of them are onomatopoeic, and some developed from various metaphors or expanded their original sense.

For curiosity's sake, I will list some words and phrases, without specifying the dialects in which they occur. German: *küssen, piepen, snüttern, -snüdeln* (*ü* in *snüttern* also appears to be long), *slabben, flabben, smacken, smukken, smatschen, muschen, bussen, bütsen, pützschen, pupen* (some of these words are colloquial, some verge on the vulgar). Many verbs for "kiss" (the verb and the noun) go back to *Mund* and *Maul* (both mean "mouth"): for example, *mundsen, mul ~ mull, müll, mill*, and the like. *Mäulchen* "little mouth" is not uncommon for "a kiss." Friesian: *æpke* (*æ* has the value of German *ä*) ~ *apki, make ~ mæke, klebi, totje, kükken*, and a few others, borrowed from German and Dutch. Dutch provides us with *zoenen* and *poenen*, about both of which more will be said below. In Swedish, two verbs compete: *kyssa* is a general term for kissing, while for informal purposes *pussa* is used.

Solomon in *The Song of Songs* mentions passionate kisses on the mouth, and Judas must also have kissed Jesus on the mouth. At least, such was the general perception in the Middle Ages (e.g., this is how Giotto and Fra Angelico, but more explicitly Giotto, represented the scene). The Hebrews and the Romans seem to have kissed as we do, and Wulfila, the translator of the Gothic Bible, probably had a similar image before his eyes while working with the Greek text.

We can now turn to the etymology of *kiss*. Siebs believed that Gothic *kukjan* "to kiss" had retained the original form of what later became

Old English *kyssan*, Old Norse *kyssa*, and their cognates. He also mentioned Modern Frisian *kok* "throat." In Old Frisian, *kokk* seems to have meant "speaker" and "mouth." He even reconstructed the Indo-European protoform *guttús*, which allegedly yielded *kyssan*. This reconstruction rests on a solid phonetic foundation, but everything in the history of *kukjan* ~ *kyssan* is so uncertain that the etymology of *kiss* cannot be considered solved.

Whenever the ritual of kissing came into being, some kisses were used to show respect, and, in other situations, they must have served a purpose comparable to a handshake sealing a bargain. Kissing the foot of a king or the Pope belongs here, too. Dutch *zoenen* has the root of a verb meaning "reconcile" (a cognate of German *versöhnen*). Consequently, people kissed to mark the end of hostilities. Later, the Dutch verb broadened its meaning and began to denote any kiss. Something similar happened in Russian, in which the verb for "kiss" is akin to the adjective for "whole": *tselovat'* (stress on the last syllable), from *tsel*. A kiss must have been a gesture signifying "be healthy." Dutch *poenen* ~ *puunen* (dialectal), with a close analog in German, seems to have meant "push, plunge, thrust; come into contact." Here, the emphasis was obviously on the movement in the direction of another person. Then there is English *smack*, believed to be sound-imitative: apparently, when one kisses someone, *smack* is heard. The presence of onomatopoeia is always hard to prove, but compare Russian *chmok*, which means exactly the same as *smack*. Latin *savium*, of obscure origin, designated an erotic kiss, while *osculum* goes back to the word for "mouth" (*os*). Neither is sound-imitative.

Where then does Old Germanic *kuss-* ~ *kukk-* belong? Many researchers have suggested that it is sound-imitative, like *smack*. Perhaps we really hear or think we hear *smack*, *chmok*, *kuss*, and *kukk* when we kiss. Alternatively, *kiss* was connected with Latin *gustare* "to taste," on the assumption that, at one time, the sought-for form began with *gw-*. Although this suggestion can be found in one of the best Germanic etymological dictionaries, it now has few, if any, supporters. More suggestive is the fact that the Hittite for "kiss" was *kuwaszi*, and it resembles Sanskrit *svasiti* "to blow; snort" (*k-* and *s-* alternate according to a certain rule, while *u* and *w* are variants of the same phonetic entity). Add to them Greek *kunéō* "kiss," in whose conjugation *-s-* appears

with great regularity: the form of the future was *kúsō* and the aorist
ékusa, earlier *ékussa*. On the basis of this evidence, several authoritative modern dictionaries posit a Proto-Indo-European form of *kiss*,
that is, follow the path trodden bravely by Nyrop. Can we imagine that
three or so thousand years ago there was a common verb for *kiss* whose
reflex (continuation) has come down to our time? Possibly, if "kiss"
designated something very common and truly important, that is, if, for
example, it existed as a religious term, with a sense like "to worship an
idol by touching the image with one's lips."

Other hypotheses also exist. *Kiss* was compared with the verb for
"speak," from which English has the antiquated preterit *quoth*; with
English *choose* and *chew*; with Swedish *kuk* "penis," with Low (=
Northern) German *kukkuk* "whore; vulva," with Irish *bel* "lip," and especially often with Latin *basium* "kiss" (noun) ~ *basiare* "kiss" (verb),
recognizable today from its Romance cognates: French *baiser*, Italian
baciare, and Spanish *besar*. All those conjectures should probably be
dismissed as unprofitable.

We are left with two choices. Perhaps there indeed once existed a
proto-verb sounding approximately like Modern English *kiss*, but
who kissed whom or what and in what way remains undiscovered.
Or, while kissing, different people heard a sound that resembles either
kuss or *kukk*. Neither solution inspires too much confidence, but, in
any case, the long consonant (-*ss* and -*kk*) points to the affective nature of the verb. Perhaps an ancient expressive verb belonging to the
religious sphere had near-universal currency, with Hittite, Sanskrit,
and Germanic still having its reflexes. If so, the main question will
be about the application of that verb. The sex-related look-alikes
("penis," "vulva," and the rest) should, almost certainly, be ascribed to
coincidence.

To prevent the Indo-European imagination from running wild, one
should remember that alongside *kiss*, English *buss* exists. Although it
sounds like Middle English *bass* (the same meaning), *bass* could not
become *buss*, and it is anybody's guess whether *bass* is of French or
Latin origin. Swedish dialectal *puss* corresponds to German Bavarian
buss, which is remembered because Luther used it. French, Spanish,
Portuguese, Lithuanian, Persian, Turkic, and Hindu have almost identical forms (Spanish is sometimes said to have borrowed its word from

Arabic), while Scottish Gaelic and Welsh *bus* means "lip; mouth." Even English *ba* "to kiss" has been recorded. This array of *b*-words seems to tip the scale toward the onomatopoeic solution, the more so because, to pronounce *b*, we have to open the lips. For millennia people have *kussed* (no pun intended), *kossed*, *kissed*, *kukked*, *bassed*, and *bussed*, to show affection and respect, to conclude peace, and just for the fun of it, without paying too much attention to origins. This is not giving a kiss of death to etymological research: it is rather a warning that some things are hard to investigate.

Honeymoon

The origin of some seemingly transparent words may pose almost insoluble problems. Obviously, *honeymoon* is a compound, whose first component means what it says. *Moon* may refer to *moon* (then the word *honeymoon* makes little sense) or *month* because *month* and *moon* share the root, and only the shortening of the historically long vowel in *month* drove a wedge between the two words. A similar change separated *holy* from *holiday*, *south* from *southern* (despite the spelling of the adjective) and *white* from *Whitsunday*. *Month* owes it origin to a lunar calendar. It is odd that we have *honeymoon* instead of *honeymonth*, but let this be the smallest trouble in the history of *honeymoon* and of the couples hoping for a lifetime of conjugal bliss and felicity.

We will see that in spite of the deceptively simple and transparent appearance of *honeymoon*, its history is anything but simple. However, let me begin with a word of warning. Nowadays, all of us look ("search") for answers on the Internet. Google provides numerous comments on the origin of English words. According to one of them, *honeymoon* derives from the Scandinavian practice of drinking Metheglin (i.e., mead or fermented honey) during the first month of the marriage (measured by one moon cycle) to improve the likelihood of conception.

Characteristically, no reference is ever given to the source of this information. Who practiced this rite in "Scandinavia," and where and when? Scandinavia is a very huge territory, and its history is known quite well. Once, even an Icelandic etymon of *honeymoon* has been offered. This is pure nonsense. In my experience, every time popular books and websites attribute the origin of an opaque English word or idiom to "Scandinavia," without saying why they think so, they should be disregarded: the authors, most likely, know nothing about northern folklore, literature, and languages, and copy their explanation from an equally ignorant predecessor. Mead and honey have of course been known to increase libido, but why in Scandinavia?

The origin of the word *honeymoon* remains a riddle, even though our early lexicographers were unaware of the problem. For example, Samuel Johnson wrote in his 1755 dictionary: "Honeymoon: the first month after marriage, when there is nothing but tenderness and pleasure." But he added: "Originally having no reference to a period of a month, but comparing the mutual affection of newly-married persons to the changing moon which is no sooner full than it begins to wane." The comment seems to have been cut out of whole cloth. Surely, he, a great expert in Shakespeare, remembered Juliet's adjuration: "O, swear not by the moon, the inconstant moon, / that monthly changes in her circled orb, / Lest that thy love prove likewise variable." Coining the word *honeymoon* with such a cruel allusion seems almost unthinkable. It would be like saying: "Enjoy the short period of mutual affection. It too shall pass." As we will presently see, Johnson did not invent his explanation (he was in general not an original etymologist), but he should have known better than to repeat it.

The oldest recorded citation of the word *honeymoon* in the *Oxford English Dictionary* (*OED*) is dated 1546. It occurs in a work by John Heywood (1497?–1540), a playwright, musician, the author of epigrams, and (especially important to language historians) the collector of *All Proverbs in the English Tongue* (1541; quite a modest title). This collection is of inestimable value. It was Heywood who defined *honeymoon* as we find it in Samuel Johnson. However, he borrowed it from Richard Huloet, the author of *Abcedarium* (*sic*) *Anglo-Latinum* . . . (1552), who referred to the "proverbial" sense of the word, as he elucidated it. Consequently, at his time, the word was in common use.

In 1656, Thomas Blount, the compiler of a dictionary titled *Glossographia*, abbreviated Huloet's rather lengthy note ("it is honey now, but will change as moon"). The *Oxford Dictionary of English*

Etymology, as usual, agrees with the *OED* but states the *honeymoon* was explained "by early authors with reference to affection of married people changing with the moon." The word *newly-married* has been replaced with *married* (which of course makes all the difference in the world), while the plural (*authors*) produces the impression that we have massive evidence on this point. Yet the evidence, as we have seen, is scanty. And let me repeat: Why should such a sweet word have been coined with such a grim message? What was the point of inventing a sweet-sounding compound, only to tell people that love is transitory?

The plot thickens. If, by 1552, *honeymoon* had become a well-known word and had stable associations with a waning moon, we wonder why no earlier reference to this allegedly proverbial association turned up in earlier authors, and why later the only people who remembered the word and its origin were dictionary makers. Juliet implores Romeo not to swear by the inconstant moon. Did Shakespeare know the treacherous compound *honeymoon*? We will never find out, but it is unlikely that the witty Heywood coined the word and that Huloet repeated somebody's joke. The *OED*'s explanation is part of the old tradition. Of course, another puzzle is why the allegedly ironic sense of *honeymoon* was forgotten and the word acquired the sweet, honeyed connotations known today.

Thus, nothing definite can be said about the circumstances in which *honeymoon* was coined. The verb *to honey* "to talk fondly, coax" existed. Our first and only memorable example of it comes from Shakespeare. Hamlet, shortly before he sees the Ghost in his mother's bedroom, keeps hurling insults at her: "Nay but to live / In the rank sweat of an enseamed bed / Stewed in corruption, *honying* and making love over the nasty sty—." Shakespeare used lots of current slang. To the extent that we can judge, *honey* "to address someone as *honey*" is roughly contemporaneous with *Hamlet*, but this fact throws no light on our problem. Although the history of *honeymoon* is opaque, I may perhaps venture a hypothesis.

Most likely, Huloet, Heywood, and others knew the original sense of *honeymoon*, and (my main point) it did indeed refer to the inconstancy of love or even had some vulgar connotations unknown to us, something like what we find in the Russian saying: "All brides are good, all the wives are bitches" (and for this reason avoided in literature). If so, it had nothing to do with newlyweds and had very limited currency. For such a word as *honeymoon* to retain its pejorative sense, it needed a community that never forgot the initial metaphor ("the moon wanes; love, too, begins like sweet honey but ends up like the moon, that is, disappears") or remembered the vulgar overtones (if such existed). It was the moon that carried the message of the compound, but later (here comes my hypothesis), *it was transferred to the honey*, the more so as stress in English compounds always falls on the first component. Such a scenario is not improbable. For example, the idiom *there is no love lost between them* used to mean that the people involved were friends (no love is lost). Later, it began to mean the opposite (there is so little love that there is nothing to lose). Thus, I suggest that the word *honeymoon* acquired the sense determined not by *moon* but by *honey* and that *moon*, which ended up in a wrong context, was misunderstood as "month."

Words corresponding to *honeymoon* abound in the languages of the world, and this is another riddle. I have not been able to find a single example of belated wisdom or grim prophesy attached to it. "Month of kissing, joy, caress, white bread, wheat bread, fine bakery, and so forth"—these are the most usual names in the European languages for the time following the wedding, and indeed, how could it be otherwise? English *honeymoon*, with its hypothesized original sad reference to the transitory nature of love, was destined to yield a more humane sense.

Frank Chance wrote in 1883: "nobody is prepared, I imagine, to assert that the French got *lune de miel* from us." For a change, he was mistaken. The expressions in Romance are, besides French *lune de miel*, Italian *luna di miele*, and Spanish *luna de miel*. English *moon* can perhaps be understood as "month," but *lune* and *luna* make sense only if we agree that they were translated from English. The route must have been from English to French and from French to several other languages, not only Romance (e.g., Russian has the same locution). I am not qualified to trace the route of this phrase from English to the rest of Europe or to account for its popularity outside England. This is something for others to do. Here, I'll only mention that, in France, it was Voltaire who used *lune de miel* for the first time in his play *Zadig* (1747). *Honeymoon*, as we have seen, predates it by two centuries.

Germans also toyed with their version of *honey* (the German for "honey" is *Honig*) in our phrase, but *Honigmonat* had no success. The German word is *Flitterwoche*, first recorded in 1539 (now in the plural: *Flitterwochen*; *Woche* means "week"). The word's literal gloss in most English dictionaries is "tinsel week," but *flittern* probably meant "to laugh, giggle." It is one of many sound-symbolic *fl*-words, like English *flitter, flutter, flatter, flirt*, and so forth. Why the time following the wedding got such a name has never been explained. Perhaps the reference is to the jubilation following the birth of a new family. Just guessing, as Walter W. Skeat used to say.

Bickering and Bitching

Respectability in etymology is determined by age: the older the recorded form, the better. The verb *to bicker* has been known since the fourteenth century, while the verb *to bitch* "complain; spoil" is a nineteenth-century coinage. By contrast, the noun *bitch* occurred in Old English, so that it is not quite clear which of the two words—*bitch* or *bicker*—should be awarded the first place.

Stephen Skinner, the author of the 1671 etymological dictionary of English, offered numerous sensible conjectures. He wondered whether *bicker* goes back to Welsh *bicra* "fight" (he wrote *bicre*) or the verb *pickereer*, which he may have understood as meaning "fight with pikes." But *pickereer* "maraud, skirmish, etc." surfaced considerably later than *bicker*. Yet Skinner's idea was sound, and so was his suggestion that a native origin of *bicker* looks more attractive. The Welsh etymon holds out little promise (the same is true of Charles Mackay's Irish *beuc ~ beic* "roar, bellow," which he cited alongside *becra*) because the origin of *bicra* has not been ascertained with sufficient clarity, and explaining one obscure word with the help of another equally obscure one is a procedure never to be recommended.

For a long time, it was taken for granted that if a hard English word resembles a similar word in Irish, Welsh, or Cornish, the path must have been from Celtic to English, and Mackay even believed that most of English vocabulary developed from Irish roots (Celtomania). Later, the opposite, equally extreme, view prevailed (only from English to Irish and Welsh). Today, historical linguists prefer to investigate the claims of each candidate for the etymon individually. All things considered, it appears that Welsh *bicra* "fight" is a borrowing of English *bicker* "skirmish," rather than the other way around.

However, a dogmatic reference to Welsh remained unchanged for two centuries. One can still find it in the 1890 edition of Webster's dictionary. A more realistic hypothesis connected *bicker* with such English words as *pick*, *peck*, and *beak*. Some such verbs and nouns have close counterparts in French and elsewhere in the Romance languages. Others don't and have never been accounted for. Why, for instance, **peak** *and pine*? To complicate matters, *pick* and *peck* can be sound imitative formations in which nothing prevents initial *p* from alternating with *b*. The woodpecker goes peck-peck-peck, and perhaps this is what we really hear, though perhaps it is a product of our imagination.

For a long time, I entertained the idea that *bicker* should be connected with *bitch* because bickering resembles yelping at one another. I was partly supported in my reconstruction by the onomatopoeic Russian verb *laiat'* "to bark." Its reflexive form *laiat'sia* (literally, "to bark at one another") means "to exchange insults, bicker" and nothing else. The late coining of English *bitch* "complain" seemed to confirm my guess. The Old English for *bitch* was *bicce*. As happens to many words for "dog," the origin of *bicce* poses problems, but they can be ignored in the present context. From a semantic point of view, the derivation of *bicker* from *bicce* leaves nothing to be desired: bickering can be easily understood as another sort of bitching.

But my etymology faced a phonetic difficulty. *Bicce* was pronounced with a consonant that later turned into *ch*; hence *bitch* (never mind *t* before *ch*: *which* and *witch* have the same final consonant, and so do *bitch* and *beach*). Just how early the change of *k* to *ch* happened is a matter of debate. But even if the change happened in Middle, rather than Old, English, it occurred before the verb *bicker* came into existence (unless it was current very much earlier than the time of its first attestation; this is possible but cannot be demonstrated). Given my etymology, *bicker* should have become *bitcher*. For this reason, I reluctantly gave up my idea.

Tracing *bicker* directly to *pick*, *peak*, *pike*, *peck*, and their likes fails to explain its meaning. To be sure, the suffix *-er* produces so-called frequentative and iterative verbs (*chatter, clatter, fritter*, and so forth), but bickering hardly conveys the idea of continual fighting, pecking, or picking; that is, *bicker* is not a remote synonym for *nag*. Bickering requires two actors. Long ago, Dutch *bikken* "cut, chip a stone" was cited in connection with English *bicker*. It has cognates in Old and Middle High German but does not shed new light on the English verb, for we have already seen *pick, beak*, and the rest. However, close to it stands Dutch *bikkelen* "to play with *bickelstenen*," that is, "play with knucklebones" or "jacks."

Here we witness the game of bones, which was called *bickelspil* in Middle High German. This would not have taken us too far, but for one word in *Tristan* by the great Middle High German poet Gottfried von Strassburg. In his survey of the contemporary literary scene (the early thirteenth century), he speaks disparagingly about a poet (or perhaps *the* poet) who expects to win a laurel wreath by jumping merrily, hare-like, over the word heath and resorting to *bickelworte* (plural). *Bickelwort* has never been explained in a satisfactory way, though no one doubts that a gamester's term is meant. Most probably, Gottfried alluded to the vulgar blabbering of the *canaille* (rabble), as opposed to the lofty diction of poets, whose art appealed to "noble hearts."

Such gamesters, he implied, play while hurling swear words at one another and resort to low slang. They *bicker*. So I suspect that English *bicker* is an import from Middle High German or rather from the Low Countries. It must have been a slang word, initially associated with the type of exchange or behavior one could hear and see in a tavern, where people played bones or dice, fought, and bandied words, not always of the friendliest type, as we, too, know from the way games of chance are played. This etymology explains why bickering needs more than one party and why its linguistic register is and has always been low. In the beginning, English *bicker* meant "skirmish, small altercation." This is exactly what one could expect.

The verb denoting "chip; cut with a pointed weapon" may have been sound imitative or borrowed from French. When dealing with such words, one never knows where they originated. "Make throws" developed from "cut with precision; engrave" and was appropriated by players at bones and dice. In German and Dutch, the suffix of iterative and frequentative verbs is -*eln*. In English, it was regularly replaced with -er. It left its initial sphere and acquired broader implications, though perhaps we are missing some of its original uses. Today, when people bicker, they only exchange venomous words. Gottfried's *bickelworte* shows that this meaning was already known in the verb's homeland.

Harlot

Some words resemble ships with merciless barnacles clinging to them. Legends about their origin are passed from generation to generation, and, though compromised and even debunked, refuse to die. Such is English *posh*, and such is our F-word. *Harlot* also travels through the world with a fanciful etymology, but, since the word is rarely used, few people remember it. Below, I will reproduce a passage from *The Life of William the First, sirnamed (sic) Conqueror*, reprinted in the third volume of *The Harleian Miscellany* (London, 1809). This passage will be found in the periodical *Notes and Queries* 2/X, 1860, p. 44: "Robert, Duke of Normandy, the sixth in descent from Rollo riding through Falais, a town in Normandy [and, the seat of the dukes of Normandy], espied certain young persons dancing near the way. As he staid (sic) to view awhile the manner of their disport, he fixed his eye especially upon a certain damsel named Arlotte of mean birth, a skinner's daughter, who there danced among the rest. The frame and comely carriage of her body, the natural beauty and graces of her countenance, the simplicity of her both behaviour and attire, pleased him so well, that the same night he procured her to be brought to his lodgings; where he begat her a son, who afterwards was named William. I will not defile my writing with memory of some lascivious behaviour which she is reported to have used, at such time as the Duke approached to embrace her. And doubtful it is, whether upon hate toward her son, the English afterwards adding aspirations [that is, *h*] to her name (according to the natural manner of their pronouncing), termed every unchaste woman *Harlot*." (A note on p. 120: "after the Conqueror obtained the crown of England, he often signed with this subscription—*William Bastard*, thinking it no abasement to his title or reputation.")

Doubtful indeed! The word *harlot* has nothing to do with King William. The name of his mother has come down to us in many forms: Herleva (usually mentioned in history books), Arletta, Arlotte, and Harlette. Her social status can no longer be determined (it was hardly so low), but the story of the girls dancing "near the way" and of her "lascivious behaviour" (who witnessed it?) is too good to be true. Though William did not enjoy the fact he was an illegitimate child, at his time, being a "bastard" was less important than being born to a noble father. Such "bastards" did not conceal their status, as the existence of the bend sinister on their shield shows.

The story goes back to the 1570s, and, as the *OED* notes, such a conjecture was possible because, at that time, no one had access to the full history of the word in question. *Harlot* turned up in English texts in the thirteenth century, acquired its present-day sense ("prostitute") two hundred years later, and ousted all the previous ones. Those "previous ones" are worthy of recording: "vagabond; rascal, low fellow; itinerant jester; churl; husbandsman; male servant; drudge; fellow." The progress of senses makes it clear that an attempt to ascribe to the etymon of *harlot* the meaning "bad woman" should not even be considered.

It may seem odd that, in the beginning, *harlot* referred to both men and women. Yet this is a common situation. In Middle English, *girl* first designated a child of either sex. In Huntingdonshire (a nonmetropolitan district in Cambridgeshire), *strumpet* means (or meant more than a hundred years ago) "a fat hearty child." At its appearance, *harlot* could have neutral connotations but was more often applied to disreputable persons, and to men rather than women. Later, the feature "disreputable" won over, and the term of abuse stuck to women. The word has close, almost identical cognates in Romance: Old French *harlot ~ herlot* "playful (!) young fellow" (hence dancing near the way?); "knave, vagabond"; Italian *arlotto* "vagabond, beggar; fool; glutton"; Old Portuguese *arlotar* "to go about begging" (thus, with the emphasis on roaming people without a definite occupation), and Old Spanish *arlote ~ alrote* "lazy," and only then "whore." Chaucer: "He [the Summoner] was gentil harlot and a kynde; a bettere felawe sholde men noght fynde." The summoner of *Canterbury Tales* is of course a scoundrel, neither gentle nor kind, but we should only note that the word is applied to a male.

Old language historians had no clue to the etymology of *harlot*. From *whore-let*? From the name of King William's mother? From Welsh *herlawd* "stripling" or *herlodes* "hoyden," from *her* "to push" and *llawd* "lad"? Yet the Welsh words were borrowed from English, and in any case, what kind of derivation is *harlot* from "push-lad"? Also, Latin *hel(l)uo* "spendthrift," Latin *ardelio* or *ardalio* "loafer" (an obscure word), Greek *ardolos* "dirty," and Old High German *harl*, a side form of *karl* "man," were pressed into service. The original *OED* refrained from guesswork. But since those days, great progress has been made in this area, especially thanks to Leo Spitzer's 1944 paper and our knowledge of the origin of *harlequin*.

It is highly probable that *Harlequin* and *harlot* have the same Germanic root and that the original harlot was either a member of the crowd known as the Wild Hunt or someone who sponged on the troops. This idea occurred to Ernest Weekley, the author of a popular dictionary of English etymology. He understood *harlot* as originally meaning "camp follower." The rest is less clear because we do not know whether the suffix in *harlot* is *-ot* or *-lot*. Weekley attempted to connect *-lot* with German *Lotter*, "as in [German] *Lotterbube*, synonymous with *harlot* in its earlier sense, cognate with Anglo-Saxon [= Old English] *loddere* 'beggar, wastrel.'" His reconstruction shatters at the fact that the form *harlo(t)er* never existed.

Harlot, after many peregrinations, returned "home" from French. In the history of English, adding a French suffix to a Germanic root occurred many times. *Strumpet* offers a good parallel: the root *strump-* is Germanic, while the suffix *-et* is French. One can certainly imagine that a Romance suffix added glamor to the name of a Germanic slut and turned her into a classy prostitute. However, Skeat, in his discussion of *harlot*, cited the Dutch suffix *-lot*, and he may have been right.

It seems probable that, as in the story of *Harlequin*, the root was *har-* "army" and that the word originally referred to a soldier of the lowest rank or anyone who followed the troops. The syllable *-lot* looks like a Dutch suffix, though indeed a rare one. Some support of Skeat's idea may come from the Middle English word *giglot* ("a prostitute or jester"?), which has never been discussed in connection with *harlot*. The syllables *gig* and *jig* arouse associations with frolicking and humble pursuits. They are typical sound-symbolic or sound-imitative complexes. Since the suffix -*lot* aroused no association in English speakers, before disappearing, *giglot* became *giglet*. Any medieval army was followed by hordes of parasites: prostitutes, disreputable vendors, entertainers, and so forth. They were harlots, giglots, and more of that type.

By way of postscript, I may mention English *harridan* "a belligerent old woman, a termagant." This item of seventeenth-century cant is presumably an alteration of French *haridelle* "old jade," another word of unknown origin. Are we dealing with one more piece of army slang, the name of another despicable creature whose name contains a Germanic root (*har-*) and a Romance diminutive suffix, whatever the middle part -*id*- may mean?

On this note, my Wild Hunt ends. We have pursued *Harlequin* and *harlot* and discovered their Germanic (in one case, English) place of origin. They traveled far and wide. Both have come a long way from their military antecedents. Harlequin, the character, has lost much of his frightening aspect, while *harlot*, though it means more or less what it used to mean, has almost disappeared from the modern language and interests only etymologists. It is curious that so many words with the root *har*- have continued into Modern English while the main one, a cognate of German *Heer*, has been supplanted by its French synonym "army."

Note

The most important works on Harlequin are Flasdieck, "Harlekin. Germanischer Mythos in romanischer Wandlung." *Anglia* 61, 1937, 225–34, with a postscript: "Nochmals *Harlekin*". *Anglia* 66, 59–69, and Kemp Malone, "Herlekin and Herlewin." *English Studies* 17, 141–45; of interest is also Leo Spitzer, "Hurlewayn." *Neuphilologische Mittleilungen* 52, 13–14. The etymology of *harlot* has seldom been discussed in comparatively late special publications. The only exception is Leo Spitzer's paper "Anglo-French Etymologies." *Studies in Philology* 41, 523–43 (see pp. 521–25).

6

Anatomy and the Art
of Consumption

Brain and Marrow

One of the areas of linguistic research is devoted to the origin of language and the connection between our ability to speak and the size and structure of the brain. It is mainly the left hemisphere that controls language. A special center, called the Broca center after the name of its discoverer (the discovery goes back to 1861), processes language information. The brain of primates differs considerably from that of other animals. However, we do not know whether a certain part of the brain evolved with the purpose of allowing us to express our thoughts in verbal form or whether it has always existed and was later used for speech.

Nor is the relation between language and thought clear. If language is the external reality of thought, should we conclude that animals, including most primates, do not think? What is the definition of thought? This is the stuff that the uneasy dreams and nightmares of linguists, philosophers, and anthropologists are "made on" (to use the phrase by Prospero, immortalized in Shakespeare's *Tempest*). But for those who coined the word *brain*, such questions, let alone such dreams, did not exist. They split the skulls of their enemies and saw gray matter oozing out of the once talkative heads. They slaughtered beasts and cattle and consumed their brains. The marrow of animals, as they soon found out, was also nutritious and good to eat.

In some languages, the same word designates "brain" and "marrow," and several distinguished language historians reconstructed a root that, in the course of time, allegedly yielded both words. Those attempts are ingenious but hardly acceptable. Latin distinguished between *cerebrum* "brain" and *medulla* "marrow." The distinction has usually been preserved in the Romance languages, though in Modern Spanish, for example, *meollo*, the continuation of *medulla*, has partly taken over for both.

Unlike the Romance words, most names for the brain in the Germanic languages trace to obscure etymons, English *brain* being one of the hardest despite the fact that it has cognates in Frisian, Dutch, and German. Sixteenth- and seventeenth-century scholars used to derive words of the Germanic languages from Hebrew, Greek, and Latin. With regard to *brain*, Greek *phrēn* was first suggested as a promising etymon. ("Mind" and "thought" are only some of the meanings of *phrēn*; compare English *phrenetic* "frantic, frenzied.") This suggestion found no support, but Greek *brégma* "top of the head; fontanel" as a cognate of brain appealed to many etymologists.

The Greeks thought that *brégma* "top of the head" and *brégma* "concoction" are two senses of the same word, but, as we now know, they are not related. The *brain-brégma* etymology was offered early and proved long-lived. Among its supporters we find many distinguished researchers. In the not too remote past, their names were well-known: Stephen Skinner (the author of the 1671 English etymological dictionary, the second such dictionary ever), Junius Wachter (whose 1737 German etymological dictionary is full of interesting suggestions), Noah Webster (the only survivor of the collective amnesia), and several other scholars whose names will mean nothing to the modern reader. The derivation of *brain* from *brégma* found a few influential supporters even in the nineteenth century. Among other things, they cited the pair Gothic *hwairnei* (pronounced *hwerni*) "skull" ~ Old Icelandic *hjarni* "brain," and a connection between the words for "skull" and "brain" does look natural.

I will leave out of consideration several fanciful hypotheses, some of which have been advanced even by our contemporaries, but one more old suggestion is worthy of mention because the train of thought seems to hold out some promise, though its phonetic component is indefensible. The German etymologist Konrad Schwenck (widely read in the first half of the nineteenth century but now forgotten) compared two German nouns *Bregen* "brain" (though this is not the main German word designating "brain") and *Brei* "mush, paste; porridge." It will be seen that, as far as semantics are concerned, the reconstruction I'll venture to offer below resembles Schwenck's.

At one time, *brain* was pronounced with *g* in the middle (German has *Bregen*, and in English *brain*, the vowel *i* is a trace of the ancient *g*-like consonant). The most ancient form of *brain* must have sounded approximately like *bragna*. And, surprisingly, this is also how *bran* allegedly sounded millennia ago! English *bran* is a borrowed word, though its source remains a matter of debate. Old French had *bran* "bran," though Modern French *bran* means "excrement, muck, filth" (!). The earliest meaning of French *bran* seems to have been "refuse, rejected matter." Alongside the French noun, we find Irish *bran* "chaff, bran." It remains unclear what the lending language of English *bran* was: French or Irish. More probably, the French word was of Celtic origin. Its expressive character (a "low" name for "refuse" or "rubbish") must have made it popular among the Celts' Germanic and Romance neighbors. Slang and obscenities cross language borders with amazing ease.

As noted, those who coined and borrowed *bragna (asterisks mark words that have been reconstructed rather that attested) had often seen the inside, the "refuse" of heads and bones, and to them brain and marrow were nothing more than "gray matter." From their perspective, brain, if at all usable, was only brains, a dish. Assuming that *marrow* (Old English *mearg*, in which *r* goes back to *z* that developed from *s*) is akin to *mast* "fruit of forest trees as food for pigs," its original meaning was "fat." Marrow looked like fat and received a corresponding name. One of the British English regional words for "brain" is *pash*, otherwise defined as "rotten or pulpy mass; mud, slush." In the remote past, people saw "mush" and called it accordingly. Since *brain* was a borrowed word, those who began to use it must at one time have had a native name for the content of heads. There are several available candidates, but we cannot be sure which one to choose.

One of the ideas present in Indo-European religion was that the gods and people used different names for the same objects. According to a Scandinavian myth, the world was made from the body parts and organs of the dismembered giant Ymir. His brain, called *heili* in Old Icelandic, became the sky. The origin of *heili* is unknown (hardly a surprise!), but it is a different word from *hjarni*, the noun that nineteenth-century linguists compared with Gothic *hwairnei*. *Heili* was the designation of a primordial brain and perhaps aroused loftier associations; *hjarni* filled the skulls of mortals. (Modern Icelanders call the human brain *heili* and thus elevated our pulp to divine dimensions.) A leading modern etymologist thought that *hjarni* might be a cognate of the Icelandic word for "gray" and glossed *hjarni* as "gray matter." I think he was mistaken, but he may have looked for an answer in the right direction. *Hjarni*, like German *Hirn* "brain" (a more common word is *Gehirn*, with the prefix *ge-*), is rather probably related to German *Harn* "urine" (!), whose original meaning was "bodily waste." *Brain* and *bran* seem to be close relatives. Such is my uncomplimentary picture of the human brain seen through the eyes of our remote ancestors.

Is this reconstruction trustworthy? Perhaps. I advanced it twenty years ago and am not aware of anyone's attempt to refute it. But neither silence nor consensus is the ultimate proof of a correct etymology. The talk, as they say at conferences, is now open for discussion. The readers are invited to use or even rack their brains(s).

Brisket

It seems reasonable that *brisket* should in some way be related to *breast*: after all, *brisket* is the breast of an animal. But the path leading from one word to the other is neither straight nor narrow. Most probably, it does not exist at all. In what follows I am greatly indebted to the Swedish scholar Bertil Sandahl, who published an article on *brisket* and its cognates in 1964. The *Oxford English Dictionary* (*OED*) has no citations of *brisket* prior to 1450, but Sandahl discovered *bresket* in a document written in 1328–1329, and, if his interpretation is correct, the date should be pushed back quite considerably. Before 1535, the favored (possibly, the only) form in English was *bruchet(te)*.

The English word is surrounded with many look-alikes from several languages: Middle French *bruchet*, *brichet*, *brechet* (Modern French *bréchet* ~ *brechet* "breastbone"; in French dialects, one often finds -*q*- instead of -*ch*-), Breton *bruch* ~ *brusk* ~ *bresk* "breast (of a horse)," along with *bruched* "breast," Modern Welsh *brysced* (later, *brwysged*

~ *brysged*), and Irish Gaelic *brisgein* "cartilage (as of the nose)." Then there are German *Bries* ~ *Briesel* ~ *Brieschen* ~ *Bröschen* "the breast gland of a calf," Old Norse *brjósk* "cartilage, gristle," and several words from the modern Scandinavian languages for "sweetbread" (Swedish *bräs*, Norwegian *bris*, and Danish *brissel*), which, as it seems, belong here, too (sweetbread is, of course, not bread: it is the pancreas or thymus, especially of a calf, used as food; -*bread* in *sweetbread* is believed to go back to an old word for "flesh"). Many words for "breast" in the languages of the world begin with the grating sound groups *br*- ~ *gr*- ~ -*khr*-, as though to remind us of our *br*eakable, *br*ittle, *fr*agile bones (*fraction*, *fragile*, and *fragment*, all going back to the same Latin root, once began with *bhr*).

At first blush, *brisket*, with its pseudo-diminutive suffix, looks like a borrowing from French. But there is a good rule: a word is native in a language in which it has recognizable cognates. To be sure, sometimes no cognates are to be seen or good candidates present themselves in more languages than one, but etymology is not an exact science, and researchers should be thankful for even approximate signposts along the way. In French, *bréchet* is isolated (and nothing similar has been found in other Romance languages), while in Germanic, *brjósk*, *bris*, *bräs*, and others (see them above) suggest kinship with *brisket*. Therefore, the opinion prevails that *brisket* is of Germanic origin. Émile Littré, the author of a great, perennially useful French dictionary, thought that the French word had been borrowed from English during the Hundred Years' War (1337–1453), and most modern etymologists tend to agree with him. Then the Celtic words would also be from English (for they, too, are isolated in their languages), and the etymon of *brisket* would be either Low (i.e., northern) German *bröske* "sweetbread" or Old Norse *brjósk*, allied to Old English *breosan* "break." The original meaning of *brisket* may have been "something (easily breakable?) in the breast of a (young?) animal." If so, contrary to expectation, *brisket* is not related to *breast*, for *breast* appears to have been coined with the sense "capable of swelling," rather than "capable of breaking." Those who insist on the Celtic origin of *brisket* have a hard time making their case. Needless to say, *brisk* is not related to *brisket*.

The reconstruction given above (an English word that spread to French, Irish, and Welsh; an anatomical term designating a brittle part of the breast in an animal's body) is acceptable, but it leaves the suffix -*et* unaccounted for. Though rarely, -*et* does occur in native English words. The best example is *thicket*, but in such cases it is usually possible to explain how the noun acquired such an unusual look. More often it seems that French -*et* was appended to native nouns, as probably happened in the history of *hornet*, *tippet*, and *strumpet*. *Brisket* could be part of that group (the simplest conjecture). Sandahl offered a most ingenious hypothesis. Middle English had the word *ket* "meat," taken over from Scandinavian, and Sandahl suggested that perhaps there was a compound like *brusk-ket* or *brust-ket* "a piece of gristly flesh."

Such a compound may indeed have existed, but we are unable to ascertain its presence and, for the time being, will stay with the suffix -*et*. Thus, it appears that *brisket* is a Germanic word of Low German or Scandinavian descent embellished with a French suffix in order to make the dish more palatable: originally, *brösk-et* or *brjósk-et*. (In similar fashion, -*et* turned a homey Germanic floozy into a classy French prostitute: from *strump-* to *strumpet*.) However, the earliest form we know is *brushet(te)*. Its vowel may have been pronounced as *ü* and reflected an unfamiliar foreign sound, which later yielded *brisket* and occasionally *bresket*.

And now a tiny piece of corroborating evidence. The origin of the word *sobriquet* (or *soubriquet*) has not been discovered, and the development of its meaning cannot but cause surprise. French *sobriquet* (earlier, *soubriquet* "tap under the chin") may go back to *souzbequet*, from *souz* (Modern French *sous*) "under." Then it means "tap under the nose." But perhaps the original form implied a chuck under the chest, the second element being *brechet* "brisket."

Note
The paper by Bertil Sandahl, "Brisket," was published in *Studier i modern språkvetenskap* 2 (n.s), 1964, 148–52.

Finger

Finger sounds almost the same in Dutch, German, and Scandinavian but, perhaps unexpectedly, lacks relatives (cognates) outside Germanic.

English also has *thumb* and *toe*, but neither can tell us anything about the mental process that resulted in coining the word *finger*. By the way, outside Germanic, the opposition of *finger* versus *toe*, which may seem so natural, even indispensable to English speakers, is uncommon. Therefore, it has been suggested that at one time *toe* meant the same as *finger*, with the later differentiation of the synonyms. To bolster up this etymology, *toe* has been compared with Latin *digitus* "finger" (the word known to English speakers from *digit*, *digital*, and *prestidigitation* "quick finger work"). However, the phonetic correspondence between *toe*, from the much older form *taih-*, and the Latin word is so imperfect that the comparison has been given up.

The German for "toe" is *Zehe*, which bears some resemblance to the German verb *zeigen* "to show; point to." Though, unlike *finger*, *zeigen* has secure related forms outside German, the connection between *Zehe* and *zeigen* is far from obvious. The idea of their being connected again stems from the suggestion that toes at one time meant the same as fingers and did the same work as those: pointed to things and were used to show something. However, it is safer to assume that *finger* and *toe* were from the start coined to designate different body parts and that, whatever the initial concept underlying *finger* might be, the two words hardly ever functioned as synonyms. Let us also bear in mind that the hand has five fingers, and, if we discount the thumb, only the forefinger is "independently active." Perhaps *finger* once referred to the index finger, and only later the name acquired a broader meaning ("finger in general"). We'll never know.

The opposition between *finger* and *toe* gave dictionary makers no end of trouble. How do you define *toe*? Some lexicographers find refuge in Latin. A toe, we are told, is a digit (!) on the foot. Only a learner's dictionary, desperate for an easy explanation, says that *toe* is a *finger* on the foot. And so it of course is. The origin of *toe* poses no problems. Fortunately, English has preserved the word *mistletoe*. The second component of *mistletoe* (*-toe*) means "twig." Toes, it appears, were described as "twigs" on the foot. The image looks credible. To be sure, fingers could also be understood as twigs on the hand, but there is no evidence for this approach. In sum, it looks as though neither *thumb* nor *toe* will furnish us with a clue for discovering the ancient impulse behind the creation of the word *finger*.

As far as we can judge, the story of *finger* began with the form *fingraz*. The modern form has lost the second syllable and, to make the word pronounceable, inserted *e* between *g* and *r*. The root has undergone no change, and it is of course the origin of this root that interests us. Some historical linguists connect *finger* with the numeral *five*. In the past, *five* had the consonant *n* in the middle (German *fünf* still has it). However, it is hard to understand where the suffix *-r* came from (*r* is indeed an ancient suffix or even part of the root, not an ending).

True enough, the hand has five fingers, but those are individualized entities, and that is why people constantly invent names for them, such as *middle finger*, *ring finger*, *little finger*, *pinky*, and the like. Among them, only the *index finger* has several old and current synonyms, like "arrow finger," for example: this digit, like a dear child—to quote a Swedish proverb—has many names. Remember nursery rhymes like "This little piggy went to market" (finger and toe play). The whole point of such songs and games is that the fingers of the hand are treated individually, rather than as a "multitude." Deriving *finger* from *five* is flawed also because the finger turns out to be one *fifth* of the hand. As Ari Hoptman, the author of the most recent research into the origin of *finger*, says: "The concept 'five' is perhaps not the most logical word to denote such an important instrument as the finger. One might expect that the finger would be named for what it can do alone, as well as what it can do together with the other fingers, and it would make far more sense to name a body part based on shape, function, or movement than on mathematics."

As a matter of fact, few etymologists have sufficient enthusiasm for the derivation of *finger* from the protoform of *five* (I have seen only one serious reference work in which the connection is called doubtless), but, since dictionaries are expected to comment on the derivation of each word they include, and since the formula "of unknown origin" is off-putting and even puzzling to those who wonder what exactly is "unknown" about the history of *finger* and so many other common words, lexicographers prefer to say something, rather than concede defeat. Personally, I very much admire Walter W. Skeat for his verdict: "Original sense unknown."

Still another dubious but well-known etymology of *finger* connects *finger* with the German verb *fangen* "to seize, catch." All the Old Germanic languages had some form of this verb. English has lost it, but *fang* contains the same root. The word was taken over from Scandinavian and meant "catch" (a noun). The sense retained in phrases like *White Fang* developed a few centuries later.

In 1929, William D. Baskett, a researcher from the then-flourishing Chicago school of etymology, brought out his dissertation titled *Parts of the Body in the Later Germanic Dialects*. Baskett found six main synonyms for "finger" in Modern German dialects, including at least one that refers to grasping, catching, and scraping (in Swabian). In his all-encompassing 2000 survey, Ari Hoptman did not miss this fact and again noted that the *fangen* connection does not recognize the finger as an independent unit, only as a set. "The act of grasping necessarily requires more than one finger, often the forefinger and the thumb; thus, it is strange that one finger would still be deemed 'a grasper,' considering all the other things the finger can do independently." Baskett cited separate words, which we never see in context. Thus, it remains unknown why fingers were sometimes understood as graspers and catchers.

Of some importance is the fact that, even though the origin of *hand* is also sometimes said to be uncertain, the connection between *hand* and the Gothic verb *hinþan* "to seize" looks probable. (The Goths were the first Germanic people to be converted to Christianity, and part of their fourth-century translation of the New Testament has come down to us; *þ* has the value of *th* in English *thick*.) If we accept the connection, this is where the "grasper" emerged in full glory: the hand, not the finger. Incidentally, *fist* probably has the ancient root meaning "five," and again this fact makes perfect sense: the fist, not the finger.

Of the other etymologies of *finger*, I'll mention only one, which goes back to the beginning of the seventeenth century: at that time, *finger* was compared with Latin *fingere* "to mold, sculpt; arrange; compose"—a clever comparison, but at that time, it was not realized that in cognates, Germanic *f* regularly corresponds to Latin *p* (as in *father* ~ *pater*). Consequently, the two words cannot be related, unless we resort to the idea of borrowing. However, Germanic *fingr*- looks like a native word, not a loan from Latin. Incidentally, in Latin, *finger-* does not refer to fingers.

In etymology, it is always profitable to cast the net as widely as possible, but in this case there is not much to be gained from looking at non-Germanic languages. For example, the origin of Latin *digitus* is also obscure and yields the sense "pointer" only if we turn it into *dicitus* and ally (equate) with Greek *dáktylos* "finger" or Latin *dactylus*, but such a process, a kind of etymological prestidigitation, carries little conviction. Perhaps more instructive is a look at Russian *palets* "finger" and its cognates elsewhere in Slavic. Originally, the word referred to the thumb (!); the finger was called *perst*. *Palets* (i.e., from a historical point of view, "thumb") has been compared with Latin *pollex* "thumb," Latin *palma* "the palm of the hand," the verb *feel* (to us, the most interesting parallel of all: Latin *p-* and Germanic *f-* go well together: see above), and a few other words in Latin and Greek. But since *palets* once meant "thumb," its connections with *feel*, so tempting at first sight, may lead us astray. The thumb is not a feeling finger, and all attempts to connect *finger* and *pollex* should probably be abandoned.

Where, then, are we at the end of our long journey? Fingers are not toes, and the etymons of *finger* and *toe* are different. Each of the five fingers of the hand is useful and necessary, and all of them are fiercely individual (the thumb and the forefinger especially so). For this reason only, the derivation of *finger* from the word for "five" is unlikely. Fingers point and "feel"; they don't catch, seize, or grasp. Therefore, no connection between *finger* and *fang* (or German *fangen* "to catch" with its related forms in Scandinavian) has probably ever existed. It seems that we are exactly where we were at the beginning, and the impression is correct.

Ari Hoptman suggested that *finger* is one of the many sound-symbolic words that designate movement. *Feel*, we may remember, is defined as "examine by touch." Hoptman's supportive material is not very impressive because not a single word he cites looks close enough to *finger*. Compare *fumble*, *flitter*, *flicker*, and so forth, including perhaps the rather opaque *fritter*. It may be that *finger* continues some verb for "fumble" or "palpate." For example, *touch*, from French, is sound-imitative and goes back to some verb like Latin *toccare*.

The uncertainty of the proposed etymology could be predicted. If the perfectly transparent sought-for cognate existed, the etymology of *finger* would have been solved long ago. And yet Hoptman's etymology is intrinsically more probable than all the previous ones. Their weakness is manifest, but their venerable age allows dictionary makers to cite them again and again, hedge, apologize for what they say, or declare victory.

Note
See Ari Hoptman, "Finger and Some Other *f*- and *fl*-Words." *NOWELE* 36, 2000, 77–91. This article is probably the most recent full-scale examination of the origin of the word *finger*. It also contains an exhaustive bibliography of the question.

Akimbo

Like all the words discussed in this book, the etymology of *akimbo* has been an object of both intelligent and futile guessing. Somebody did coin *akimbo*, but once it became known, it may have succumbed to folk etymology, which obliterated all ancestral traits. This is the reason the most cautious dictionaries say: "Origin unknown."

Among others, the Italian phrase *a sghembo* "awry, aslope" has been proposed as the etymon of the English word. The similarity is unmistakable, but several circumstances cast doubt on this connection. One is of a general sort, and I regularly refer to it when a borrowing is suggested. Why should the English have taken over a foreign word to designate a gesture common to people all over the world? When the answer is missing, the hypothesis loses all attraction. It is known why and under what circumstances English appropriated a multitude of musical terms from Italian, but why *akimbo*? Were Italians famous for having their "hands on the hips and the elbows turned outward," to quote the standard dictionary definition? The worst thing about this etymology is that the Italian phrase has nothing to do with the position of the arms. Consequently, the English are supposed to have borrowed *a sghembo* and endowed it with a sense remote from the original one. As we will see, this argument will also prove fatal for another attempt to trace *akimbo* to a foreign source. Finally, we cannot help observing that Italian *gh* designates "hard *g*" (as in English *get*), while *akimbo* has *k*. The parallel form *a schembo* (*sch* = *sk*), was dialectal, so that its popularity among English-speakers could not have been significant at any time.

Akimbo surfaced as *in kenebowe* (1400). More than two centuries later the variants *a kenbol(l)* ~ *a kenbold* turned up. For their sake, we will leave Italy for Scandinavia. The Icelandic words *kimbill, kimpill,* and *kimbli* "bundle of hay; hillock," which were once compared with *akimbo*, exist. According to some old dictionaries, they mean "the handle of a pot or jug," but they do not. Their root is related to English *comb*, and it was used in Germanic for coining the names of barrel staves, fastenings, and so forth. Similar names (*kimble, kemmel,* and many others) for various vessels (not handles!), are also current in modern British English and Swedish dialects. For this reason, Ernest Weekley, the author of a popular English etymological dictionary, set up Middle English *kimbo* "pot ear, pitcher handle." The metaphor, from a pitcher with two handles to a person with arms akimbo, is indeed widespread. Also, according to Weekley, who was always on the lookout for the French sources of English words and phrases, *in kenebowe* may have been a conscious translation of the French phrase *en anses* "on the handles" but does not explain why it is so different from English *akimbo*, especially if we remember that Middle English *kimbo* has been reconstructed rather than recorded and that seventeenth-century authors knew the form *kembol(l)*. What happened to final *-l*? Weekley did not provide an answer to any of those questions. *Akembol* could not develop from *in kenebowe* in a natural way, though it could perhaps have been a product of folk etymology because of an association with the names of pots and jugs.

A third putative source of *akimbo* is Gaelic *cam* "bent, crooked"; the English adverb *kim-kam* "all awry, all askew" has been attested. Since *-bowe* in *kenebowe* means "bend" and is identical with *-bow-* in *elbow* and *rainbow*, *kimbo*, from *ken-bow* ~ *kin-bow* ~ *kinbo*, emerges in this reconstruction as "bent bend," a tautological compound (both of its parts mean the same), like many others in the Indo-European languages. For example, numerous place names, which, when deciphered, yield "white-white water," "hill-hill," and so forth. (Incidentally, while reading the entry *akimbo* in Skeat's dictionary, I discovered, much to my surprise, his passing statement on the popularity of such compounds, as though this fact were the most obvious thing in the world. It is not, and few researchers are aware of them.) The suggestion that just one component of *akimbo* is Celtic has little to recommend it. In sum, *akimbo* would be easy to explain if its earliest form were not *kenebowe*. Lost among so many putative sources, we will return to Scandinavia.

The form that allegedly might generate *akimbo* is Icelandic *kengboginn* "bent into a crook." (Icelandic is important because it tends to preserve the most archaic of all the Scandinavian forms). British dialectal *kingbow* looks like a variant of it (*-bowe* is not incompatible with *-boginn*). This etymology is given in most dictionaries as final. A late fourteenth-century English word may have been borrowed from Scandinavian, but Italian *a sghembo* hastens to take its revenge. *Kengboginn* never meant "akimbo," and a change from "bent, crooked" to such a highly specific meaning ("with one's hands on the hips") looks suspect. Also, *keng-* in *kengboginn*, like *kimble*, bears little resemblance to *kene-*. Once again, we wish there were no *kenebowe*.

At first blush, *kene-* in *kenebowe* is the adjective *keen*. If so, *in kenebowe* must be understood as "in keen bow," that is, "in a sharp bend, at an acute angle, presenting a sharp elbow" (such are the glosses in the *Century Dictionary*). In Middle English, *keen* "sharp-pointed" "was in common use as applied to the point of a spear, pike, dagger, goad, thorn, hook, anchor, etc., or to the edge of a knife, sword, ax, etc. . . . In its earliest use, and often later, the term connotes a bold or defiant attitude, involving, perhaps, an allusion to *keen* in its other common Middle English sense of 'bold.'" The quotation is from the same dictionary, which calls all the previous explanations erroneous.

Skeat defended the *kengboginn* etymology and kept repeating that Middle English *kene* was not used to denote "sharp" in such a context. He never elaborated on his phrase *in such a context*. Despite Skeat's objection, the etymology of *kenebowe* defended in the *Century Dictionary* seems to be the least implausible of all, assuming that the first vowel of *kenebowe* was long; the vowel in *keen* undoubtedly was. *Kene-* with short *e* has no meaning. Later, this *e* must have been shortened (a usual process in trisyllabic words, to which we owe short *o* in *holiday*, as opposed to long *o* in *holy*, for example), and the change destroyed the tie between *kene-* and *keen*. The second *e* was shed—another common process in Middle English. The new form (let us spell it *kenbow*) began to resemble words for vessels with two handles and *in kennebowe* became *akingbow, akingbo, akimbo,* and so forth. In the disguised compound *akimbow*, the idea of a bow also disappeared (even an association with *elbow* did not save it); hence the spelling *-bo*. The influence of Gaelic *cam* need not be invoked in the history of *akimbo*.

Faced with many hypotheses, we are still not quite sure where *akimbo* came from, but "origin unknown" would be an unnecessarily harsh verdict. In 1909, the first edition of Webster's *New International* opted for *keen-*, the second (in 1934) cited *kingboginn*, and the third (1961) gave the earliest form (*kenebowe*) and stopped. Such is the sad progress of etymological lexicography.

Ache

An etymologist cannot help concluding that words tend to live up to their meaning. Even a cursory look at the many attempts to find the origin of *ache* will confirm the truth of that statement. Although *ache* goes back to Old English, its unquestionable cognates are few. Low (i.e., northern) German dialects have *äken* "hurt, fester," *ake* "finger inflammation; whitlow; secretion from the eye," and the like. Bavarian *acken* "hurt" is isolated in the south, and therefore its status in relation to English *ache* is unclear. Finnish *äkä* "hatred" is, not improbably, a borrowing from German. Many Finnish linguists have discussed this idea.

We wonder whether the short English and Low German words are related, and, if they are, do they have cognates outside their restricted area? Assuming that *ache* and *äken* have a common ancestor (a *protoform*, as such ancestors are called), did its meaning (today it is "dull, steady pain") develop from an abstract notion referring to discomfort, or was its starting point the name of some painful symptom, as suggested by "fester" and "inflammation"?

Modern etymological dictionaries sometimes offer minimal discussion or supply all kinds of useful and interesting information that has no direct bearing on the origin of our word. For example, they often mention the fact that at one time *ache*, verb, and *ache*, noun, had different forms in Old English, that the noun was pronounced with *ch*, that the immensely influential lexicographer Samuel Johnson was unaware of the true state of affairs, and that his ignorance is the main reason we have the preposterous spelling still used. Some dictionaries confine themselves to the verdict "origin uncertain," which is true but uninspiring.

The earliest English etymologists, from the seventeenth century on, believed that *ache* is derived from Greek *ákhos* "grief, pain." Even though there is no need to assume that *ache* goes back directly to Greek (why should it?), if we assume that both words arose under the influence of some interjection like German *ach!* (i.e., *akh!*), the similarity will receive a rather plausible explanation. This etymology has been proposed by such different people as Hensleigh Wedgwood, a scholar who attempted to trace too many English words to sound imitation, and (tentatively) by Ferdinand Holthausen, a cautious researcher who never allowed fantasies to run away with him. All things considered, an exclamation is perhaps an unlikely source of *ache*, though *akh! okh!*, *ukh!* can serve as the foundation of words for moaning, groaning, and the like. (Gothic *auhjan* "make a noise," if pronounced as *ohjan*, is perhaps one of them.)

Since outside Germanic, English *k* corresponds to *g*, etymologists exploring the origin of *ache* looked for Indo-European words beginning with *ag-*. Greek had *ágos* "a great sin incurring a curse." The Old English for *ache* was *æce* (*æ*, as *a* in Modern English *man*) ~ *ece*, and *ágos* is a tolerably good match for it, except that one expects Proto-Germanic *ákis*, not *ákos* (only *i* in the second syllable would have caused the change of *a* to *æ*). This etymology occasionally turns up in modern dictionaries, though with some hedging. More about *ákhos* and *ágos* will be said below. Some of our most authoritative sources state that *ache* is related to Latin *agere* "drive," with an unexplained change of meaning (via "impel, force"). The frequentative form of *agere* is *agitare* "agitate," which seems to provide a link between "drive" and "pain"; a few moderately convincing Scandinavian and Finnish parallels of a similar semantic shift have been cited. Despite the near consensus on the *agere-ache* etymology among many distinguished scholars (but the *OED* offers no conjecture on the origin of *ache!*), it does not sound fully convincing. With respect to physical pain, and that is what *ache* seems to be about, we may remember the questions doctors ask when they want to find out what is wrong with us: "Will you describe your pain as burning, piercing, stabbing, or throbbing?" Some concrete notion like "burn" or "throb" would be a more acceptable basis for "ache" than "drive."

Two circumstances may be relevant to our search. In the Germanic languages, we find a group of similar-sounding words referring to unpleasant sensations. Such are German *Ekel* "nausea; disgust," which at one time competed with a synonym having *r* in the middle (*erken ~ erkeln* "to abhor, loathe"), Dutch *akel* "grief" (the common word is the adjective *akelig* "dismal; nasty"), German *heikel* "tricky, delicate" (said about a situation; known only since the sixteenth century), Old Icelandic *eikinn* "raving mad," corresponding to Old English *acol* (with long *a*, that is, the vowel as in Modern English *spa*) "frightened," and *ekla* "lack."

Also, there is no shortage of analogous *ag-* words: for instance, Gothic *aglo* "anguish; affliction" (its English cognate is *ail*) and *agis* "fear" (here, the English cognate is *awe*). Old English *āg-lǣc ~ āglāc* (both vowels were long) meant "grief, distress"; *āglǣca* "monster" is familiar to the readers of *Beowulf* in the original. With other vowels we find Old Icelandic *uggr* "fear" (the root of English *ugly*); in Norwegian and Swedish, *agg* "anger" corresponds to it. In Icelandic, *agg* means "squabble, quarrel," and one can easily imagine the character of the Icelander who once had the nickname *Aggi*. Incidentally, the Indo-European root *ak-* meant "sharp," and its reflexes are many, for example, Latin *acutus* "acute" (from which English has, via French, *ague*). It is as though, all over Europe, from Greece to Scandinavia, *ag- ~ ug-* and *ak- - ~ aik- ~ eik ~ ek- ~* (?) *heik* were at one time the favorite syllables for designating things causing pain or arousing fear, and things loathsome and "icky"; those about which we say *yuck*. It has been pointed out to me that an ancient Turkish root also meant "pain."

Another consideration is this. In Indo-European, the vowel *a* occurs with some regularity in words denoting lack and physical defects. This has been noticed by Ferdinand de Saussure, a great language historian, though most of his examples are not from Germanic. Such observations are too general to furnish a clue to individual solutions, but it is characteristic that hardly any word mentioned above has an established etymology. The same can be said about words for "illness," including *smart*, *sick*, and especially *ill* (English *ill* is a borrowing from Scandinavian). In this area, taboo must have been rampant: don't call an ailment by its name and the spirit controlling it will be kept at bay.

What, then, is the conclusion? *Ache* is indeed a word "of uncertain etymology," and such it will remain. It might be a symbolic coinage of sorts, with the vowel *a* playing some role in its early history, and it might be part of a sizable group of words beginning with *ag-*, *ak-*, *-aik*, all of them referring to guilt, fear, suffering, and disgust. If so, Greek *ákhos* and *ágos* belong with it in a loose way, but neither can be called its cognate. (A conclusion along these lines must have appealed even to such a serious scholar as Jan de Vries, the author of, among many others, two etymological dictionaries: of Dutch and of Old Icelandic. He compared Old Icelandic *ögurr*, allegedly "pain," and Greek *ákhos*.)

If I may venture some sort of conclusion, I would stay away from reconstructing an Indo-European root of *ache* (I doubt that such a root existed) and dissociate *ache* from Latin *agere* ~ *agitare*. Some primordial impulse seems to have connected words for "ache" with the sound complex *ak* ~ *ag*. The rest is obscure.

Booze

Booze is an enigmatic word, but not the way *ale*, *beer*, and *mead* are. Those emerged centuries ago, and it does not come as a surprise that we have doubts about their origin. The noun *booze* is different: it does not seem to predate the beginning of the eighteenth century, whereas the verb *booze* "to tipple, guzzle" made its way into a written text as early as 1300 (which means that it turned up in everyday speech some time earlier). The riddles connected with *booze* are two.

First, why did the noun appear so much later than the verb? A parallel case will elucidate the problem. The verb *meet* is ancient, while the noun *meet* is recent, and we can immediately see the reason for the delay: sports journalists needed a word for a "meeting" of athletes and teams and coined *a meet*, whose popularity infuriated some lovers of English, but, once the purists died out, the word became commonplace. But the noun *booze* is not a technical term and should not have waited four hundred years before it joined the vocabulary. *Second*, the verb *booze* is a doublet of *bouse* (it rhymes with *carouse*). *Bouse* has all but disappeared, while *booze* has not gone anywhere. Mr. John Cowan has pointed out to me that A. E. Housman used the spelling *boose* in *Last Poems*, suggesting that the spelling had not stabilized by 1922, when the book was published.

However, it is not so much the death of *bouse* that should interest us as the difference in vowels. The vowel we have in *cow*, *round*, and their likes was once "long *u*" (as in today's *coo*). Therefore, *bouse* has the pronunciation one expects, whereas *booze* looks Middle English, that is, with its long *u* intact. However, in northern English dialects, long *u* did not become a diphthong, and this is probably why *uncouth* still rhymes with *youth*, rather than *south*. Is *booze* a northern doublet of *bouse*? One can sense James A. H. Murray's frustration with this hypothesis. He wrote: "Perhaps really a dialectal form" (and cited a similar Scots word). It is the most uncharacteristic insertion of *really* that gives away Murray's dismay. His style while composing entries was business-like and crisp. He did not strew his explanations with *really*, *actually*, *definitely*, *certainly*, and other fluffy adverbs.

Whatever the causes of the modern pronunciation of *booze*, one etymology should cover both it and *bouse*. What, then, is the origin of *bouse*? This word is surrounded by numerous nouns and verbs, some of which are, and others may be related to it. First of all, its Dutch and German synonyms *buizen* and *bausen* spring to mind. Both are rare to the extent of not being known to most native speakers, but, at one time, they were current. Some other words refer to swelling, violent or erratic movement, and noise: for instance, Dutch *buisen* "to strike, knock" and, on the other hand, *beuzelen* "to dawdle, trifle," Norwegian *baus* "arrogant; irascible" and *bause* "put on airs" (which partly explains the sense of Dutch *boos* and German *böse* "bad, wicked; angry"), and English *busy* (Dutch *bezig*). *Busybody* shows that *busy* did not always mean "occupied": it rather referred to meddling and doing things in an irritating way.

We can probably see the pure root of such *b*-words in English *boo* (compare it with *bo-* in *Bo-peep* ~ *peek-a-boo*) and Dutch *bui* "gust, squall," as well as Russian *bystryi* "quick" and *boi-us'* "I am afraid" (stress on -*us'*). When it comes to swelling and puffing up, German words ending in *sch* (from *s*) present themselves, such as *bauschen* "swell." Not improbably, English *bustle* "a frame or pad thrusting out a woman's skirt," an obscure eighteenth-century word, must be related to German *Bausch*, which formerly meant "handful; armful" and now means only "ball" (of paper or wool)," "puff" (on a sleeve), and so forth.

Scholars dealing with the oldest stages of language reconstruct Indo-European roots to which they add numerous "extensions" (also called *enlargements* and *determinatives*), along with prehistoric laryngeal sounds, and obtain nests of seemingly related words of great antiquity. But when it comes to later periods, which, one would think, pose fewer problems, they become much more cautious and even timid. One can read in our best etymological dictionaries that German *böse*, English *busy*, its Dutch cognate *bezig*, and English *bustle* (the noun, as above) are words of unknown origin. The same holds for English *boast*, which rather obviously belongs with swelling and puffing up (the Old English for "boast" was *boi-an*, a word like Dutch *bui* "shower; squall" and Russian *boi-us'* "I am afraid," a mere root, as it were) and *boost* (a nineteenth-century "Americanism," most likely, a word brought to the New World from some northern British dialect).

Old dictionaries were full of fanciful derivations. The discovery of sound correspondences turned etymology into a semblance of an exact science, but words do not always march like soldiers on parade. German linguists coined the term *sound gesture* (*Lautgebärde*) for such vaguely symbolic groups as the one being discussed here. In our case, the "gesture" is *bo-* ~ *bu-* for naming things and actions that refer to swelling and noise. The consonant *s* appended itself to *bo-* ~ *bu-*, and, as a result, we have all the words mentioned above. There is a temptation to co-opt more and more look-alikes into this group. One wonders where to stop, but this is a perennial problem in the study of related words. I don't think that the "gesture" stops at *bouse*. For comparison, see what is said on *bizarre* in this book (Chapter 2).

If this conclusion is right, *bouse* meant approximately "to revel noisily." What begins as a show of conviviality often ends in a brawl. In Browning and other poets, the word meant "feast, carouse" and had no vulgar connotations. The *Century Dictionary* quotes Keats: "As though bold Robin Hood / Would, with his Maid Marian, / sup and bowse [sic] from horn and can" (*Lines on the Mermaid Tavern*). Later, a noun was formed to match the verb. One has to agree with Murray: *booze* probably reached the Standard (in his days the phrase was *the literary language*) from the North, retained its dialectal pronunciation, and stayed as "a low word" (perhaps also thanks to its pronunciation!) for liquor and all kinds of cheap swill.

A short postscript is due here. Russian has the noun *buza* "an alcoholic drink" and the verb *buzit'* "to brawl" (both stressed on the second syllable). Their origin need not delay us here, but the connection is instructive: from "liquor" to "brawl."

Cake

It is not immediately clear whether once you have your cake, you always want to eat it. Anyone who begins to learn Swedish soon discovers that the Swedish for "cake" is *kaka*. How can anyone eat a thing called *kaka*? Apparently, one can. (To be sure, the first vowel in the Swedish word is long, as in English *spa*, so that the scatological association exists only on paper.) Nor does a broad look bring us reassurance. Latin *cacare* (the infinitive; the first person singular is *caco*) "to defecate" has spread far and wide. It occurs not only in Romance but also in Slavic and Celtic. The rarely used and all-but-forgotten English verb *cack* (the same meaning) has some currency only in regional speech, but bookish borrowings with this root from Latin, usually via French, were at one time rather numerous. Obviously, the sound-imitating *cackle* has nothing to do with *cacare*.

Cacare looks like a typical baby word (*ka-ka, pee-pee, poo-poo, tut-tut*, and so forth are near-universal). One can easily imagine that not only the action but also the product of defecation was called *ka-ka*. I began my story with Swedish because *cake* in the form *kaka* first turned up in Middle English texts only in the fifteenth century. It must have been a borrowed word because, were it native, it would, most probably, have occurred in some English text much earlier.

The exact source and the route of penetration remain unclear. Icelandic, though it still has the form *kaka*, cannot be considered as the lending language (English did not borrow any Icelandic words in the Middle Ages), but Swedish and Norwegian can. Swedish final *a* would have become *e* in Middle English. Nor was it probably, in late Medieval Swedish, a fully articulated *a*, reminiscent of Modern English *way*. The Modern Norwegian form is *kake*, and it may have sounded the same more than half a millennium ago (another perfect fit, as far as we are concerned). In Modern Danish, we find *kage* and would like to rule it out as the etymon of English *cake* for phonetic reasons. Yet long ago, Danish *kage* was also pronounced as *kake*. Thus, despite some geographical uncertainty, the Scandinavian source of *cake* looks secure.

We can now leave phonetics behind and turn to the history of meaning. To begin with, in the modern language, English *cake* does not always designate food. For example, *cow cake*, also called *pat*, means "a piece of dung." This circumstance rules out the possibility of kinship between *cake* and *cook*, a borrowing of Popular Latin *cōcus*. Second, the oldest cakes, made with dough and water, were flat. Actually, they were pan*cakes*, even though today, we do not associate pancakes with cakes. This is where we probably detect the original sense of *cake*, namely, "a flat object."

If we take into consideration that, outside English, *kak-* coexists with *kok-* as the name of the cake, we will notice Swedish *koka* and Norwegian *kok ~ koke* "lump of earth; lump of snow; cow cake" (i.e., something "caked together," indeed, not necessarily flat and not necessarily cooked) for "cake" may be any heap, more often small. Such is English dialectal *cock* "a heap of hay in the field; of dung or turf (rarely of grain)," another word with *o* in the middle, and also borrowed from Scandinavian. Even *coke(s)* "charred coal" may, despite some difficulties its vowel presents, be part of this family, though dictionaries, ever fearful of disagreeing with the *OED*, offer a derivation from English dialectal *colk* "the core of an apple" or say "origin unknown."

In trying to discover the past of sounds, words, and grammatical constructions, linguists resort to two methods. One is called *internal reconstruction*. This method presupposes juxtaposition of facts in the same language. Thus, when we notice that *cake* is food, possibly flat (as in *pancake*) or something flat, though not food at all (as in *cow cake*), stay within English, and draw conclusions from our observations, we use internal reconstruction. But when we look at other languages (in our case, Scandinavian) and note that some close cognates of *cake* designate small heaps, lumps, and round stones, we use the *comparative method*.

The ideal situation occurs when the results of both methods point in the same direction. This, it appears, is what has happened in our attempt to penetrate the historical development of *cake*. *Cake* and its related forms (having the vowel -*o*-) seem to have been coined with the senses "lump; heap; mud cake," possibly, a baby word (*kaka* ~ *koka*) and, possibly, with reference to a child's poop. It could hardly be expected that the unappetizing meaning of *kaka* would be allowed to coexist with the specialized meaning "a food item" and even become its main one. Yet this is, apparently, what happened early on.

A similar case is German *Fladen* "fritter" and "a piece of cow dung" (again "something flat"). The connection between Germanic *kaka*, Latin *cacare*, and the Romance names for "cake" is less clear, but *kak-* ~ *kok-* are so firmly integrated into the vocabulary of English and its sister languages that they appear to be native. Words beginning with and ending in the same consonant (*bib, bob, boob, dad, dud, dude, gig, gag, cock, kick, cook, cake, mum, mom, pep, pap, tit, tat, teat, toot*, along with such almost humorous verbs as *babble, bubble, cackle, diddle, giggle, gaggle, google*, and their likes) are sometimes sound-imitative but more often sound-symbolic, and baby language, emotional and picturesque by definition, is their natural soil. Therefore, they sound so much alike all over the world. *Cake* shows that, with time, such formations may lose their "symbolic" nature and develop respectable "adult" senses.

This is the end of the story. It may be a bit off-putting to discover that *cake* is Scandinavian, while *cookie* is Dutch. For those who feel slighted, here is a short postscript. Consider the phrase *to take the cake* "to carry off the honors." Supposedly, the custom has Irish roots. The Irish are said to have taken the phrase to America, where it contributed to the creation of the "cake walk dance."

If everything said above is true, the readers may rejoice: they have eaten a rather crummy cake and still have it as a reward for their interest in word origins.

Note
In the periodicals, the Irish-American hypothesis of the origin of *cake walk* was suggested in *American Notes and Queries*, vol. 1, 1888, p. 147,

and twice in the British periodical *Notes and Queries* 8/I, 1892: 60 and in vol. 200, p. 1957, p. 357. Dictionaries tell the same tale.

Rum "Drink"

The most obvious law of etymology is that we cannot explain the origin of a word unless we have a reasonably good idea of what the thing designated by its word means. For quite some time, people pointed to India as the land in which rum was first consumed and did not realize that in other European languages, *rum* was a borrowing from English. The misleading French spelling *rhum* suggested a connection with Greek *rheum* "stream, flow" (as in *rheumatism*). According to other old conjectures, *rum* is derived from *aroma* or *saccharum*. India led researchers to the rare Sanskrit word *roma* "water" as the etymon of *rum*, and this is what many otherwise solid nineteenth-century dictionaries said. Webster gave the vague, even meaningless, reference "American," but on the whole, the choice appeared to be between East and West Indies. In the first edition of his dictionary (1882), Walter W. Skeat suggested Malayan origins (from *beram* "alcoholic drink," with the loss of the first syllable) and used his habitual eloquence to boost this hypothesis. Was Malaysia the home of the beverage? This is a crucial question. Without answering it, we are doomed to find words divorced from things. (*Words and Things* [German *Wörter* und *Sachen*] was the title of an excellent journal devoted to etymology.)

Then *The Academy*, a periodical that enjoyed well-deserved popularity throughout the forty years of its existence (1869–1910), published the following paragraph. (The *Imperial Dictionary* gives it in full, but few people have access to or ever use it, and I will therefore reproduce the paragraph in full.) *The Academy*, September 5, 1885, p. 155: "Mr. N. Darnell Davis has put forth a derivation of the word *rum*, which gives the only probable history of it. It came from Barbados, where the planters first distilled it, somewhere between 1640 and 1645. A MS. 'Description of Barbados' in Trinity College, Dublin, written about 1651, says: 'the chief fudling (sic) they make in the Island is *Rumbullion*, alias *Kill-Divil* (sic), and this is made of sugar-canes distilled, a hot, hellish, and terrible liquor.' G. Warren's description of Surinam, 1661, shows the word in its present short form: '*Rum* is a spirit extracted from the juice, . . . called *Kill-Devil* in New England!' '*Rumbullion*,' is a Devonshire word meaning 'a great tumult,' and may have been adopted from some of the Devonshire settlers in Barbados; at any rate, little doubt can exist that it has given rise to our word *rum*, and the longer name *rumbowling*, which sailors give to their grog." Also in 1885, *berummaged* "confused" was recorded on Dartmoor, and still later it became clear that French *guildive* is an alteration of English *kill-devil*. According to Halliwell's *Dictionary of Archaic and Provincial Words* (an excellent book), many of the settlers in Barbados, at the time when sugar making was being established there, came from Devonshire.

Skeat accepted Davis's etymology unconditionally, and, since that time, it has become commonplace. However, some dictionaries, including the original *OED*, show caution, supply the explanation with a question mark, or even say that the origin of *rum* is "uncertain." The etymology of *rumbullion* will concern us here only in so far as it may be a combination of the adjective *rum* and French *boullion* "hot drink." That adjective has been rather convincingly traced to Romany *rom* "male" (= "Gypsy man, good man"), a once ubiquitous cant word. *Romeville* (i.e., *Rumville*) was London, and so on. Hensleigh Wedgwood, the main etymologist of the pre-Skeat era, thought that *rum* is a curtailed form of *rum booze* "great drink." Indeed, in 1567, wine was called *rum booze* in Elizabethan slang.

It may not be out of place to mention an article whose title promises nothing to word lovers but that contains numerous ingenious etymologies (John P. Hughes, "On 'h' for 'r' in English Proper Names," *The Journal of English and Germanic Philology* 53, 1954, 601–12). A strong bond unites *h* and *r* in the history of all the Germanic languages. Alternations of the *Hob* ~ *Rob* type are the thin edge of a very big wedge. Hughes suggests that *rum booze* was taken for a plural (*rumboes*); then the new singular *rumbo* "strong punch" allegedly came up, from which *rum* would be a shortened form. However, *rumbo* was attested only in the middle of the eighteenth century. Though *rumbo* is a rather improbable source of *rum*, in Hughes's opinion, *hum* "alcoholic drink" is a stub of *humbooze* and a doublet of *rumbooze* or *rum booze*.

The way to *rum* from *rum booze* is shorter than from *rumbullion* (or *rumbustion*, also "tumult, hubbub, etc."), but the fact remains that rum reached England from Barbados. It is, however, not improbable that the phrase *rum booze* had existed in the speech of the English settlers on the Caribbean island and was taken overseas. If so, *rumbullion*, from *rum* (adjective) and French *boullion* "hot drink," was a verbal joke, a pun. (In England, rum was known very little before 1685. Yet, on July 7, 1685, after the battle of Sedgemoor, the vanquished Duke of Monmouth tasted the drink. It must have been one of the last pleasures the rebellious duke enjoyed before his execution.) Most importantly, *rum* "a drink" and *rum* "odd" cannot be separated. There was quite a fashion for *rum-* coinages in the eighteenth century: compare *rumgumption*, from which we have the stub *gumption* "common sense" (originally perhaps "*rough* common sense"), while *rumbustious* "boisterous, violent" sounds suspiciously like *rambunctious* "mischievous, self-asserting." Leo Spitzer believed that the French argot word *rogomme* "strong drink" goes back to English *rumgumption*. Some details remain hidden, but one thing never changes: excessive consumption of rum can result in violent behavior.

Note

Leo Spitzer, "Anglo-French Etymologies." *Modern Language Notes* 59, 1944, 223–50 (see pp. 243–46). The title of the dictionary contains a mistake: in Spitzer's work, the *Imperial Dictionary* is called *Universal*.

Cocktail

This is a story of a recent but puzzling word, explained so clearly that no one will ever say that its origin is unknown or debatable. But this is also a story of sticks and stones breaking the bones of uninformed etymologists.

The earliest dated citation of *cocktail* "an alcoholic drink" in the first edition of the *OED* goes back to 1809. The volume of the *OED* with the word *cocktail* appeared in 1893. The examples are preceded by the fateful comment: "A slang word, of which the real origin appears to be lost." Why this comment is fateful will become clear toward the end.

At the moment, we should keep in mind only one incontrovertible fact: *cocktail* spread to the rest of the world from the United States.

As could be expected, fantasies and folk etymology ran wild trying to explain where such a strange name for a beverage came from. "the term was suggested by the shape which froth, as of a glass of porter, assumes when it flows over the sides of a tumbler containing the liquid effervescing." I don't know enough about porter, but the etymological froth effervesced in many directions: "The old doctors had a habit of treating certain diseases of the throat with a pleasant liquid, applied with the tip of a long feather plucked from a cock's tail, etc." This was a nice habit, especially considering that the liquid poured down the patient's throat "consisted of bitters, vermouth, and other appetizers." On the other hand, it is quite possible, or so some people thought, that we owe the exotic name to Mexico: "The Aztec word for 'pulque' is pronounced much like *octail*, and General Scott's troops called the liquor 'cocktail' and carried the word back to the United States." (The famous general Winfried Scott, 1786–1866, is meant.)

Those who looked to Mexico for inspiration ignored the fact that all things good to eat and drink were supposedly invented in France or under the influence of French speakers. We are now told that *coquetel* (whatever its origin), a mixed drink known in the vicinity of Bordeaux for centuries, was introduced to America by French officers during the Revolution or that the first cocktails were served from eggcups (never mind the long feather plucked from a cock's tail) and that the French for "eggcup" is *coquetier*. The custom is said to have originated in New Orleans soon after 1800, a date that accords well with the Bordeaux hypothesis. *Coquetels* were, quite naturally, served from *coquetiers*, and one of those French words must have been the etymon of English *cocktail*. That cocktail consisted of cognac, brandy, and bitters made from the inventor's secret formula.

Predictably, we are offered no evidence confirming the role of eggcups in the history of cocktail and the introduction of the French drink into the United States or references to historical sources, even anecdotal. Indeed, there was something called *cock ale* "ale mixed with the jelly or minced meat of a boiled cock, besides other ingredients," traced by the *OED* to the middle of the seventeenth century. This dainty went out of fashion in England but would have been the right thing for the colonies. Another kind of cock ale is defined as "a mixture of spirits and bitters fed to fighting cocks in training." Inebriated fighting cocks—that is what we need! It is of course unclear how *cock ale* changed to *cocktail*, but plus or minus a letter seldom bothers amateur etymologists. The clinching piece of evidence (evidence at last) comes from the circumstance that, in the days of cock fighting, the spectators used to toast the cock with the most feathers left in its tail after the contest, and the number of ingredients in the drink corresponded to the number of feathers left; hence *cocktail*. This is the second time a cock's feather appears in our tale. We have already heard about the patients suffering from a sore throat.

Cocktails are inseparable from bars and restaurants, and *cocktail* may be an abridged form of *cock tailings*, the name of a mixture of tailings from various liquors, thrown together in a common receptacle and sold at a low price. According to a slightly different version of the bar-and-restaurant etymology, in the early American days, they used to empty the last ounce or so of miscellaneous bottles of liquor into one bottle, the cork of which was decorated with a cock's tail feathers. *Cocktail* emerges as *cockcork*.

All those conjectures are hopeless not only because they are so silly, but rather by definition. If any of them had any foundation in reality, the drink would have almost certainly been called *cock's tail* (cf. *coxcomb*, that is, *cock's comb*). Some people realized this and suggested a connection with the word *cock-tailed*. They were close to the truth, but *cock-tailed* means "having the tail cocked, so that the short stump sticks up like a cock's tail." Where does the beverage come in?

Further events developed in this manner. In 1946, a Swedish scholar read attentively the relevant entries in the *OED* and came to a reasonable conclusion about the origin of *cocktail*. But etymology as a branch of scholarship suffers from a peculiar disadvantage: it is extremely difficult to collect the literature on the attempts to explain the origin of any given word. For decades I have been collecting such literature pertaining to English. My database is rather full but of course not complete, and I, too, have been more than once hauled over the coals for missing the latest publications. The second problem is the language barrier. It would be naïve to expect that a student of linguistics can read the relevant works in every language. Nowadays, English is fine.

In the past, specialists were expected to be able to read German and French. But woe to a researcher who publishes only in Dutch, Russian, or Japanese! Finally, there are major, visible periodicals, and such as are seldom or never noticed by the world at large. How many people in the wide world have heard about *Lincolnshire Notes and Queries* or *Cheshire Sheaf*? And what if the most ingenious guess appeared in a footnote to an article on cockfighting, published in a sports magazine? To return to the beginning. Swedish is not a language that everyone interested in English etymology can read, and the article, though featured in a general linguistic bibliography, has not been noticed.

In 1960, a Belgian scholar read the same entries and arrived at the same conclusion as his predecessor about fifteen years earlier. Yet he did not know an important citation his Swedish colleague had unearthed in 1946, and this weakened his case. Although he repeated his results four years later, he did not fare better than the Swede. Finally, in 1978, a spirited article by a professor from Cornell appeared. Once again, the same entries were examined and the same etymology was offered, unfortunately, again without the benefit of the most cogent citation. Needless to say, the last author did not realize that he had walked a well-trodden path, but he had his reward: no one seems to have read his contribution, and he fell into the black hole shared by the Swede and the Belgian. All dictionaries kept repeating that the origin of *cocktail* is unknown. Only now, probably under the influence of my publications, online versions of reference books give a succinct explanation that reflects the research of many years ago. Etymologies are not theorems and cannot be proved by means of syllogisms, but the suggestion by the three scholars seems to be right.

Their proposal is not as charmingly simple as Eric Partridge would prefer it to be ("*Cocktail*. Any creature with tail resembling a cock's, hence a lively cheerful, basically spirituous drink"), but, by way of compensation, it makes sense. In the past, the tails of horses that were not thoroughbred (e.g., of hunters' and stagecoach horses) were docked. They were called cocktailed horses, later simply cocktails. By extension, the word *cocktail* was applied to a vulgar, ill-bred person raised above his station, a person assuming the position of a gentleman but deficient in gentlemanly breeding. Let us note that, according to the 1806 citation given in the Swedish article (it antedates Murray's examples by three years), "cocktail is a stimulating liquor, composed of spirits of any kind, sugar, water, and bitters" (*Balance*, Hudson, N. Y., May 13, 1806; the citation appeared in the *Supplement* to the *OED*, but its value was not appreciated). Water was an ingredient of the original cocktail! According to an 1836 anecdote, a wounded duelist was carried into a tavern and revived by a mixture of liquor, egg yolk, sugar, lemon, and crushed ice (presumably a cocktail), and, as we know, ice is frozen water. Cocktail then was an acceptable alcoholic drink, but diluted, not a "purebred," a beverage promising more than it could deliver, a thing "raised above its station." Hence the highly appropriate slang word applied earlier to inferior horses and sham gentlemen.

Some tales have a happy end.

Note

The articles mentioned above appeared in *Moderna språk* 40, 1946, 2–8; *Notes and Queries* 204, 1959, and 205, 1960, 306; *Le français moderne* 29, 1961, 285–87; *English Studies Presented to R. W. Zandvoort. . . . A Supplement to English Studies* 45, 1964, 31–32, and *Linguistic and Literary Studies in Honor of Archibald A. Hill*, vol. 3, 1978, 147–53.

7

In the Air, on the Ground, and in the Sea

Butterfly

Some compounds begin to make sense only after we have discovered their history. A typical case is the names of the days of the week. Except for *Sunday*, none of them is fully transparent to modern speakers (only *day* poses no problems). Most often, a look at their history provides convincing answers. This holds not only for such very old words as *Tuesday* and *Thursday* but also for the likes of *nickname* and *breakfast*. Yet one also runs into a sizable group of compounds whose separate elements make perfect sense while the whole remains a riddle. What is the connection between *strawberry* and *straw*, *jackpot* and *jack*, *doughnut* and *nut*? *Butterfly* belongs with *strawberry*. Why *butter*?

The few popular hypotheses have been recycled in numerous articles and books. Perhaps *butterfly*, originally the name of the yellow species, such as the cabbage butterfly or the brimstone butterfly, was extended to all lepidopterous insects. Variations on this theory are that the first butterflies one sees in spring are butter-creamy or that butterflies come in "butter season," from March to November. Or vats containing butter have special attraction for butterflies. (Here is part of a description: "I have seen Polish women churning butter in the old-fashioned wooden churns in the farmyard, surrounded by a cloud of butterflies of all kinds. The smell of buttermilk, byproduct of churning, contains some aroma which is irresistible to butterflies.") Also, it has been observed that butterflies, during their larval stage, store lots of fat. Or their excrement resembles butter. Or (perhaps the most common explanation) the popular superstition has it that witches turn into butterflies and steal milk and butter (hence the name). Or *butterfly* is a "corruption" of *flutter-by*. In the past, some of those who had the courage to translate Dutch *boterschijte* (the main support for the excrement etymology) into English bemoaned the degradation of the butterfly: from Psyche (in Greek, *psyche* is both "soul" and its incarnation "butterfly") to a butter-shitter.

Except for the flutter-by joke, none of the conjectures cited above is fanciful. The butterfly is at the center of numerous superstitions the world over, and, in some parts of Germany, it is called "milk thief." *Schmetterling*, the Standard German word for "butterfly," sounds so much like the Slavic word for "(sour) cream" (consider the family name of the Czech composer Smetana, the author of the opera *The Bartered Bride*) that it is usually classified with borrowed words, and we get one more tie between butterflies and dairy products. Russian *babochka* "butterfly" (nearly the same form elsewhere in Slavic) seems to be a diminutive of *baba* "(old) woman," a doublet of *babushka* "grandmother"—a fact that seems to strengthen the alleged connection between witches and butterflies. (In Russian, both nouns are stressed on the first syllable.) Romance scholars also have trouble explaining the origin of their word for "butterfly," such as French *papillon* (Latin *papilio*), Italian *farfalla*, and Spanish *mariposa*.

This is where Wilhelm Oehl, a prominent Swiss linguist, comes in. He studied the phenomenon he called elementary, that is, primitive, word formation. His approach was inspired by the gifted but controversial scholar Alfredo Trombetti, whom he called a genius. Today, we know that languages form families and that every family goes back to a proto-, or mother language. For example, English is a member of the huge Indo-European family. It remains a matter of discussion who the Indo-Europeans were, where they came from, and how they managed to spread from Ceylon to Norway, but the fact that such a family exists is certain. Other families are smaller, and their early history is sometimes more transparent, but, regardless of size, comparison within families follows the same principles: related forms (cognates) are recognized because their meanings match while their sounds coincide or differ according to certain rules. Yet words occur that, although they sound amazingly similar, violate sound correspondences and cannot be looked upon as borrowed (the languages in question have never been in contact), seem to be in some way connected, and Trombetti considered a broader framework than a set of mutually isolated families. Oehl examined hundreds of such words and ascribed their similarity to people's identical verbal reaction to certain movements. For instance, when speakers, wherever they live, catch a ball, they cry out *gop*, *kap*, *hop*, or something like it. Such words may be short-lived, but, after they disappear, they are coined again. Creating them is like following an instinct. This is what Oehl understood by primitive word formation. Modern students of sound symbolism have not yet discovered Oehl (one never sees references to him), though he is certainly their ally.

The Old English for *butterfly* was *buttor-fleoge*, for all intents and purposes the same word as today. Since in English, the component -*fly* is added freely to the names of various winged creatures, from *gadfly* to *dragonfly*, only *buttor-* "butter" has to be explained. While investigating the names of the butterfly from all continents, Oehl noticed that it tends to be a symbolic representation of the butterfly's opening and closing its wings. The "ideal" names are simple reduplication: *popo*, *pepe*, *pupu*, *dudu*, *buom-buom*, *kupu-kupu*, *firi-firi*, and so forth. Some reduplicated words have additional syllables: *bebele*, *palpalut*, *liblikas*, *kukupo*, *yakukek*, *odefufu*, and the like. We immediately recollect Russian **babochka** (-*ochka* is a suffix), Latin **papilio**, and Italian *farfalla*. *Papilio* is not an exact counterpart of *bebele* (the vowels in it differ from syllable to syllable), and in *farfalla* -*r* and -*l* alternate, but those look like insignificant complications.

The main difficulty with Oehl's lists is that classic types never exhaust his material, and "mixed types" are pressed into service. *Peme* and *lablok* are slightly less persuasive than *pepe* and *liblikas*, while *pete* (disyllabic), *mbudi*, *futie*, and *naphitka* do not even make one think of reduplication. However, Oehl was convinced that *butterfly* does not owe its origin to *butter*. He had shown that once words like *babochka* arise, they tend to be reshaped or reinterpreted under the influence of folk etymology: *babochka*, naturally, aligned itself with *baba*, whereupon milk-stealing witches appeared on the scene, and the word's "primitive" origin was forgotten. According to Oehl, *butter-* in *butterfly* should be understood as an alteration of the "mixed" *pete ~ bete* type. The cause of the alteration might be the belief that butterflies steal butter or the color of their excrement, or whatever. The implication is that at one time the insect was called approximately *buto* or *boto*. Such hypotheses cannot be proved, but Oehl's material makes his reconstruction not entirely improbable. He also listed a type based on the combination *m + t*, widespread in Slavic, and believed that German *Schmetterling* is a borrowing of some such word. Initial *sch-*, he suggested, was added to the *met*-word later, to connect it with *smetana*. *Schmetterling* retained the status of a loanword from Slavic, but its history emerged in a new light.

It will cause no surprise that Romance etymologists accepted Oehl's conclusions, for *farfalla* and *papilio* are such obvious cases of reduplication, while those who attempt to trace the origin of *Schmetterling* and *butterfly* ignore them. Oehl was the creator of a most impressive panorama, but, not unlike an oil painting, its effects are partly lost if the onlooker comes too close to the canvas. No one will bet on his derivation of *butterfly*, but, who knows! It may be right, for, when all is said and done, we should admit that butterflies have relatively little to do with butter. To an etymologist, beautiful, fluttering butterflies are sometimes more dangerous than flying dragons: they don't spit fire but are harder to catch.

Foxglove

The origin of plant names is one of the most interesting areas of etymology. I have dealt with *henbane*, *hemlock*, *horehound*, and *mistletoe* and know how thorny the gentlest flowers may be for a language historian. It is certain that *horehound* has nothing to do with hounds, and I hope to have shown that *henbane* did not get its name because it is particularly dangerous to hens (which hardly ever peck at it, and, even if they did, why should they have been chosen as the poisonous plant's preferred victims?). On the face of it, the word *foxglove* makes no sense because foxes do without gloves and even without hands. The scientific name of *foxglove* is *Digitalis* (the best-known variety is *Digitalis purpurea*), apparently because it looks like a thimble and can be easily fitted over a finger (Latin *digitus* "finger"). See more about it below. The puzzling part is *fox-*. It was such even in Old English (*foxes glofa*). Even if, as some people think, the name was applied to a different plant, all the problems remain.

It is amusing what fierce battles have been fought over the origin of the outwardly insignificant word *foxglove*. Walter W. Skeat broke many a spear defending the simplest etymology (*foxglove* is *fox* + *glove*), but neither he nor anyone else has been able to explain how the Anglo-Saxons came by this name: Why *fox*? Skeat produced an impressive list of Old English plant names with obscure references to animals in them, for example, *fowl's bean*, *cow-slip* (not *cow's lip*!), *ox-heal*, *catmint*, and *hound's fennel*. And we know *dog rose* and *wolfsbane*, to mention just a few oddities. Each of them needs an explanation, and Skeat may have pooh-poohed the question too hastily: "[to us] such names as *fox-glove* and *hare-bell* seem senseless, and many efforts, more ingenious than well directed, have been made to evade the evidence. Yet, it is easily understood. The names are simply childish, and such as children would be pleased with. A child only wants a pretty name, and is glad to connect a plant with a more or less familiar animal. This explains the whole matter, and it is the reverse of scientific to deny a fact merely because we dislike or contemn [sic] it. This is not the way to understand the workings of the human mind, on which true etymology often throws much unexpected light." Unfortunately, the Anglo-Saxons were not children, and though, like us, they certainly enjoyed playing with language and inventing "pretty names," those names cannot be written off as silly or irrational. So let me repeat: *foxglove* does go back to a word that means exactly this (*fox-glove*), and all attempts to explain it as a "perversion" of some other compound or phrase are misguided, but the reason for endowing the flower with such an incomprehensible name has not been discovered.

The unfortunate idea to trace *foxglove* to *folk's* (or *folks'*) *glove* is relatively recent. It may have gained popularity after the publication of the book *English Etymologies* by Henry Fox (!) William Talbot (1847). We read the following in it: "In Welsh this flower is called by the beautiful name of *maneg ellyllon*, or the fairies' glove. Now, in the days of our ancestors, as every one knows, these little elves were called in English 'the good folks.' No doubt, then, these flowers were called 'the good folks' gloves,' a name since shortened into foxgloves [sic]. The plant is called in French *gantelée* (little glove); in Latin, *digitalis*, and in German, *fingerhut* (thimble). It is worthy of remark, [note the comma!] that the Greeks appear to have called it by a name which is different from the above, but not inappropriate, 'the trumpet flower.' At least, so I conjecture from the name *salvinca* applied to it in the middle ages, which is doubtless from the Greek *salpigga*, a trumpet. In addition to what was said before, it may be reminded that these flowers are called in Teviotdale [Scotland] *witches' thimbles*, agreeing partly with the Welsh; the witches, however, taking the place of the fairies."

Talbot, the inventor of photography, was a well-read and talented man, but it would have been better if he had not written a book on word origins. Practically, all his suggestion are fanciful and sometimes silly. Even in 1847, one could have done much better. His Greek derivation is also more than suspicious. By an amusing coincidence, the Latin name *digitalis* was coined in 1542 by Leonhart Fuchs (1501–1566), one of the founders of modern botany (German *Fuchs* means "fox"). The flower *fuchsia*, whose pronunciation is a torture to foreigners, and the color *fuchsia* (the color of *digitalis purpurea*!) are named after him. According to the *Century Dictionary*, Fuchs called the flower *digitalis* inspired by German *Fingerhut* "foxglove." French *gantelée* was already known in the thirteenth century. History's little joke connected Fuchs, H. Fox Talbot, and *foxglove*.

Belief in fairies, as in *Midsummer Night's Dream*, has no roots in Old English, so that all talk about good folk's glove(s) lacks foundation. R. C. A. Prior, the author of *Popular Names of British Plants* (1863), was a first-rate specialist in botany, but not in etymology, and his assertion (*foxglove* from *foxes-glew*, allegedly, meaning "folk's music," "in reference to the favourite instrument of an earlier time, a ring of bells hung on an arched support, the tintinnabulum, and thus answering to Norwegian *Revbielde*" [i.e., "foxbell"]) is also sheer fantasy. *Glew*, or rather *gliew* (Modern English *glee*), designated the sound of musical instruments, so that the ringing of bells should be dismissed as irrelevant. One wonders again what the fox has to do with our flower, but first a correction and a warning. The Norwegian for *foxglove* is *revebjælle* or *revebjølle* (one letter in the middle is missing from Prior's form). Also, at his time, the literary norm in Norway required that Norwegian words be spelled according to the rules of Danish orthography, and the Danish for *bell* is *bjælde*. Prior may have found *bielde* in some dictionary or he may have copied the word with two mistakes. Even the *Oxford Dictionary of English Etymology* cited the nonexistent *revbjelde* (from the *Oxford English Dictionary* [*OED*]), and I see it occasionally surfacing on the Internet (the *Century Dictionary* did much better). Old English *foxesclīfe* "foxglove? greater burdock?" (*ī* designates a vowel like the one we hear today in *lea*) has also been pressed into service, but *cl-* would not have yielded *gl-*.

Thus, a few wrong etymologies have been debunked, but what the fox has to do with the foxglove remains a mystery. An echo of the once well-known tale, North Germanic or Classical? To my regret, no Scandinavian dictionary I have consulted discusses the Norwegian word. In Dumfriesshire (south-central England), *foxglove* is called *tod-tail*, and *tod* means "fox." The second element poses no problems, for the bells of this plant bear some resemblance to fingers, and thus to gloves. There is a kind of grass called *fox grass*. The *Century Dictionary* gives several names for *Digitalis*: *fox-fingers*, *ladies' fingers*, and even *dead-men's bells*. In sum, *foxglove* means *foxglove*, and this disturbing fact has to be accepted. "One of the queerest crazes in English etymology," said Skeat, "is the love of paradox, which is often carried to such an extent that it is considered mean, if not despicable, to accept an etymology that is obvious." He cited attempts to invent a clever explanation for *foxglove* as an instance of the "queer craze." But, with due respect to the great scholar, it must be said that obvious etymologies are often wrong, that *foxglove* causes legitimate surprise, and people's attempts to dispel the mystery of etymology is the result of their healthy rebellion against the impenetrability of the words they use.

Note
Skeat wrote about *foxglove* many times. His latest letters to the editor on this word will be found in *Notes and Queries* 8/VIII, 1895, 495–96 and 1896 8/X, 462–63. Worth consulting is also St. Swithin in *NQ* 8/VIII, 452–53.

Shrimp and Shrew

It is amazing how expressive ("sound-symbolic") some initial consonant groups are. We hear *slump*, *smirk*, *sneak* and, on finding out what those words mean, feel that their meaning somehow "fits" them.

This reaction, unlike what happens in dealing with sound-imitative words (*boom, crash, shoo!*, and so forth), is language-specific because what works for English may and usually does not work for Russian or Chinese.

My interest in the history of the word *shrimp* was aroused by chance, when, years ago, I looked up the etymology of *scrumptious* in a reliable modern dictionary. It turned out that the word's origin is unknown. The usually sensible *Century Dictionary* suggested that *scrumptious* is an alternation of *scrimptious*, from *scrimption*, the noun going back to *scrimp* "to pinch pennies; to make small." The original *OED* thought so, too. The semantic shift from *scrimptious* to *scrumptious*, it explained, needn't worry us because adjectives occasionally change their meaning to the opposite: compare the history of *nice* (from "ignorant" to "stupid," to "minute and scrupulous," to "dainty" and "delightful"). One can also cite the seriously ameliorated adjective *pretty*: from "tricky, cunning, wily" to "astute, sagacious, ingenious," even "brave," and finally to "good-looking." But it took *nice* and *pretty* several hundred years to "turn around" (and there is the evidence of cognates), while *scrumptious* is slang, hardly predating the first quarter of the nineteenth century, and the intermediate stages in its history, including dialectal use ("mean, stingy, close-fisted; fastidious, hard to please; stylish, handsome") shed little light on the change. In a more general way, one can note that words sometimes combine opposite senses, especially across related languages ("hot" and "cold," "high" and "low," "beginning" and "end," and so forth). There is even a learned term for it (*enantiosemy*: a recent Greek compound modeled on German *Gegensinn*). Terms and parallels notwithstanding, every case needs an explanation.

Some modern reference books say that *scrumptious* is probably an alteration of *sumptuous*. Can *cr* ~ *kr* be used as a reinforcing infix, like *damn* in *fan-damn-tastic*? The English *scr-* words that do not go back to Old French or Latin (*script, scrofula*, and so forth) are invariably of Scandinavian origin. This makes sense, for the native *scr-* would have become *shr-*: compare *shriek* (English) and *screech* (Scandinavian). Still puzzled by the etymology of *scrumptious*, I began to look at other *shr-* words and took a note of *shrimp* and later, of *shrew*.

Shrimp entered English only in the late Middle period and meant "a dwarfish creature." The verb *shrimp* "shrink" also exists. The closeness of *shrimp* and *shrink* is apparent. *Shrink* derives from Old English *scrincan* "wither; cower, huddle." The senses "to become reduced in size or extent; retreat, recoil" were attested or developed later. The crustacean that interests us seems to have had a different name, but, when we begin to look for the linguistic environment of *shrimp*, we invariably find references to shriveling and emaciation.

Scandinavian dialects are especially rich in such words. We find Norwegian *skramp* "lean man or horse" and *skrumpa* "big lean cow," along with Danish *skrimpe ~ skrampel* "thin cow" (also said about other cattle). Dutch cognates usually mean "wrinkle" (arguably, a small thing), whereas German *schrumpfen* means "shrivel"; at one time, English also had the verb *shrump* "shrug, shrink." As though to remind us of the *scrimptious ~ scrumptious* alternation, we learn that German *schrumpfen* replaced the earlier form *schrimpfen* and that Norwegian *skrumpe*, an exact counterparts of German *schrumpfen*, must also have ousted the verb *skrimpa*. But the German-Scandinavian vowel game is old and has an easy explanation: there, we deal with a verbal root of the same type as English *shrink—shrank—shrunk*. If the new infinitive *to shrunk* suddenly emerged in English, we would have stated that the vowel of the past participle crept illegitimately into the infinitive. It would still be a rather bizarre development, but its source would be evident. By contrast, the change of *scrimptious* to *scrumptious* had no environment to justify the substitution because the analogs of *shrimpfen ~ shrumphen* did not exist in nineteenth-century English.

We discover that *scr-* is a common modification of *cr-* (which does not come as a surprise because, in the Indo-European languages, *s-* constantly attaches itself to various roots, and there is even a learned term for this phenomenon, namely, *s-mobile* "movable *s*"). Various *scr- ~ skr-* words may perhaps be related to *shrimp*, but each of those words has its own history, which is sometimes far from clear.

No doubt, the noun *shrimp* belongs with the verb *shrimp*, almost certainly with the verb *shrink*, with their doublets having no *s-* (for example, *crimp*), with Norwegian dialectal *skramp* and *skrumpe*, German *schrumpfen*, and quite a few others. When *shrimp* surfaced in English, it probably meant "diminutive creature." The slight difference in the dates of our first records does not make it clear whether there was enough time for the transfer of the name from "tiny marine creature" to "puny human being." Also, no Germanic language associates the shrimp with its size. German *Garnele*, Norwegian *rekje*, and its close cognates in Swedish, Danish, and Icelandic have nothing to do with dwarfs; their etymons should probably be sought among foreign words. The same holds for Romance: French *krevette* and Spanish *camaron* ~ Italian *gamberetto* (possibly, very old borrowings), let alone Spanish *quisquilla* "trifle; shrimp" (Latin *quisquillae*, plural, means "rubbish"). By way of consolation (if any consolation is needed in an etymologist's search), we note that shrimp may be large, as evidenced by the tautological compound *shrimp scampi* (*shrimp-shrimp*; Italian *scampo* means "lobster"; thus, a lobster-sized shrimp, as it were).

Returning to English, we wonder in what circumstances the name was applied to the crustacean. Along the way, we have encountered lean cows, horses, and people but not a single inhabitant of the sea. When we call someone small and unimportant a shrimp, it sounds like a metaphor, but, viewed historically, the name coined to designate dwarfs seems to have been transferred to the animal in an undocumented process. Spanish *quisquilla* shows that shrimp and trifles may be inseparable in our mind. *Shrimp* remains without a definite etymology, but, like *scrumptious*, it seems to be an expressive word. With the result being so uncertain, it will be useful to look at the history of *shrew*.

We are again turning to the *Century Dictionary*. According to it, "there is no foundation in fact for the vulgar notion that shrews are poisonous, or for any other of the popular superstitions respecting these harmless little creatures." However, research shows that "[U]nlike most mammals, some species of shrews are venomous. Shrew venom is not conducted into the wound by fangs, but by grooves in the teeth. The venom contains various compounds, and the contents of the venom glands of the American short-tailed shrew are sufficient to kill 200 mice by intravenous injection." The shrew is an insectivorous mammal. An old etymology traced *shrew* to a root meaning "cut" (as in *shear*) and glossed the word as "biter" on account of its reportedly venomous bite. Another version of this etymology refers to the shrew's pointed snout. The Old High German cognate of *shrew* meant "dwarf" (a figure cut short?). We suddenly find ourselves in close proximity to *shrimp*, which also first meant "tiny creature" (or so it seems), and this suggests that *shrimp* and *shrew* are related. But some chronological difficulties remain. *Shrimp* entered English in the fourteenth century. Its siblings are Middle High German *schrimpfen* and Middle Dutch *schrimpen*; both verbs meant "shrink." Unlike *shrimp*, *shrew* has an Old English etymon: its first known form is *scrēawa*. It would be tempting to explain *shrew* as "diminutive animal" because some shrewmice are the smallest mammals in nature, but *scrimp-*, the putative etymon of *shrimp*, and *scrēawa* share only the first three sounds. Even if we disregard *-m-* in the middle of *scrimp* (nasal sounds are often mere "infixes"), the part the ancestors of *shrimp* and *shrew* share is hardly sufficient for setting up a common root and positing affinity between them.

English *shrew* "malignant person," known in texts since the thirteenth century, seems to be the same word as the animal name. "Biter" fits its meaning in light of the creatures' folklore, but evil people do not have pointed snouts, and this circumstance calls into question the etymology offered above, even though it has been popularized in some of our most authoritative dictionaries. Another venue suddenly opens up and leads us to emaciated men (we have seen the reference in the story of *shrimp*), unclean spirits, and wild beasts. Swedish *skragge* and Middle High German *skröuwel* mean "devil." Here are a few more Scandinavian words (naturally, beginning with *skr-*, not *shr-*): Norwegian *skrubb* "wolf," its homophone Norwegian dialectal *skrubb* "old lean man" (visualized as the Devil?) and *skrogg* "wolf" (again!), Icelandic *skröggur* "old man; ghost" (in Old Icelandic, *skröggr* was used as one of the names of the fox), and a certain giant was called this (another devilish creature). In some rural areas of Norway, *skrugg* is a counterpart of *skrogg ~ skröggur*. English *scrag* "lean man or animal" and *scraggy* obviously belong here, too. The consonants *gg*, as in the Scandinavian languages, and *w*, as in Old English *screawa* and Middle High German *scröuwel*, are compatible. The rest is less clear.

To begin with, one wonders how Norwegian *skrubb* and *skrogg* (the latter with its respectable Old Norse heritage) are connected. In etymological research, it is customary to amputate final consonants and compare the stumps. The severed limbs, so-called *extensions*, are supposed to have been added to the root in the process of word formation, but since such consonants (in our case, *b* and *g*) have no identifiable meaning, the procedure does not arouse much confidence. Also, the shorter the stub, the easier it is to find words seemingly belonging together. For instance, English *scrub* means "low stunted tree" and "dwarf cattle"; it is an etymological doublet of *shrub*. Are they related to Norwegian *scrubb* and English *shrimp*, as well as other words for "people of delicate build" and "lean cattle"? And *scrub* "rub hard"? Is it *rub* "augmented" by *sc-* in order to sound expressive? If *shrimp* has the root meaning "shrink, shrivel" (by the way, should we consider *shrivel* in our tale?), the names of dwarfs and lean creatures will get a reasonably convincing explanation. However, we observe wolves, foxes, devils, and thin old men coexisting peacefully in the same semantic cage. Did they have a single progenitor? Wolves are especially puzzling. According to one hypothesis, Norwegian *skrogg* designates the wolf as a particularly lean creature. It is true that wolves are always hungry, but among the words for "wolf" in various languages I have not been able to find a single one that emphasizes the beast's lack of flesh: the idea underlying the name has usually something to do with the wolf's ferocity, readiness to attack, and less often color (gray). Yet *lean beast* has been used as a euphemism (a taboo word) for the dangerous and ever-hungry predator.

Words designating pagan devils are notoriously hard to trace to their roots. In disentangling the Germanic knot, we should perhaps begin with the sense "demon, ghost." There must have existed in people's imagination a terrifying creature called approximately *skrogg*, *scrauw*, or something like it. *Skr-* ~ *scr-* was, as noted above, sound symbolic. This initial consonant group tends to occur in words for scrambling, scraping, scratching, scrubbing, and many other harsh and precipitous actions, or it refers to screaming, screeching, and shrieking. Therefore, a sumptuous thing looks doubly sumptuous when it is called scrumptious.

The ghost is easy to associate with any of those things: it could screech, scramble, and scratch. We have little chance of discovering how *-ogg* and *-ubb* in *skrogg* and *skrubb* originated. From "devil, demon, ghost" we may perhaps get to "emaciated old man," a figurative use of the original meaning. The much-feared wolf must have been viewed as another incarnation of the devil. For example, the most ferocious beast in Scandinavian myths was the terrible wolf Fenrir. The fox, though a feared hen-snatcher and the traditional embodiment of slyness in folklore, seems to have ended up in this company by mistake, but language history shows that wolves and foxes were often confused. Thus, Latin *lupus* "wolf" is akin to *vulpes* "fox."

Even though "emaciated old man" looks like an extension of "(poor) devil" or "(lame) devil," the path from this meaning to "lean cattle" and "stunted tree" is not straight. Could references to small size have been borrowed from other *scr-* nouns? *Shrink* at one time meant "huddle" and so did *shrug* (in addition to "shiver"), a cognate of Swedish dialectal *skrugge* "crouch" and Danish *skrukke* ~ *skrugge* "walk lamely, hobble; duck the head." *Shrink* is related to *shrimp*, while *shrug* is evidently akin to Norwegian *skrogg*. Proximity in form and sense resulted in overlap and confusion. Some words are like a bunch of grapes on a vine (they are fed by the same root), whereas others resemble a batch of mushrooms huddling together on a stump and owing their origin to the same mycelium (so one may say that they are related), but they are still rootless. For all those vague reasons, it is safer to keep *shrew* away from *shrink* despite the fact that the devils of popular tradition may be shrunken, old, and lean. But if the shrew (the animal) got its name because of the venomous bite ascribed to it, one can risk the conjecture that the little mouse was identified with the devil. In this case, biting and pointed snouts should no longer interest us here.

The hypothesis offered above resolves itself into the following. The etymon of *shrew*, with its sound-symbolic beginning (*scr-*), meant "devil." The origin of the word's remaining part remains undiscovered. In the Middle Ages, the devil was often represented as ugly, lame, and so forth. Perhaps this is how the figurative meaning "emaciated old man" came into being. People believed that the shrew had a venomous bite and therefore looked upon this creature as an incarnation of the Devil. They were wrong; the wolf has a much better right to be called "devil." The application of *shrew* to cantankerous human beings has the same cause. The senses "lean cattle" and "stunted tree" seem to go back to a different but similar *scr-* word. *Shrew* was not coined with the meaning "biter," "short" (from a root for "cut"), or "with a pointed snout." *Shrimp* is unrelated to it.

English *shrewd* may be an adjective like *crabbed*, *dogged*, and *wretched*, but it may be a disguised past participle because the verb *shrew* "curse" (extant in *beshrew*) existed. The way covered by *shrewd* since the fourteenth century goes from "wicked, hurtful, dangerous, grievous, serious" to "cunning, artful, astute, sagacious." Like *nice* and *pretty*, this word has been greatly ameliorated. I hasten to add that *screw*, whatever its meaning, has nothing to do with *shrew*, and its history is as full of dramatic events as the one told above.

8

Multifarious Devilry

Rogue

This is a supplement to the stories of *scoundrel* and *ragamuffin*. As with *scoundrel*, most sources tell us that the word *rogue* is of unknown origin. This conclusion could be expected, for *rogue*, a sixteenth-century addition to the English "word-hoard," meant "a wandering mendicant." (In his etymological dictionary, Walter W. Skeat attributed the original sense "a surly fellow" to it but did not adduce sufficient evidence in support of his statement.) Even assuming that the rogues of five hundred years ago called themselves rogues won't take us too far because, once again, we will be facing the almost impenetrable slang (cant) of the underworld, English or international.

Rogue surfaced in an English text in 1561. Most likely, it was a product of that century. Quite early, *rogue* acquired the senses "knave" and "villain" and became a facetious term of endearment. Today, we mainly apply it to scamps and mischievous persons, especially to the individuals prone to displaying a roguish smile. The main stumbling block (though, at first sight, it should have been a steppingstone) in reconstructing the history of *rogue* is its French twin *rogue* "arrogant, haughty," a word, strange as it may seem, evidently unrelated to *arrogance*. *Arrogance* and *arrogant* go back to the root of Latin *arrogare* "to claim for oneself," from the prefix *ad-* and *rogare* "ask" (compare English *interrogate* and *prerogative*).

Friedrich Christian Diez (1794–1876), the founder of Romance comparative linguistics, suggested that the French had borrowed *rogue* from Scandinavian and cited Old Icelandic *hrókr* "rook; long-winded talker." This rather improbable etymology has been questioned again and again, but it still appears, though not without a good deal of hedging, in a few authoritative dictionaries of French. Our greater concern is that, according to an opinion that has long since become dogma, French *rogue* is neither the source nor a cognate of English *rogue*. Only the great German etymologist Friedrich Kluge thought otherwise (but he devoted a single line to the English word in an insignificant booklet on English etymology), and Skeat believed that the meaning of *roguish* had been influenced by French.

Similar Celtic words, such as Scottish Gaelic *rag* "villain; a thief who uses violence," with a cognate in Breton, were noticed long ago. Judging by their geographical distribution, they are not loans from French. Nor does the French word look like a borrowing from Celtic. The *Oxford English Dictionary* (*OED*) offered no etymology of *rogue* and did not mention the oldest hypothesis on its origin. William Lambarde, a famous sixteenth-century English antiquarian and author on legal matters, traced *rogue* to Latin *rogator* "asker, beggar" (thus drawing a bridge from *rogue* to *arrogance*) and found several supporters.

However, for a learned Latinism, *rogue* is too widespread in British dialects. This fact did not stop Ernest Weekley from writing in his 1921 *Etymological Dictionary of Modern English*: "Distinct from F[rench] *rogue*, arrogant, but perh[aps] connected with *rogation*, petition. Cf. F[rench] *roi Pétaud*, king of the beggars, which some connect with L[atin] *petere*, to ask." The *Oxford Dictionary of English Etymology* found the connection between *rogue* and *rogare* probable, but the *OED* online did not support that conjecture. The rare late Middle English noun *roger* "a begging vagabond pretending to be a poor scholar from Oxford or Cambridge" (with *g*, possibly as in *go*) must, as it seems, be allied to *rogue*, but since nothing is known about its history, *roger*, according to a commonsense rule, cannot shed light on its look-alike, the almost equally impenetrable *rogue*.

The poet and amateur etymologist Charles MacKay believed that thousands of English words go back to Scottish Gaelic (one can find his fanciful derivations in several short notes and in the dictionary he brought out in 1877). Predictably, he also traced *rogue* to Scottish Gaelic (this idea lacks merit, and there is no need to discuss it here), but he also compared it with **ragman** (as in *ragman's roll*) and **ragamuffin**, and this is what Leo Spitzer, an astute professional Romance etymologist, suggested seventy years later. Few people ever consult MacKay's dictionary. I suspect that Spitzer, despite his great erudition, was not aware of its existence. (Perhaps a short digression can be allowed here.

The origin of English words has been investigated by professional scholars and amateurs for more than four centuries. During that long period, researchers have offered numerous conjectures, sometimes inspiring, sometimes fanciful. Occasionally, an author, all of whose ideas are demonstrably wrong, would hit on a useful solution. Therefore, an etymologist should always expect to find a jewel in a dung heap. My experience confirms this conclusion. Unfortunately, life is too short to explore all such heaps. Be that as it may, MacKay seems to have guessed well.)

As we have seen, *ragamuffin* is also a word of debatable origin, but it certainly consists of three elements: *rag-*, the inserted *-a-* (as in *cock-a-doodle-doo*), and the somewhat enigmatic *-muffin*. The French name *Rogue* was applied to traitors and infidels, whereas *Ragamont* and *Rageman* occurred among the names of the devil. The vowels (*a* versus *o*) alternated in the Devil's name: *Ragomant* ~ *Rogomant*. We also find such medieval proper names as Rogan and Ragon.

It appears that *rogue* originated in France, where it meant "traitor, infidel" and where its etymon meant "Devil." From France it presumably spread to late medieval England (*rogue, roger*) and the Celtic-speaking countries. In *ragamuffin*, we find one variant of the Devil's name and in *rogue*, the other. Latin *rogare*, I believe, should be left out of this story, even if someone at one time made a connection between beggars pretending to be students at Oxford and Cambridge and a verb meaning "to ask."

Note
Leo Spitzer, "Ragamuffin, Ragman, Rigmarole and Rogue." *Modern Language Notes* 62, 1947, 84–93 (see p. 91 on *rogue*).

Ragamuffin

There is some similarity between *hobbledehoy* and *ragamuffin*. The words are symmetrical: both fall into three parts (*hobble-de-hoy* and *rag-a-muffin*) and refer to young males of questionable standing. In addition, both have been written off as formations of unknown origin. We'll soon see that they also belong together in that both fell victim to folk etymology. Finally, it is not for nothing that *ragamuffin* "a poorly dressed child" and *hobbledehoy* "an unwieldy youth" ended up in the chapter dealing with devils and demons.

In the tale of *hobbledehoy*, I noted that the date of such words' first appearance in writing cannot tell us when they surfaced in the language. With *hobbledehoy* and *ragamuffin*, the situation is especially complicated because both words are "popular"—that is, vulgar or perhaps regional. They might exist for a long time without making their way into manuscripts and books. However, this observation should be taken with caution: many words, recorded, for example, in the fourteenth century, may indeed have been coined just then. Such is probably the history of *ragamuffin*, which turned up first in William Langland's poem *Piers Plowman* (1399). I wanted to write "in Langland's *famous* poem" but then thought better of it. Only good specialists in Middle English can read Langland's text in the original, and how many others have read its translation into modern language? Yet the poem is indeed famous, and reference to it graced the first essay in this book (*Alairy*) and the essay on *Cockney*.

In it, a devil called Ragamoffin (*sic*) is mentioned. The name Isabella Ragamoffyn occurred in 1344. This is a typical case: in the Middle Ages and later, many slang words surfaced as derogatory nicknames before they merged with the rest of the vocabulary. We know nothing about Isabella Ragamoffyn, but she probably deserved the moniker that stuck to her. Numerous nondescript and unsavory family names originated this way. For two centuries, *ragamuffin* (with any spelling) did not appear again in written documents. Its uninterrupted history in texts goes back to 1581. This means that, but for Langland and Isabella Ragamoffyn, we would have dated the word to the end of the sixteenth century!

Whatever the origin of *ragamuffin*, its present-day sense was influenced by *rag*, just as *hobbledehoy* inevitably makes one think of hobbling. In thirteenth-century France, the devil Rogemon le bon (or Rogamont) was a well-known figure, and there is every reason to suppose that he made his way into England and was there folk etymologized into *Ragman*. *Le bon* is again the product of taboo. The etymology of the French word has never been ascertained to everybody's satisfaction, but *Rag-* may be of Germanic origin. If so, the

Germanic word traveled to French and later returned to English (a not uncommon scenario).

For a long time, I have entertained the idea that Italian *ragazzo* "boy, youth" has the same root, followed by a Romance modifying suffix. *Boy* "imp" is just what one expects. (Later, I discovered that I have a predecessor, Eduard Mueller or Müller, but few people consult his dictionary. Even he may not have been the first to notice the similarity between *ragazzo* and *ragamuffin*.) Probably no other word of Italian has been discussed so often with such meager results. The Germanic root *rag-* "fury" seems to have existed for many years, as evidenced, for example, by Dutch dialectal *(lopen en) raggen* "run around in a state of violent excitement," said about animals in heat. Also consider *rigmarole*. This word is of dialectal origin, perhaps like *ragamuffin*, and goes back to *Ragman's roll*, the name of a game of chance. The Devil was often portrayed as having a ragged appearance, so that *Ragman* did fit the character of the Evil One, and, quite probably, this is how people understood the word, but I have a strong suspicion that Ragman had as little to do with rags as the original ragamuffin and that *ragamuffin* also referred to the Devil. A word with such a root seems to have been known rather widely because Lithuanian *rãgana* and Latvian *ragana* mean "witch." If Germanic *rag-* existed, it must have met with and interacted with French *rage*, a word of different origin.

In dealing with *hobbledehoy*, we first looked at *hobble*, then at *hoy*, and finally at *de*. We'll follow the same strategy here; that is, forget -*a-* for a while and turn to *muffin*. The German nickname *Mof* (again a nickname!) and the dialectal verb *muffen* "smell musty" exist, and so does English *muff* "stupid person." English *muff* "a covering for hands" and the verb *muff* "to handle awkwardly" are late and obscure words as far as their origin is concerned. The same holds for *muffin* "a cake" and *muffle* "the thick part of the upper lip and nose." Some of them came to English from Dutch and French, and they only show that a syllable like *muff* and *moff* may mean whatever people want it to mean, from "fool" to "cake." This statement will remind some of Humpty-Dumpty's attitude toward language. Or was the sound complex *moff ~ muff* sound-symbolic and could therefore refer to any object lacking substance?

A promising explanation of -*muffin* in *ragamuffin* seems to have been suggested in 1910, by A. Smythe Palmer. He came across the obsolete regional phrase *Auld Muffy* "Devil." Old French *maufé* "ugly" was applied to Satan (*Satan le maufé*). It may well be that *ragamuffin*, like *hobbledehoy*, consists of two elements, both meaning "devil," with the connecting element *a* in the middle. This element occurs in many English words, both of native and French origin. In trying to account for the etymology of *ragamuffin*, we can of course dispense with -*a*- by going back to *of*, as in *Tom o'Shanter* and *five o'clock*. Nor should we be interested in the influence of such French words as *vis-à-vis* and *cap-à-pie*. More probable as models are words like *chickabiddy*, *cock-a-leekie*, and *cock-a doodle-doo*. This intrusive *a* might be used for rhythmical purposes or because such words existed and provided a model. There was perhaps an element of humor in coining such compounds.

One still wonders where final -*n* came from, but so many nouns ended in -*an* and -*en* (like *guardian* and *warden*), along with "funny" words like *slabbedegullion* and *tatterdemal(l)ion*, that a neologism like *ragamauffi* must have looked too bare. Shakespeare, in *1Henry IV*, iii: 272, has *rag of Muffin* or *rag of Muffian*.

Etymology is a very serious branch of linguistics, but people know nothing about scholars' doubts and enjoy playing with words. Slang bears witness to this attitude toward language. By the middle of the fourteenth century, *ragamuffin* or some similar form of this noun must have been well-established if it could be used as a nickname. Whatever the origin of the connecting element *a* in it, the result was "Devil-a-Devil," a close relative of the later *hobbledehoy* "Devil-de-Devil." Naturally, as time went on, *ragamuffin* acquired the sense "a ragged person." The initial connotation was forgotten, and the origin of the word became impenetrable. King rag(e)man, Auld Maufi, and King Robert were full-grown devils, but the loss of status resulted in their loss of stature, so that *hobbledehoy* and *ragamuffin* began to refer to adolescents, rather than full-grown men. Those who have read James Greenwood's novel *The True Story of a Little Ragamuffin* will learn a great deal about the London slums and criminals of long ago, but not notice that Greenwood added *little* to *ragamuffin* in the title. Apparently, the protagonist's age was not taken for granted.

Note

The rarely used book mentioned above is an etymological dictionary by the German scholar Eduard Mueller (or Müller) *Etymologisches Wörterbuch der englischen Sprache*. Coethen: Paul Schettler, 1865–1867; 2nd ed., 1878. It is the only etymological dictionary of English published before the appearance of Walter W. Skeat's work that is still worth consulting for its conclusions and material, rather than for what is euphemistically called "historical interest." Abram Smythe Palmer was a self-taught philologist, today remembered, if at all, for his book on folk etymology. His article "Folk-Lore in Word-Lore," referred to above, appeared in the periodical *The Nineteenth Century and After* 68, 1910, pp. 545–57 (see pp. 545–46). I did not mention several publications that deal with *ragamuffin* that, in my opinion, hold out no promise for solving the word's origin.

Hobbledehoy

Hardly anyone uses this word today. Yet most native speakers of English know that it refers to a gawky, clumsy youth. Though our sources usually say that the origin of *hobbledehoy* has not been discovered, this statement should be interpreted as meaning: "No consensus exists on the word's etymology." Conjectures on the derivation of "hard words" always exist, and we will see that *hobbledehoy* is perhaps less opaque than it seems. *Hobbledehoy* conjures up a picture of hobbling (hence the reference to clumsiness), but, most likely, this association goes back to so-called folk etymology, that is, to an attempt to decipher an incomprehensible word. We'll return to folk etymology below.

Hobbledehoy appeared in English texts in the middle of the sixteenth century, and, even at that time, its form must have caused confusion because *hobble-* varied with *hobba-*, *hobby-*, and *hobbard*, among others. Apparently, people tried to make sense of a strange compound and failed. We may never know in what milieu this word surfaced (in street performers' lingo? In vagabonds' cant? In a remote rural dialect or in urban slang?). Yet one thing is clear: *hobbledehoy* consists of three elements: *hobble*, *de*, and *hoy*, though *hobble* perhaps falls into *hob-* and *-le*.

In dealing with such "funny" words, chronology is not necessarily a decisive factor because they may exist for a long time before, by a lucky chance, they make their way into a written or printed book. There is nothing specifically late Middle English about *hobbledehoy*, and indeed, the similarly sounding fiend's name *Hobbididance* surfaced in 1603, and *hobidy-booby* (a single occurrence in the *OED*) goes back to 1720 (it may mean "scarecrow"). Regional *hubble-te-shives*, a synonym of sixteenth-century *hubbleshow* and *ubbleshoo*, means "commotion." Fiends of all kinds tend to make a lot of noise, and this circumstance may provide a clue to the origin of *hobbledehoy*.

Long ago, it was suggested that *hob-* in *hobbledehoy* is a variant of *Rob*, or *Robert*, the name of the Devil, because *h* and *r* vary in English with great regularity. *Hobby* has been a pet name for *Robert* from time immemorial (the noun *hobby*, that is, a hobby horse, has a similar origin). Our hobbledehoy begins to look like a petty devil. The same *hob* occurs in *hobgoblin*. Robin Goodfellow is the name of an evil spirit (*Good-* in *Goodfellow* was supposed to dupe or propitiate the demon: you call an evil and dangerous creature good, and it will do you no harm; such is the explanation of taboo). The spelling *hobbledehoy* probably goes back to *hober-* (i.e., *Robert*) *-dehoy*, with *hobble* being (again!) a folk etymological reshaping of that form. From the end of the sixteenth century, we also have a mention of Sir Hobbard de hoy, a devil arousing lust, an uncontrollable sexual urge. (Old Mother Hubbard has nothing to do with that gang.)

More puzzling is the origin of *-dehoy*, though the element *-de-* can be left for further discussion. *Hoyden*, which first meant "a rude fellow" rather than "a boisterous girl," seems to have been a term of abuse and meant "heathen." In this form, the English word was apparently taken over from Dutch. Swear words travel light. In any case, *hoy-* in *hobbledehoy* could not be borrowed from *hoyden*. Also, the exclamation *hoy!* makes little sense in this context.

With the rest we are on slippery ground. In an attack on a word about which most authorities say "origin unknown," nothing else could be expected. I believe that the best suggestion about *hobbledehoy* traces it back to *Robert le Roy* "Robert the King." The alliteration binding the elements *hobble* and *hoy* is obvious. When in popular speech, *Robert* changed to *Hobert* or some such form, Roy, apparently, followed suit. The existence of King Robert is probable (remember the opera *Robert le Diable* by Meyerbeer!), and there must have been an element of humor in giving Robert Bruce the affectionate name King Hobbe. Hobbard-de-Hoy looks like a good sibling of three fiends mentioned in *King Lear:* Hobberdidance, Obidicut (also known as Haberdicut), and Flibbertigibbet.

If the story seems to have begun with Robert le Roy, where did *de* come from? The number of words with this infix is small, and they tend to be deliberately funny. Such are the defunct *simper-de-cocket*, an obsolete mild term of abuse for a woman (i.e., "a simpering coquette"?), *gobbledegook* ~ *gobbledygook*, *fiddlededee* "nonsense," and their likes. French words must have provided inspiration for some coinages because words of the *Cœr de Lion* (Richard the Lionheart) type were known widely. Another lion, namely *dandelion*, from *dent-de-lion* "lion's tooth" came into existence in a similar way. In fiends' names, this infix seems to feel quite at home: see the three names (*Hobberdidance* and others), mentioned above. Incidentally, the form *Flibberdigibbet* has also been recorded.

Here are some more words with *de* in the middle, some of them dialectal: *hagger-de-cash* "in a disorderly state," *flipper-de-flapper* "noise and confusion," *grizzle-de-mundy* "a stupid person who is always grinning," *tatterdemalion* "a ragged person," and *slobberdegullion* "lout." The infix *de-* could be not only of French but also of Dutch origin; in Low German, quite a few words of this type occur. *Hobble-de-poise* "easily balanced" is half-Germanic, half-French. This background (facetious coinages and compounds referring to fiends) makes it clear that *hobbledehoy* was a so-called popular word. English *de* is unlike French *de-*: it does not necessarily mean "belonging to." Sometimes it simply points to a connection between the parts of a compound, but its function is too vague to be defined in unambiguous terms.

Evil sprites are often associated with fiends of small stature, that is, imps. That is why above I referred to a petty devil. The step from such a petty devil to a naughty, mischievous, deformed, or simply small boy is short. When *Hobert-de*-hoy became the designation of an unwieldy adolescent, *Hobert*, one can imagine, turned into *hobble*, and the word acquired its present form. One thing is rather obvious: hobbledehoys do not hobble and never did.

Should lexicographers delete the fateful line "of unknow origin" from their dictionaries? The answer to this question is a matter of opinion. I did not *prove* anything. It was only possible to make suggestions, cite parallels, and celebrate intelligent guesses. Anyone is welcome to agree with my reconstruction or say that the question remains open. In the essay on *henchmen*, we have seen how Frank Chance tried, for ten years, to persuade his colleagues that *henchman* does not go back to *hengstman* "horseman" but hardly convinced anyone. The same will hold for *hobbledehoy*. Yet now the reader has a full picture of the problem, and this is already a step forward. The next section (on *ragamuffin*) may provide some ammunition to the argument presented above.

Note

No special articles on the etymology of *hobbledehoy* have been written, but there is an entry "Hobbledehoy" in my dictionary. Other than that, a useful and even inspirational paper is by John P. Hughes, "On "h" for "r" in English Proper Names." *The Journal of English and Germanic Philology* 53, 1954, pp. 601–12.

Harlequin and Harlot

This section is about the adventures of *harlot* and *Harlequin*. The main clue to their origin is hidden in the syllable *har*. Let us look at the dictionary page with the words in the title and begin with *harrow*, as in *harrowing of hell*. This verb, a near-twin of *harry* "to attack," goes back to Old English. We may wonder why *har(r)-* was chosen as the root denoting the opposite of peace but note that *harrow* "rake" probably has a sound-imitative origin from the grating noise its teeth make. Close by is *harp*. The harp, unlike the rake, has no teeth. Yet the inspiration for coining the instrument's name could be the noise from pulling strings. Although this instrument is often a source of sweet music, the verb *harp* "to irritate by going on again and again on the same subject" tells a different story. The effect from plucking strings need not always be mellifluous.

Latin *harpa* "harp" is believed to be a borrowing from Germanic. However, Latin also had the word *harpago* (stress on the first syllable) "grappling-hook," from which, via French, English got *harpoon* "a barbed missile." Hence also the name of Harpagon, the French miser, immortalized by Molière, and the Greek harpies, Zeus's merciless snatchers. As is known, certain consonants of Germanic languages have regular correspondences outside this group. For example, Latin *pater* is related to English *father*, and the correspondence *p ~ f* is just what we should expect. Harpies got their name from Greek *harpázein* "to snatch." Since the word's root ends in *p*, as does English *harp*, the correspondence is too good (*p* in both cases): the words cannot be related. Nor does it seem likely that Germanic borrowed *harp* from Greek (in a borrowing, *p* would of course have been preserved intact). Probably the same jarring sound suggested similar names to speakers in different corners of the continent. A leap from an Aeolian harp, with its dulcet music, to a harpoon gives one pause.

The root we are inspecting also turns up in the Germanic word meaning "army." In the fourth-century Gothic Bible, the noun *harjis* "army" occurs. German *Heer* (the same meaning) is a recognizable modern cognate (related form) of *harjis*. The Baltic cognates of *harjis* and *Heer* mean "war." The ultimate origin of *harjis* is unknown, and the same holds for *Krieg*, the Modern German word meaning "war." Yet perhaps the solutions are not too far to seek. As a result of several excellent investigations, we now know the origin of the main Indo-European words for "peace." The reference is usually to harmonious communal living. Human beings have warred ever since they emerged on the surface of the earth, but always prayed for peace. The medieval Scandinavians, amazingly, did not even have a separate word for "war": they called it "un-peace."

War was (and is) inseparable from tumult. Numerous *kr- ~ cr-* words—*croak, creak,* and *crash* (German *Krach*) among them—are sound-imitative. Russian *krik* "a shout" also belongs here, and I suspect that English *cry* (from Latin via Old French) does, too, and that the ingenious derivation of the Latin word, suggested by the great Roman scholar Varro and often repeated in modern dictionaries as at least possible, is a case of folk etymology. *Krieg,* too, looks like one of such words. All of them refer to din, uproar, noise, and the impression they produce. Some were coined in Greek, others in Latin, and still others in Germanic. The syllable *har-* is a member of the same loud military family.

A few more words, directly connected with war, are worthy of our attention. German *Herberge* "inn, hotel," that is (literally), "army shelter,

shelter for an army," made its way into Medieval Latin as *herbergium*; hence Italian *albergo*, French *auberge*, and their kin elsewhere. The Romance languages had enough native words for "barracks" (the ancient Romans called them *castra* "camps"). Yet the German noun conquered most of Western Europe. Someone who provided lodgings, a purveyor of lodgings (for an army), was called *her-berg-ere*. Today, *harbinger*, the modern continuation of *Herberger*, denotes a person or phenomenon foreshadowing the arrival of someone else or of a future event, a forerunner, and the ancient association with the army is forgotten. Shakespeare was fond of this word. His harbingers more often promoted the advent of good things than disasters.

An instructive case is English *harangue* "a long, passionate oration." The word reached England from France, but in French and elsewhere in Romance (*arrenga*, *arringa*), it is from Germanic. It referred to a crowd of armed warriors standing in a ring (and, apparently, listening to an oration by the leader; oaths were also sworn in this environment). Next comes *harness*, recorded in English texts around 1300 with the sense "baggage, equipment; trappings of a horse." At around the same time, it could also mean "body armor; tackle, gear." The route is familiar: from Old French to Middle English. *Harness*, like *harangue*, is an ancient compound, ultimately from Old Norse, in which *herr* meant "army" and *nest* (so!) meant "food, provision."

Mention can also be made of *herald*, originally *hari-wald-*, in which *har-* is "army" and *wald-* means "rule," as it still does in English *wield*. A herald is an envoy, someone who delivers proclamations, thus, a person not so different from a harbinger. The little remembered noun *heriot* is, by contrast, "pure English." It emerged with the sense "feudal service consisting of military equipment restored to the lord on the death of a tenant." The origin of *-ot* needn't delay us here.

Such then is the "military" environment of *harlot* and *Harlequin*. *Harlot*? Well, perhaps, but Harlequin, a buffoon, rather than a warrior. Is it possible? We will see.

Harlequin

Harlequin, Italian Arlecchino, one of the principal characters in the Italian *commedia dell'arte*, a witty amorous servant, captivated audiences for centuries. His mask and tight-fitting costume made him immediately recognizable. He was a buffoon, a combination of naïveté and shrewdness, stupidity and common sense, Columbine's lover, a servant always in trouble for one reason or another. In England, Harlequin played a noticeable role in the literary life of the Elizabethan period, that is, at the close of the sixteenth century, but in Padua, Italy, he entertained spectators almost a century earlier. Though he ended up as a memorable character in Leoncavallo's tragic opera *Pagliacci* (1892), traditionally, unlike Leoncavallo's character, he never sings or speaks, and some mimes achieved greatness while impersonating him. It follows that he came to the theater world not from *commedia dell'arte*, with its famed art of improvisation, but from pantomime.

Predictably, it is his name rather than his tricks and *batte*, or *batacc(h)io*, a clublike object, known as *slapstick* (hence our *slapstick*, an illegitimate offspring of the Italian comedy!) that captivated word hunters. Henry Cecil Wyld, the author of an English dictionary containing numerous nontrivial notes on word origins, wrote about a hundred years ago that all ideas about the etymology of *harlequin* are mere speculations. This is not true and was not quite true even when Wyld's dictionary was being put together. At least one thing is clear. Though Harlequin reached England from Italy via France, his old name must have begun with an *h*. This circumstance will play a decisive role in our story. Italian lost initial *h* very long ago. The English had no need to add it and would not have done so. When they began to speak about Arlecchino, they, predictably, did not turn him into Harlecchino. It follows, surprisingly, that the original name was not Italian (nor French, for the same reason, but then no one derives it from French).

At least seventeen sources of the mysterious name have been proposed. The number comes from a German dissertation that gives a survey of old scholarship. It is, naturally, not my aim to go over all of them because several present minimal or no interest. Some are memorable only because they serve as illustrations of wild etymologizing. Thus, *Harlequin* has more than once been derived from the name of the French town Arles! Yet it is worth mentioning that a nimble demon in Dante's *Inferno* (XXI, 118) was called Alichino. More likely, *Alichino* is a garbled variant of *Harlequin*, rather than the other way around. If so, Harlequin's name is older than Dante, who was born in 1265 and died in 1321.

In our short survey, we did not miss a mention of a devil residing in hell because that is where this story will eventually end up. The infernal origin of Harlequin may sound incredible to those who have not followed the development of this character and the scholarship devoted to it, but, as early as 1844, Jacob Grimm, the elder of the two world-famous brothers and the founder of medieval Germanic scholarship (language, literature, myths, laws, and folklore), suggested that *Harlequin* is an alteration of German *hellequin* "little hell." If so, *-quin*, like *-kin*, would be a diminutive suffix, as in *manikin*. Grimm seems to have looked in the right direction, but both the meaning (little hell?) and the form he reconstructed inspire little confidence.

With some regularity, the ghost of King Charles Quint appeared in the studies of Harlequin. Charles V (1500–1558), Holy Roman Emperor, was a famous personality, and a merry old soul was he, a great fighter and traveler. According to the traditional explanation, he acquired the nickname Arlequin, "as he delighted in meddling, like Harlequin, in the affairs of others." At one time, Max Müller (1823–1900), a renowned mythologist and linguist, found this source of Harlequin's name worth mentioning, but the king's soubriquet only shows that, in the sixteenth century, the word *Harlequin* was known far and wide.

Another temptation to an etymologist is the existence of Erlkönig, celebrated in Goethe's ballad and Schubert's song. In it, a man rides with his son who imagines that he hears and sees the king of the forest calling him, inviting him, tempting him with rich gifts and the love of his daughters. The distracted father tries to explain to the youngster that it is only the wind or the mist, that no forest king lives there. He flogs the horse, hurries, and finally reaches home, to find the child dead in his arms.

The source of that plot is the Danish ballad *Elveskud* (*Elve-skud* "Elf-shot"), one of many tales about the evil and vindictive elves destroying people. The original text reached the German poet and philosopher Johann G. Herder in the form *Ellerkonge* (an assimilated form of *Elvekonge*), which he misunderstood as "Alder-King." The mistranslation was perpetuated by Goethe. In the oldest version of the story, an elf-*daughter* keeps tempting the *rider*, not the rider's son. The English public tends to remember elves mainly from Shakespeare's *Midsummer Night's Dream*, but those are playful, even if mischievous products of British folklore. They are quite different from their Scandinavian namesakes, friendly or dangerous as the case may be.

There is nothing for Harlequin to do in Goethe's enchanted forest, but, curiously, we keep running into fear-inspiring creatures the moment we begin to chase Harlequin. Divine and demonic names often sound alike across the entire Eurasian continent, sometimes by chance, sometimes because the powers beyond our control are usually thought to be menacing. The feared Turkic (and broader: Siberian) Erlik-khan, a demon of death, has been cited in connection with Harlequin, but the coincidence is probably due to chance. In Old French, the word that interests us was spelled *harlequin* and *hellequin*, both with minor variations. It survived in some French dialects as the name of the evil will-of-the-wisp. In Dorset, southwest England, *harlican* is (or was) an abusive term for a troublesome youngster. Its occurrence in Thomas Hardy's novel *Jude the Obscure* was noticed long ago. It follows that the variation *rl ~ ll* in Harlequin's name should be taken in stride, perhaps even for granted.

We are now approaching the solution of the riddle. In 1937, Hermann M. Flasdieck, a German philologist and a first-rate expert in the history of the English language, brought out a book on Harlequin. It first appeared as a long article (125 pages) in the periodical *Anglia*, which he edited. Flasdieck explored all the hypotheses about the origin of this figure and came to what looks like an almost irrefutable conclusion. I don't know how many months or years he spent while writing that book, but when he had completed it, he discovered a short 1935 essay on the same subject and with the same conclusions by the outstanding American philologist Kemp Malone. He added a few paragraphs recognizing Malone's study, whose contribution did not make his own detailed survey redundant.

In broad outline, the devious history of *Harlequin* was known long before 1934, as the entries in such fully reliable reference works as Walter W. Skeat's *An English Etymological Dictionary*, the *OED*, and the *Century Dictionary* show, but none of them was quite sure of the name's exact origin and formulated their conclusions as probable or at least possible. Above, I have quoted Henry Cecil Wyld's pessimistic formulation on this score and registered my disagreement with it.

Incidentally, among the authorities, the *OED* mentioned Carl A. F. Mahn. All those names—Wyld, Flasdieck, Malone, and Mahn—mean nothing to the public. Very rarely does a philologist become known to the wide world and is not forgotten soon after his or her death (except of course in professional circles). Posthumous fame followed the Grimms (because of the tales they published), Noah Webster, to a much lesser extent James A. H. Murray (the *OED's* first editor), and perhaps Jean-François Champollion, the decipherer of Egyptian hieroglyphs. But, in 1864, Mahn revised the etymologies in Webster's original dictionary, and his contribution was valued so highly that that edition was known as Webster-Mahn, not a mean honor. Beginning with Jacob Grimm, all serious investigators derived the buffoon's name from Germanic, even though the theater that made the figure famous is Romance. But Flasdieck and Malone showed that the source was not just Germanic but English.

For the record: the word *harlequin*, without capitalization, first occurred in the 1092 *Ecclesiastical History* by Orderic(us) Vitalis (1075–c. 1142), an English monk (Vitalis is a late monastic name). He, naturally, composed his important book, now available in translation, in Latin. Orderic recounted the experience of a certain priest, also an Englishman, who, while in Normandy (i.e., in northern France), met the *familia Herlequini*, a troop of damned souls from hell. Their leader had a club and was terrible to look at. Walter Map (1140–c. 1209), another English cleric and author, possibly of Welsh descent, also heard about the existence of the creature and in his work *De Nugis Curialium* "Of Priests' Trifling Occupations" (look up the English adjective *nugatory!*) spelled the name as *Herlething*. The copyist must have misread the original word *Herleching*, that is, *Herleking* (the spelling of *ch* for *k* was not too rare in Middle English). Map did indeed tell a story of King Herla, allegedly, an old king of Britons and (!) the leader of the Wild Host.

The story of the Wild Host goes back to antiquity and shows remarkable longevity. Modern folklorists recorded it widely in the Germanic-speaking world. In the extant legends, the troop consists of dead people (not sinners from hell!) led by a horseman named Wod(e). This name reminds us of the god Wotan ~ Wodan (Scandinavian Othinn). *Wode* has nothing to do with *Harlequin*, but the tale is the same. The Roman historian Tacitus, who lived in the first century CE, already knew one version of it. He even mentioned the warriors Harii, resembling "the family." In French, the troop is known as *la mesnie Hellequin* (with several variants; *mesnie* means "family").

Two circumstances troubled etymologists. First, the variation *ll* ~ *rl* in Harlequin's name. That is why some researchers believed that *hell* is the name's root. We have dealt with this problem above. Second, the variation *-kin* ~ *-king* misled them, and even Jacob Grimm considered the possibility of *-kin* being a diminutive suffix. This circumstance has also been touched upon earlier. Hermann Flasdieck went a long way toward clearing the ground in both cases. By contrast, Kemp Malone spent no time on these problems. The solution seemed so obvious to him that he did not bother to refute his deluded predecessors. Such was his choice, but being apodictic is perhaps not the safest way of convincing opponents, and, in etymology, clearing the ground is crucial. Thanks to Flasdieck's painstaking analysis of every detail, we may say something that is exceptionally rare in the study of word origins: namely, that the solution he offered is not merely clever, ingenious, highly probable, or (the worst of such epithets) thought-provoking, but correct.

The Wild Host is the same as the Wild Hunt. The modern legends of the horseman Wode refer to some hunt. Surprisingly, the procession, though frightening, is hardly ever dangerous: one should only keep out of its way. We may remember that the eleventh-century witness of the hunt was also unharmed, just frightened. In the older scholarly literature, one can read that the belief in the Wild Hunt has a meteorological foundation: a powerful storm allegedly evoked images of a furious procession of airborne spirits. But, more likely, the procession was believed to have caused tempests: the Wild Hunt might be primary.

All this sounds convincing, but where does Harlequin come in? Herla King was a pagan demon, whose name referred to war. Predictably, after the conversion to Christianity, Herla was associated with the Devil, but the Devil of folk belief is a complicated figure. One of his functions is to dupe people by promising gifts in exchange of salvation (the Faust plot). Yet quite often the Devil and imps are outsmarted by the clever protagonist. This is how he acquired the role of a trickster, successful or frustrated, another complex figure, because his functions vary between those of a wily deceiver and a culture hero. One short step separates a trickster from a buffoon.

Ordericus Vitalis said that, in Normandy, no one would believe his story. Yet the English demon did cross the sea and became domesticated in northern France and beyond. Predictably, his name lost the initial *h*. From France the *h*-less Arlequin traveled to Italy, to end up as a major character in the pantomime of the early modern period. In Shakespeare's England no one recognized that descendant of their own old demon. Arlequin is still untrustworthy, still a trickster, and his black mask reminds us of his long-forgotten infernal origin.

A Few Obstreperous Demons

Enter multifarious devils, these heroes of so-called lower mythology. Unexpectedly, *boy* occupies a prominent place in this crowd. Two words seem to have merged in the history of English: one denoted a male child and the other a supernatural creature of dread. Male infants, even the most intractable ones (*boys will be boys*, we once used to say), will not concern us here, but perhaps we should not miss the exclamation *at(t)aboy* and the less dramatic *(oh,) boy!* Some facts from early Modern Dutch seem to point to the original status of both as (mild?) curses: devils, not children were invoked. At the end of the fifteenth century, youngsters in the streets of Amsterdam used to throw stones at one another and shout "Boye, boye, egellentir." *Tir*, the second component of *egellentir*, possibly seems to have meant "animal," and the first possibly stood for "hedgehog." Apparently, we are dealing with two gangs: one was called "Boys," that is, "Daredevils"; the other, not improbably, "Hedgehogs." The rock-throwing youths encouraged one another by shouting their gangs' names in the same spirit in which modern fans encourage their teams at games. This is not an isolated Middle Dutch example of this type.

English *boy* "devil" has disappeared from English, but perhaps it has found its last resort in hunters' language, in which it means "hunted animal." Other calls to the dogs (besides *ataboy!*) are *hoicks a boy!* and *yoicks Bewmont. Bewmont* looks like a fanciful extension of *boy*. These, then, are the possible relics of the once common word *boy* "devil."

We find ourselves on firmer ground when we note that, all over Eurasia, the combination of *b ~ p* with *o* and *u*, often followed by *g* and *k*, produces the names of devils, ghosts, and other supernatural creatures. *Boo* alone suffices to scare a timid soul, someone who, according to one old idiom, cannot say *boo* to a goose. The braver ones hiss and boo in a theater or at a meeting. Booing creatures make a lot of noise, and so do some inanimate things. Russian *boi-* is the root of several words for boasting and fear, Modern Dutch *bui* means "squall," Old English *boia* meant "to boast" (Modern English *boast*, we observe, also begins with *bo-*), and the number of such nouns and related verbs—in Germanic, Celtic, Slavic, Latin, Greek, and Sanskrit—is almost endless.

Here are a few characteristic examples: Swedish *troll-* or *trullbacka* "witch," English regional (i.e., dialectal) *bog* "boastful," *bug* (such as we find in our computers), Russian *buka* "bogeyman," and Swiss dialectal *boi* and *bögk*, alongside English *bogeyman* and *boggle*, all meaning the same. I suspect that *bogus* belongs here, too. The word surfaced in nineteenth-century American English. In 1827, it was applied to an apparatus for coining false money. A nice coinage, we may say. It probably existed in some dialect and stayed dormant until it turned up in criminal slang. At present, this obnoxious devil produces all kinds of suspicious things.

Knowing nothing about golf, I notice that the number of strokes a good player may be supposed to need for each hole is called Bogey, allegedly from an imaginary partner Captain Bogey, a twin of the familiar demon. The *Oxford Dictionary of English Etymology* notes that *bogey ~ bogy*, dialectal *boggart*, and the verb *boggle*, all recorded since the sixteenth century, seem to be connected with *bug*, but the connections of the group are uncertain. They will never become more certain than they already are. Metaphorically speaking, we witness a huge mass of rootless mushrooms on a stump (mushrooms, it should be noted, have no roots), but nevertheless constituting a family.

Apparently, the demons mentioned above tried to scare and deafen people, and the words denoting them are sound-imitating, or, to use a technical term, *onomatopoeic*. That is why it is so hard to pinpoint their place and time of origin: they are panhuman and can be coined in any language in any century. Moreover, they can appear, disappear, and reemerge in the same or similar form. One wonders whether some of those "twins" (like English *bogey* and Russian *buka*, for example) arose independently of each other or whether perhaps at least a few are borrowings. Their history resembles the history of baby words. For instance, *mama* is a near-universal word for "mother," and some other kin term (*baba*, *daddy*, and so forth) are of the same type. They were coined by grownups in imitation of their infants' babbling. Incidentally *babble* belongs here, too.

Many names of otherworldly creatures refer to their ability to inflate, rather than to making loud noises, because monsters and bogeymen frighten their victims not only by deafening them but also by their huge size. They may become so angry that they burst, Rumpelstiltskin-like. Not unexpectedly, some such words have nothing to do with demonology, but they belong here in some vague way because the objects they denote can puff up, spread, or look big. Such are *bud*, *body*, *butt*(*ocks*), *button*, *bubble*, *pug* (Low German *Pogge* means "frog"!), *pack*, *pock*, *poke*, *poodle*, *pot*, and so forth, with numerous similar formations in German, Scandinavian, and elsewhere. Being swollen and being noisy are often inseparable.

Here we may ask whether Puck belongs to that group. The word emerged in Old English as one of the names of the Devil. Later, the name was applied to a mischievous sprite, also called Robin Goodfellow and Hobgoblin, about whom more is said above. As could be expected, Puck has close relatives elsewhere, namely in Old Norse and Celtic. It is not clear whether the Old English word had a short or a long vowel in the root. The modern pronunciation of *Puck* suggests a short vowel, but Puck's lookalikes in Old Icelandic, Irish, and Welsh point to length, and in English dialects, *Pook* and *Pooka* turned up, a possible doublet of *Puck*. Perhaps the original form was closer to *Pook*, reminiscent of Winnie the Pooh. We observe that such a northern demonic creature existed in people's imagination, but its place of origin is impossible to pinpoint. I suspect that *Puck ~ Pook* impressed people by its ability to grow rather than by deafening them.

One more supernatural creature is perhaps worthy of mention here. English *pixy* "little fairy" is a west country word (Cornwall,

Devonshire). And it would be tempting to detect "little Puck" in it. But its initial form seems to have been *pisky*, and its Scandinavian look-alikes also have *-sk-* in the middle. Since in the south of Sweden, *Pus* "devil" is known, *pisky* seems to contain the root *pus-* and the very common diminutive suffix (*-ky*, *-ke*). If *Pus*, like *Puck*, was sound imitative, the two devils are "cousins." Some researchers think that *pixy* is of Celtic origin (just as they trace *Puck* to Celtic) but do not advance persuasive arguments for their conjecture. Still another possibility is that *pixy* is a phonetic variant of *pisky*: *ks* and *sk* occasionally play leapfrog (e.g., *dusk* goes back to Old English *dox*). We are on safer ground with regard to the noun *pickle* "urchin." This word is of Low, that is, Northern German (possibly, Frisian) descent, and its earliest meaning must have been "little Puck." The last two letters in *pickle* (*-le*) designate one more widespread diminutive suffix, as in dialectal English *puckle* "goblin."

Many roots beginning with a consonant have variants with initial *s*. This enigmatic *s*, which appears across language barriers as well as in seemingly related forms in the same language—*s-mobile*, that is, "mobile s,"—has been mentioned more than once above. Usually, *s-mobile* turns up in dealing with old words, and indeed *Puck*, as we have seen, is old, but *spook* is not. Like *bogus*, it surfaced in American English in the nineteenth century and is believed to be of Dutch origin. If this idea is correct, *spook*, too, must be rather old because American English would hardly have borrowed a word from Dutch so late. Is *spook* really *Pook* with *s-mobile*? I am inclined to think so.

These, then, are the demons lined up to introduce us to a crowd of their relatives: boy, bug, Puck, Bogey, and Spook. But our gallery would be incomplete without their odd relative Tantrabobus, whose name has many variants: Tantrumbobus, Tantraboobs, and so forth. Tantrabobus and the rest are guests from British dialects. They are the names used for noisy children and the noise they make, that is, they designate ruckus, rumpus, or fracas (look up those three words in etymological dictionaries to increase your embarrassment). In American English, Tantrabobus has been attested as a jocular term of endearment.

Whatever the origin of those mysterious words (ruckus and others) and their pseudo-classical endings, Latin is not their source.

Tantrabobus and its kin probably belong with other noise-producing demons. The din must have been so deafening that some people went mad when exposed to it. English *dander* means "to walk around" and (!) "to talk incoherently." Most people know the word from the idiom *to get one's dander up* "to become furiously angry." The Dutch origin (among a few others, hardly deserving credence) has been proposed also for this word. In Old High German (the German language roughly before 1200), *tantaron* "to be out of one's mind" turned up. It is amazing how old some such words are and how late most of them were recorded from all kinds of nondescript sources. *Tantra-* took care of the noise effect, but coupled with *-bobus*, the name could grace any demon.

In the *English Dialect Dictionary* by Joseph Wright, the mysterious triad *antrims ~ antruns ~ anthrun*, a close synonym of *tantrum*, occurs. *Tantrum* has the variant *dandrum*, defined by Wright as "a whim, a freak, ill-temper." Dutch *dunder* means "thunder," but there is no certainty that the *dander ~ dunder* group is of Low German origin. *Dunderhead* means "fool," and, even if *dunder* in it means "thunder," the reference is to someone deafened by a lot of noise. Quite possibly, two words coalesced here: some old noun for "din," as in *Tantrabobus*, and a Low German (or Dutch) word for "thunder."

I am sorry that I cannot explain the etymology of *dandruff*. Dandruff, often shortened to *dander*, is a great nuisance, but it has nothing to do with noises. There is no certainty that this compound is *dand-ruff* rather than (less likely?) *dan-druff*. The word was recorded in English texts in the middle of the seventeenth century, and next to nothing is known about its origin. By way of compensation, I would like to suggest that in the universally condemned idiom *to get one's gander up*, *gander* is perhaps a scurrilous replacement of *dander* in *to get one's dander up*. Since long ago, *gander* has been a facetious euphemism for "penis; amorous man," as follows from the narrator's peregrinations in the nursery rhyme about the innocent-sounding goosey-goosey gander, who (which) ended up in his lady's chamber. This idiom was also coined in America.

Demonology is rich, and we'll go to the next horror chamber expecting more encounters with supernatural beings.

9

Our Habitat and Disposable Stuff

House and Home

It is astounding how mysterious the origin of some such simple words as *house* is. They are old, even ancient. Over time, their form has changed very little, and sometimes not at all, so that we do not have to break through a thicket of sound laws to reconstitute their initial form. They have been monosyllabic for millennia, and, even in the reconstructed protolanguage, they were only one nonradical syllable longer. Yet, two thousand years ago, they would have puzzled an etymologist as much as they do today. Conventional wisdom suggests that to call a man a man and a house a house, people chose some easily available language material; yet we can seldom recover it.

If we look at the origin of such well-known words for "house" as French *maison*, Italian *casa*, and Russian *dom*, we will see that they once referred to covering and hiding somebody or something or to being "put, fitted together." Users of English dictionaries will find some information about them in the entries on *mansion*, *case* "holder," *casement*, and *dome*. Going further, they will discover the current connection between Latin *domus* and English *timber* and *tame*. In light of such facts, the etymology of *house*, recognized by most language historians, even though sometimes with an ill grace, makes sense.

The oldest recorded form of *house* is *hūs*, with long *u* (long *u* is the vowel we hear in Modern English *too*), and it seems to be related to the verb *hide* (Old English *hȳd-an*: *ȳ* is the umlaut of *ū*) and through it to the noun *hut*. Even though *hut* came to English from French *hutte*, French borrowed it from Old High German *hutta ~ huttea*. Therefore, the comparison (*house ~ hide ~ hut*) is, in principle, legitimate. Trouble comes from the final consonant *-s*, for, if *hide* and *hut* are cognates, one expects *-t* or *-d*, rather than *-s*, at the end of *house* (*hūs*). Though the riddle has not been solved in a perfectly convincing way, some hypotheses look acceptable. (Not improbably, final *s* and *d* alternated in this root.) We have a better chance of finding out what kind of a place the speakers of Old Germanic called *hūs* than of disentangling the consonants.

In the fourth-century Gothic text, which is a translation from Greek of the New Testament, *hūs* occurred only as an element in the compound *gud-hūs* "(Jewish) temple." (*Gud*, of course, means "Christian god"; Germanic also had several words for "pagan temple.") In Gothic, the word for what we today call "house" was *razn*. It corresponded to Old English *ærn* ~ *ern*, still preserved in *saltern* "salt works" and *barn* (*b-* appears to be all that is left of *bere* "barley": the barn must have been a place for storing barley; this etymology has been challenged but looks plausible).

The Old Icelandic cognate of *razn* was *rann*, and it, too, lingers in English as the first element of *ransack*, originally, "search for plunder," a borrowing from Scandinavian. There also were other Gothic words for "house," namely, *gards* and *hrot* (English *yard* and, quite possibly, *roost* are related to them). No doubt, all of them referred to different structures and buildings, but we should note only one thing: the oldest Germanic family hardly lived in a place called *hūs*.

This conclusion is borne out in a rather unexpected way. There must have been something special about the function or appearance (or both) of the Germanic *hūs* that distinguished it from its counterparts elsewhere because the word for it made its way into Old Slavic. The Slavs lived in a *dom*. The *hūs* served other purposes. Since the borrowing goes back to a remote past, we may assume that the word taken over from the Germanic neighbors meant in Slavic approximately or even exactly what it once meant in the lending language. The noun in question is extant practically all over the Slavic-speaking world (though more often in regional dialects than in the Standards). The present-day senses of its reflexes do sometimes mean "house" and "home," but those senses are swamped by "earth house," "hut" (as in obsolete Polish *chyz* and Russian **khizhina**; I have highlighted the stressed root), "the place for building a house," "a winter shed," "a shed in the woods," "storehouse," "hayloft," "marquee," "barn (granary)," "closet," and "storehouse." Thus, we find all kinds of names for "outbuildings." Even "monastery cell" occurs in the list, and, characteristically, this meaning was ascribed to Gothic *hūs* (allegedly, a one-room structure) in *gud-hūs*. If originally *hūs* denoted a place for temporary protection of people from the elements ("a hut") or for sheltering grain and other things, the connection of *house* and *hide* looks unobjectionable. As noted, it is only the last consonant that spoils the otherwise rather neat picture.

Old Germanic had three grammatical genders, and the word *hūs* was neuter. It is still neuter in Modern German (*Haus*). The assignment of *hūs* to this gender might be an accident of grammar, but it might be caused by its sense. Two circumstances made me mention the fact that *hūs* and, incidentally, both Gothic *razn* and *hrot* were neuter. First, the situation in Icelandic comes to mind. What was called *hús* in Old Icelandic (in that language, *ú* designates a long vowel, that is, *ū*, not stress) was not a separate building but a string of "chambers" that made up the farmhouse. Next to the living quarters, often without a partition, a sheepfold was situated; in winter, sheep's breath served as "fuel" and warmed the room. Therefore, I wondered whether perhaps the old *hūs* looked like the medieval Icelandic farm, with the word being coined as a collective plural. Later, a singular may have been formed from it. This would have been a common process: neuter plurals quite often developed into singulars.

Then there is the word *hotel* (French *hôtel*), with its older form *ostel*, from which English has *ostler* "a person taking care of the horses and mules of the guests at an inn." *Hotel* is related to *hospital, hospitality, hospice*, and *host*. The medieval "hotel" first designated any building for human habitation, though the modern sense is also old. I am not jumping to conclusions, but, to return to the statement above, it so happens that in my work I, on various occasions, keep encountering neuter plurals, and, to the best of my knowledge, in the huge literature on the word *house*, no one asked why the Germanic noun for "house" was neuter. Therefore, I thought that there would be no harm in mentioning this detail.

As could be expected, etymologists spent some time hunting for distant cognates of *house*. A Hittite and an Armenian word have been proposed as related. Neither has aroused much interest and probably for good reason. *House* appears to have been a local (Germanic) coinage, but whether we have discovered its etymon remains somewhat unclear. That is why the most cautious dictionaries call *house* a word of uncertain etymology. May it stay long in its relative obscurity, but it seems quite probable that the Germanic *hūs* protected (covered) the goods and the people "hiding" in it and consisted of several adjoining structures, more or less like the Old Icelandic *hús*.

After reaching some conclusions, however shaky, about the origin of the word *house*, it is only natural to look at *home*. Once again, no convincing answer is in view. *Haims*, the Gothic noun allied to English *home*, occurs in the text of the Bible twice. It glosses two Greek nouns for "village" (as opposed to "town")! This clarifies the idea of what the Goths called home and contains no surprises. Indeed, Modern German **Heim**at means "homeland, native land" (-*at* is a suffix). No less instructive is Old Icelandic *heim-r* (-*r* is an ending) "(the whole) world," though it could also refer to a narrower space. Old English *hām* (with long *a*, as in Modern English *spa*) also denoted a village, an estate, and sometimes a house. The progression was evidently from "abode" to "one's native place." Perhaps the most general senses of *home* have been retained in two Gothic adjectives with prefixes: *ana-**haims** "present," that is, "at home" and *af-**haims** "absent," that is, "not at home" (each has been recorded only once and only in the plural). Dutch has close analogs: *in-heems* "native, homebred" and *uit-heems* "foreign" (*heem* "home").

Perhaps we can also remember the convoluted history of English *hamlet* "small village" (no connection with Shakespeare's hero!). Old English had the noun *hamm* "a piece of pasture land; enclosure; house." The Middle Low [= northern] German cognate of this word, with a diminutive suffix, made its way into French and returned to English with -*et*, a diminutive French suffix! The etymology of *hamm* is disputed, and one can sometimes read that it has been confused with *ham*, the word known from place names like *Nottin**gham*** and *Birmin**gham*** (the same in German: *Mann**heim***, etc.). Allegedly, *hamm* is akin to *hem* "edge." This etymology invalidates the seemingly good comparison of words like *Nottin**gham*** and *Mann**heim***. I have always thought that *hamm* had nothing to do with *hem*: the word, I believed, referred to a place smaller than a "hām"; to emphasize the difference, speakers shortened the vowel. Serious historical linguists treat such guesses with disdain, and I would not have dared to mention mine but for a partial support from Skeat. He indulged in none of my semiotic fantasies; yet he also wrote that *hām* and *hamm* are related. He was a man of rare common sense. (We always tend to agree with those who agree with us, don't we?) Be that as it may, wherever we look, "home" returns us to a village or a piece of pastured land, apparently owned by a village community.

Today, the words of the song "Home, Sweet Home" and phrases like "there is no place like home" epitomize the idea of home quite well, though clearly the beginning was less poetic. Yet one's home, even if not "a castle," is indeed "sweet," and perhaps the idea of the "sweet" comfort associated with one's dwelling need not be old. *Home*, some researchers suggested, is allied to Irish *cóim* "pleasing, pleasant." This connection is often ignored, but I have never seen it refuted. No doubt, the concept of "the place owned by the community; village; settlement" preceded the idea of satisfaction of communal living, but home was as dear to its inhabitants long ago as it is to us. Not a parallel but an instructive case is the Slavic word that means both "world" and "peace." If we remember that Icelandic *heimr* means "world," we will understand that, contrary to the dream of privacy in today's overpopulated, overcrowded world, in the past, being together in a place open to the members of the community and to no one else was the source of peace and pleasure.

Above, I made much of the fact that *hūs* "house" was neuter. The word for "home" was feminine, but it showed a rare irregularity: in Gothic, *haims* belonged to one declension in the singular and to another in the plural. This oddity has a close analog in Greek, and it has often been discussed but never explained. Perhaps the true etymology of *home* will be revealed only when we account for that irregularity and realize that the speakers of Old Germanic looked on *one home* and *a multitude of homes* as different entities.

The old Indo-European root of *home* remains a matter of dispute. At one time, Gothic *haims* was compared with an Indo-European verb for "live." Although phonetically and semantically not implausible, today, this etymology has no advocates. Most dictionaries state that *haims* is a cognate of Greek *kóme* "village" and reconstruct the root with the sense "to lie, to be situated" (other cognates of *kóme* are Latin *civis* "citizen" and Russian *sem'ia* "family"; the latter sounds similar elsewhere in Slavic). However, the path from "lie" to "settlement" is far from obvious. Besides, for *kóme* to match *haims*, its *o* should have gone back to *oi*, and the possibility of this change has been challenged with seemingly good reason. As noted, still other researchers consider the relationship between the word for "home" and English *hem* "edge." I'll pass over some fanciful suggestions, even when they have eminent proponents. Let us rather remember the main things: *home* is a local Germanic coinage (whether it has an ancient Indo-European root is interesting but not very important); speaking about one home and about many homes was marked in a nontrivial way, and, on Germanic soil, *home* probably had positive connotations in the remotest past. By contrast, *house* designated a structure where something could be stored or hidden. Perhaps the difference between them is not so great.

Key

Now that we have looked at the distant history of the words *house* and *home*, it is natural to ask a question about the etymology of *key*. After that, we'll cross the *threshold* and go to sleep in a *bed*. But first we should unlock our habitat.

Key has been known from texts since the year 1000. Yet dictionaries refuse to say anything definite about its distant origin. The reason for specialists' extreme caution is not far to seek. In most cases, a word for *key* means "opener" or "closer" (in the remote past, all kinds of tools were sometimes used for locking and unlocking the door), but *key* cannot be associated with any word meaning "open" or "close." Desperate attempts to derive *key* from Latin *clavis* "key" by eliminating the consonant *l* (*claudo* means "shut, close") were doomed to failure. However, they did not lose their attraction even in the second half of the nineteenth century. Equally futile were the references to English *quay* (from French, from Celtic) and to Welsh *cau* "close, clasp, etc." Several other unpromising hypotheses need not delay us here. The most serious complication in our search consists in that *key* lacks indubitable cognates except *kaei* "key" in Frisian (the old forms and numerous variants in Frisian dialects have also been recorded), and, in the absence of *dissimilar* related words, it is usually impossible to draw any conclusions in etymology.

I'll skip numerous technical details and state dogmatically that the etymon of English *key* sounded *kaigjo-* (*j* stands for what would be *y* in Modern English), and this form excludes many tempting comparisons. German and Dutch scholars have more than once tried to connect English *key* and German *Kegel* "skittle, ninepin," but the match is unsatisfactory from the phonetic point of view. In this case, we have only phonetics to guide us. Consequently, the suggested interplay of *key* and *Kegel* leads nowhere. *Kegel* and most other words that have been used in the hope of shedding light on the derivation of *key* have another flaw: their origin is either equally debatable or even beyond reconstruction.

Let us look at some seemingly promising facts. In addition to the noun *key*, English has the adjective *key* "twisted," as in *key-legged* "knock-kneed, crooked," at present known only in northern British dialects, and even there sometimes few people still recognize it. The verb *key* means "to twist, to bend." Those regional words seem to have come to English from Scandinavian. In Swedish dialects, *kaja* "left hand" occurs. It is allied to Danish regional *kei* "left-hand"; in the Danish Standard, the corresponding adjective is *kejtet*. Old Icelandic *keikja* "bend back" belongs here, too. The left side is often looked upon as weak and deficient. "Left" interpreted as "bent, twisted, crooked" and of course "sinister" is a common occurrence.

The most primitive keys, when they were keys rather than bars, had bits. In many languages, the root of the word for "key" means "curvature." Wattle doors of the ancient speakers of Germanic had openings in the front wall. They were not real doors and did not need elaborate locks. Their function was to keep the cattle from entering some quarters rather than saving the house from burglars. Laws against thieves were severe. I believe that English *key*, both the noun and the adjective, goes back to the same source and belongs with the Scandinavian words cited above. *Key*, it appears, designated a stick, a pin, or a peg with a twisted end. It must have been a northern word from the start. The modern pronunciation of *key* (unpredictably, *key* rhymes with *see*, rather than *say*) may be of northern origin as well.

Before the Scandinavian noun was borrowed, Old English, quite naturally, had a native word for "key," namely, *scyttel ~ scyttels*, allied to the verb *scēotan* "to shoot." (It has been observed that Old English *scyttel* meant "bolt" and that we still shoot a bolt; I can add that the proverb "a fool's bolt is soon shot" was known as early as the thirteenth century!) The disappearance of *scyttel* "key" may have been due to the noun's broad range of senses: *scyttel* also meant "dart, arrow, missile" (i.e., not only "bolt" but anything that could be shot). However, its modern reflex is *shuttle*! The Old Frisian word was probably likewise a loan from Scandinavian. Perhaps the borrowing happened at the epoch vaguely referred to as Anglo-Frisian. The Old English form of the word *key* behaved in a strange way: it could be masculine or feminine, and it vacillated between the so-called strong and weak declensions. All this might be the consequence of the fact that *key* was a guest in the language, and people were not quite sure of its grammatical categories. For the sake of historical justice, I should add that Eiríkr Magnusen almost guessed the source of *key* as early as 1881, but he was led astray by his idea that *key* is a congener of *akimbo*.

If my reconstruction is correct, the word came to English very early, and one wonders why it did not turn up in texts before 1000. Possibly, *key* was first known only in the north and spread to southern dialects much later. Even if both English and Frisian borrowed the word from their northern neighbors, its source in English was hardly Frisian; a Frisian loan would have taken less time to reach Wessex, whose dialect of Old English we know especially well.

But why was the word borrowed? Probably the Scandinavians had keys whose construction differed from those the Angles and Northumbrians used. Here we enter the sphere of "Words and Things," an indispensable field for the etymologist, but we don't know enough about the keys of medieval England to offer an intelligent guess.

Key in place names like *Key West* is an entirely different word. It is an adaptation of Spanish *cayo* "shoal, rock, etc."

Ajar

All modern dictionaries state that *ajar* goes back to the phrase *on char*, literally "on the turn" (= "in the act of turning"). This is, most probably, a correct derivation. However, such unanimity among even the most authoritative recent sources should be taken with caution because reference books tend to copy from one another. Recycling a plausible opinion again and again produces an illusion of solidity and solidarity in an area notorious for debatable results. That is why it is so interesting to read books published before the first edition of Walter W. Skeat's etymological dictionary (1882) and the *Oxford English Dictionary* (*OED*) (1884–1928) came out. After their appearance, the lines of English etymological research hardened, and few people risked questioning the giants' conclusions, though additions and improvements never stopped.

First, let us look at the accepted explanation. As noted, the etymon of *ajar* is said to be *on char* (the earliest citation goes back to 1510; cf. *at char*, 1708: Jonathan Swift). *Char(e)* is related to Old English *cierran* "to turn." Its root can be detected in *charwoman* and *chore*. Today, we remember the latter word only with the sense "an unpleasant task" ("a job of work"), and it usually occurs in the plural (*chores*). Its meaning accords well with that of *charwoman*, even though the cause of the variation *char ~ chore* remains unclear (however, see below).

In its present form, *ajar* surfaced in a printed text only in 1786. For that reason, it does not occur in pre-nineteenth-century dictionaries, and it is absent even from the first edition of Webster's (1828) and its reprints. Later editions listed the word without any derivation, but in 1864, C. A. F. Mahn revised Webster's etymologies, explained *ajar* as *a* + *jar* (a self-evident move), and cited its Dutch synonym *akerre* (*sic*), but he also referred to *jar* "harsh sound." In his opinion, the connecting link between "harsh sound" and "partly open" was provided by Shakespeare's usage: *jar* "a vibration of the pendulum of a clock." However, *jar* "turn" and *jar* "vibrate" are different words, and if *ajar* is related to Dutch *op een kier* (this is the modern gloss for *ajar*), it has nothing to do with a discordant noise. To be sure, when a door is ajar it often vibrates (and, while vibrating, creaks) and turns on its hinges, but only one of the two verbs, namely "to turn," is akin to Old English *cierran*, Dutch *keren*, and German *kehren*. The other *jar* is a sound-imitative verb (or so it seems).

Along the way from *on char* to *ajar*, *ch* must have undergone voicing. James A. H. Murray, while editing the letter A for the *OED*, suggested that the association with *ajar* "in a jarring state, out of harmony, at odds" caused the confusion. In a way, it is a variation on Mahn's idea. The confusion is quite possible, the more so as the Holstein phrase *in de Kirr* indicates both being not tightly closed and creaking (and see what is said above!), but the story of a door at war with itself does not end here.

Later scholars tried to find a phonetic analog of the change. According to a well-known rule, *s* sometimes alternates with *z*, depending on the place of stress in a word: compare *'exhibition* (*ks*) ~*ex'hibit* (*gz*), *'execute* (*ks*) ~ *ex'ecutor* (*gz*), and so forth. In such examples (note the value of *x* in the word *example!*), *s* acquires voice when it stands after an unstressed syllable. It has therefore been surmised that in the string *on char*, in which *ch* also stands after an unstressed syllable, it yielded *j* for the same reason. Even though the events may have developed this way, the question remains open or, if I may take such liberties, ajar. Initial *ch-* hardly ever became *j-* in the history of English. The only two instances may be *jowl* in "cheek by jowl" and *jaw*; neither is certain. To complicate matters, the local variant *jarwoman* "an occasional assistant in the kitchen" exists. One should also bear in mind that English *j-* often has a strong expressive value in both word-initial and word-final position, as in *jig*, *jog*, *job*, *budge*, *nudge*, *grudge* (see p. 36), and many others. To account for its emergence, one does not always need a phonetic law—that is, reference to a rule-governed regularity.

I ventured to attack *ajar* because I would like to point to an amazing, even baffling number of similar-sounding synonyms of *ajar* in the Germanic languages. The closest of them is Scottish *ajee* (also spelled *agee*). It means the same as *ajar* but has a different root. *Gee* (*jee*) is a call to a horse. It also functions as a verb and means (at least in some British dialects) "to move (to one side), stir, alter one's position," as in *fowls go gee* (or *chee*, as it was generally pronounced in Kent!) when they go to roost; the evidence at my disposal is dated to 1875. *Agee* is less limited in its use than *ajar*, for in Scottish, one can also look "agye," that is, aside, while in English only doors and windows can be (or stand) ajar. Then there is British dialectal *ashore* (with the variants *ashard* and *ashare*) with early antecedents. In reference to a door it means "ajar" (this *ashore* is not allied to *ashore* "on a shore"). If *sh-* in *ashore* acquires voice, it will become *ajore*, a form not too different from *ajar*, especially in light of the fact that English *char* alternates with *chore*.

In Low (northern) German, we encounter *enkarich*, corresponding to Dutch *aankerre* (their southern German cognate is *achar*), while Frisian has *in 't kier*. As we have seen, the Old English verb related to *char* was *kierran*. Middle English *k* regularly became *ch* before *i*. Once again, if *ch* in the German, Dutch, and Frisian forms, cited above, acquires voice, we'll get something like English dialectal *ashore* with *j* in place of *ch*. This *ashore*, different from *ashore* "to on the land," may be related to Modern English *askew* (a word of French origin). In any case, it is not a cognate of *ajar* "on the turn." Of the several Icelandic phrases corresponding to *ajar* I'll mention only *á gaur*, with its variant *á gaul* (*á* has the value of *ou* in English *out*). Kentish *chee ~ gee*, English dialectal *jarwoman*, and the Scandinavian *g-* forms weaken the idea that *jar* for *char* in *ajar* is the product of final stress.

As long as we analyze the words featured above one by one, each seems to have an acceptable etymology, but the group in its entirety gives us pause. Is it possible that *on char* (which must have passed through the stage *achar* before becoming *ajar*), *agee* (*ajee*), *ashore* (*ashare*), and *á gaur* are quite unconnected? And whence this fixation on half-open doors? Outside Germanic, it is hard to find even one word with such a meaning. Why was it so important to have a multitude of synonyms for this situation? What superstition is behind such questions? In English regional speech, we find phrases like "Are you from Seaford?" (Sussex) and "Do you come from Topsham?" (Devonshire). In the United States, one can hear "Were you born in a barn?," and in Germany, the question is *"Haben Sie Säcke vor den Türen?"* ("Do you have sacks in your doorway?"). All such questions are asked of those who leave the door open. Apparently, a migratory formula occurs here, and the place name (in the English questions) is more or less arbitrary. In Nottinghamshire, they say: "I see you come from Warsop way; you don't know how to shut doors behind you." Whence this obsession with doors not shut properly?

Perhaps, at least initially, the word(s) referred to doors that refused to close well, and phrases with the senses "askew, aslant, on the turn, on the go, off the beam," to mention some of them, served the purpose well. In English, such doors were also "out of harmony," and this circumstance may have contributed to the survival of *ajar*. Carpenters were employed to make repairs, and the term for "half-open" (or rather, "not closing properly") may have become part of their lingua franca, a common language of wandering handymen. See what is said about the history of *adz(e)*, in Chapter 10. The initial term may have been coined in northern Germany or elsewhere and, once adopted, changed in every land by folk etymology.

I realize how shaky my hypothesis is, but, in my opinion, it is almost unbelievable that so many look-alikes designating a marginal state of a door and a window should have sprung up independently and acquired a similar form. Even if what I suggested here cannot be accepted as the basis of a viable etymology, people may start thinking anew about the origin of the enigmatic English adverb *ajar* and the strange idioms cited above.

Threshold

One does not have to be a specialist to suggest that *threshold* is either a disguised compound or that it contains a root and some impenetrable suffix. Disguised compounds are words like *bridal* (originally, *bride + ale* but now not even a noun as in the past because *-al* was taken for the suffix of an adjective) or *barn*, a blend of the words for "barley," of which only *b* is extant, and Old English *earn* "house." I cited *æren* ~ *earn* in the previous section on *house*. Nor is it immediately clear whether we are dealing with *thresh-old* or *thresh-hold*. Some of our earlier scholars (among them, Franciscus Junius, the author of a serious English etymological dictionary, 1743, and C. A. F. Mahn, the 1864 editor of etymologies in Webster) thought that *threshold* was indeed *thresh + hold*. They were mistaken. An attempt to identify *-shold* with *sill* is a solution born of etymological despair. This Germanic word for "threshold" was opaque as far back as the time of the oldest written monuments.

Stepping over the threshold is an important event in numerous myths. The hero leaves home, and the threshold stays forever behind him. The door of hell may cut off the hero's heel. It is not for nothing that we speak of threshold situations. But the Germanic word for "threshold" does not seem to contain any mythic allusions. It has been recorded in rather numerous forms. Old English had *þrescold, þerxold,* and even *þrexwold* (*þ* = *th* in English *thick*), which shows that the word's inner form made little sense to the speakers. Thus, *-wold* meant, as it more or less still does, "forest." Hence the persistent belief that the threshold is a board or a plank ("something wooden") on which one thrashed. This interpretation survived the first edition of Skeat's dictionary (about which more will be said below) and surfaced in numerous books derivative of it. But *wold* never meant "wood, timber." As a matter of fact, it did not even always mean "forest"; for instance, its Icelandic cognate means "field."

Swedish *tröskel* and Norwegian *terskel* go back to Old Norse *þresk(j)öldr,* which, like its Old English cognate, underwent several changes under the influence of folk etymology; the second element was associated with the Old Norse word "shield." The fact that the threshold has nothing to do with shields did not bother anyone: folk etymology gets its nourishment from outward similarity and ignores logic. The continuations of Old High German *driscubli ~ driscufli* live on only in dialects. The Standard Modern German word for "threshold" is *Schwelle,* a cognate of English *sill,* as, among others, in *windowsill.*

The Scandinavian forms look like the English ones, but those of the Low (= northern) German—Dutch—Frisian area bear almost no resemblance to them. Modern Dutch has *drempel* and *dorpel.* The suffix *-el* causes no problems. The fact that in *drempel* r precedes the vowel, while in *dorpel* r follows it, can be explained away as a typical case of *metathesis*—that is, of transposition of sound (see Old English *þrescold* and *þerxold,* above and compare English *curd ~ crud* or English **burn** versus German **brennen**). An extra *m* in *drempel* need not embarrass us either, for such nasalized forms are plentiful. Thus, English *find* may be allied to Latin *petere* "to seek," and, if it is not, there are dozens of other examples; consider *stand—stood*; though, when one word requires so much special pleading, some feeling of unease cannot be avoided. The English noun makes us think of *thrash* and its doublet *thresh,* while Dutch *drempel* seems to be cognate with English *trample.* Now the threshold comes out as that part of the floor on which we *tread,* rather than *thrash,* though neither *trample* nor especially *thresh ~ thrash* are close synonyms of *tread*. In making this argument, Germans often glossed *threshold* as *Trittholz* (*Tritt* "step," *Holz* "wood").

Jacob Grimm, who sometimes made mistakes but never said anything that failed to provoke and enrich thought, believed that *threshold* designated the part of the house in which corn (grain) was threshed or stamped upon (stamping constituted the primitive system of threshing) and had some following, but Charles P. G. Scott, the etymologist for the *Century Dictionary*, noted that "the threshing could not have been accomplished on the narrow sills which form thresholds, and it was only in comparatively few houses that threshing was done at all." Some time later, Rudolf Meringer, who devoted much energy to researching people's material culture in the German- and Slavic-speaking areas, said the same. He pointed out that, as a general rule, the oldest Germanic threshing floors were situated outside (!) living houses and that the only exceptions could be found in Lower Saxony.

Not without some reluctance, we should accept the conclusion that, in the remote past, the threshold denoted an area next to the living quarters, rather than what we today understand by this word, assuming of course that *thresh-* in *threshold* is identical with *thresh ~ thrash*. However, this assumption seems inevitable. The verb in question could perhaps at some time mean "rub," as shown by the possible cognates of *thrash ~ thresh* in Latin (*terere*) and Russian (*teret'*; stress on the second syllable), not "beat repeatedly and violently." Yet this nicety will only obscure the picture, for the threshold was not a board people's feet "rubbed."

We should now turn our attention to *-old*. The original *OED* cautiously identified *thresh-* with the corresponding verb and called the residue of *threshold* (i.e., *-old*) doubtful. The much later *Oxford Dictionary of English Etymology* shifted accents somewhat: the first element is said to go back to Old English *þerscan*, retained as Modern English *thrash* in the primitive sense of "tread, trample," while the second element is called "not identifiable," which sounds more ominous than "doubtful." The *OED* online adds nothing new. In my opinion, the situation with the second element is not so hopeless.

The famous German linguist Eduard Sievers isolated the ancient suffix *-ðlo* (*ð* = *th* in Modern English **the**). Its existence cannot be put into question, and it is still almost discernible in words like *needle, ladle,* *saddle*, and the rest. Sievers reconstructed the etymon of *threshold* as *þersc-o-ðl(o)*. Old High German *drisc-u-bli* (see above) looks almost like his etymon made to order. In that form, *ðl* changed to *dl* and allegedly underwent metathesis: *dl* to *ld* (a common process: even *needle* has been recorded in the form *neelde*); hence *threshold*.

Bed

In a book like this one, discussing words whose origin is supposedly known (i.e., agreed upon) would be a waste of time. One can look them up in any dictionary or on the Internet. Though the etymology of *bed* has reached the stage of an uneasy consensus, the accepted explanation has recently been called into question. Also, the history of *bed* is so interesting that it may not be entirely pointless to return to this thrice-told tale.

Bed and its cognates have been attested in all the Germanic languages, including Gothic (a fourth-century translation of the New Testament), where it sounded *badi*. The passage in the King James Bible is: "Take up thy bed (couch), and go (walk)." A modern "bed," unless it is a sleeping bag, would be impossible to take up and carry, so that some modern versions offer *pick up* (or *take up*) *your mat* (*pallet, couch*). The relevant place occurs in Luke V:18, 24 and Matthew IX:6. The Old Germanic form must have been *badjo- ~ baðjo-* (*ð = th* in English *this*).

Since the bed that could be picked up and carried was not a modern bedstead, *mattress* makes good sense. Old Icelandic *beðr* meant "bolster; feather bed," and we know from the sagas that beds were indeed mattresses put on benches at night and taken away in the morning. Several words for "bed" exist in the old and modern Scandinavian languages; they are usually unrelated to *bed*. However, "bolster, mattress" is not the beginning of the story. Both language and material culture point to objects quite different from mattresses and pallets.

A first complication comes from the fact that *flowerbed*, *seabed*, and even such a late coinage as *bedrock* have nothing to do with our idea of sleeping. German *Beet*, which is a phonetic variant of *Bett*, is an exact analog of English *flowerbed*, while Danish *bed* means *only* "flowerbed."

It is improbable that such a sense should have been retained and a much more general one ("a place for sleeping") lost over the centuries. The allied forms in Norwegian and Old Swedish denote "lair of an animal; nest." The conclusion suggests itself that the original bed was a place dug in the ground.

This idea seemed unacceptable to Jan de Vries, one of the main etymologists of the second half of the twentieth century. Human beings are not animals, he reasoned. As a result, he preferred to connect *bed* with *bath* and reconstructed the word's original meaning as "warm place." His objection would have carried more weight if he had studied primitive culture with the same attention with which he studied the history of words. But even words examined without any connection to archaeology show how unpredictable the routes for the names of our sleeping arrangements are. English *litter*, a borrowing from Anglo-French (cf. French *lit* "bed") was recorded in the thirteenth century and, predictably, meant "bed." Some time later, the senses "portable couch; straw, etc., for bedding; number of young brought forth at a birth" were recorded. Probably they were known earlier but did not come to light in the extant manuscripts. Reference to "trash" ("things lying about") does not antedate the seventeenth century. Latin *lectus* and Anglo-French *litere* are allied to English *lie*; hence all the attested senses. A common development is from "things strewn, scattered" (*straw* is related to *strew*) to "camp" (i.e., tents, shelters, etc.) and further to "sleeping place" (I translate German *Lager* as "camp," but it is a most inconvenient word to gloss in this context because it means both "camp" and "bed").

For a change, Jacob Grimm did not guess the origin of *bed*. He connected *bed* with *bid* (thus, the place on which one is invited to lie down and sleep). This etymology was repeated several times and then politely forgotten. If I am not mistaken, the first who saw the light in the history of *bed* was Friedrich Kluge, Walter W. Skeat's German counterpart. He connected this word with Latin *fodio* "dig" and received the support of his great contemporaries Karl Brugmann and Evald Lidén. Digging returns us to holes in the ground; however, long before Jan de Vries, this idea seemed indefensible to Wilhelm Braune, another light of Germanic philology. He believed that *bed*, as in *flowerbed*, emerged late. But Kluge's suggestion took root, and, in today's dictionaries, it is repeated as the best there is, though with a usual array of cautious parenthetic adverbs (*probably, apparently*, and the like).

As far as I can judge, the investigations by Hadwig Posch, Harri Meier, Peter Maher, and Johannes Hubschmid make this caution unnecessary. All the works mentioned above, except Maher's, are in German. The latest inroad on this subject, by A. E. Man'kov, is in Russian, and his results are the same as those by Posch and others. The Celtic cognates of *bed* mean "grave," and Peter Maher says the following: "the Germanic words for 'bed' have been generalized to mean 'sleeping place' for the living from an older usage . . . [which] was to name the grave with a word from the paradigm of Proto-Indo-European **bhedh-bhodh* 'cut (especially in the earth' " (an asterisk marks an unattested, reconstructed form). I realize that one needs a complete demonstration to believe the conclusion of this type, and anyone seriously interested in the subject is welcome to open the *Journal of Indo-European Studies* 9 (1981), 341–49, and follow the argument. In my judgment, given the present state of the art, this comes as close to the solution of the origin of *bed* as one can hope for.

It would be unfair not to mention the latest dissident voice, especially because it belongs to Elmar Seebold, the editor of Kluge's etymological dictionary of German. He points out that the second part of Greek *krábbatos* "bed" bears a strong resemblance to the Germanic protoform of *badi*, and this is an interesting observation, but, as he himself notes, nothing is known about the Greek word's origin, so that the next step cannot be made. Also, Seebold believes that "sleeping hole" is an improbable etymon for *bed*. This is true, but he should have looked at "grave," not "sleeping hole," the more so as he mentions Maher's article in the list of the works he used. He also observes that the succession of the consonants *b-d* in the protoform suggests a word imitating the sound of trampling. A similar onomatopoeic origin has been proposed for English *dig*, as well as for *path* and its German cognate *Pfad*. Cutting and digging were certainly associated with trampling, and *bed*, like dig, can indeed be sound-imitative, but this circumstance does not invalidate the conclusion that beds were once graves. Another of Seebold's ideas that, given the complexity of the problem, *bed* can be accounted among substrate words (i.e., a loan from some indigenous pre-Germanic language) carries little conviction for the lending language remains a mystery.

In German, they say that high climbers and deep swimmers never grow old and don't die in their beds. By contrast, most etymologist do. It is their problems that never grow old.

Dregs

It is amazing how rich the vocabulary of junk is! This verbal riffraff is sometimes native and sometimes borrowed, as if the native resources for describing refuse were insufficient! It is amazing how many words English has for things thrown away or looked upon as useless! The origin of some such nouns is transparent. Obviously, offal is something that falls off, but even this word was borrowed from Dutch *Afval* (and compare German *Abfall*). Other histories are more intricate. *Litter* started its life in English with the sense "portable couch." Next, we find "straw for bedding" (hence "number of young brought forth at a birth": "a litter of puppies, kittens, pigs"), and finally, "trash." The ultimate source is Medieval Latin *lectus* "bed," recognizable from French *lit*. What a sad process of degradation! Some such words pretend to be related, for example, *dross* and *trash*, but they are not. *Dregs* and *dross* begin with *dr*, while *trash* begins with *tr*. One is tempted to posit a common origin for all of them, but it is better not to yield to this temptation, even though, as we will see, the prominent role of initial *tr* ~ *dr* in this group is hardly due to chance.

Dross goes back to the root one finds in the Old English verb *drēosan* "to fall." This makes sense: what falls off becomes offal. Some things drop with a loud noise, so that *dr-* in *dross* may be sound-imitative. In dealing with sound-imitative words, one never knows where to begin and where to stop. Old English *drēosan* "to fall" reminds us of *drizzle*, but *drizzle* surfaced in texts only in the sixteenth century, and one wonders what to do with such a late relative. It has a synonym and two look-alikes, namely, regional *dozzle* "to drizzle; confuse" (different meanings of the same word or homonyms?) and *sizzle* and *fizzle*, both obviously sound-imitative. To complicate matters, *fizzle* is known to have come to English from French: words of this type sound alike all over the world. Another word that turned up late (only in the fifteenth century) is *drowsy*, not inconceivably akin to *drēosan*. *Dregs*, unless used figuratively, means "sediment, lees." Apparently, no sound imitation here despite initial *dr*.

This short introduction will prepare us for what follows, especially for the discussion of the origin of English *trash*.

Trash

This word surfaced in English only in the sixteenth century. The original *OED* refused to commit itself to any etymology, but it did mention an array of similar Scandinavian words having approximately the same meaning. As a rule, borrowing from Scandinavian into Middle English goes back to a much earlier period, and that may be the reason James A. H. Murray, the *OED*'s first editor, showed such restraint. However, a few Scandinavian words did make their way into English (or at least into English texts) relatively late. Be that as it may, the *Oxford Dictionary of English Etymology* (1966) removed the doubtful Scandinavian look-alikes and made do with the curt statement "of unknown origin": safe but uninspiring.

Below, I'll quote the entry *trash* from the latest (1911) edition of Walter W. Skeat's *A Concise Etymological Dictionary of the English Language*: "The original sense was bits of broken sticks found under trees. . . . Cf. Icel[andic] *tros* rubbish, twigs used for fuel; Norw[egian] *tros* fallen twigs, half-rotten branches easily broken; Swed[ish] *trasa*, a rag, tatter, Swed[ish] dial[ectal] *trås*, a heap of sticks. Derived from the Swed[ish] *slå i tras*, to break in pieces, the same as Swed[ish] *slå i kras*, to break in pieces; so that *tr* stands for *kr*, just as Icelandic] *trani* means a crane (see **Crane**).—Swed[ish] *krasa*, Dan[ish] *krase*, to crash, break; see **Crash**. *Trash* means 'crashings,' i. e. bits readily *cracked* off, *dry twigs that break with a crash or snap*." In 1910, Skeat wrote a long article about the word *trash*, but his point was that, alongside the noun *trash* "refuse," the verb *trash* "to impede, hold back" exists, a word of French origin. That verb needn't interest us here.

Long before the publication of *The English Dialect Dictionary* by Joseph Wright, a work of perennial value, a correspondent to the

British biweekly *Notes and Queries* (3/IX, 1866, p. 400) noted that, in Suffolk, *truck* means "odds and ends; miscellanea; rubbish." A child "too fondly devoted to sweetmeats" is told not to eat "such nasty truck." Is this another variant of *trash*? The Scandinavian hypothesis of the origin of *trash* looks attractive despite the late occurrence of the word in English texts, but why *trash*, rather than *tras*? Naturally, it has been suggested that the Scandinavian noun was influenced by Anglo-Norman, the version of French spoken in early medieval England. This hypothesis is reasonable but unverifiable.

By contrast, the *tr-* ~ *kr* (*cr*)- alternation to which Skeat referred causes no surprise. We witness it in bird names, which often have an imitative base. In dealing with sound-imitative words, we should always expect variation. The question is whether *trash* is indeed sound-imitative. Skeat mentioned Icelandic *tros* "rubbish." The source of that word is not improbably French *trouse* "baggage," known to English speakers from *trousseau*. The Icelandic synonyms of *tros* are *trys* and (!) *drasl*. *Tros* turned up in books only in the eighteenth century, but *trys* is old. English *dross* has a history of its own.

Trash refers to what we throw away or what goes to waste, what is dismissed and discarded. Other kinds of "trash" are leftovers and lees, the remainder of the valuable part of an object. All kinds of "shavings" are also trash, so that the name for them may go back to various labor activities (such is probably the case of English *trash*). One expects words for "trash" to be "low" and therefore native, but since they often have a derogatory tinge, they travel widely as slang from land to land, like other terms of abuse.

Judging by the facts at our disposal, the origin of English *trash* is not entirely "unknown." Collecting twigs and branches was once an important activity. Those bits were collected "by hook or by crook" (see the later section on the origin of this idiom). In the Middle Ages and some time later, special regulations existed for appropriating such pieces of wood because they constituted valuable "trash." Trash probably did get its name from the crashing sound involved in breaking twigs and branches. The short word *trash* was easy to imitate and told its sound-imitative story. Therefore, or so it seems, speakers of Middle English took a fancy to it. Later, the loanword *tras* passed through many a French mouth, emerged as *trash*, and finally (in the sixteenth century), after many years of existing only in "popular speech" or regional English, turned up in texts. This reconstruction looks reasonable, but the closeness of such unrelated Icelandic synonyms for "trash" as *tros* and *drasl* invites caution.

Rubbish

Words for things wasted or thrown away tend to denote some concrete, narrowly specified refuse and only later acquire a generic meaning. Yet, when several synonyms share the field, they are seldom fully interchangeable. Thus, *trash, rubbish, junk, offal,* and *garbage* either refer to different kinds of discarded objects or have different stylistic overtones. One also notices with some surprise that in Modern English, all such words are borrowings.

Except for Skeat, the authors of other reliable dictionaries inform us that the origin of *rubbish* is unknown or uncertain, even though this word has been current since the fourteenth century. The fourteenth century means Middle English. To be sure, people never stop coining words, but, if *rubbish* had existed in Germanic since time immemorial, it would have had a different look. A loanword? Probably. But before trying to find the source of *rubbish*, we should decide whether it has anything to do with *rubble.*

To the public, etymology is an anonymous area of knowledge. Those who have heard the names of Walter W. Skeat, James A. H. Murray, and Ernest Weekley probably realize that those scholars did not single-handedly find the origin of all the words included in their dictionaries, even though their contributions must have been significant. The less famous figures, to whom the study of the English vocabulary owes so much, belong to history, as the phrase goes, and even professionals seldom refer to them. About 150 years ago, James A. Picton, Abram Smythe Palmer, and especially Hensleigh Wedgwood were well-known to the public (the Internet has preserved the images of Picton and Wedgwood, and I hope that Picton is still remembered not only in his native Liverpool). In the periodical *Notes and Queries*, we can find their conflicting views on the etymology of *rubble* and *rubbish.*

Picton insisted that *rubbish* and *rubble* are, from an etymological point of view, different words. *Rubble*, he argued, goes back to Old French *robeus* or *robows*, which refer to "the stone chippings mixed with mortar used in Roman and medieval buildings to fill in the core of a thick wall. . . . So far as my researches go, I can find no instance of *rubble* having any other meaning than that of undressed stone fragments or chippings. The derivation suggested by Mr. Wedgwood [in his dictionary] from French *repous* is a very probable one. . . . I maintain, therefore, that *rubble* cannot, under any circumstances, be identified with *rubbish*." One can see that *rubble* has never changed its meaning. Picton may have had a point, but *robeus* looks suspiciously like *rubbish*. Also, the evidence at Picton's disposal suggested to him that *rubbish* had appeared in English almost two centuries after *rubble*, but in fact, the two words are almost contemporaneous.

Murray and his circle treated Picton with the respect that scholar deserved, and perhaps the formulation on *rubbish* in the old *OED* owes something to him (mere guessing). In any case, we read there that *rubbish* is of obscure origin, though related in some way to *rubble*, but that there is no certainty that Anglo-Norman *robel* and *ruble*, the earliest attested English forms of *rubble*, are of French origin.

The other school was represented by Wedgwood and Smyth Palmer. I'll skip their musings on chronology and quote Skeat, who, like those two scholars, insisted on the identity of *rubble* and *rubbish* and even defined *rubbish* as "broken stones, waste matter." Skeat looked on Middle English *robows*, *robeux* as the plural of the unattested word *robel*, "clearly represented but Modern English *rubble*." Let us not forget that *robel* did not show up in any text, a circumstance that explains the *OED*'s caution. Skeat went on by saying that *rubble* is *obviously* the diminutive of French *robe* "trash" and cited Italian *roba*, one of whose oldest senses was (alongside "gown" and "robe") "trash." *Robaccia* still means "old goods, rubbish," and *robiccia* means "trifles, rubbish," from *robe*. Every time a researcher, even one of Skeat's stature, says *obviously*, we are probably in trouble. When everything is clear, there is no need to say "obviously." And let me repeat for the third time: *robel* has not been attested. Now, it appears, we should look at *rob* and *robe*, but this part of the investigation can wait because still another hypothesis on the origin of *rubbish* deserves our attention.

In 1946, Leo Spitzer, a distinguished Romance philologist and an astute word historian, pointed to the Old French *reborser*, familiar to English speakers from the word *brush* (*re-* is a prefix). The senses associated with *reborser* are, among others, "to brush the hair the wrong way; stem the tide" and "retrace one's steps." In one of the modern French dialects, *rebroh* and *rebrost* mean "an accumulation of tree branches, tree stumps," the reference being to the debris in a forest. Let it be noted that English *brush* "wood thicket," quite possibly identical with *brush* "utensil," another borrowing from French, appeared in English in the same fourteenth century and meant "lopping of trees." In British English, this noun seems to be relegated to regional speech, but in American and Canadian English, *brush(wood)* is a familiar word. This is Spitzer's suggestion: "The heap of debris to which rubbish originally referred was a pile not of stone [as is the case with *rubble*] but of branches, and the main idea was not that of worthlessness but of obstructiveness."

Updating great dictionaries is slow and sometimes thankless work: no sooner a new entry seems to be ready for publication than someone comes up with another ingenious hypothesis. To exacerbate the situation, in most cases, several perfectly reasonable solutions compete. Did Spitzer guess well? We remember that the earliest meaning of *trash* was "broken twigs." Spitzer, I suppose, did not connect *rubbish* (as he understood it) and *trash*, and hardly anyone else has noticed the similarity. I am not saying that the riddle has been solved, but it would be nice to arrive at a single explanation for *rubbish* and *trash*. *Rubble* would then have its own etymology, even though *rubble* and *rubbish*, close in sound and meaning, may or even must have influenced each other in the course of their long coexistence. If we accept this result, Picton will be vindicated, though not for the reasons he cited. He wrote: "The two words *rubble* and *rubbish*, which are continually confounded, have really nothing to do with each other. Their origin is different, and their meaning entirely separate."

Garbage

Of all the English words for "waste" *garbage* is perhaps the most obscure. Judging by its suffix (compare *cottage, voyage, umbrage,* and so forth), it has a French look. Its appearance in texts does not antedate late Middle English, and its first recorded sense is "offal of an animal, entrails of fowls," which confirms the statement made at the beginning of this short series: though at present, *trash*, *rubbish*, and some of their synonyms refer to "waste matter in general," in the past, each of them had a more concrete sense.

At first blush, *garbage* is the closest kin of *garble* "distort the meaning," the verb that goes back to an Arabic term of Mediterranean trade. It once meant "to remove the rubbish from an imported consignment of spices." For chronological reasons, it could not become the source of *garbage*. The two words were later associated because they sound so much alike, and both have negative connotations. Here again we find ourselves in a sound-imitative quagmire, but in place of *r-b* words, *g-r* and *gr-b* turn up at every step. Such formations refer to grabbing, scratching (like German *krabbeln*), disorderly movements, and the like. French *grabuge* means "confusion; wrangling" and is probably a borrowing from North Italian (though some earlier dictionaries reconstructed the opposite direction: to Italian from French). Incidentally, *grab* is related to Russian *grabit'* "to rob," and we return to *rubbish*, *rubble*, and its obscure kin.

Alongside *garb* "dress" (a Romance word of ultimately Germanic origin: something made, prepared, adorned), English has *garb* "sheaf," a cognate of German *Garbe* (the same meaning). *Garb¹* and *garb²* may be "obscurely related," as dictionaries like to call such cases. Skeat thought that a sheaf was something that could be "grabbed," and German etymologists share this opinion. But *garbage* as "handful" does not sound too convincing. Even if it is correct that *garbage* emerged as a word of sound-imitative origin, with *gr-b* referring to things grabbed, selected, sorted out, and thrown away, such was only the remote beginning of the noun, whose root traveled between Germanic and Romance and which in the Romance-speaking world, too, occasionally crossed language borders.

This is what the *Century Dictionary* says about *garbage* (with the abbreviations expanded here): "The form is like Old French *garbage*, *gerbage*, Medieval Latin *garbagium*, a tribute or tax paid in sheaves, from Old French *garbe*, Medieval Latin *garba*, a sheaf; there may be a connection similar to that shown in German *Bündel*, the entrails of fish, literally a bundle, = English *bundle*. There can be no connection with *garble*, a much later word in English, and one which could not have produced the form *garbage*." Skeat's influence on this etymology is obvious, but the formulation is not trivial, and the result sounds promising.

At this juncture, I would like to mention Dutch *karwei* "entrails of animals given to the hounds." Two excellent etymological dictionaries of Dutch exist. Both give nearly the same explanation of *karwei*. Those explanations would take us too far afield but add nothing to what has been said above because the authors' reasoning is entirely different from that found in English sources. However, once, in 1893, Jacob Verdam, one of the greatest experts in the history of Dutch, compared *karwei* and English *garbage*. The similarity is striking. Are the current explanations of *karwei* a product of folk etymology? Verdam's suggestion has never been noticed, let alone discussed in any detail.

And here comes my plea. While discussing *trash* and its synonyms, I called attention to Leo Spitzer's hypothesis on the origin of English *rubbish*, and now I have unearthed Verdam's idea that Dutch *karwei* may have something in common with English *garbage*. Perhaps someone will comment on the forgotten findings by those two outstanding researchers. Resuscitating valuable ideas buried in the depths of old journals is an important part of etymologists' work. Convincing refutation is as valuable as agreement.

Note

Here are the references to the papers mentioned in the discussion of *trash* and *garbage*: 1) Leo Spitzer, "Three Etymologies." *Philological Quarterly* 25, 1946, pp. 273–77 (see pp. 276–77); 2) Jacob Verdam, "Verklaring van Nederlandsche woorden." *Tijdschrift voor Nederlandsche taal- en letterkunde* 12, 1893, pp. 112–30 (see p. 113).

Those references tell an important story. Pay attention to the titles of both articles: "Three Etymologies" and (in translation) "Explanation of Dutch Words." Hundreds of papers on etymology bear such and other similar unrevealing titles. To find out which words are discussed in them, one has to read or at least look through the entire text. How could even such extremely well-informed scholars as Walter W. Skeat and James A. H. Murray notice the relevant page in Verdam's article?

And half a century later, who would benefit by Spitzer's idea? A bibliography of English etymology, published in 2010 by the University of Minnesota Press, allows any researcher to find the relevant references. The voluminous book features thousands of papers published between 1692 and 2000, with a few items that appeared in 2001–2003. Thanks to this resource, I could find both Verdam's and Spitzer's suggestions.

Gibberish

Gibberish, though not slang, like *hogwash* or *baloney*, is an undignified word because it refers to undignified, unintelligible speech and may therefore have an origin in an attempt to convey the word's "low" meaning by its form. *Gobbledygook* (a witty individual coinage) is a typical example of such an attempt. Popular culture, be it Greek, Roman, or contemporary, produces numerous words and expressions whose etymology puzzles even the contemporaries.

No citations of *gibberish*, which has also been recorded with *e* in the first syllable (*gebberish*) and *-dge* at the end (*gibberidge*), predate the 1450s. The word resembles an adjective (compare *bookish*, *childish*) and also makes one think of the names of languages (*English*, *Pictish*, and so forth). Nouns do not end in this suffix (*-ish* in *radish* and *varnish*, to cite two random examples, only looks like a suffix). The other recorded variants of *gibberish* can be passed over as presenting no interest, except for *guibbridge* (a seventeenth-century form), which indicates the pronunciation with so-called hard *g*, that is, with *g* as in *give*. Though all of us hear a lot of gibberish, the word *gibberish* has low frequency in everyday speech.

The prevailing pronunciation of *gibberish* in today's English (everywhere) is with initial *j*. This has not always been so. Walter W. Skeat, who died in 1912, was not aware of *gibberish* ever having initial *j*. In the middle of the twentieth century, Daniel Jones, the author of the groundbreaking pronouncing dictionary of British English, listed the variant with *j-* as rare. The second edition of the *Century Dictionary* (1911), an American reference work, also favored hard *g-*. By contrast, Henry Cecil Wyld, an Englishman and another outstanding linguist, gave *gibberish* with *j-* in his 1932 dictionary. In the *Oxford Dictionary of English Etymology* (1965), under the verb *jibber*, a variant of *gibber*, both pronunciations appear, but *g-* is the first, while in the 2007 edition of the *Shorter Oxford Dictionary*, the order is reverse. There can be no doubt that the variant with *j-* has won over. *Gibberish* was first recorded in the sixteenth century, and Shakespeare, judging by his pun (*Jupiter-gibbeter* "gibbet-maker" in *Titus Andronicus* IV: 3,80) know the variant with initial *j*. The evidence is confusing. Perhaps when *gibberish* arose, *g-*, rather than *j-*, was at least more usual in it.

If so, a wedge is driven between *gibberish* and the verb *jibber*. Besides, *jibber* was first recorded in 1824, and, if at that time *gibberish* had a variant with *j-*, *jibber* should be looked upon as a back formation on *gibberish* rather than its etymon. To be sure, a word like *jibber* may exist for years before it makes its way into a book, but a gap of nearly five centuries of unrecorded history between *jibber* and *gibberish* is perhaps unbridgeable even for slang. The variation of final *-sh* with *-dge* in *(-i)dge* is trivial. An anthologized example is *Greenwich*, but there are many others, such as *hodgepodge*, a doublet of *hotchpotch*.

The oldest conjectures on the origin of *gibberish* still hold, at least up to a point. These are the facts relevant to our discussion. To begin with, we notice that *gibberish* is surrounded by a considerable number of words like *gibber*, *jibber*, *jabber*, *gab* (the latter as in *the gift of gab*), and *gobble*, all of which refer to rapid chatter. Icelandic synonyms of *gibber* have similar structure and belong to the extended *jibber-jabber* family outside the British Isles. In the 1882 edition of his etymological dictionary, Skeat went so far as to reconstruct *gab-* or *gap-* (as in the verb *gape*) "mouth." Later, he never returned to this bold idea. Second, a few Old French words resemble their English look-alikes and have the same meaning. Stephen Skinner, whose English etymological dictionary appeared in 1671, derived *gibberish* from French *gaber* "to cheat."

Both observations—on the similarity between *gibberish* and *gab-* ~ *gib-* words and on the French connection—are valid. It is therefore possible that we are dealing with loanwords (whatever the direction of borrowing) or with a sound-symbolic formation common to both Germanic and Romance. Here I would again like to mention the contributions of Wilhelm Theodor Braune (1850–1926), a celebrated German philologist. He published a series of articles on the Germanic element in the Romance languages. They appeared in a major journal devoted to Romance philology, and, although the journal was published in Germany and in German, Germanic scholars, unless they study the etymology of French, Spanish, or Italian, have an insufficient knowledge of them. Incidentally, he signed his Germanic works "Wilhelm Braune," while his Romance articles appeared under the name of Theodor Braune. Perhaps he wanted to emphasize his "Romance" orientation in those works, but Jekyll-Hyde games are sometimes confusing. I also realize that authors do not care about the plight of bibliographers. Yet this looks like a nasty trick on the part of someone whose full name, as indicated, was Wilhelm Theodor Braune.

With regard to *gibberish*, Braune had no doubt that the lending language was Germanic. He was probably right because the Germanic *gib-gab* family is larger and more ramified than its Romance counterpart. The words mentioned above may have constituted part of international slang, with Germany being a likely center of dissemination. Leo Spitzer, a very knowledgeable etymologist, thought that *gibberish* was a borrowing of French dialectal *aguibre(e)* "a dull, mind-boggling thing." Since he did not reconstruct the ways of penetration, his hypothesis cannot be of much interest. (I may add that in etymological research, the scholar's expertise sometimes plays a negative role. Spitzer, an outstanding specialist in Romance philology, was prone to finding Romance roots in too many cases.)

Gibberish, pronounced as *jibberish*, is better suited for denoting nonsense than *gibberish* with hard *g*, because, in English, *j* often has an expressive function. This is true, regardless of whether it stands at the beginning or at the end of a word. Here is a fraction of a much longer list: *budge, grudge, drudge, dodge*; *jab, jaunt, jog, jaunt, jitter*, and *jinks*. Most of those words are of unknown or of uncertain origin. *Gibberish* (with *j-*) is in good company, if *grudge, drudge*, and *jitter* can be called such.

Unlike Stephen Skinner and those who came after him, Samuel Johnson, in his 1755 dictionary, believed that *gibberish* should be traced to the name of Geber, an eighth-century alchemist. Apparently, people looked on Geber's technical jargon as incomprehensible to outsiders (as though every unschooled person is expected to understand chemistry!). Johnson's etymologies were never original, and, unlike his definitions and citations, present no interest. Thanks to the research by Gwin J. Kolb and Robert DeMaria Jr. (*Notes and Queries* 243, 1998, 72–74), we now know where Johnson found his idea and can dismiss it as untenable. *Gibberish* is certainly not a derivative of a proper name. It is a formation imitating prattle, but the details of its history remain unclear.

The suffix *-ish* in *gibberish* has never been accounted for. If it was added to *gibber*, one wonders why no early record of this verb has come down to us. Also, no other word designating prattle, babble, chatter, and other kinds of nonsensical talk ends in *-ish*. Perhaps there once was a Franconian word (let us say, *gibber*, a noun) that reached the language of the speakers of Old French. In French, it retained its original meaning but added a suffix and later returned to English with other words ending in *-s ~ sh*, such as *finis ~ finish* and *skirmish*. The French form could have begun with *gi-* (spelled *gui-*) or *ji-* (spelled *gi-*). This is a reconstruction with too few documented elements. The current hypotheses (those mentioned above) are more solid but not wholly convincing because so far no light has fallen on the cause of the word's unstable pronunciation and on the social milieu in which it was coined. Sometimes an etymologist can only present a full picture of available facts and hypotheses and stop on the threshold of a solution. It is a bit embarrassing that, of all words, *gibberish* happens to be a good case of such a situation.

10

Tools, Implements, and Professions

Ax(e) and Adz(e)

By a curious coincidence, both nouns in the title have final *e* in British English but are usually *e*-less in the United States. Despite the difference, the tools' cutting edge is the same everywhere. Since an adz is a kind of ax, the question arises whether the two words are related. It is more profitable to begin with a look at the origin of *ax*. This word's oldest Germanic form is known from the text of the Gothic Bible, translated from Greek in the fourth century CE. The Gothic for "ax" was *aqizi*, that is, *akwizi*. Its cognates (related forms) are Old English *æx* ~ *eax* (*æ* has the value of *a* in Modern English ax; *eax* is a phonetic variant of *æx*) and *æces*, along with Old Saxon *akus* (Modern Dutch *aaks*), Old High German *ackus* (Modern German *Axt*, *-t* does not belong to the root), Old Frisian *axa*, and Old Icelandic *øx*. The Old English and other forms were recorded half a millennium and even nine hundred years later than Gothic *akwizi*. We may assume that the oldest known form is close to the "original" one. Along the way, the word seems to have lost one syllable, though it is not improbable that the earliest West Germanic and the Old Norse forms were always slightly different from the Gothic one. (Old English and its neighbors were dialects of the same ancient language, and dialectal variation is a universal phenomenon.)

Although *æx* was the main Old English word for "ax," it was not the only one. *Taper-ax* has also been recorded, a typical so-called tautological compound: each component means the same (*ax-ax*). This was the name of a formidable weapon, borrowed from Old Norse, where the "tapar-øx" served its purpose very well: one constantly reads in the sagas how enemies' skulls were cloven with its help all the way to the neck. But the medieval Scandinavians did not coin this word: it migrated to them from the Slavs: compare, for example, Russian *topor* (stress on the second syllable). Finnish *tappara* "ax" also goes back to Slavic. Even this is not the end of the journey because the Slavs must have taken over that word from their eastern neighbors: its probable source was (or so it seems) Old Persian *tabar* "pickax." Turkic *täbär* looks amazingly similar. Nor has the ancient pre-Indo-European word *taba* "stone; rock" from Asia Minor escaped the attention of language historians.

Are we dealing with an old migratory word traceable to the Stone Age? Here I may repeat what is written in the later essay on "awl": a study of the names of instruments and tools provides rare and precious insights into the history of civilization. The wanderings of *taba ~ tabar ~ täbär ~ topor ~ tapar ~ tappara* all over Eurasia tell us a good deal about the spread of material culture but little or nothing about etymology. Even if at one time *taba* or *tapa* meant stone, we still do not know what the origin of this word is. Did our remote ancestors go tap-tap-tap with their pieces of rock? Is *taba* a sound-imitative word? We'll never know.

The same question arises in connection with the word *ax*. To be sure, Greek *axíne* "ax" and Latin *ascia* (presumably, from *acsia* "adz") make us think of *acute* "sharp" (from Latin *acūtus*), but is this how the ax got its name? Gothic *aqizi* had three syllables. If, as is believed, its earlier form was approximately *ak-wes-j-ō*, with a suffix (*wes*) meaning "belonging to," perhaps *ax* did mean "something sharp, a member of a class of sharp objects." Long before the nouns of the Indo-European languages acquired grammatical genders, they were classified by their features: soft, warm, round, and so on. This system is well-known from some modern African languages. In Germanic, the word for "ax" (*aqizi*, and all the others) was feminine, and the same holds for Modern German *Axt*. This fact says nothing about the origin of *ax*. Why should axes be referred to as "she"? Because the male owner was so fond of this object? Does "she" in reference to a ship provide an analogy?

A migratory word does not have to be a worldwide traveler. For example, French *hache* "ax" reached France in the twelfth century from its German-speaking neighbors. The etymon was some form like *happja* (Old High German *happa ~ heppa*, etc., the name of a sickle, rather than an ax; Modern German *Hippe* means "pruning knife"). This means that, when we look for the origin of a word like *ax*, we need not concentrate only on its native and foreign close synonyms: a simple association will sometimes do quite well (both sickles and axes cut). Finally, by way of exception, the word we are investigating may be transparent. For instance, another French name meaning "ax" is *cognée*, that is, "fastened with a wedge." At one time, this participle was used with a noun; later, it began to function as a self-sufficient name of the tool. The root is familiar to English speakers from the word *coin*. It meant "wedge" and "a die for stamping money." *Coign of vantage* "a favorable position of observation," revived by Walter Scott, and *quoin* (pronounced as *coin*!) "cornerstone" also remind us of the Latin word.

Armed with such an amount of information, we will approach the history of *adz* with due caution. This history is rather obscure because *adz* does not seem to have any cognates in any language, which probably means that the word was *coined* in Old English. Such words are rather numerous, and nearly each of them is an etymological crux.

The word *adz(e)* surfaced more than once in Old English texts. It had several local variants, and its gender fluctuated: *adesa* was masculine, while *adese* was feminine. Also, *eadesa* and *adusa* have come down to us. Apparently, the tool had wide currency. As we will see, *adusa* may be the form that provides the best clue to the etymology of *adz(e)*. The consonant *s* in all those forms should have been voiced (i.e., *z*), but, until the seventeenth century, the standard spelling was *addice*, and Samuel Johnson, the author of the great 1755 dictionary, considered the spelling and the pronunciation *adze* to be a reprehensible corruption of *addice*. We do not know why *s* in *adesa* and its likes remained voiceless in Old and Middle English. The pronunciation with *z* became the norm only after *i* in *addice* was lost; hence the modern spelling.

The form *atch* turned up in the seventeenth century, and some people who said *an adz* occasionally made the familiar mistake of misdivision and turned *an adz* into *a nadz*. A few other regional forms of *adz* are also known. They are more or less predictable and shed no light on the word's origin. *Adz* has no established cognates, even though it is an old word. Most likely, it was coined "locally" and had no currency outside England. If the speakers of Old English had brought it to their new home from the continent, some related forms would probably have turned up in Frisian, Dutch, or German. Also, the texts in which *adesa* appears owe nothing to the language of the Vikings, and indeed no similar word exists in Scandinavian.

The process of formation must have been simple, and even transparent, and it is reasonable to suggest that its name, a technical term, was coined by those who dealt with it. Although *adz* seems to have been a neologism, quite a few of its possible cognates have been offered: some by over-imaginative authors, others by reliable ones. The search was for words denoting either something sharp or related to manual skills: German *Ader* "vein," German *ätsen* ~ English *etch*, English *thixle* ~ German *Dechsel* "adz" (pay special attention to this pair!), Latin *astutus* "sharp, astute," Latin *ador* "spelt" (a cereal plant) and *asser* "stake," Lithuanian *vedegà* "adz, icepick" (related to Sanskrit *vádhar-* "some deadly weapon"), and a few others.

One look-alike has attracted special attention. In Hittite, a dead language of ancient Anatolia, the word *ateš* (pronounced as *atesh*) occurred. Its meaning has been a matter of debate; at present, it is usually glossed as "ax." This is indeed a remarkable coincidence, but, according to the opinion of the most reliable modern specialist, the Hittite word is not related to *adz*. This conclusion is intuitively correct because, if *adz* were a migratory word, it would probably have turned up somewhere between Anatolia and Anglo-Saxon England. Even if the two forms were related as items of the ancient Indo-European stock, the occurrence of a carpentry term only in Hittite and Old English would have been a minor miracle. A Basque cognate or even the source of *adz* has also been proposed; again, perhaps there is no need to go so far.

In the story of *ax(e)*, among many other words, Old Saxon *akus* turned up. Old English *æces* seems to have developed from some such form. Walter W. Skeat, in the first edition of his etymological dictionary of English (1882), "suspected" that *adesa* was a "corruption" of *aces* or *acwesa*; he should have added *acusa* as a possibility. We now wince at the old term *corruption* (see its use by Samuel Johnson, above!), and indeed, linguistic change is always an act of "corruption." If, however, we substitute *alteration* for Skeat's *corruption*, his idea will look reasonable. Yet we are not told why the original form was "corrupted," altered, or simply changed. That is perhaps why Skeat gave up his early suggestion (it does not appear in the fourth, latest edition), and *adz* joined the long list of words of unknown origin, where it stays to the present day.

Yet, if we begin with Old English *adusa* (rather than *adesa*; *adusa* "ax," as noted above, has been recorded), Skeat's idea may be rescued. *Adusa* resembles Old English *æx* and especially Old Saxon *akus*. In Old English, this similarity was, quite naturally, noticed, with the result that *æx* and *adesa* sometimes even formed an alliterative pair. And here comes my tentative etymology. I believe ("suspect") that Old English *adusa* is the continental *acusa* "ax," with *d* substituted for *c* (*k*) under the influence of some form like Middle Low German *dessele* "adz" (see *thixle* ~ *Dechsel*, above), that is, I suggest that *adusa* was a blend. The blending happened because the names of the two tools were frequently mentioned in single breath, like our modern alliterating *pots and pans*, *sticks and stones*, and the like.

The process of blending can be established only when it is occurring under our eyes. Thus, *sitcom*, *Eurasia*, and *workaholic* are certainly blends. This fact can be "proved" by reference to the memory of the native speakers still living and the dictionaries that recorded the act. A historical blend is doomed to remain a hypothesis. The same holds for my reconstructed blend, but, as the starting point for a further search for the etymology of this word, it will probably do.

Awning and Tarpaulin

The famous sailor Captain John Smith wrote in 1607: "Wee did hang an awning (which is an old saile) to . . . trees to shadow us from the Sunne." This is the earliest citation of *awning* in the *Oxford English Dictionary* (*OED*). In 1609, we find the following sentence: "A trar [sic]-pawling; or yawning." Since Smith considered it necessary to explain what *awning* meant, he did not expect the word to be known to his readership. Yet he must have had some reason for using it because, otherwise, he would have made do with *an old saile*. The use of *yawning* remains a puzzle (a spelling mistake?). By contrast, *trar* is certainly a misprint for *tarre*, which occurs elsewhere. *Awning* and *tarpaulin* appeared in print at approximately the same time, which perhaps suggests that a new way of processing canvas was introduced early in the seventeenth century. Even if this suggestion is true, we do not know who coined the words.

The French for "ell" is *auln* or *aun*. Stephen Skinner, the author of the second English etymological dictionary, brought out his work in 1671. He was a younger contemporary of Captain Smith, and we might expect that, being so close to the events Smith described, he would have had more information about the source of the neologism than we do. And perhaps he did. He also called *awning au(l)ning*. Did he know the word's origin, or was it a clever guess? And why should anyone use a measure of length to name a piece of sailcloth?

This is the comment I received from Mr. Laurel Wilson: "In medieval England, there was an official whose job it was to make sure that linen and canvas were sold in the correct lengths. The lengths indeed were 'aunes' or 'aulnes' and the official was the a(u)lnager. The measurement itself was in use for many different things, but since the aulnager was specific to linen and canvas, it does seem possible that there is a relationship there." Judging by the citations in the *OED*, in Skinner's days the word *a(u)lnager* was still known. It has also been pointed out that, in the food industry, the measure becomes the name. Such are the Italian *cinque e cinque* after the cost of the ingredients: five lire for the wrap and five lire for the inside. The name is extant (e.g., in Tuscany and Liguria) despite the fact that the lire no longer exists. Surprisingly, John Minsheu, the compiler of the first dictionary of English etymology (1617), missed this word, but its absence of course does not mean that he did not know it.

Unsatisfied with Skinner's etymology, researchers continued their exploration. Since Captain Smith said that the awning was hung to trees to shadow people from the sun, *heave*, *haven*, and *heaven* have been tried as the words that might lead to *awning*. But even the most resourceful etymologists did not know how to get rid of the initial consonant: *awning* never appeared as *hawning*, so that reference to dropping one's aitches did not go too far. The suffix (*-ing*) caused little interest. It was the root that bothered most people, though the addition of *-ing* also needs an explanation.

We may perhaps skip the suggestions that *awning* is a borrowing from Hindi or Persian (the latter idea had the support of Walter

W. Skeat, but he soon gave it up) and several other unpromising guesses. The only breakthrough seems to have occurred in 1862. In the area of English etymology, the main contemporary predecessor of Skeat was Hensleigh Wedgwood. Between 1859 and 1885, Wedgwood's dictionary of English etymology was appearing in installments, and George P. Marsh, a distinguished American historical linguist, formed a high (partly undeservedly high) opinion of that work, even though he was aware of its drawbacks. He discussed every installment in *The Nation* and decided to bring out an American edition of "Wedgwood" that would incorporate his corrections. Only the first volume (A through D) came out.

Marsh offered a French etymology of *awning*. Allegedly, *awning* was a reduction of *auvening, auven*, from French *auvent* "a penthouse of a cloth before a shopwindow," as defined in *A French and English Dictionary* by Randle Cotgrave (1611). As we can see, the timing is perfect: with Cotgrave and Captain Smith we are at the beginning of the seventeenth century. Wedgwood found Marsh's idea convincing, but did not reject his own original etymology; he simply added *auvent* as a more likely source of *awning*. In the later editions, he skipped reference to Marsh, and the new etymology was known as his, which is most unfair.

The trouble with Marsh's suggestion is that the posited intermediate forms (*auvening* and *auven*) have not been attested, and *auvent* has never been used as a nautical term. Enter Ernest Weekley, the author of numerous excellent books on the history of English words and of scholarly articles on etymology. His main field was Romance (especially French) linguists. Weekley pointed to the weaknesses of Marsh's reconstruction and cited Italian *alona*, Spanish *olona*, and so forth, all meaning "sailcloth." Cotgrave also featured *alone* "canvas for the sayle of a ship." According to Weekley, "*aulone* . . . instead of *olonne*, may have been mixed up with another *aulonne, aulomne*, which . . . is a woollen cloth named for Alone in Beauce. I suggest, as a pure conjecture, that it is the origin of the *awn-* in *awning*, and that the latter is a sailor's corruption of an unrecorded *aulonning*." Note how close *aulonning* is to Skinner's *au(l)ning*! As time went on, Weekley must have felt disillusioned with his idea because in his etymological dictionary, published fifteen years later, he only said "of unknown origin."

It would have been instructive to learn why he rejected his older "pure conjecture."

Borrowings pose an unavoidable problem. It does not suffice to find a French, Italian, or Persian look-alike of an English word. As long as nouns are concerned, we should explain why the name of a certain object was taken over from a foreign language because words travel with things. For instance, silk came all the way to English from the East, and the word *silk* traveled with it. Few people have encountered the adjective *sericeous* "silky," but the alternations *i ~ e* and *l ~r* tell a story of silk that can be reconstructed in minute detail (not only the word for it but of the once famous Silk Road: the Greek for *silk* is *sēres*), but, as regards *awning*, why French, why Italian? Was awning invented in the Romance-speaking world or imported from there?

Wedgwood, a great master of obscure allusions, wrote in passing that *awning* should be compared with Danish *avn* "awn" without explaining how exactly the two should be compared. Did he mean that an awn, a bristle on a grass spike, hangs like an awning suspended from its support? As early as 1826, John Thompson, the author of the otherwise useless book *Etymons of English Words*, also derived *awning* from *awn* because both, as he put it, in their different ways are coverings or hulls. Wedgwood of course knew the book: in his days, there was very little to read on English etymology. Perhaps that is all there is to it, even though Thomson's derivation is almost too good to be true. Not improbably, in the 1620s, *awning* was nautical slang or part of newfangled professional jargon, and that is why Captain Smith found it necessary to explain the word to lay readers. If *awning* was a coinage by Smith's crew, it is surprising how soon the word became common property.

Tarpaulin, for which the earliest citation in the *OED* goes back to 1607 (thus, another seventeenth-century word), may be less opaque than *awning*. Yet some doubts remain, though Skeat had none. The word, he says, "means *tarred pauling* or *tarred palling*; a palling is a covering, from the verb pall, to cover." But the *OED* is more cautious: "The blackness of tarred canvas may have suggested its likeness to a funeral pall; though, in the absence of any instances of *tar-pall*, this origin must remain conjectural." The reference to *tar* in *tarpaulin* is probably noncontroversial, and the occasional spelling *tar pauling* shows that such was the popular understanding of the word in the seventeenth century.

Curiously, now the connection with *tar* seems to be lost because, in at least American English, *tarpaulin* has been clipped to *tarp*.

Captain Smith used *awning* and *tarpaulin* as synonyms, and it does not come as a surprise that Ernest Weekley devoted some time to both. He suggested that *paulin* is the same word as Middle English *palyoun* "canopy." Its cognate in all the continental Scandinavian languages is *paulun*, a popular variant of *pavilion*. Low German exhibits nearly the same form. Given this reconstruction, *tarpaulin* is half-English and half-Scandinavian (or German, though more likely Scandinavian). We of course wonder where Smith learned this odd hybrid and who combined the components of *tarpaulin*. The captain did not coin this word, just as he did not coin *awning*. *Aulnin(g)* and *tarp-aulin* sound oddly alike (i.e., if we divide *tarpaulin* in a different way!). No one seems to have noticed their likeness, and perhaps it is not worth our attention because the word *tarp* did not exist even in British dialects.

This, then, is what the phrase "of undiscovered origin" means: a thicket of naïve and ingenious hypotheses, none of which is fully convincing but some of which hold out promise. One wonders: should we return to the trodden and abandoned paths? The answer depends on our attitude toward the subject. If we are interested in the origin of words, the more we learn about the attempts to penetrate their past, the more enlightened we come away. In etymology, perhaps more often than in any other historical discipline, people constantly suggest seemingly ingenious hypotheses without realizing that the same hypotheses were offered and rejected or called into question long ago. While retracing the steps of past researchers, we may formulate new hypotheses. The best flowers bloom on dung, and nothing grows on barren ground. Last but not least, history is always breathtakingly interesting for its own sake. We are human because we are endowed with the power of speech. How then can etymology leave anyone indifferent?

Note
See the discussion of *awning* in *Notes and Queries* 2/XII: 248, 299, and 400–401 (the third contribution is by the distinguished scholar Frank Chance); in *Academy* 76, 1919, 760–61 and in *Transaction of the Philological Society* 1909: 275 (the last two publications are by Ernest Weekley).

Mattock

Some of our simplest tools often have undecipherable names. Even when their origin poses no problems to a professional language historian, the answer may come as a surprise. For instance, *hoe* is related to the verb *hew*, but this connection is far from obvious to a modern English speaker. In the course of time, the once apparent ties between *hoe* and *hew* have been severed. The story of *ax(e)* and *adz(e)* (see above) showed how far one should sometimes go to discover the hidden root and how dubious the result of the search may be.

Mattock has been known since the Old English period. In the extant texts, the forms vary: *mattuc, meattoc,* and *meottoc.* The variation of this type need not surprise us. Old English preserved the pronunciation of several dialects, and also scribes were often uncertain about the spelling of the words they knew. There is nothing particularly astounding in those forms. I am saying all this because it has been suggested (wrongly, I believe) that the recorded forms look unusual, even exotic, and that therefore, the word must have been borrowed from some lost indigenous language, or, to use a technical term, from the "substrate."

Before the Germanic invasion, Britain was a Celtic-speaking country. Welsh and Scottish Gaelic forms resembling *mattock* exist, but they may have been borrowed *from* English, rather than serving as the source of *mattock.* This uncertainly in dealing with Celtic and English words is typical, and, not unexpectedly, opinions on the origin of *mattock* differ. To exacerbate matters, even in Celtic, such an obscure word may have been taken over from an even deeper substrate! The Celts were not the first inhabitants of the British Islands. However, nothing is known about the language of the Picts, who lived in what is Scotland today, and, as far as we can judge, mixed with the Celts and forgot their language. Suggestions about the pre-Germanic substrate in the history of English words inevitably resolve themselves into the chilling verdict: "Origin is not and can never be known." Before admitting defeat, we should try to explore all the facts at our disposal.

In its Modern English form, *mattock* rather obviously, though perhaps deceptively, consists of the root *mat(t)-* and the diminutive suffix *-ock,* as in *bullock* "young bull," *ballock* "testicle" (regional?), *hillock,* and a few more nouns. Yet one can easily understand why people need words like "little bull," why a testicle looks like a tiny ball, and why a hill can be small, but the reference to a small mattock makes less sense than, for instance, to a small ax or a small hammer. However, let us assume, even if only for the sake of argument, that -*ock* is a suffix. If necessary, we can give up this idea later.

The most puzzling circumstance, which seems to bolster the idea of the word's substrate origin, is the isolation of *mattock* in Germanic: it occurs only in English. There is no word like it in Frisian, Dutch, German, or Scandinavian, and, if it is true that the Celtic look-alikes are loans from English, the origin of *mattock* begins to look like an insoluble puzzle. To increase our puzzlement, we discover that *mattock* has excellent relatives "abroad," namely, in Slavic: *motyka, motyga,* and the likes (stress on the second syllable). The meaning of the Slavic noun is the same as in English.

Unfortunately, no light will come from the East because Slavic etymologists cannot agree about the word's origin. Quite common is the derivation of the oldest form *motyka* from the ancient root *mat-* "to dig." Sanskrit *matyá* "harrow" (noun), Latin *mateola* "rod, club, mallet," and perhaps a few verbs meaning "to toss, mix up, etc." may be related. A different but similar etymology of the English word connects *mattock* with Vulgar (i.e., late and popular) Latin *matteŭca* (rather than *mateola*) "club, stick." The only reference book that traces English words to reconstructed Indo-European roots is the *American Dictionary of the English Language*. The information there is not original. It goes back to the dictionary by the late German scholar Julius Pokorny, the successor of his teacher Alois Walde, who traced *mattock* to the root *mat-*, as in Latin *mateola*. In 1929, he even wrote a short article about this word. A few other words that may be related to *mattock* also exist. German *Steinmetz* means "stonemason." *Stein-* is "stone," but what is -*metz*? Is its root the same as in English *mete (out)* or in *mattock*? This connection has often been suggested and denied.

Perhaps the most unexpected turn in our plot has been caused by a suggestion in the Norwegian etymological dictionary by Hjalmar Falk and Alf Torp, two distinguished Scandinavian language historians. Theirs is a wonderful work. It was written in Norwegian and later expanded and translated into German because, before the First World

War, German was the main language in which articles and books on Germanic historical linguistics appeared, and the use of Norwegian limited the book's access to an international market.

This is the reasoning in Falk and Torp's dictionary. There was a Middle English word *maddock* "larva," borrowed from Old Norse and slightly reshaped. We have seen the syllable *-ock* as the suffix in *bullock*, and the root occurs in almost all the Germanic languages. Even Gothic, a fourth-century language, preserved in a translation of the New Testament, knew the suffix-less noun *maþa* "worm" (*þ* has the value of English *th* in *thin*). This *maddock*, apparently, "a little worm," later became English *maggot*. No one knows why such a radical change occurred (a product of taboo?), but *maddock* did exist and it meant "maggot." The origin of *maþa* "worm" is unknown. Yet we notice that the word sounds amazingly like English *moth*. There must have been something in the *math* ~ *moth* syllable that the speakers of the oldest Germanic languages associated with such creatures. Obviously, *mattock* sounds very much like the aforementioned *maddock*. It is almost the same word.

According to Falk-Torp, the root of *maddock* and *mattock* was approximately "to crush" (Slavic etymologists suggested "*dig*": see above!): the mattock, maggot-wise, allegedly worms its way through the ground. Scandinavian linguists endorsed Falk and Torp's idea, while English and Slavic sources do not seem to have noticed it. We can easily understand why the original *OED* and the books depending on it state that the origin of *mattock* is unknown. I would prefer to side with the *OED* online and say that the word's origin is uncertain rather than unknown. Yet the *OED* online does not refer to Falk-Torp.

No less interesting than the reconstruction of a word's ancient root (always a dubious enterprise) is the question about why English *mattock* is so similar to its Slavic look-alikes and, if somewhere along the way one language borrowed from another, why, in the Germanic group, only English has *mattock*. As far as I understand Falk and Torp, they looked on *maddock* ~ *mattock* as native Germanic words. This may be true, but the situation remains unaccounted for.

The names of tools are often borrowed from other languages. Medieval artisans traveled from land to land, and the names of their implements became part of what is known as *lingua franca* (see the earlier section on *adze*). Curious blends sometimes appeared, and garbled forms came up. If Falk and Torp guessed well—that is, if the mattock got its name because it behaved (figuratively speaking) like a maggot, inching its way through hard ground—we will still wonder at the geography of this word. Why English and Slavic? Why almost ubiquitous in Slavic while, in the Germanic-speaking world, only English? The Slavs certainly did not borrow their word from English, and English speakers hardly borrowed it from Slavic, unless they did so before the Germanic invasion of the British Islands by the Angles, Saxons, and Jutes in the fifth century. We have an elegant solution (the one offered by Falk and Torp), but it hangs by a rather unsafe thread. It also remains unclear whether *-ock* in *mattock* is a diminutive *suffix*. In the science of etymology, the way to the truth is often no less interesting than the solution.

Awl

This short section explores a truly intractable word. The near-futile attempts to discover how the awl got its name will highlight the perils of the journey we are determined to undertake. All that is known about *awl* resolves itself into a few hazy hypotheses. By contrast, the sections that follow hold out more promise. Even though the names of weapons, tools, and all kinds of appurtenances are hard to reconstruct, they provide a rare insight into the history of civilization. Soldiers and journeymen travel from land to land, and the names of their instruments, whether murderous or peaceful, become so-called *migratory words* (*Wanderwörter*, as they are called in German: words errant, as it were).

We observe that not only *awl* but also the very word *tool* ends in *-l*. This *-l* is a remnant of several once living suffixes. We detect them, for example, in *bridle, girdle, saddle, satchel,* and *needle*. As far as we can judge, the root of *tool* meant "to produce, prepare." Many Romance words also end in *-l*; there, it is a diminutive suffix (for instance, in *satchel* "little sack" and the like). The Latin for "awl" is *sūbula*. Its *sū-* is akin (related) to English *sew-*; apparently, the word meant an instrument for sewing. Russian *shilo* (i.e., *shi-l-o*) is a close analog of *sūbula* (*shi-t'* "to sew"). Whether -*l* in *awl* is also an ancient suffix remains to be seen.

The Old English for "awl" was *æl*, more likely, though not certainly, with a short vowel. It occurred only as a translation of (gloss on) Latin *sūbula*. The word figures in the biblical texts in descriptions of torture: for example, people's ears are said to be pierced with an *æl*. It continued into Middle English, but for phonetic reasons the form *awl*, homonymous with Modern English *all*, cannot be its reflex: such a modern word would have become *ale*. *Awl* goes back to Scandinavian *al-r*, a cognate of *æl*. This is a common situation: an English word competed with its Danish relative and look-alike and was ousted by it. After the end of the highly successful Viking raids, the Danes ruled over two-thirds of medieval England.

A similar instrument was called *prēon(e)* in Old English. It means "pin; brooch," and the regional word *preen* still means "pin" or "pincers for removing clothes pegs" (unrelated to the verbs *preen* and *prune*), but German *Pfriem(en)* and Dutch *priem* designate the same instrument as *awl*. Their origin is as obscure as that of *awl*. A word cognate with *æl* was known elsewhere in West Germanic. Old High German *ala* became *Ahle* (*h* in it is only a graphic sign of vowel length). The length of the vowel in *æl* is of some importance because dictionaries give partly misleading information on this subject and because the etymology of *awl* depends on our knowledge of the value of *æ* in *æl* and of *a* in Old High German *ala*.

The spelling of the attested forms provides no information on how those *æ* and *a* were pronounced because, in later periods, they would have been lengthened anyway. Therefore, when some of our most authoritative sources reconstruct the ancient Germanic and Indo-European form with a long vowel, this information should be taken with a grain of salt. *Awl* has close counterparts in Baltic, Finnish, and Sanskrit (a typical situation when one deals with the names of instruments and tools), and *in those languages* the root vowel is indeed long. Yet when a word travels from one part of the world to another, its pronunciation is liable to change. Perhaps Old English *æl* and Old High German *ala* did have long *æ* and long *a*, but perhaps not. Migratory words are vagabonds wearing similar clothes, and Old English *æl*, Lithuanian *ýla*, Finnish *ora* "thorn," and Sanskrit *ārā* "awl" need not go back to an Indo-European root. Some speakers of an extinct language that invented a thorn-like instrument may have taught the inhabitants of India how to use it, and the tool, along with its name, began to move west.

The form *ala* enjoyed obvious popularity because it also existed with an additional instrumental suffix. Alongside Old High German *ala*, in later northern German texts *elsene* and *elsen* were recorded (hence Modern Dutch *els*). The suffix is familiar from the German noun *Sense* "scythe." It appears that one instrumental suffix (*l*) in *ala* did not suffice, or perhaps -*l* was no longer understood as a meaningful element. This detail would not have been worthy of mention if some Germanic form like *alasno* had not migrated to the Romance-speaking world: hence Spanish *alesna*, French *alène*, and Italian *lesina*.

Obviously, not the word but the tool and the people who wielded it "migrated." However, we cannot ascertain the epicenter of its spread in the enormous territory between India and the Baltic Sea. It seems more reasonable to reconstruct the starting point in the East, but what was so special in that first awl, and who carried its fame to the remotest borders of Europe? We have no answer, and that is why the etymology of *awl* remains "unknown." Awls are used for piercing small holes in leather, wood, etc. and can be bent- or straight-pointed. Hence the distinction between bradawls and sewing awls. It has also been suggested that some ancient awls were used as weapons. Is this what made them so well-known over most of Eurasia?

A curious episode unites the history of *awl* and *augur*, another piercing instrument. *Augur* is what remains of the once long compound *nafogār*, from *nave* (as in the name of the hub of a wheel) and *gar* "spear" (as in *garfish* and others). A *nauger* became *an auger* because of misdivision. By contrast, *an awl* has often been attested in dialects as *a nawl*. Phonetics played a decisive role in the name of another boring instrument, namely, *wimble*. The well-known alternation of French *gw* and English *w* (as in *Guillaume* versus *William*) produced *gymble*. A diminutive suffix turned it into *gimlet*, remembered mainly from the phrase "eyes like gimlets."

Alongside *æl*, Old English had *āwel* "flesh hook," this time definitely with a long vowel, which developed because of the loss of *h* after short *a* in the original sound group. Its root is akin to *ac-* in *acute*.

Consequently, the flesh hook was simply "a sharp instrument." Yet the similarity with the word for "awl" is almost uncanny. For some time, historical linguists believed that they were dealing with the same word. Yet James A. H. Murray, the *OED*'s first editor, sensed the difficulty. In 1905, a special article dealt with this small problem, but it took the authors of even dependable manuals and dictionaries quite some time to represent facts in their true light.

Is the story disappointing? The answer depends on what one expects from an essay devoted to etymology. People ask: "What is the origin of awl?" and are provided with a few vague ideas on the word's origin instead of an answer. But such is the state of the art. It would be unrealistic to expect that scholars have discovered the absolute truth in any area of knowledge. Etymology is no exception to this rule.

Theodolite

Few people know the word *theodolite*, and no one knows its origin. Writing about it is art for art's sake, the most beautiful kind of art. The word turns up in one of the songs by Flanders and Swan, as Professor John Considine pointed out, and of course dictionaries list it and encyclopedias provide illustrations of this surveyors' instrument for measuring horizontal and vertical angles. Yet when I explain what the word means, I usually hear the question: "Is it the same thing as a level or bubble?" Well, not quite: just look at the picture in Wikipedia. Though the surname Theodoli is Italian, the name of the instrument arose in England and seems to have greater currency in Germany and other European countries than at home. Since most people live happily without having ever seen a theodolite or being aware of the word's origin, why, one might ask, bother? And this is where the idea of art for art's sake comes in. People are curious (or, let us say, inquisitive) and enjoy knowledge for its own sake. What's Hecuba to them, and what is a theodolite to most? Don't rush to conclusions.

At one time, the etymology of *theodolite* was a matter of a protracted discussion. It began in 1798, in the pages of *The Gentleman's Magazine*, in the letters to its immortal editor "Mr. Sylvanus Urban" (the amusing pseudonym of Edward Cave). And an excellent journal it was (1731–1907). I have mined the entire set for my database and enjoyed reading the florid letters, highbrow reviews, and vituperative comments printed there. Later, the debate over the etymology of *theodolite* was continued in the pages of *Notes and Queries* and, with less vigor, in *The Philosophical Magazine*. Mid-nineteenth-century German books on geometry also devoted some space to the derivation of *theodolite*. I have thirty-one citations (counting only articles) on the subject. A word that aroused so much interest in the past (even a few famous scholars participated in the exchange) does deserve our attention.

Theodolite, along with a description of the instrument, first appeared in *A Geometric Practice Named Pantometria* by Leonard Digges, published posthumously by his son Leonard Digges (1571). The word occurring in the book has the Latinized form *theodelitus*. A long excerpt from *Pantometria* will be found in the *OED*. There is every reason to believe that the word, like the instrument, was Digges's invention, but he left no explanation on this score and neither did his son. Many instruments have enigmatic names. One of them is *skirret*, a homonym of the plant name (it is used for measuring land, aligning trenches, etc. working on a revolving center-pin). A mason's term, it surfaced in a special book in the middle of the nineteenth century, and no one seems to know where it came from. For years, I have been trying to find corroboration of the architectural term *kibosh*. It seems to have existed, but no source confirms this ghostly twin of the kibosh we "put" on something.

Three approaches to *theodolite* have been tried.

1. The word has a strong Greek look, so attempts to decompose it into two or three Greek elements could be expected: *thea* "prospect" + *delo-* "make visible"; *theaomai* "see" + *dolos* "stratagem" or + *dolikhos* "long," or + *delos* "manifest" + *itus* "circumference." Or perhaps the last syllable should be understood as *litos* "simple, smooth" *theomai* "see" + *odos* "path" + *litos* = "scanner of exact (or finely drawn) lines of direction." Conversely, *-litus* may be equal to Greek *lithos* "stone" (compare English *monolith*); then we obtain "stone devised as a path to good observation." The common feature of those etymologies is the root meaning "see." Or take

obelos "pointed stick, rod, spit" (as in *obelisk*), transmute it into Aeolic *odelos*, and get *odelited* "graduated," whatever, *th-* means (perhaps the English definite article). Still another possibility is *theou + dolos* "god's counsel": "As the *astrolabe* had its derivation from the Greek *astro* and *labe*, taking the stars, the inventor of the *theodolite* thought he could do no less than seek in that language for some equivalent for Jacob's staff" (actually, *dolos* means "bait; trap"). Some of the aforementioned proposals are fanciful, while the others are not unreasonable. If *-us* is a spurious Latin ending, *litos* and *lithus* present no interest as putative components of *theodolite*. In the original edition of the *OED* we read: "Can it have been (like many modern names of inventions) an unscholarly formation from *theomai*, I view, or *theo*, behold, and *delos*, visible, clear, manifest, with a meaningless termination?"

2. "'*Theodelitus*' . . . consists of a graduated circle, with a diametral [sic] bar, furnished with a couple of sights. This bar always had the name of *alhidada*, or *alidade*. . . . Now *theodelitus* has the appearance of being a participle or adjective; and may therefore seem to refer to the circle as descriptive of an adjunct. A circle with *alidade*: could it be possible that, in the confused method of forming and spelling words which characterised the vernacular English science of the sixteenth century, an *alidated* circle should become *theodelited*?" (Professor A. De Morgan, 1863). This hypothesis (*theodolite* as an Arabic word; *th-* as the article) had a few supporters and has been periodically revived. However, it is hopelessly convoluted and presupposes numerous changes, which are the more surprising as *alhidada*, an old word in English, never appeared in the garbled form reconstructed by De Morgan. Frank Chance, an extremely knowledgeable researcher of that time, disposed of this etymology in his typically ruthless way.

3. As early as 1865, it was suggested that the word *theodolite* goes back to the proper name *Theodolus*. One of its bearers was active in 1685, much too late for Digges, but Theodolus's family had a reputation for being good mathematicians (J. C. J.). Walter W. Skeat, writing in 1895, did not remember the old note, for he stated: "My own guess . . . is quite a new one, unlike any that has

ever yet been suggested. My belief is that it [the word] is derived from the personal name *Theodolus*, which, as every schoolboy knows, means 'servant of God.'" Today not every schoolboy knows the meaning of *Theodolus* (in British public, that is, private schools of Skeat's day, there even existed a slang word *dolos* "slave"), but one thing is certain: an etymologist can never be sure that his or her conjecture is new. At that time, Skeat had no clue to the persona of the mysterious Theodolus. However, this is the pronouncement in the last edition of his English etymological dictionary: "Generally said to be Greek. Formerly *theodelitus*, meaning 'a circle with a graduated border'; used A.D. 1571. Also *theodolet, theodelet*. Apparently imitated (it is not known why) from Old French *theodelet, theodolet*, the name of a treatise, literally 'a work by Theodulus.'" Ernest Weekley offered a similar version of this etymology: "It is just possible that Digges, for some fantastic reason now unknown, named the instrument after the famous Old French theological poem called the *Tiaudelet*, translated from the Late Latin *Theodulus* (9 century)."

A sorry tale: a half-forgotten word of undiscovered origin. It reminds me of old pictures one sometimes sees in great museums: "Portrait of an unknown man by an unknown artist."

Dildo

There is something childish, humorous, even demeaning about disyllabic words whose first and second syllables begin with the same consonant: *bimbo, babble, bubble, cackle, diddle, pimple, pamper, pompous, tittle-tattle*, and their likes. They seem to be either sound-imitative or sound-symbolic because they suggest repetitive or circular movement: you begin with *d, k, p, t*, and no sooner are you through with them than they crop up again.

There has been some discussion about the origin of Mr. Bumble's name (this scoundrel is Oliver Twist's tormentor in the early chapters of the novel and gets his comeuppance at the end). Though all the conjectures known to me are reasonable, I would like to add my own. Obviously Mr. Bumble has nothing to do with bumblebees, but what if Dickens knew the now obsolete word *pumple* "pimple" (apparently a big pimple)? He liked such names. For example, Pip's uncle (*Great Expectations*) was Mr. Pumblechook, and Paul Dombey's dry-as-dust teachers were Dr. Blimber and his daughter Cornelia Blimber. Those are speaking names, not as obvious as Fielding's Squire Allworthy but suggestive enough. I needed this long introduction to justify the proposal that *dildo* also betrays its function by its name.

This word had its heyday in England in the seventeenth century (no citations in the *OED* before 1593) and then disappeared from texts. However, it stayed in the underworld, as the citations from 1785 and 1886 show. In our time, the word returned in force, but, at the end of the 1850s, it was remembered so little (if at all) that James A. H. Murray, the *OED*'s first editor, included it in the dictionary despite the prudish attitude toward such vocabulary prevalent in his day. He must have been sure that no one would *look for* it in the dictionary. The 1886 citation is especially interesting because it gives the names for the dildo in several languages, Italian *diletto* among them, and states that *dildo* is the English variant of it. But this etymology arouses suspicion because *diletto* (i.e., "pleasure; beloved," a *delightful, delectable* thing) would probably have remained *diletto* in English (as can be seen from *stiletto*) or yielded *dilto*.

It usually causes surprise when we find an old low word like *dildo* with the meaning current nowadays. Yet such is the case here. *Dildo* was also used as part of refrains: *dildo-lee, dildo-doe,* and *dildo-dill.* There is no way of knowing whether people grinned when they heard those "burthens." In *The Winter's Tale* (Scene Four), a servant praises a balladeer: "he has the prettiest love-songs for maids: so without bawdry, which is strange; with such delicate burthens of dildos and fadings, 'jump her and thump her'; and where some stretch-mouthed rascal would, as it were, mean mischief and break a foul gap into the matter, he makes the maid answer, 'Whoop, do me no harm, good man;' puts him off, slights with 'whoop, do me no harm, good man.'" (*Burthen,* or *burden,* means "refrain"; *fading* was the name of a dance, apparently Irish, and *with a fading* occurred as the refrain of a popular song of an indecent character.)

We will reserve judgment about the propriety of the song, the modesty of dildos and fadings ("without bawdry"), and the innocent character of the "burthen" "jump her and thump her." *Dildo* seems to be *dil-do*, with *dil* meaning *swive*, as Shakespeare would have put it, and what is now expressed with the help of the *F*-word. Or the syllable *dil* is followed by another syllable beginning with *d* and a vowel (*o*) added, as in the words, cited above (*bimbo* and the like). The "etymological" meaning of the English *F*-word is "move back and forth," and *dil* seems to have meant the same. *Dalliance* and *dilly-dally* come from French, but the original home of *dally* is Germanic (archaic German *dahlen* means "dilly-dally"). In words of this type, vowels vary freely. For instance, the German for the English *F*-word is *ficken*.

Therefore, *dilly-* in *dilly-dally* is not a meaningless syllable appended to *-dally*, as some etymologists believe, but a native (Germanic) twin of *dally*, the one we see in *dil-do*. The original meaning of both must have been "move back and forth." Perhaps the obsolete cant word *dell* (once written *dill*) "wench; whore" is akin to *dill-* in *dilly* and had the connotations of Modern English *Bobby-dazzler* (a British or Australian term meaning "a person or thing that is outstanding or excellent"). The sound group *dil*, along with *till-*, seems to have suggested something frivolous and alluded to meandering and useless work.

At the time of dildos and fadings, there was an exclamation *tilly-vally* "nonsense, fiddlesticks." Martin Luther used the German compound *tillens-tellens* with the sense "dilly-dallying." In England, the hot-dumpling sellers' cry was: "Diddle, diddle, dumpling," memorable from *Mother Goose*: "Diddle, diddle dumpling, my son John, / Went to bed with his trousers on; / One shoe off, and one shoe on, / Diddle, diddle dumpling, my son John." (The youngster, as has been suggested, was too befuddled to undress.) From a phonetic point of view, *diddle* is not too far from *dildo*—a similar combination of sounds denoting moving about and looking alive.

Curiously, a Russian almost identical twin of *dildo* exists, namely, *dylda* "lanky youth," a noun that is somewhat humorous, but not obscene. *Dylda* has no cognates in any other Slavic or Baltic language. Therefore, borrowing in either direction (from English into Russian or from Russian into English) is out of the question. If *dildo* were part of common European slang, it would probably have turned up somewhere between Russia and England. The Russian word was first recorded in a dictionary only in 1847. The hypotheses about its origin are few and uninspiring. In light of what we observe in English, it may not be too bold to suggest that *dylda* is a formation of the same type as English *dildo*, *dilly-dally* and their kin.

Perhaps in some other dialects, at an earlier time, *dylda* referred to a tramp, a hobbledehoy or conversely, to an idler, or gadabout. *Dild ~ dyld*, *dald*, and *dold* can mean almost anything. The Russian (partly dialectal) *dyl(d)-* and *dol(d)-* refer to repetitive actions that command no respect, for instance, *dyldit'* "to behave foolishly; loaf" and *doldonit'* "to prattle; say the same thing again and again in a boring way" (the boldface letters show the place of stress). "A lanky youth" is the only sense that has survived. It is not related to English *dildo*, the way English *dally* is to German *dahlen*, but the impulse that resulted in coining the two words may have been similar. In etymology, coincidence proves nothing, but it should not be dismissed as unworthy of note, especially in dealing with sound-symbolic formations.

Haberdasher

Haberdashers sell hats and other furnishings for men. Milliners cater to women. They are called "milliners" because their wares used to come from Milan, a town once famous for textiles, but no one can tell for sure how haberdashers got their name. The merchandise known in the English-speaking world as haberdashery is called *Galanterie* in German. French *galanterie* means "gallantry." Nothing in the word *haberdashery* makes one think of elegance or refined behavior. The closeness of *-dashery* to *dashing* is accidental. The same holds for *balderdash*, a word of undiscovered origin with which *haberdashery* has once been compared on account of its referring to all kinds of trifles ("nonsense").

In the first quarter of the eighteenth century, gentlemen wore burdashes, or berdashes, around the waist, that is, fringed sashes (another recorded meaning of *burdash* is "lace cravat"), and *haberdasher* has been repeatedly derived from *berdash*, but the comparison should be rejected for three reasons: (1) *haberdasher*, although a rare word, was in use as early as the fourteenth century, whereas *berdash* ~ *burdash* emerged in the reign of Queen Anne (1702–1714); (2) if we agree that *berdash* and *haberdasher* are related, the syllable *ha-* will be left unaccounted for; (3) *berdash* itself lacks a convincing derivation, and a word of obscure origin cannot be expected to throw light on another obscure word.

The first etymological dictionary of English was published in 1617, by John Minsheu. He thought that *haberdasher* goes back to the German phrase *habt ihr das* "have you (got) this?"—allegedly, "the expression of the shopkeeper offering his wares to sale." This is folk etymology, but such phrases do occasionally become words. For instance, *was ist das?* "what is it?" traveled from German to French and became *vasistas* "little window." From French it reached Russian. Apparently, people used to hear some noise, open their window, and ask: "What is it?" Dutch *haberdoedas*, gibberish, but an exact counterpart of Minsheu's invented question, means "a box on the ear" (!). It is a facetious reshaping of German *hab' du das* (approximately, "you've got one"), a phrase that presumably existed.

Other phrases suspected of giving rise to *haberdasher* are French *avoir d'acheter* ~ *haber d'acheter* "to have to buy," German *Habe* "goods, wares" + *tauschen* "to exchange," Dutch *kopen* "to buy" + *d(w)aas* "silly, foolish" (the Dutch etymology is Stephen Skinner's; Skinner was the author of the second etymological dictionary of English, 1671); the Latin verbs *habere* ~ *deber* used in bookkeeping, and Irish Gaelic *ambach* (*avach*) "neck" + *deise, deas* (*dash*) "clothes; fitting, symmetrical, suitable; hence *haberdashery* "things suitable for the neck"; so Charles MacKay; and even the nonexistent compound *sabretacherie* ("the haberdasher being the man who, in an age, when all men who could afford to buy anything, went more or less armed, purveyed those kickshaws of man's attire, which were not furnished either by the silk mercer or the armourer").

Haberdasher has come down to us in several forms, including *haburdassher*. One of the older spellings of *avoirdupois*, whose earliest recorded meaning was "merchandise sold by weight" and which often turned up with initial *h-*, for instance, *(h)aberdepeis*, looks like a reasonable source of *haberdasher*. The comparison of *-eis* with French *ais* "a board on which the dealer in small wares would display his goods" reminds one of a statement Richardson, the author of the once-popular nineteenth-century dictionary, made about his illustrious predecessor: "Skinner runs away." The *avoirdupois* etymology still has supporters. The others have long since been forgotten, though Minsheu's phrase turns up every now and then in modern publications.

We don't expect haberdashers to sell their wares by weight, and an attempt to explain *haberdasher* through *avoirdupois*, with or without initial *h-*, seems to be a long shot, but in the Middle Ages haberdashery included "daggers, swords, ouches [i.e., *owches* "clasps, brooches, etc."], aiglets [i.e., *aglets* "stay-laces"], Spanish girdles, French cloths, Milan caps, glasses, painted cruizes [crosses], dials, tables, cards, dolls, puppets, ink-horns, tooth-picks, fine earthen pots, pins and points, hawks' bells, salt-cellars, spoons, knives, and tin dishes." A 1595 author speaks of a "fellow" loading his sleeve with "fuel from the haberdashers." Even in that interminable list, we do not find a single item that could have been put on a scale.

It is no wonder that Hensleigh Wedgwood, an active etymologist of the pre-Skeat era, distinguished between *haberdasher* "peddler" and *haberdasher* "maker of hats" and offered separate etymologies for them. For the same reason, *haberdasher* has often been compared with *haversack*, a word that English borrowed from French, and French from German. In German, it designated a bag in which cavalry carried the oats for their horses (*haber-* is "oats" in German). It is a late word in both French (no attestations before 1612) and English and an improbable source of *haberdasher*. The chance is also small that we are dealing with two different words, as Wedgwood preferred to think.

The only breakthrough in the research into the origin of *haberdasher* happened in 1862, when Henry T. Riley, a most reliable editor, discovered Anglo-French *hapertas*, occurring once in a legal document and, in close proximity, the word *haberdashrie*, mentioned along with wool, fur, etc. He defined *hapertas* as "a cloth of a peculiar texture, probably coarse and thick." Ever since it has been believed that hapertas is a fabric from which the original haberdashery was made. Such was Riley's opinion ("[i]n the word *hapertas* there can be little doubt that we have the origin of our present word *haberdasher*"), and his etymology can be found in nearly all our dictionaries that dare offer the origin of the modern English word.

Riley's suggestion violates the law that prohibits explaining one obscure word by referring to another equally obscure one (see above).
The meaning of *hapertas* is unknown (it is not even quite clear why
Riley decided that the stuff was coarse and thick), and the difference
between *p/t* in it and *b/d* in *haberdashery* has not been explained. Also,
one should beware of the phrase "no doubt," while suggesting an etymology unless the fact cited is indeed above doubt. Skeat devoted a
special article to this problem, but no trace of it remained in the last
edition of his dictionary. The idea that hats were made from hapertas is
uninspiring guesswork, and we are left in the dark about the two early
meanings of *haberdasher* that worried Wedgwood (in my opinion, it is
the main question, for the original haberdasher seems to have been a
peddler or badger, rather than a hatter).

I will skip discussion of the words *haberjet(t)* (it is *haberject* in
dictionaries "a kind of cloth made in very early times in England, said
to be of a mixed color, and also to have been worn chiefly by monks"),
ha(u)bergeon, and *hauberk* (both mean "a piece of armor; neck protector"). They are phonetically close to *haberdasher*, but their history
does not overlap that of *haberdasher*. Today we are not a whit closer to
understanding the origin of *haberdasher* than we were in 1617. A good,
predictably inconclusive survey of the main conjectures appeared in
the *Century Dictionary*. Despite the support of Riley's etymology by
Skeat and the *OED*, *hapertas* appears to have nothing or very little to
do with *haberdasher*. Some German word may be its etymon, or, to put
us all to shame, it may go back to the phrase *habt ihr das*?

Note
These are the most important contributions to the discussion of the word
haberdasher: Henry T. Riley, "Haberdasher." *Notes and Queries*, 1/X, 1854,
p. 304; William W. Skeat, "Haberdasher." *Academy* 72, 197, pp. 513–14;
and J. Blundell Barret, "Haberdashery." *Academy* 73, 1907, p. 662.

Mad as a Hatter

This phrase has bothered English speakers for quite some time, and
the Internet is abuzz with explanations. The hypotheses are varied. For

starters: the earliest citation of the idiom in the *OED* goes back to 1829. My colleague Stephen Goranson unearthed an 1827 example. We may agree that the enigmatic simile arose in the 1820s and start sifting the explanations.

Some of those who tried to explain the origin of *mad as a hatter* referred to phonetics. Since English speakers are apt to drop their aitches, *hatter* may stand for *atter*. English *adder* "viper" is sometimes cited in this scenario, though the change from *dd* to *tt* remains unexplained. The merger of *t* with *d* between vowels is typical mainly of American English, in which *sweetish* and *Swedish*, *Plato* and *playdough*, *futile* and *feudal*, and the like are homophones in the pronunciations of many. Attempts to trace our idiom to America have been unsuccessful. Another approach relies on the circumstance that the German cognate of *adder* is *Natter*, but *mad as a hatter* is English, not German. English has the noun *attercop* "spider" (Old English *āt(t)or* meant "poison"). Obviously, those facts are immaterial for our discussion.

Still other conjectures can be summarized under ther heading "Linguistic legerdemain and borrowing." The verb *to hatter* "bruise with blows; harass, etc." exists. Perhaps, we are told, this verb was substantivized (i.e., turned into a noun; compare: *read*, the verb, and *it is a good read*), and an angry hatter came into being. Though the origin of the verb *hatter* is unknown, it means approximately "to batter" and hardly throws light on the idiom. Also, dialectal *gnattery* "irritable," related to *gnatter* "to nibble; grumble; talk foolishly," has been pressed into service. What if people used to say *mad as a gnatter* and changed the rare *gnatter* to *hatter*? Did they ever say so?

A citation has been found for *as mad drunk as a hatter*, so that the current idiom might be an abridgement of a more sensible one. Finally, *as mad as . . .* need not end in *a hatter*; among several other candidates, the best-known one is *a March hare*. Of note is the fact that *mad*, in addition to "crazy," can mean "angry; wildly excited." However, the problem of the ill-tempered hatter remains. The phrase has been traced to a borrowing. I am leaving out of consideration Charles Mackay, who derived the phrase (at *hatter*) from Irish Gaelic. His etymology is fanciful. The French say: *"Il raisonne comme une huître"* ("He reasons like an oyster"). Couldn't the French oyster, while crossing the Channel, turn into a mad hatter? Really, why not?

The main problem with this idiom is not its inherent silliness but its late attestation. Even if it was current some time before the 1820s, it certainly did not exist in Old or Middle English, so that tracing *hatter* to some ancient word is an unrealistic procedure. Rather probably, *mad as a hatter* appeared as slang in English approximately when it was first recorded. If the idiom was indeed slang, it may be useful to see whether real mad hatters are known. Indeed, some candidates have turned up.

Two of them deserve mention. "William Collins, the poet, was the son of a hatter . . . at Chichester, Sussex. The poet was subject to fits of melancholy madness, and was for some time confined in a lunatic establishment at Chelsea. The other lunatics, hearing that his father was a hatter, got up saying, 'Mad as a hatter.'" Alas for the chronology! Collins (1721–1759) died before the idiom became known. Around 1830, a Mr. Harris was elected at the head of the poll for Southwark. He was a hatter in the Borough, and proved to be out of his mind. According to another version the "day on which he was 'chaired' in his own carriage was exceedingly hot, and his head during the whole time of the procession being uncovered by removing his hat, he was attacked by brain fever." He died soon after that, but earlier, one of Mr. Harris's canvassers addressed the crowd so: "You've a shocking bad hat on. I'll send you a new one." During election campaigns, changing hats, with reference to changing one's views, was a well-known procedure. "A considerable number of hats consequently changed owners, and the saying having been put into the mouths of so many persons, it was taken up by the *gamins* [street urchins], and was in vogue for some time." This is entertaining but probably useless stuff for discovering the origin of the idiom.

Somewhat more promising is the reference to a hatter as a profession. Professional shepherds in Australia lead a lonely life and are considered "to be to a certain degree mad." "shepherds and hut-keepers . . . are very fond, wherever they can get the materials, of making cabbage-tree hats. The industry distracts their thoughts, and the hats are sold at a good price." Conclusion: the idiom is an import from Australia. Unfortunately for this derivation, the idiom did not turn up in Australia before it was recorded in England. "A lead miner in Derbyshire or a gold miner in Australia who works alone . . . is called a hatter." He is said to work under his own hat and "is looked upon as eccentric; and it seems to be presumed that the solitary worker does not work in partnership with other miners because he is a little mad." Once again, we can see that the roots of the idiom are supposed to be hidden in some local custom. The migration of a phrase or a word from one part of the country to another and becoming slang in the capital is not improbable, for just the foreignness of the item may contribute to its becoming part of the "street urchins'" language.

Hardly anyone remembers those guesses. It is the reference to medicine that has won the day, and the next conjecture known to me is the favorite of many good dictionaries. The hypothesis was offered in 1900, and its author (Thomas J. Jeakes) published it twice. I'll reproduce his second note: "the hatter's madness was dipsomania [alcoholism], induced by working with hot irons in a heated atmosphere and in a standing position. The tailor works under similar conditions, but seated; his condition is therefore less aggravated, and he accordingly gets credited only with pusillanimity and lubricity [i.e., lechery or wantonness?]." Poor mean-spirited, promiscuous tailors, a favorite target of English folklore!

Equally well-known is the reference to the disease caused by mercury poisoning. Hatters used inorganic mercury in making felt hats and allegedly suffered from a debilitating disease (in France, this happened in the eighteenth century and in England later, just around the time when the idiom cropped up). If this fact was widely known, why did people keep offering ever new conjectures about the pernicious phrase? The earliest queries and hypotheses in my database go back to 1869 (I worked with journal publications), and the latest was published in 1913. No one mentioned the poisoning (or alcoholism, for that matter)! Also, Mr. Pascal Trégeur pointed out in a comment on my original post that *as a hatter* and *like a hatter* often functioned as a reinforcing phrase, mainly in northern English dialects, Scotland, and Ireland. See *drunk as a hatter*, above.

As a final flourish, I would like to mention the British writer Joseph Archibald Cronin. One of his novels is titled *Hatter's Castle*. The cruel hatter in that story is not mad (angry) but certainly crazy. I don't think Cronin chose the protagonist's occupation (he deals in hats) by chance. (I may not be the first to offer this guess.) As to Alice's mad hatter,

I decided to leave him in peace: the idiom emerged in the language before the publication of the famous book, and Lewis Carroll only made
use of it.

What then is the corollary? Well, nine *tailors* make a man. One may
be as jealous as a couple of *hairdressers*, and a thing is sometimes not
worth a *tinker's* dam. With such a panoply of denigrated professionals,
why can't one be as mad or drunk as a hatter? This sounds like an
embarassing anticlimax, but, most probably, hatters have (had)
nothing to do with their proverbial madness.

11

History and Geography

Viking

The first documented raid by the Vikings goes back to 793. For more than two centuries, they were the terror of Europe. A good deal is known about their conquests, ships, and morals. The Old English chronicle and the sermons written at that time are full of heartbreaking descriptions of the pagan Norsemen's cruelties. But the origin of the word *viking* remains a matter of debate, as dictionaries put it. To us the Vikings are Scandinavian sea robbers who looted the treasures of Europe, conquered great territories, and settled in England and France. It is not for nothing that one of the northern provinces of modern France is called *Normandy*. And William the Conqueror, the triumphant Bastard, defeated the Anglo-Saxons in the battle of Hastings at the head of a *Norman* army.

However, on the continent, by 1066, the erstwhile Vikings had become French barons and spoke a northern dialect of Old French, so that the ethnic "Normans" overpowered medieval Britain twice: as Danes (hence the existence of hundreds of Scandinavian words in Middle and Modern English) and as the French (from whom English has countless French words). But the word *viking* predates the raids quite considerably. It was common to Old Norse and Old English, and some scholars suggested that Old English had lent it to Old Norse.

At the end of the seventh century, almost exactly a hundred years before the rapacious Vikings sacked Lindisfarne Abbey, an Old English word that can be modernized as *viking scathe* turned up. It meant "piracy." Christine Fell, an excellent researcher and a fully dependable authority, explained: "In the seventh century *wicing* appeared [in Old English prose texts] without national overtones. In the ninth century it could be used of piracy in any context, including the Scandinavian, but in the late tenth century the association with northerners became more pronounced." In Scandinavia, the name *vikings* was given to the brave men who made military expeditions to foreign lands. The points of view of the attackers and the attacked were, not unexpectedly, different.

For a long time, taking part in such "expeditions" remained an almost indispensable rite of passage. It was part of growing up, a sign of maturation, a recognized way of showing one's mettle. One could spend several years in plundering the English, the French, the Germans, or the Slavs, amass great wealth, come home, marry, and become a respectable farmer, a role model for his community and sons. Or the doughty warrior might perish. Then his mother or sister would erect a stone in his memory and have a runic inscription carved stating that so-and-so was a good *drengr* ("valorous man") and that he had lost his life abroad. Numerous such stones have come down to us, and a thousand years later, we read the inscription and meditate on the fortunes of that fellow and on the grief of his relatives.

When military expeditions of the Viking age had lost their importance, the word *viking* deteriorated and began to mean "a figure of fun." It thus shared some ground with *berserkr* "berserk." The most ancient berserks, about whom we know almost nothing, were, apparently, great fighters, the rulers' elite troops. Yet in the Icelandic sagas, recorded in the thirteenth century, berserks appear as crazy, almost invulnerable bandits, and we know that laws were issued against them. In this day and age, we, too, have witnessed what happens to professional soldiers when their army is suddenly disbanded. By contrast, the Viking past was first romanticized, and descriptions are not uncommon of old men saying that in their youth they were on "viking" (i.e., on expeditions), but now they are decrepit and unfit for such deeds. The image of a venerable old viking was popularized by nineteenth-century literature and the admirers of Macpherson's *Ossian*. However, even in the sagas, the image of the brave viking gradually lost its allure.

A serious etymological difficulty is the relation between two Old Norse words: *víkingr* (masculine) "Viking" and *víking* (feminine) "Viking expedition" (the accent mark over *í* designates the length of the vowel, not stress). Those almost identical words must be connected, but we don't know which was derived from which. Nor do we know whether the word originated in Scandinavia because, as noted, the

Anglo-Saxons and, we should add, the Frisians knew it long before it surfaced in Old Norse. But prose in Old Norse (or Old Icelandic; in this context, they are synonyms) is so late that the language in which *víking* or *viking* was coined cannot be determined. *Viking* may have become part of the sailors' common language long before it was recorded in texts, and the etymology I am ready to support confirms this conclusion.

These have been the main lines of research. From Old Icelandic the word *víc* "bay" and a place name *Víc* are known. *Víkingr* can be traced to either of them, with the meaning "people living in a bay area" or "people of Víc." But not all Vikings were born in the same place and their main occupation was not "haunting bays, fjords, and creeks," as an old but excellent dictionary put it. Besides, a good etymology of *viking* has to account for two similar but distinct words rather than one. There was also Old English *vic* "town," a borrowing from Latin. The conjecture that this is what the Vikings called their camps (whence the word *víkingr*) strains belief. Equally improbable is the hypothesis that *viking* has something to do with the word *king*. But as we will presently see, the attempt to trace *víkingr* to the verb *víkja* "to go seafaring" (it dates to 1944) has potential.

The Norwegian scholar Eldar Heide established a connection between *víking-* and the Old Scandinavian noun *vica* "one shift of oarsmen changing places with another at the oars" (2004); this noun is related to the verb *víkja* "to turn" (and to English *week*). The ships of that time were propelled with oars, and it is credible that the word for "sea voyage, expedition" owes its existence to the idea of an oarsman's duty, the shift spent at the oars. The line was blurred between what we today sometimes euphemistically call "explorers," armed medieval traders undertaking sea voyages and ready to defend themselves or obtain their booty by force, and sea robbers, so that the narrowing of meaning in a word like *víking(r)* is natural. A *víkingr* (or his English or Frisian counterpart) would be someone on a rowing expedition. The occurrence of nearly the same word in Old Norse and Old English would then find a plausible explanation. Thus, we end up with the aforementioned verb *víkja*, but look at its other sense.

It may perhaps be premature to declare the riddle solved, but Heide seems to have been on the right track. In another context, the Vikings were called Varangians. From an etymological point of view, the two appellations have nothing in common. The Internet has not yet noticed Heide's contribution, and the only post-2005 paper on the etymology of *víkingr* is mere guesswork.

Incidentally, there is no logical reason why we spell *Viking* with a capital letter. The word is not and has never been a proper name.

Note

Most of the vast literature on the word *Viking* is in languages other than English, and I'll refrain from listing it. But Eldar Heide wrote his essay in English: "Víking—'rower shifting'? An Etymological Contribution." *Arkiv för nordisk filologi* 120, 2005, 41–54. Also, Christine E. Fell wrote in English. Her two papers relevant to our subject appeared in *Proceedings of the British Academy* 72, 1986, 295–326, and in *Leeds Studies in English* 18, 1987, 111–22.

Yeoman

Everything, beginning with its spelling, is odd about the word *yeoman*. Today, the English digraph *eo* occurs only in some bookish borrowings like the prefix *neo-* and in such rare French loanwords as *feoff* (which is a little-remembered synonym of *fief* "a feudal estate") and *people*. However, since *yeoman* replaced French *valet* in the fourteenth century, there must have been a need for a native (English) noun of comparable meaning. Surprisingly, it left no trace in Old English.

Most probably, *yeoman* turned up in our texts soon after it became known. We note that *-man*, as the second element of a few compounds, is sometimes added to a root that no longer means anything to us. Such are, for example, *leman* "lover," *chapman* "itinerant salesman; huckster, badger" (now current only as a family name), and *henchman*. We have no other choice but to assume that if, in the fourteenth century, *yeoman* was a neologism, its inner structure was transparent to those who coined it. However, *yeo-* turns up in neither Old nor Middle English extant manuscripts. The researchers who tried to explain the derivation of *yeoman* referred to Frisian, German, and earlier English words. Their attempts presuppose that at one time *yeoman* did make good sense to the speakers but has come down to us in an altered form. If so, with regard to history, *yeoman* resembles *leman* and *chapman*. It is incomprehensible why then we have no record of it before the fourteenth century. If the institution of yeomanry had existed much earlier, some mention of it would almost certainly have turned up in the extant texts.

As could be expected, attempts to decipher the enigmatic *yeo-* are rather numerous. Indeed, it is so typically English, and not even particularly old! Perhaps, it was said, *yeo-* is related to Middle English *yemen* "to care" (Old English *iemen* "to care"). We naturally wonder whether the original yeomen were overseers or caretakers. As the *Oxford English Dictionary* (*OED*) and historical documents inform us, in the fifteenth century, yeomen were guards and gentlemen attendants in a royal or noble household, rather than overseers.

German has the noun *Gau* "region, area" (memorable to some from *Gauleiter*, a high-ranking official under the Nazis). Its English cognate has not been recorded (Bengeo in Hertfordshire goes back to Belingeho, "a ridge over the river Beane"), and the reconstructed form *ga-man* or *gea-man* (a suspicious creation under the best of circumstances) carries little conviction mainly because, as just noted, *Gau* has no cognates in English, but also because yeomen were not responsible for ruling any areas, and the tentative meaning "villager" is both strained and ill-suited to the role yeomen played in society. However, Walter W. Skeat and several other distinguished scholars failed to propose a more convincing etymology of the intractable word, and it is natural to prefer returning with a poor catch to coming home empty-handed.

"Forefather" (from *iu*, the adverb, "of yore") is an even worse candidate for the etymon of *yeoman*. Tracing *yeoman* to an adjective related to German *gemein* "mean, common" (its Old English cognate exists) and operating with *gem-* as a putative root carries even less conviction because separating *-man* in *yeoman* from the word *yeo* deprives us of the only foothold we have in search for the word's origin. Besides, what was so "common" about the early yeoman? *Yeoman* never functioned as a synonym for *a common man*.

According to the derivation that won the guarded approval of the first editors of the *OED*, *yeo-* is a variant of *young-*; according to this analysis, *yeoman* emerged as *young man*. The semantic leap is unobjectionable, and there are good parallels for servants and attendants being called young men, but the phonetic change from Middle English *yeong-* "young" to *yeo-* inspires little confidence. However, the *OED* almost guessed the origin of *yeoman* when it cited the British English dialectal (southern and southwestern) word *yeomath* "a second crop of grass in the same area; aftermath" (*-math* in *yeomath* and *aftermath* is akin to the verb *mow*) and concluded that *yeomath* also means "young grass," with the same unusual phonetic development from *young-* to *yeo-*.

Today we know more about the history of *yeomath*, and this is where luck and serendipity played a role in my research. I was reading an old book on Dutch etymology and ran into an exact Dutch equivalent of *yeomath*. It turned out that *yeo-* has nothing to do with *young* but is related to a prefix with respectable Indo-European ancestors meaning "additional." In several languages, including Old English, it occurs in the form of *ā, ō* (both vowels are long), and *uo* (the latter goes back to *ō*), for example, Old English *owæstm* "shoot" (i.e., "an additional branch"), Old High German *a-mahd* "yeomath, aftermath" and *uo-wahst* "crop; additional growth" (the root is *wachsen* "grow"; cf. the English verb *wax*), Middle Low (i.e., northern) German *o-herde* "a shepherd helper," and many others. The Dutch scholar whose book appeared in 1859, a noted German dialectologist who also knew that prefix, and, finally, the author of a dissertation on the words for "second crop" in modern German dialects missed English *yeoman*, though, obviously, *yeo-* in *yeomath* and *yeoman* have the same etymology, as the *OED* suggested in the first place. This is where my luck came in: my learned predecessors left something for me to add.

Thus, *yeoman* seems to have meant "an additional man." However, several questions have not received an explanation. Neither recorded form of the prefix should have yielded English *yeo-*: *ee-* or *yea-* could be expected, and indeed, the pronunciation "yeeman," a variant of "yoman," continued into the eighteenth century. Yet it is not the form we use today. It also remains a riddle who coined *yeoman* for the prefix *yeo-* never had wide currency, and why, despite this handicap, the word gained popularity. *Yeomath* makes the etymology of *yeoman* secure; it is regarding its history that we are still in the dark. As time went on, the connotations of *yeoman* vacillated between the dignified ("a gent-leman attendant; landowner") and the ignoble ("beefeater"), but those vagaries of its semantic history have nothing to do with the process that in the fourteenth century resulted in the rise of our word.

Note

The origin of *yeoman* has been discussed almost solely in nu-merous letters published in the periodical *Notes and Queries* be-tween 1831 and 1903, and of course in all English dictionaries. The essay above depends on my contribution to a *Festschrift* in honor of R. W. McConchie (*Words in Dictionaries and History*. Amsterdam, Philadelphia: Benjamins, 2011, pp. 108–33). There, all the references mentioned above can be found.

Cockney

In the nineteenth century, the origin of hardly any other English word was discussed so often and with so much passion in both professional and lay circles as that of *cockney ~ Cockney*. The earliest attestation of *cockney* goes back to William Langland, the author of the poem *Piers Plowman* (1362; see reference to it in the essays on *alairy* and *raga-muffin*). The relevant line sounds so: "Every v and v had a cockenay." The symbol v means "five," and James A. H. Murray, while working on the letter C in the *OED*, explained *cockenay* in that sentence as *cocken-ay* "cock's egg," that is, "bad, spoiled, defective egg." He translated the line: "Every group of five guests was given the measly repast of a bad egg." Earlier commentators took *cockenay* for "cook," which made little sense. The translation of "ay" cannot be challenged. Modern English *egg*, a word of Scandinavian origin, like many others ending in *-g* (*leg*, *tug*, and so forth), supplanted the native form *ay*: compare German *Ei* "egg." However, Murray failed to explain the syllable *en* in *cocken*. He took it for the ending of the genitive case, though in Middle English, *cock* belonged to a declension in which such an ending was impossible.

In Chaucer and later authors, *cockney* means "milksop; pet child; fool; effeminate man; simpleton" and, finally, "(a pampered) inhabitant of a town; Londoner." The path from "bad egg" to "fool," "simpleton," and the rest is not unthinkable, even if not quite straight. Yet, in addition to the syllable *en*, there is another hitch. Murray's reconstruction presupposes that *cockenay* "bad egg" was a familiar word, which, as time went on, developed numerous figurative senses. But the picture is different: the sense "bad egg" never had great currency, was at best known in a few dialects, disappeared rather soon after Langland, and did not survive even in regional speech (the two extant attestations go back to 1568 and 1592), while *cockney* ~ *Cockney* "simpleton; Londoner" has had an uninterrupted history until our time. The phrase *cock's egg* (always with predictable derogatory senses) did turn up in later periods, but we need the archaic *ay*, not today's *egg*. The main question is whether the story of *cockney* began with two Middle English homonyms or with one word endowed with two rather incompatible meanings.

The origin of *cockney* puzzled Murray's predecessors, but those predecessors appeared long after Langland's days. In 1617, John Minsheu published the first comprehensive etymological dictionary of English. Though Langland seems to have lived in London for some time, we cannot even begin guessing where he learned the word *cockeney*. In any case, neither Minsheu nor those who came after him seem to have known *cockeney* "bad egg," so that all attempts revolved round the senses partly familiar to us today. Minsheu recounted an anecdote about a London child who, after being taken to the countryside and informed by his father that horses neigh, heard a rooster and asked: "Does the *cock neigh* too?" Hence, allegedly, *Cockney*, a derisive name for the stupid Londoner. This anecdote has been repeated innumerable times. Of course, it must have been told tongue in cheek, for no one could grow up in London without seeing and hearing horses. Yet, even two hundred years later, some credulous people who touched on the origin of *Cockney* referred to Minsheu as their authority.

When a word poses an almost insoluble riddle, scholars and amateurs tend to offer many explanations. Some of them look reasonable. For instance, it has been proposed that a word meaning "defective egg" could be applied to men with small or misshapen testes and hence to any man who lacked virility; thus, from "effeminate" to "pampered, spoiled." Still another derivation traced *cockney* to English *cockered* "spoiled, pampered," a word of dubious origin. For a long time, etymologists tried to connect *Cockney* with Latin *coquina* "kitchen" (or rather with the French noun *coquin* "a person fond of cookery" and the reconstructed French past participle *coquiné*, which allegedly yielded the sense "a vagabond who hangs around the kitchen" or "a child brought up in the kitchen").

Some of those suggestions, even though they always take cognizance of only part of the word *cockney*, turn up in respectable old reference works; for example, in Hensleigh Wedgwood's and the early editions of Skeat's dictionary. Wedgwood, it will be remembered, was the main authority on English etymology before Skeat. Later, he receded into the background, while Skeat, an extremely prolific writer, changed his opinions more than once. Of course, *cockney* must have some connection with *cock*; it was *-ney* that refused to yield a reasonable meaning. *Cockney* has also been understood as the name of someone living in the land of Cockaigne, a fabulous country of abundance and, by inference, London, where, as everybody knew, streets were paved with gold. Yet *Cockaigne* is a Romance word, and its association with *Cockney* is late. Though the nature of their interaction remains undisclosed, *cockney* cannot be derived from *Cockaigne*. I will skip about a dozen old and new conjectures that died without issue and deserved their fate.

Etymology is politicized more often than nonspecialists may think. Words travel from language to language in happy disregard of national, confessional, and other borders. Unfortunately, it is often believed that taking over a term of material or intellectual culture from a neighbor or a distant land lowers the prestige of the borrowing nation. When ideological battles are fought over this nonsense, hot-headed linguists and journalists defend the greatness of their country with the help of dictionaries and reconstructed forms. But *cockney* is a special case, for it caused the only etymological war between England and the United States. And a bitter war it was, with casualties on both sides. It broke out when Murray, who viewed with unconcealed disapproval the progress of the *Century Dictionary* (he looked upon the American project as a competitor of the *OED*), accused the American editors of the ignorance that "would not be tolerated even (!!) by female extension students at Oxford," and all because he disapproved of the *Century's* derivation of *cockney* from French. The conflict raged for several years and all but antagonized Murray's American collaborators, who otherwise treated his work on the *OED* with unconcealed admiration. Later, oil was poured on troubled waters, and the countries became allies again, never again to indulge in open hostilities.

Shakespeare, Minsheu's contemporary, knew the word *cockney* and used it twice in his plays. When King Lear, stung by his daughters' ingratitude, exclaims: "O me! My heart, my rising heart! But down!," the Fool retorts: "Cry to it, Nuncle, as the cockney did to the eels when she put'em i'th'paste alive; she knapp'd'em o'th'coxcombs with a stick, and cried 'Down, wantons, down!' 'Twas her brother that, in pure kindness to his horse, buttered his hay." *Cockney* seems to mean "idiot" in both pronouncements. In *Twelfth Night*, Feste (so again a fool) meets Sebastian, whom he takes for Cesario (i.e., for his twin sister Viola in disguise), and addresses him. Sebastian does not understand what Feste wants and says: "I prithee vent thy folly somewhere else, / Thou know'st not me." Feste, amused by Sebastian's pompous phrase "vent thy folly," answers: "Vent thy folly! He has heard that word of some great man, and now applies it to a fool. Vent thy folly! I am afraid this great lubber, the world, will prove a cockney." The sentence, which probably contains a pun, is obscure, but in it, too, *cockney* means "idiot." Chaucer, two centuries before Shakespeare, used *cockney* in the same way ("idiot, simpleton").

The question about the origin of *cockney* remains partly open. The most convincing division of the old word is *cock-e-ney*, with -*e*- being a spelling variant of intrusive -*a*- (as, for example, in *cock-a-doodle-doo*, *rag-a-muffin*, and other such words). The sound *n*- in -*ney* seems to have the same origin as *n*- in *nuncle* "uncle" (from *an* or *mine uncle*), *nanny* (from *mine Annie*), and many other words of this type.

Was the reference to "cock's egg" medieval slang? The word was certainly vulgar. Street slang is often borrowed, and the word may have reached England from France. Perhaps *cockney* "fool," a homonym of *cockney* "bad egg," does go back to an Old French participle *acoquiné* "pampered, idle," as was suggested long ago, but French *é* does not become English *ei*. This phonetic difficulty seemed insurmountable to Murray, and he had a good point. Yet it seems reasonable to suggest that not all the recorded senses of our word ("bad egg" and "fool, milksop, etc.") go back to the same etymon. However, the division of

Langland's form into three parts (*cock-e-ney*) is correct and will remain the starting point of all future endeavors to etymologize *cockney* ~ *Cockney*.

Most sources say that the origin of Cockney is unknown (which is not a true assessment of the situation); cite Murray's etymology (from "defective egg"), or add their own, often fanciful, cognates; or give two derivations supplied with question marks. Though part of the solution escapes us, the story, even in its curtailed form, was, I believe, worth telling.

Note

The bibliography of *Cockney* is huge. Here are the main titles pertaining to the "etymological war": James A. H. Murray in *The Academy* 37, 1890, 320–21, 357, and 426–27, and Charles P. G. Scott (he was the etymology editor of the *Century Dictionary*) in the *Nation* 50, 468–69 (reproduced in *American Notes and Queries* 8, 1890, 92).

The Buckeye State

The origin of *Buckeye*, as applied to Ohio, is no secret (though some stories on the Internet smack of folk etymology), and I will add only a few details that may not be universally known. But first, a short bibliographical digression for the benefit of those who may be interested in how the relevant material is collected for producing essays like this one. The sources at our disposal are full of irresponsible references. For example, I once found a mention of *Etymological Journal*. Naturally, I wanted to read such a promising periodical. Yet, most probably, it never existed, and the article containing the material I needed did not come to light. In the *Magazine of American History*, volume 19, 1888, p. 82, an anonymous author says this: "Mr. A. A. Graham, Secretary of the Ohio Archaeological and Historical Society, has recently published in the *Ohio State Journal* an answer to the question repeatedly asked, 'Why are the Ohio people called Buckeyes?' Mr. Graham quotes from a brilliant after-dinner speech by the celebrated Dr. Daniel Drake, the botanist of the Ohio Valley, at a public dinner given on the forty-fourth anniversary of the city of Cincinnati." A summary of Dr. Drake's answer follows.

For my work, I needed both the original and a retelling of the speech. However, it appeared that the *Ohio State Journal* is as elusive as the aforementioned *Etymological Journal*. With the help of an experienced reference librarian, I found *Ohio Archaeological and Historical Publications*. Volume 2, and indeed for 1888, carries the article "Why Is Ohio Called the Buckeye State?" However, its author is William M. Farrar, not A. A. Graham, who was the Society's secretary and, true enough, often appeared in *Publications*, but none of his contributions dealt with the nickname. Farrar does quote Dr. Drake, and it is easy to assume that the editorial assistant on the staff of the *Magazine of American History* made a mistake. But how could that feckless person give a wrong title and a wrong name? Some members of the Society who read the *Magazine* should have detected the error; yet no correction appeared in any of the later volumes. Moreover, the summary in the note does not match what Farrar says! Samuel Johnson, the author of the 1755 English dictionary, defined *lexicographer* as a harmless drudge. This definition has been quoted to death. Yet the readers of books like this one may sometimes want to know what it takes to offer some seemingly most trivial statement. When moving into a new house, we should sometimes think of those who built it, and not only when we encounter problems with heating.

And now to business. The first volume of the *OED* was published in 1884. At that time, the editors knew that *Buckeye* meant "an inhabitant of Ohio" but had no citations; this is one of the rare cases of a word in the *OED* not supported by examples. In the first *Supplement*, several citations turn up, none of which predates 1822. I have at my disposal two reports of the tree called buckeye. J. H. J. wrote in 1861: "The name Buckeye was never applied to the State or its people by the early inhabitants, and the tree itself was not held in such estimation as to induce it. The early settlers found it utterly useless for most domestic purposes. It was unfit for building, or fences; the wood could not be split, and when green, made the worst of fuel. Its abundant fruit was utterly useless; while in one respect it was reckoned a nuisance, being injurious to cattle, which sometimes ate them, causing a kind of vertigo, called staggers" (*Historical Magazine*, volume 5, 1861, pp. 286–87).

The nickname of the state and its inhabitants, J. H. J. emphasized, owes nothing to the qualities of the tree. This conclusion was made all the more persuasive by being formulated first in Latin and then in English.

The anonymous author in the *Magazine of American History* quotes Dr. Drake, according to whom the wood is soft, and "when the first 'log cabin' was to be hastily put up, its softness and lightness made it precious; for in those times laborers were few and axes once broken in hard timber could not be repaired. It was, moreover, of all the trees in the forest, that which best arrested the rifle bullets of the Indian. When the infant Buckeyes came forth to render these solitary cabins instinct with life, cradles were necessary, and they could not be so easily dug out of any other tree." Compare the phrase *utterly useless*, used twice in the previous passage. However, the two authors agree on the texture of the tree. In a postscript to his first publication, J. H. J. adds: "The name of Buckeye was a term of reproach, applied in a very early day to lawyers and doctors, who happened to be regarded a little *soft*" (volume 6, 1862, p. 37). They also agree that the nickname is connected with the presidential campaign of 1840, even though an association between the buckeye and Ohio arose before that time.

When General William Henry Harrison was nominated for President, an opposition newspaper said that he was better fitted to sit in a log cabin and drink hard cider than rule in the White House. Harrison became "the log cabin candidate," and his supporters ("the merry buckeye boys") sang the song: "Oh where, tell me where / Was your buckeye cabin made," and so on. The buckeye achieved the status of a popular emblem and was commercialized. Crowds of men and boys went to the woods in the morning and returned later in the day "carrying great bundles of buckeye sticks, to be converted into canes and sold to travelers, or sent to adjoining states to be used for campaign purposes." This part of the story can be easily found in the Internet. As far as I can judge, its source is Farrar's 1888 essay. Both *OK* and the nickname *Buckeye* existed before Van Buren's and Harrison's campaigns but rose to such prominence thanks to them. It is a curious fact that we are dealing with the same period. Van Buren and Harrison, it will be remembered, were the eighth and the ninth presidents of the United States, respectively.

Note

My colleague Stephen Goranson discovered the sources that mystified me. As I suspected, the reference to *Etymological Journal* and the article I vainly tried to find in it was a hoax. He also pointed to the booklet titled *Celebration of the Forty-Fifth Anniversary of the First Settlement of Cincinnati and the Miami Country: on the 26th Day of December 1833 by the Natives of Ohio*. Shreeve & Gallager, 1839. It contains some information that reached me secondhand. The paperback booklet is now available in a modern reprint.

Hoosier

Anyone interested in the etymology of *Hoosier* should read Jeffrey Graf's essay, published on the website of *Indiana Notes and Queries*. It is an exhaustive survey (revised in February 2007) of the surmises about this nickname. In 1995, William D. Piersen, and, in 2007, Jonathan Clark Smith devoted articles to *Hoosier*'s early days (both appeared in the *Indiana Magazine of History*). I am returning to this chestnut, mainly because all three authors, though extremely well-informed, missed a work that, in my opinion, deserves attention. Now, fifteen years after my initial inroad on the word *Hoosier*, I see that, since 2008, several authors have again dealt with it but, apparently, none of them has discovered my blog. Even the omniscient Wikipedia took no notice of it. This is a pity because the facts I discussed in that post are worthy of attention.

The starting point for everyone interested in the history of Indiana's nickname is a brochure with the title *The Word Hoosier* by *Jacob Piatt Dunn and John Finley by Mrs. Sarah A. Wrigley (His Daughter)*. Indiana Historical Publications (volume IV, number 2. Indianapolis: The Bobbs-Merrill Company, 1907, 29 pp.). John Finley was the author of the poem *The Hoosier's Nest* (1833) that seems to have made the soubriquet recognized by a wide audience. The poem takes up three pages of small print. The painstaking research was carried out by Dunn, who knew most of the silly conjectures, as well as the few plausible ones, on the etymology of *Hoosier*, and offered an explanation of his own. He had a healthy attitude toward etymological folklore, for he realized how little trust one can put into stories of the type "I was there and know the facts."

Thus, in 1929, Oscar D. Short brought out his recollections in the *Indiana Magazine of History* (volume 25) that begin so: "There has been a tradition in our family, which I have known since boyhood, that Aaron Short, an older brother of my grandfather, gave to the inhabitants of Indiana the name 'Hoosier.'" The story appeared four years after Dunn's death, but, if he had read it, he would have found nothing new for himself in it: a very strong man, so Short recounts, was victorious in a fight, jumped up, and shouted: "Hurrah for the Hoosier" (perhaps he tried to say: *husher* or *hussar*). Both versions—of *Hoosier* going back to *husher* or being a "corruption" of *hussar*—were familiar to Dunn. The editors of the *Indiana Magazine of History* had no illusions about the verisimilitude of Short's recollections; yet they decided to add a new piece of legendary material to the Hooseriana. (*Cockney*, it will be remembered, has once been attributed to the phrase "Does the cock neigh." *Hoosier* suffered from a similar nonsensical etymology: its source was allegedly the question: "Who's here?") The authors of tales like Short's believe in them wholeheartedly, but such is the reception of all folklore. Even the storytellers who tell the most fantastic fairy tales, when asked about enchanted castles and boys becoming ravens at the will of an evil stepmother, tend to answer evasively that, of course, such things do not happen here, but at one time and elsewhere.

Smith accords Short's story a measure of respect. However, *Hoosier*, as far as we can judge, has always been pronounced with the vowel of *hoo*. For this reason alone, the suspicious word *husher* "stiller" (a person so strong that he can "hush, still" anyone) is an unlikely etymon of *Hoosier*. Likewise, *hussar* could hardly have been such an active word in the man's vocabulary that he would recall it in midair. It is also Smith's contention that *Hoosier* reflects "local pride" rather than "southern scorn." The *OED* quoted from a letter allegedly written in 1826, the first extant text believed to have the word in question. However, the date seems to be wrong, and we have to accept Smith's conclusion that there is no documented use of *Hoosier* before the 1830s. His other contention, namely, that *Hoosier* emerged with reference to the Indiana boatmen and, far from being a "slur," showed how people reveled in being called Hoosiers, is harder to accept. (Those with a taste for the topic "Boatmen and Etymology" are advised to turn to the essay herein on the idiom *by hook or by crook*.)

According to the traditional theory, *Hoosier* originated in the South as a term of contempt, a word like *yokel, hayseed, rube, bumpkin, hillbilly, clodhopper, jake, backwoodsman*, and dozens of others; and that in Indiana, it lost its offensive connotations even though it retained its negative sense outside the state. This reconstruction agrees with what we know about such situations. Peripheral areas usually preserve archaic features, be it phonetics, grammar, or vocabulary. The adoption by political parties and religious groups of the opprobrious names that in the beginning their enemies and denigrators coined in contempt has often been recorded: such is the history of *Tory, Whig*, and *Quaker*. The ties of *Hoosier* to the rest of the South are too numerous to be ignored, and, outside Indiana, references to those who are called Hoosiers are never complimentary.

Dictionary of American Regional English (*DARE*), a splendid reference work, treats the word in depth (but offers no etymology), and Graf, naturally, consulted it. *Hoosier* can mean "a rustic, especially in such combinations as *country hoosier* and *mountain hoosier*; an unmannerly or objectionable person; a White person considered to be objectionable, especially because of racial prejudice; an inexperienced or incompetent person among those skilled in a particular field, especially logging." The verbs *hoosier* "to be a farmer" and *hoosier up* "to work incompetently; to slow down or shirk on a job, usually on purpose" also exist. According to Smith, *Hoosier* came to mean "an inept person, a bad worker, etc." later, and it is true that the word's pejorative uses in written and printed documents do not antedate 1836. Yet the time gap is minimal, and slang makes its way into books and letters sporadically. Also, the connection between *Hoosier* and "Indiana boatman" will appear strong only if we disregard all other contexts. On the whole, it is easier to accept the fact of late attestation than of the development from "a doughty boatman" to "hillbilly, jerk."

Several times those who investigated the origin of *Hoosier* have mentioned a similarly sounding family name and made it responsible for the rise of the Indiana nickname. Their hypotheses (Piersen is among the most recent advocates of one of them) do not go far and carry little conviction. But, in 1999, Randall Hooser published an article in *Eurasian Studies Yearbook* (pp. 224–31), and this is the article even Graf missed. The author documents the history of his extended family. The Hausers came to the United States from Alsace. In their dialect, the diphthong designated in spelling by *au* had the value of English *oo* in *hoo*. Consequently, *Hauser* and *Hooser* are variants of the same name. According to the author, the Hoosers migrated to Indiana from Salem, North Carolina, and were mocked for their beliefs and customs. He does not explain under what circumstances the nickname was extended to the rest of the inhabitants of the state, why the meaning of the slur was forgotten exactly where it should have been best remembered, and why such an obvious origin did not occur to the people who wrote about the subject in the 1830s of the nineteenth century, but all etymologies of *Hoosier* are marred by similar inconsistencies (hence the never-ending debate). Especially baffling is the circumstance that, even in Finley's days, no one knew why Hoosiers were called this. Nicknames are invented to belittle or tease their bearers even when applied to kings: consider such cognomens and *Harald Bluetooth* and *Charles the Bald*. The case is certainly not closed, but, if the first Hoosiers were the Hausers and "foreigners," we begin to understand why there was no love lost between them and their new surroundings, why they chose Indiana as their place of residence, and why other southerners stick to what seems to be the word's original meaning.

It is not for an outsider to solve the question that puzzled so many specialists in Indiana history, but I hoped that Randall Hooser's article would become part of the debate. This did not happen, and I am sorry for it. It is extremely hard to discover all the relevant literature on the history of any word. I know this from bitter experience, and that is why, three decades ago, I embarked on the compilation of an exhaustive bibliography of everything written about the origin of English words. This bibliography was published in 2010, and one could hope that any researcher would start reading on the subject by opening this voluminous book. Neither the contributor to Wikipedia nor the author of a detailed article in the *Chicago Tribune* (it appears at once when you Google for *Hoosier: origin of the name*) looked up the word in that bibliography.

DARE records the following spelling variants of *Hoosier*: *hoogie*, *hoojy*, *hoodger*, *hoojer*, *hushier*, and *hooshur*; from older sources *hoosher* has come down to us. They reflect two pronunciations: *hooser* and *hoosier* (*-sier* as in *hosier*). If the etymon is *Hooser*, a third variant emerges. All three can be reconciled. The use of *sh* for *s* is old in the history of English. The roots of *banish*, *nourish*, *bushel*, and so forth had final *s* in French, but they were borrowed with *sh*. This alternation can also be observed in living speech. In Minnesota, where I live, people say *groshery* for *grocery*. The same alternation affects the voiced partners of *s* and *sh*. For instance (drawing on what one hears in Minneapolis), *Fraser* is pronounced *Frasier* (the University has Fraser Hall on campus, an often-visited building, so that *Fraser* is a high-frequency word on campus). It takes an effort to convince students that the name of Sir James Frazer, the author of *The Golden Bough*, should rhyme with *razor*. *Hooser*, that is, *Hoozer*, may have become *Hoosier*, as *Fraser* became *Frasier*.

Dunn's attempt to derive *Hoosier* from a word recorded in Cumberland, with the resulting meaning "a large man," has little to recommend it: the connection is tenuous, and the original Hoosiers hardly got their name for their physique. The other explanations rarely go beyond exercises in folk etymology.

Mr. Randall Hooser, the author of the contribution to *Eurasian Studies Yearbook*, discovered my blog in 2010 and sent me a lot of material supporting his etymology. I learned nothing new from it because the facts pertaining to the history of the Middle High German vowels can be found in all relevant textbooks. The original derogatory meaning of *Hoosier* is certain, and the word's adoption by Indiana should cause no surprise. Let us remember Suckers and Pukes for the inhabitants of Illinois and Missouri, respectively. Later, I was a guest of Mr. Hooser and the members of his family, and we talked about the indifference of the world to their etymology of *Hoosier*. As usual with such intractable words, the truth is evasive, but the derivation of *Hoosier* from the family name Hooser is, to my mind, not improbable.

12

Suspicious Usage and Troublesome Phonetics

Ain't

Ain't is like Robert Burns's John Barleycorn: condemned but inerad-icable. One must be a teacher (at any level) to realize the amount of vitriol and passion inspired by this short word. It has been vilified and admired, attacked, and defended. Countless pages in periodicals are devoted to *ain't*: professors of linguistics, language historians, and interested individuals used to flood periodicals like H. L. Mencken's *The American Mercury*; *Word Study*, *American Speech*, and the *English Journal*, fighting one another and justifying or (more rarely) condemning *ain't*. Passions seem to have run higher in the United States than in Great Britain (all the titles listed above are American). Of late, the condemnation has been tempered because we don't like being judgmental. Yet my American spellchecker still underlines *ain't* in red. The other similar forms (*isn't*, *don't*, *didn't*, *shan't*, *won't*, *can't*, and a few more) never aroused protest. A social stigma is attached only to *ain't*, though the word is easy to pronounce, rhymes with *faint*, *quaint*, and *saint* (let us ignore *taint*), and one wonders where the stigma originated. Did or does the condemnation come from the word's in-clusiveness? *Don't* means only *do not*, *won't* stands for *will not*, and so forth, while *ain't* is short for *am not*, *is not*, *are not*, *has not*, and *have not*. Perhaps guardians of linguistic purity wince at such linguistic promiscuity?

It has been shown that the best nineteenth-century British and American authors did not shy away from using *ain't*. Dickens's characters use the form freely, and not all of them are country bumpkins and the inhabitants of London slums. The same is even more true of Anthony Trollope, a writer who, as is known from his journalistic prose, was extremely sensitive to the mishandling of English. In his novels, aristocrats use *ain't* as often as so-called common people. Likewise, in Thomas Hardy's prose, people from all walks of life show no fear of it. Returning to America, we can read in letters to the editor that, in Boston, for example, the best educated people do not avoid *ain't*. All that is interesting and instructive, but remember my spellchecker! Apparently, we owe the perennial open season on this form to editors and teachers, that is, to those representatives of the middle class whose lips are never polluted by *ain't* and who took it upon themselves to guard English from corruption. Where did *ain't* come from? Nobody knows for sure. Yet some conjectures are more attractive than others.

One suggestion is perhaps safe. Though *ain't* stands for a half-dozen forms, **it hardly originated many times** (as a substitute for *amn't*, for *isn't*, for *haven't*, and so forth) to become a jack-of-all-trades. More likely, *ain't* surfaced as a substitute for some one form and, with time, spread far and wide. Judging by the recorded material (it is of course available in the *Oxford English Dictionary* [OED]), **the fashion for *ain't* and its kin (*can't*, *isn't*, and others) does not predate the middle of the eighteenth century**. This fact, as we will see, is of some importance for our reconstruction. The question is: Where was the epicenter of the change?

Ain't seems to occur especially often after *I*: *I ain't*, that is, "I am not" or "I have not." It has therefore been suggested that *ain't* traces to *am not*. Nowadays, *amn't* is a rather unpronounceable group and never occurs in conversation. Such it must also have been in the past. However, if at any period it occurred in oral speech with some regularity, *amn't* would certainly have lost *n*. The modern pronunciation of words like *damn*, *autumn*, *column*, and *solemn* leaves little doubt on that score. (The simplification of final *mn* began in late Middle English.) However, *amn't* should have yielded *amt* or *ant*! Alongside *ain't*, the form *cain't* (i.e., *cannot*) has been recorded. It has been suggested that the length of *nn* in such words was transferred to the preceding vowel, so that *annot* (from *amnot*) and *cannot* later became *ānot* and *cānot* (*ā* designates long *a*, as in Modern English *spa*). By a well-known rule, long *a* became a diphthong (as in *lame*, *cane*, and the rest). This reconstruction looks rather precarious.

Another putative source of *ain't* is *aren't*. But there is a hitch here, too. We have seen that the contracted forms hardly predate the 1750s. By that time, American English had existed for more than a century. American English (particularly on the East Coast) is not an *r*-less dialect. Yet *ain't* sounds the same on both sides of the Atlantic. *Aren't*, with *r* preserved, would not have yielded *ain't*. But it was also hardly its source in British English, where, given the loss of *r* after vowels, it would have produced *aunt* or perhaps *ant*. (*Aren't I* and *ain't I* still coexist in informal American English, but this circumstance has no bearing on the history of *ain't*.)

Even *isn't* has been considered as the source of *ain't*. Older texts show that *s* was occasionally lost in *isn't*, *wasn't*, and *doesn't*. The form *i'n't* alternated with *ent*, and "if we imagine [!] a lowering and lengthening of the vowel (corresponding pretty exactly to what happened in *don't* and *can't*, etc.), this would result in a pronunciation *eint*." Let no one think that, in trying to emulate Jack Sprat and his wife, I made a heroic attempt to lick the plate clean and for the sake of completeness cited the suggestions by some unreliable amateurs. It was Kemp Malone, a distinguished American philologist, who defended the idea that *ain't* goes back to *amn't*. The quotation in this paragraph is from *A Modern English Grammar on Historical Principles* by the celebrated Danish linguist Otto Jespersen. *Aren't* has been promoted as the source of *ain't* in numerous works.

Finally, some researchers believe that *ain't* goes back to *haven't* or *hasn't*. It will be remembered that, in the past, the ending of the third person singular was *th*, not *s* (*he giveth*, he *goeth*, etc., familiar from Shakespeare and the Revised Version of the Bible). Thus, *haven't* and *hathn't*, or given the dropping of *h*'s, *'aven't* and *'athn't*, should be retained, in my view, as possible sources of *ain't*. Moreover, the old infinitive corresponding to the modern form *have* was *han* (*han* in Chaucer and *ha'* in Burns). As seen in *behave*, the root *have* sometimes occurred with a long vowel. Of all the possible sources—from *amn't* to *ain't*, from *aren't* to *ain't*, from *isn't* to *ain't*, and from *'a(th)n't* to *ain't*—the last one presupposes the least amount of guesswork of the *if we imagine* type. (Jespersen did not object to deriving *ain't* from *amn't* and *haven't*, but, much more probably, *ain't* had a single source.) Still another circumstance should not be overlooked: *am*, *is*, and *are* go with one person only each, while *(h)a'(th)* fits all of them, in the singular and the plural. The form's ambiguity must have contributed to its staying power and spread.

Such is the history of *ain't* as I see it. Other people see it differently.

Note

Among the reference books, an especially detailed entry on *ain't* can be found in the *OED*. Charles P. G. Scott, the etymology editor for the *Century Dictionary*, was perhaps the first to insist that the main source of *ain't* is *haven't*. Today, many researchers gravitate toward this view. As pointed out above, the papers on the history and use of *ain't* are numerous. The most informative recent work on this subject is by Michael Montgomery, "Hain't We Got a Right to use *Ain't* and Auxiliary Contraction? Toward a History of Negation Variants in Appalachian English." *Southern Journal of Linguistics* 38, 2014, 31–68. Though the focus is on regional American speech, pp. 54–64 deal with broad historical issues. I can also recommend Harold H. Bender's letter to the editor of *Word Study* XI/4, 1936, 1–2 and the paper by Martin Stevens, "The Derivation of 'ain't.'" *American Speech* 29, 1954, 196–201. Two contributions explain why today no one says *amn't*: Richard Hudson, "*I amn't.*" *Language* 76, 2000, 297–323 (the asterisk means that such a form does not exist!) and Liselotte Anderwald, "*I amn't Sure: Why Is There No Negative Contracted Form of First Person Singular Be?" in *Anglistentag 2001 Wien* (Dieter Kastovsky, Gunther Kaltenböck, [and] Suzanne Reichl, eds.), 8–17 (with references to an earlier discussion of this form). Wien: Trier, 7–17. There is also an important article in German by Hans Pinsker, "Neuenglisch *ain't*" in *Festschrift Prof. Dr. Herbert Koziol zum siebzigsten Geburtstag*. (Gero Bauer, Franz K. Stanzel, and Franz Zaic, eds.). Wien, Stuttgart: Wilhelm Braunmüller, 1973, 238–54. Of interest is still Harry Warfel, "Fire in our Ears." The *English Journal (College Edition)* 22, 1933, 411–16. (Warfel, 1899–1971, was a literary scholar and a first-rate expert on American culture.) The book by David Skinner, *The Story of* Ain't: *America, Its Language, and the Most Controversial Dictionary Ever Published* (Harper Collins, 2012) is about the history and reception of *Webster's Third*. But in the index, p. 333, *ain't* is featured, and one can glean a good deal of information about various people's views on *ain't* and the treatment of this word in Webster's dictionary.

Sneak—Snack—Snuck

In the triad *sneak—snack—snuck*, it is of course *snuck* that will interest us most, but the origin of this "illegitimate" past tense of *sneak* should not be handled in isolation. The recorded history of *sneak* is relatively short. In texts, the earliest examples with it turned up about four hundred years ago. Old English had *snican* "creep," with short *i*, as in Modern English *nick*, and this form could have yielded *sneak*, just as Middle English *crike*, from Scandinavian, yielded *creek*. But for *snican* to become *sneak*, it had to pass through a stage with a vowel like *e* in German *geben* "to give" (such is the phonetic regularity), which has not been attested.

On the other hand, there was a Scandinavian verb *snikja* "hanker after; ask silently for food as a dog does," which, if it had been borrowed into English, would have yielded *snick*. *Snick, snick and snee*, along with *snicker* ~ *snigger* are living words. All of them are expressive but none of them refers to longing or creeping. Though an Old Scandinavian verb with a long vowel in the root also existed, as follows from the participle *snikinn* "covetous," it would have become *snike*, not *sneak*, in Modern English. For all these reasons, dictionaries say that the origin of *sneak* is uncertain. Its etymology seems to be within reach, but at every step something goes wrong.

Such complications need not surprise us. *Sneak* "go stealthily, creep furtively," like all the other verbs mentioned above, is an expressive word, and in such words both vowels and consonants often behave erratically: they shorten, lengthen, change, and alternate in defiance of the rules valid for the rest of the vocabulary. Hensleigh Wedgwood, a distinguished etymologist of the pre-Skeat era, paid special attention to the expressive nature of *sneak*. He wrote: "The radical signification seems to be going along like a dog scenting his way with his nose to the ground, sniffing for victuals or what can be picked up. . . . The idea of meanness arises from the dog being deterred by no rebuffs when he is sniffing after food. . . . The metaphor is distinctly seen in the slang term of an *area sneak*, one who pries into areas for what he can pick up."

Language historians feel secure only while dealing with recurring situations; exceptions can be neither predicted nor accounted for with certainty. Most verbs resembling *sneak* are also expressive because they refer to actions describing strong emotions, the use of force, or nontrivial behavior. Such are Dutch *snaken* "crave, hanker," Icelandic *snaka* "rummage about," and especially English *snooks* that surfaced late in the nineteenth century (*cock a snook* "make a derisive gesture with thumb to nose"), along with *Snooks*, the hypothetical family name of an unidentifiable person; the English dialectal verb *snook* "hanker" also exists. The closest kin of the *sneak ~ snick ~ snack ~ snook* family is *snoop* (from Dutch) and its cognates, which mean "mooch, cadge; loiter, loaf." Most of them have presumably been around since the seventeenth or the end of the sixteenth century (though the meaning "creep" is old) and make the impression of being part of the early modern North European cant (the language of the underworld) that "sneaked" into colloquial German, Dutch, and English and with time acquired a measure of respectability. This is a common occurrence with low slang.

Dictionaries, while trying to account for the obscure past of *sneak*, do not refer to *snoop* and its Dutch source, apparently, because the barrier between final *k* and *p* looks insurmountable, but fearlessly compare *snack* and *snap*. This is a valid comparison. *Snack*, like *snoop*, is a loan from Dutch. Before it began to mean "light meal," it meant "bite (especially of a dog); share, portion; drop of liquor; morsel of food." "Share" can still be recognized in the phrase *go snacks* "divide the spoils." Consequently, a snack is "a bite." *Snatch* is an etymological doublet of *snack*; the alternation *-k ~ -(t)ch* is the same as in *seek ~ beseech*. Contrary to the alternation *-k ~ p*, it is regular. A snack is thus something snatched up. The protoform of the verb *snatch* must have been *snakkan*. Modern Dutch *snakken* means "grab" and "chatter." Quite probably, *snap* is a sound-imitative verb and was coined to represent the snapping of a dog's jaws or some other quick action. Just as English *snack* means "hasty meal," German *Schnaps*, more often spelled *Schnapps* in English, denotes "a kind of gin"; originally it referred to a dram of spirits, so much as is tossed off at a swallow; compare German *schnappen* "seize, snatch" and Dutch *snaps* "gulp, mouthful."

We can now turn to *snuck*. The form is puzzling. As is known, English verbs, like the verbs in all the Germanic languages, are divided into two groups, conventionally called strong and weak. *Strong verbs* change their root vowel in forming their principal parts (e.g., *ride ~ rode ~ ridden, sing ~ sang ~ sung, give ~ gave ~ given, take ~ took ~ taken,* and so forth), whereas *weak verbs* only add an ending, as in *miss ~ missed, beg ~ begged,* and *land ~ landed.* The number of strong verbs is relatively small, but they are among the most common in the language: *see, stand, sit, come, go,* and so forth. Only the weak type is productive, that is, a new verb will form its past tense and the past participle according to the *miss/beg/land* pattern.

For example, it is unimaginable that a verb like *drum* should develop the forms *drum—drame—drum* on the analogy of *come—came— come,* or that anyone would coin the past *kuck* (from *kick*) because the past of *stick* is *stuck.* Analogy works almost exclusively in the opposite direction: numerous strong verbs have become weak over the centuries, as opposed to a tiny group of weak verbs that have joined the strong conjugation. The past of *sneak,* a late addition to the vocabulary of English, is, naturally *sneaked,* but *snuck* is widespread in American English (it is also current in British English), and its emergence causes surprise. Another weak verb that has gone over to the strong class is American English *dove* for *dived,* and the two are often discussed together. But whatever explanation can be offered for the change from *sneaked* to *snuck* will hardly hold for *dove.*

English has at least three preterit forms with the vowel of *snuck,* namely, *dug, stuck,* and *struck.* However, the verbs *dig, stick,* and *strike* have not become weak. An eminent British scholar devoted a long article to *snuck* and came to the conclusion that *snuck,* from the way it sounds, describes its action better than *sneaked.* No arguments in this area are final, but his conclusion may be right. *Snuck* is shorter and therefore more "final" than *sneaked,* but *sneak* differs from *snack* and *snap* in that it does not presuppose abruptness (the opposite is true). Consequently, the substitution of a strong form for a weak one still remains partly unexplained.

Obviously, most people who care about propriety in language are interested not in the origin of *snuck* (its origin is destined to remain a mystery, whatever we write about it) but in whether an educated person is "allowed" to say *snuck*. This is a moot question. If the majority of the population has chosen *snuck*, who cares what editors and teachers think? The popular, "uncultured" forms (the weeds) always win in the long run. Were it not so, we would still be speaking some version of Proto-Germanic. For centuries, people said *he hath, giveth, cometh*, and so forth. Today, we know about the existence of such forms only because we still read Shakespeare and the Revised Version of the Bible. Someone who has grown up with *sneaked* winces at *snuck*, but the *snuck* crowd does not care, while linguists are kept busy evaluating the status of this illegitimate form and reconstructing its history. Everybody has something to do, and the story seems to have a happy end.

Note
This is the reference to the paper mentioned above: Richard M. Hogg, "Snuck: The Development of Irregular Preterite Form" in *An Historic Tongue: Studies in English Linguistics in Memory of Barbara Strang*. Graham Nixon and John Honey (eds.). London, New York: Routledge, 1988, 243–47.

The Parasite Like

When did people begin to say: "I will, like, come tomorrow" and why do they say so? It may seem that the filler *like*, along with its twin *you know*, are of recent date, but this impression is hardly correct. Yet, indeed, both became a plague in recent memory. Occasionally an etymologist discovers that a word was current in Middle or early Modern English, disappeared from view, and then seemingly resurfaced in the modern language. One wonders whether this is the same word or its homophone "born again."

Of some interest is the fact that the adverb *belike* once existed and may still exist, at least in regional speech. Consider the following: "All these three, belike, went together" (1741; *OED*). Take away *be-*, and you will get a charming modern sentence: "All these three, like, went together." *Belike* meant "in all likelihood." *Like* occurs in comparable contexts. A few instances of it will be found in the first edition of the *OED*, under *like*, marked as "dialectal and vulgar": "Of a sudden like," "In an ordinary way like"; those and a few other similar examples are from the nineteenth century. After the verb *to be*, *like* may be indistinguishable from *likely*. Henry W. F. Talbot, the inventor of photography, was also interested in the history of words. I will reproduce three examples, whose accuracy I did not verify, from his book *English Etymologies* (1847): "He is like to die for hunger, for there is no more bread" (Jeremiah XXXVIII: 9), "You are like to be much advanced" (Shakespeare), "I wish that I were dead, but I am na like to dee" (*Auld Robin Gray*). In such sentences, *like* means "likely" ("he is likely to die," etc.). Talbot was a polymath and dabbled in etymology. His derivations have no value, but his material is often of interest.

My hypothesis is that, at a certain moment, *like* freed itself from the verb *to be* and became an independent filler. It has been used in British dialects as it is used in American English for quite some time and was perhaps brought to the New World, where it stayed "underground" until approximately fifty or so years ago. Assuming that such is the state of affairs, one wonders why Bret Harte, Mark Twain, and Jack London (among many other writers who reproduced the speech of common people) did not notice the parasite. The *Second Supplement* to the *OED* cited the sentence: "And I thought like wow, this is for me" (1970; no earlier citations). The editors of the dictionary assigned this usage to "less analysable constructions," and indeed *like* is redundant in *like wow*. It need not be called an adverb, for it is a parenthetical word and should be flanked by commas (as is done in most modern editions that contain samples of such usage). The part of speech called "adverb" has always served as a trashcan for grammatical misfits, but this practice has nothing to recommend it.

Even if a bridge can be drawn between *like* after *be/am/is/are* (and perhaps *belike*) and our free-floating *like*, we still do not know why, close to the end of the twentieth century, the modern filler left its modest home and succeeded so singularly in contaminating the Standard. Nowadays, linguists are not supposed to be judgmental, so that I should have said *penetrating* instead of *contaminating*. Allegedly, their duty is to describe language with equanimity and detachment, as a geologist examines rocks or, even better, as an entomologist studies insects. Indeed, it would be ridiculous to accuse mosquitoes or scorpions of the harm they do their victims. That is why the multiple papers devoted to *like* retain absolute detachment. *Like* is called a discourse marker or a pragmatic marker. Its uses by native speakers and by foreigners are classified, tabulated, and summarized. Foreigners, I may add, were quick to learn and introduce this parasite (sorry, pragmatic/discourse marker) into their speech.

However, language, in addition to being a means of communication, is an object of culture, a garden in which flowers coexist with weeds, and there is no joy in hearing from a native speaker or a learner from afar: "She may, like, come later" and "Did you, like, attend college?" To be sure, the egalitarian motto—be descriptive, not prescriptive—is a hoax, for teachers and editors exist (are even paid) for instilling certain values into students and authors, and when we are not sure of a word's meaning or of some niceties of usage, we still say (are, like, expected to say): "Let us look it up in a dictionary." Therefore, I am ready to describe *like* and condemn it.

Although I cannot explain why *like* won its victory when it did (and this makes my reconstruction vulnerable), perhaps we may agree about why this victory occurred. There is a branch of linguistics called *pragmatics*. It deals with the ways people organize their speech; the use of *like* belongs to it. Whatever the source of the filler, it seems to function (or at one time to have functioned) as a marker of uncertainty and resembles *as it were*, a common parasite in British English. People tend to safeguard themselves from a possible rebuttal and do it instinctively. "Will you, like, pay me later?" It means: "Will you pay me later? Of course, I am not even suggesting that you will, so that if you have no such plans, I am quite happy, but perhaps you will." *You know* plays a comparable role. "This is a strange thing, you know." Read: "I believe it is a strange thing, and you will not contest my statement, for *you know* that I am right, you yourself think so, don't you?" (One of the Barnacles in the Circumlocution Office in Dickens's *Little Dorrit* says indignantly: "He wants to know, you know"—a rather early instance of *you know* in later English literature, 1857.) A classic example of pragmatic humility is the use of *oder* "or" as a "finisher" in German: once the sentence is finished, the interrogative *oder* is added to it (comparable to English "isn't it?" and so forth).

The democratization of life in the free world did not abolish disparities in cultural level and status. People continue to be cautious and instinctively defensive. But after *you know* and *like* gained ground, those tags began to be repeated unthinkingly. Every successful change passes through three stages: introduction, acceptance, and spread. Language change is no exception to this rule. (Those living in the American Midwest constantly hear a rising intonation at the end of declarative sentences. An administrator said to a group of faculty: "There will be a freeze on hiring this year," and one could not understand whether it was a statement or a question, even though the speaker had no doubts about the budgetary woes of the college. Less enlightened people use this intonation all the time. Is this another feature of what used to be a deferential attitude toward the interlocutor or a sign of instinctive self-effacement, now reproduced automatically on a par with *like* and *you know*? Has this phenomenon been observed outside American English, in which it supposedly originated in women's speech in California?)

I am far from certain that I managed to account for the triumph of the parenthetical *like*. Particularly disconcerting is the fact that the analogs of *like* swamped other languages at roughly the same time or a few decades later. Germans have begun to say *quasi* in every sentence. Swedes say *liksom*, and Russians say *kak by*; both mean "as though." In this function, *quasi*, *liksom*, and *kak by* are recent. The influence of American *like* is probably out of the question. So why, and why now? Delving into the depths of Indo-European and Proto-Germanic requires courage and perspicuity. But here we are facing a phenomenon of no great antiquity and are as puzzled as though we were trying to decipher a cuneiform inscription. Change baffles researchers: they can observe and describe it but often fail to explain its causes.

From Dodge and Nudge to Kitsch: A Case of Effective Affinities

Dickens's Artful Dodger and the car "Dodge" made the word *dodge* famous beyond its merit, especially if we consider the fact that *dodge* is an upstart, originally perhaps criminals' slang. Dickens, ever-sensitive to the language of the street, must have had a good reason for giving such a sobriquet to the crafty young scoundrel Jack Dawkins, and *Oliver Twist* is full of the words current in slums and among thieves. Nothing is known about Jack's parents, and nothing is known about the origin of the words *dodge*, *nudge*, and *kitsch*, except that *kitsch* is a loan from German. The noun *dodge* surfaced in English texts a century before the verb: 1575 versus 1680 (those are the dates of their first occurrence, as given in the *OED*). The verb was first recorded as meaning "to palter, haggle, trifle." Later, the senses "to shift one's position" and "to play fast and loose" emerged. The earliest citation of *dodge* "to jog" (now dialectal) is dated to 1813. As we will see, it is a fact of no small importance that *dodge* competed with *jog*.

Our story hangs by a single thread, namely, by the role of the consonant denoted in writing by the letters *j* and *ge*. We will pass by words like *large* (taken over from French) and *bridge* (native). Everything is known about their history and about the history of their final consonants. It is the likes of *dodge* and *jog* that will occupy our attention. We observe with some curiosity the surroundings of *dodge*. *Budge* and *fudge* "to fake, patch up" (the latter with the earlier variants *fadge* and *fodge* "to adjust, fit") and their relative *fidget* are words of dubious or even unknown origin, that is, they do not have recorded earlier forms and resemble only one another.

Drudge may be a continuation of *drugge* "to drag or pull heavily" (related to *drag*?). *Trudge* once had the variant *tridge* and *tredge* (a typical variation in such words). They probably belong with *tread*, a verb recorded long ago and having related forms elsewhere, but old age and an extended family do not seem to have contributed to its etymological transparence: it is still part of the same group. Scottish *dod(d)* "to jog'" may belong with *dodge*, but of course there is no certainty. One cannot help noticing that all the verbs cited above are expressive, almost suggesting their meaning, that is, sound-symbolic. When we hear such words, it seems that they mean just what we expected. It is of course an illusion but not a groundless one.

The words with initial *j* make a similar impression. Dictionaries have little or nothing to say about their origin except for again calling them sound-symbolic or imitative. Here is a short list of such words: *jabber*, *jade* "a worn-out horse; slut," *jam* (verb), *jamboree* "noisy revel," *jangle*, *jar* (verb), *jargon*, *jaunt*, *jeer*, *jejune*, *jerk*, *job* "to prick" and "work," *jiggered*, *jilt* (in high) *jinks*, *jostle*, *jump*, *junk*, and quite a few more. The history of *jazz* and *jig* (of *jazz* especially) has been researched in great detail, but their origin remains obscure (sound-symbolic, sound-imitative?).

Armed with such poor ammunition, we, predictably, have little to say about the origin of the word *dodge*. It can go back to an unrecorded form with the root *dog-* or *dod-*, followed by *i* or *yod* (*yod* is the name of the initial sound in words like *yes*). Then the development will have been as in *bridge* and *soldier*. Or it may be a continuation of a French word (such as *large*, *huge*, *rage*, *siege*; incidentally, *huge* is a word of unknown origin!). Finally, it can be a reshaping of a loanword from some other language. For example, *ledge* and *ledger* are believed to have been borrowed from Dutch or a "reinforced" form of an English word, even though the details of such a change are bound to remain unclear; yet *tredge* is probably indeed a "reinforced," emphatic form of *tread*. Such ideas have occurred to both professional historical linguists and amateurs. *Dodge* has been compared with the verb *dog* because to dodge is "to shift and play tricks like a dog." It was also said that a young or favorite dog will attempt to follow its master or mistress in the rambles after only being beckoned or driven home, that is, "dodge." However, final *-g* turned into *-dge* only in words going back to Old English, like *bridge* and *wedge*, while *dodge* is an upstart, a contemporary of Shakespeare.

French *douger* "to stumble slightly" and Middle Dutch *docken* "to duck" perhaps resemble some senses of *dodge*, but the sounds match badly. *Dodder*, a doublet of *totter*, is another plausible semantic fit, but the problem of *-d* becoming *-dge* remains. The derivation of *dodge* and its northern English look-alike *dadge* "saunter aimlessly" from *dod* and *dad* "jog" looks promising (let us remember that "jog" is one of the recorded meanings of *dodge*), **but only if we are ready to admit that *-dge* appeared as an expressive variant of *-d*.** Here is the rub.

Let us forgive ourselves the vice that Shakespeare, in the opening line of Sonnet 62, called the sin of self-love. Etymology stopped being guesswork after linguists discovered the existence of regular sound correspondences. Thus, English *milk* is indeed related to German

Milch because the *k* ~ *ch* alternation between those two languages is regular. But Russian *moloko* (stress on the last syllable) does not belong to this family: English *k* should correspond to Slavic *g*, not *k*. The pair is too good to be related! Perhaps the Slavic word was borrowed "whole-sale" from Germanic, or Germanic took it over from Slavic or both received it as a loan from a third language.

In the "prescientific" past, such a conclusion would not have occurred to anyone because nothing could be too good for the researchers of old: the closer the resemblance, the better. Reference to sound symbolism, to expressive and emphatic variants, and other more or less intangible factors is not proof, and etymologists fear to watch their self-love crumble and turn into self-indulgence. However, words obey the so-called laws of historical linguistics only up to a point because people have always treated language as a favorite toy and created words in many capricious ways. This process is especially obvious in the history of slang. The more picturesque a word is, the easier it is to play with it, and *dodge* is certainly a "playful" verb. It also seems that, in some epochs or centuries, speakers are apt to treat their language with more freedom than in the others. The age of Shakespeare was (though this view may be an illusion) one of such epochs.

Hensleigh Wedgwood, who dominated the English etymological scene before the emergence of Walter W. Skeat, offered many promising solutions, but often (too often) allowed his excessive trust in the role of sound imitation and sound symbolism to run away with him. Be that as it may be, he cited northern English *dodge* "a small lump of something moist and thick" and compared it with German (Bavarian) *datsch* ~ *dotsch* having almost the same meaning: "a mass of something soft; a fat person." He connected the German (also dialectal) verb *datschen* "to press down something soft" with English *dodge*. The *OED* did not ignore English dialectal *dodge* but gave it a special entry and offered no etymology. This *dodge* surfaced roughly at the same time as the verb that interests us. German *dotsch* and English *dodge* "lump" are probably connected in some way and the parallelism *datsch* ~ *dotsch* and *dadge* ~ *dodge* is unmistakable. However, we have not yet arrived at an etymology. If we are dealing with some conversational words known in English and German, what is their origin, and why are they known in two languages? Were they part of common European army slang or international thieves' cant?

Verbs meaning "press" often develop the sense "press on." If we assume such a starting point, the path may have been from "press" to "press on; press through a soft substance without a well-defined direction" (because in dealing with such a body the knife or the hand will go every possible way) and "shift." "Palter" (= "act nervously") and "haggle" would have been later figurative senses. *Jog* aligns itself with "pressing on" quite naturally. Wedgwood's etymology has several advantages: it connects *dodge* "shift" with its German near-homonym and with *dodge* "lump"; it encounters no phonetic difficulties (the final voiced sound is of the same origin as in *sludge* and *hodgepodge* from *slush* and *hotchpotch*) and the development of senses, though not obvious, does not look fanciful. Cautious reference to this etymology is perhaps preferable to the now standard verdict "of unknown origin." James A. H. Murray, the *OED's* first editor, had the same opinion but could not overcome the *-d/-dge* barrier.

Wedgwood compared *dodge* with both German *datsch* and northern English *dod/dodder* ~ Scots *dad* "a slam; tick," Skeat cited English dialectal *dade* "to walk unsteadily," *dod* "to jog," along with *dadge* and *dodder*, and remarked: "Very doubtful." He also mentioned *dither* "act nervously" in connection with *dodge* but later gave up this comparison. The reconstructed Middle English form *dodien*, developing phonetically like *soldier* (so still in the otherwise cautious and usually reliable *Century Dictionary*) is fiction. In light of what we know about the role of *j-* ~ *-dge*, it does not seem too bold to suggest that *dodge* is a reinforced, sound-symbolic variant of *dod* "to jog."

This conclusion is borne out by at least two parallel cases. The verb *nudge* appeared in a text in 1675. Not unexpectedly, its origin is unknown. A similar German verb exists but does not clarify the situation. Next to *nudge*, we find *nud* and *nuddle*. Both refer to beating, pummeling, pushing, and so forth. Equally obscure is the origin of *nod*. Yet the word *nodgecock* "simpleton" has been recorded. It seems that there is very little one can say about the origin of that family, except that once such monosyllabic verbs—*dod*, *nod*, *nud*, and their likes— emerge, they tend to develop more emphatic twins like *dodge*, *nodge*, and *nudge*. Theirs is a rootless but powerful family. Yet its history gives us an idea of how the earliest words in language came into existence.

Perhaps the suggestions offered above may help elucidate the origin of *kitsch*, a borrowing of a nineteenth-century German word. There will be no reinforced forms because German lacks the consonant English has in *jog* and *budge*. But some light may come from the obscurity of the words for "mud." *Kitsch* "art in poor taste" emerged in Munich in 1870, and in the full light of history, was, apparently, slang, and, not unexpectedly, is a word of unknown origin. Attempts to derive it from English *sketch* or from a Hungarian word with a similar meaning carry little conviction. Only a third etymology seems to make sense. German *Kitsche* designates a kind of rake used for removing mud, from which *kitschen* "to rake together street mud" has been derived.

Kitsch was probably coined with the sense "smoothed out mud." German language historians did not pay attention to English *keech*, first recorded in Shakespeare and meaning "fat of a slaughtered animal rolled into a lump" (applied mockingly to a butcher's wife and a butcher's son!). It will be remembered that German dialectal *datsch* ~ *dotsch* also mean "a mass of something soft; a fat person." Not improbably, *Datsch* and *Kitsch* are words of a similar type. Perhaps *dadge* and *dodge* came to English from German, like *Kitsch*, whatever the homeland of *keech* may be, but the itinerary of such monosyllables from land to land is hard to trace.

13

A Few Idioms

By Hook or by Crook

By hook or by crook means "by any means available." Why do we say so? What could be obtained by those tools and where? The origin of idioms may be as enigmatic as the origin of words. *It rains cats and dogs*. Do cats and dogs ever fall from the sky in a violent torrent? *To get one's dander up*. What is *dander*? *By Jingo*. Who is Jingo? Some such questions have never been answered.

According to the *Oxford English Dictionary* (*OED*), *by hook or by crook* appeared for the first time in a written text around 1380 in the works of the great philosopher and theologian John Wyclif (c. 1330–1384). As we will see, the dating is important for debunking some fanciful hypotheses of the origin of this idiom. To be sure, if, in 1380, the phrase *by hook or by crook* could be used in a written text by such a popular writer as Wycliff, we may conclude that by that year it had become common enough to be understood by a broad audience.

Conjectures about the idiom's background are many. In periodicals, they began to appear around 1850. Perhaps the best-known explanation one can find in old journals, popular books, and sometimes even today on the Internet runs as follows. As is well-known, Cromwell's fleet invaded Ireland. Hook and Crooke are places in the port of Waterford, Wexford, and the invaders allegedly declared that their fleet would safely land *by Hook or by Crook(e)*. Ireland was besieged twice: in 1649 and 1650, and Cromwell may have promised to conquer it by hook or by crook (though we have no documents to prove it), but, even if in one of his joking moments he did so, he used the idiom long known to him and everybody else. The pun suggested itself at once. This explanation of the phrase is at odds with chronology, as James A. H. Murray used to say.

The same flaw marks the next "theory" with all its ramifications. Enter Messrs. Hook and Crook. Here are some ghosts of those gentlemen. In the Great Fire of London, many boundary marks were destroyed. We are told that disputes about the sites of different properties arose and hindered the rebuilding of the city. It was therefore decided to appoint two arbitrators, whose decisions should be final in all cases. The surveyors appointed were allegedly a Mr. Hook and a Mr. Crook, and they gave so much satisfaction in their decisions that the rebuilding proceeded rapidly. Hence, allegedly, the idiom. Now, the Great Fire of London lasted from September 2 to September 6, 1666. We are obliged to repeat: by that time, our idiom had been current for a very long time. Only a decade and a half separate Cromwell from the Fire.

According to another version, there once (in what century?) were two judges who in their days decided "most unconscientiously" whenever the interests of the crown were affected, and it used to be said that the king could get anything by Hooke or by Crooke (note the spelling), though perhaps the correct form of the second gentleman's name was Croke. Or such judges, though not crooks, were famous for the perpetual *diversity of opinion*. Consequently, every suitor was sure to have either Hook or Crook (once again spelled Croke) on his side. Finally, an old London legend has it that the numerous families of Hook and Crook formerly did the ferry business for the whole of the British metropolis. Thus, whichever boat was chosen to cross the Thames, one was sure to ride with either Hook or Crook.

Urban folklore has for a long time interested students of oral tradition. The Hook and Crook legends resemble those that claim to account for the origin of some obscure place names, and some of them need not be dismissed out of hand because the popular memory often preserves a garbled version of the truth. A serious researcher's business is to study documents (evidence). Have any traces of the Hook-and-Crook couple been found? It would be curious to account for the tenacity of what at first sight looks like sheer nonsense. The history of the ferry business on the Thames has probably been traced by specialists. A complete roster of British judges may also exist. Any Hook and Crook? Here we cannot afford going so far afield. Yet one thing is clear: *by hook or by crook* surfaced in writing toward the close of the fourteenth century, and even if later Mr. Hook and Mr. Crook ever existed in some capacity as a team, the idiom could at best reinforce the idea of their association rather than being the source of the phrase. But more probably, those gentlemen are pure fiction.

Those who wrote letters to the editor and volunteered to tell the world what they thought they knew about this or that phrase never referred to their sources because they only repeated the versions they had once heard. Occasionally they found their information in books whose authors also did without references. Bizarre conjectures acquired the status of common knowledge. Such is, for example, the idea that *by hook or by crook* means "foully like a thief or holily like a bishop," the hook being used by burglars, the crook being the bishop's crozier. Very ingenious but quite untrustworthy, even if some wit applied the idiom in that context.

Two hypotheses on the origin of *by hook or by crook* look reasonable. One appeared in *Manchester Notes and Queries* for 1882. In the past, we are told, a man living beyond reach of the few cart-roads of the country could take home his merchandise only in one of two ways: on his own back or on that of a beast of burden. As late as the 1880s, in some places, packmen still carried their bundles at the end of a hooked stick. The simplest pannier was formed of bent poles and was called a crook. Thus, a man's goods were conveyed from place to place either on his own shoulder or by means of a packhorse, and all he wanted "had to be got either by hook or by crook." Though this hypothesis makes sense, the practice described looks like a justification rather than the source of the idiom. We should also remember how long ago that idiom was coined.

The suggestion that looks attractive and that has been accepted, even if cautiously, by several good authorities appeared in 1872, in the biweekly *Notes and Queries*, Series 4, Volume IX, p. 77. Its author was Edward Smirke (1795–1875), an English lawyer and antiquarian. He explained that, in the Middle Ages, people were allowed to collect dead wood for fuel and other purposes as long as their actions did not interfere "with the more substantive use and profits of the timber for the general purposes of the landowner." It was permitted to carry away any refuse (i.e., dead or damaged portions of the trees) if that refuse was removable by simple means, *without using axes, bills, or saws*. Among the tools allowed were *crook-lugs* (in this word, both components seem to mean the same: a kind of crook for lugging). Thus, one could get that fuel only by hook or by crook and, consequently, not by any means available! The modern sense must have developed later when speakers no longer remembered the legal motivation for the phrase. Perhaps this is the true story of *by hook or by crook*.

Two factors must have contributed to the survival of the idiom. *Hook* and *crook* rhyme, and English is fond of such sayings (compare even our modern *snail mail*, *stop and shop*, *Polly Wolly*, and so forth). Also, *hook* and *crook* mean approximately the same, and, judging by expressions like *safe and sound*, *fine and dandy*, and quite a few other, tautology holds certain attraction in such cases: it reinforces the message without burdening the listener with more content. *Hook* and *crook* were at one time interchangeable synonyms. For instance, *a shepherd's hook* meant the same as *a shepherd's crook*.

As so often, we should end our investigation on a cautious note. Perhaps the truth is now known, but of course there is no absolute certainty. Edmund Smirke seems to have guessed well. If so, we know not only the origin of a curious English idiom but also the name of the person who discovered its source. Such a double discovery is rare in the science of etymology.

Raining Cats and Dogs

Some phrases exist that all or most native English speakers know but hardly ever use. Such are, for example, *to kick the bucket* and *to pay through the nose*. *Raining cats and dogs* is part of this moribund set. Everybody who is interested in matters etymological has experienced the disappointment at being told "origin unknown." What is true of the undocumented history of words is doubly true of proverbial sayings and idioms, even though most of them are comparatively recent. Apart from the familiar quotations from the Bible and Greek and Latin classics, they are usually post-medieval. The *OED* is reticent when it comes to their origin (because its conclusions are based on hard facts, and those are few), whereas books meant for the so-called lay reader don't shy from supplying fanciful information. References (beyond "some people think") are seldom given, and all kinds of improbable guesses are passed off as theories worthy of attention.

A case in point is the "theory," according to which the source of *it is raining cats and dogs* is Nordic. Allegedly, in Norse mythology, cats were supposed to have great influence on the weather, while dogs were a signal of the wind; or cats were a symbol of heavy rain (whatever *symbol* means in this context), while the dog, an attendant of Odin, the storm god, represented great blasts of wind; or witches in the guise of cats rode upon the storm and followed Odin and his dogs. Yet in Norse mythology, Odin is not a storm god, his "animals" are an eight-legged horse and two wise ravens, while cats have nothing to do with either Odin or witches, and rain is not connected with any divinity. A demon, whose figure very probably goes back to Odin, presides over the Wild Hunt (a procession of dead riders) in Scandinavian *folklore*, not mythology. The Wild Hunt, which is known in most of northern Europe, is associated with stormy weather, but Odin's following is made up of flying corpses. Cats, dogs, and witches do not participate in it. Under no circumstances can the English idiom be traced to any scene in Scandinavian oral tradition. Apparently, no one who refers to Scandinavian tales seems to have read them.

The idea that *it is raining cats and dogs* is an alteration of some foreign model has occurred to many. The Greek phrase *káta dóksa*, approximately, "contrary to expectation" (compare English **cata**clysm, and *ortho*do**xy**), seemed especially worthy of note because even, allegedly (I cannot judge), in Modern Greek, one sometimes uses it in describing a downpour, and the same phrase has reportedly been heard from Romani (the country is never specified).

However, in Greek (assuming the information is reliable), *káta dóksa* can be applied to any phenomenon that is unexpected. An additional point should be made. When a loan is suggested, reference to a similar-sounding word or idiom in a foreign language will never suffice because the ways of its reaching a new home have to be traced. How did Greek *káta dóksa* reach English? Did the English phrase originate among schoolboys or university wits? Another Greek etymology derived *cats and dogs* from **Katadoupoi**, the name of the great cataracts on the Nile (perhaps via French). Here, we would like to be told how the Greek cataracts were transferred from the Nile, directly or via

France, to the foggy skies of England. And what has happened to the dogs (or is *doupoi* the last remnant of the canine pack)?

A correspondent to *Notes and Queries* wrote in 1919: "I think I have heard somewhere that this phrase is a corruption of *tempo cattivo* (bad weather) and that it was introduced into England by Nelson's sailors who had served in Italian waters." Dogs have again disappeared from the scene, and it is amazing how often it is believed that the origin of the English phrase would be explained if only the source of its first half were explained. Yet some people were aware of the problem. We read " 'Cat-and-dog weather.' I consider that these sayings [*sic*] have more to do with the cat than with the dog. *Cattivo tempo* . . . is bad weather, and cat weather is probably a bad pun derived from *cattivo*. The *dog* has been, we may presume, introduced by some genius who, having read or heard of the 'warring elements,' deemed the dog a fitting companion for pussy!"—an 1870 "theory."

Here is another variant of the cat-and-dog weather derivation, this time, bypassing the epithet *cattivo*: "[T]he elements of nature in their disarray fly at each other as if a cat and dogs met at a barn door." Italians also say *freddo e vento e acqua a catinelle* "cold and wind, and water in basins" (a common image: raining in buckets). Quite true, but where are the dogs? Perhaps if one can say *acqua a catinelle*, one can also say *a catinelle e dogli* . . . (*dogli* is the plural of *doglio* "large jar; barrel"). The author of that hypothesis admitted that he had never heard such a phrase, but why not presume?

We are now ready to make a trip to the Netherlands. John Bellenden Ker (1764–1842) produced a set of incredibly ingenious books (six volumes) on questions of etymology. He looked at hundreds of English words, proverbial sayings, and nursery rhymes as "corruptions" of something existing in Dutch (Ker's Dutch is as mind-boggling as the content of his works). His explanation must be quoted in full: "IT RAINS CATS AND DOGS. That is, the rain is violent and drives to the face. '*Et reyn's ketse aen d'oogs;* q. e. this is a proper current in the eyes; it is a thorough drive upon the eyes; it is as if its only object was our eyes; how properly it besets one's eyes! The phrase is evidently jocular in both travesty and original; and evidently spoken by one who had been peppered by some driving storm of rain. '*Et, het*, this, it. *Reyn*, pure, unmixed, proper, sheer. '*S, is,* is. *Ketse*, as the participle present of *ketsen, kitsen*, to chase, to drive on after, to pursue, to hunt. *D'oogs, de oogs*, the eyes." Etymology has always attracted lunatics (some of whom happened to be medical doctors). A similar recent Hebrew derivation of the English phrase also exists, but I will spare the readers the details. By the way, Ker was a distinguished botanist, and one wonders why an ability to do serious research did not prevent him from producing such stuff.

Back to England. "*Raining Cats and Dogs.*—'During a heavy, but genial shower toward the end of this March [this was published in early April 1857], and old stone-breaker said to me: "This is the rain, Sir, to make the *cats and dogs* grow!" pointing as he spoke to the hedge-side willows, which were covered with the bursting *catkins*, which are called by some people 'cats and dogs,' and which were used on Palm Sunday to represent the branches of palm. Does this throw any light on the singular saying which heads this note?" I have serious doubts.

We are finally moving from the realm of linguistic games to real life. "Has the expression an origin with cats and dogs pattering across a bare boarded floor, strangely resembling the sound of a heavy downpour of rain?" I cannot judge. Rather frequent is the reference to Jonathan Swift's description of a heavy shower in London: "*Drown'd puppies*, stinking sprats, all drenched in mud, / *Dead cats*, and turnip tops, come tumbling down the flood." While viewing the trophies of the rain, we are told, people must have believed that it had "rained cats and dogs." Clever, but far-fetched. Swift did know the phrase. The *OED* quotes him as saying "it would rain cats and dogs" (1738), and this is the earliest literary attestation of the idiom in the dictionary, but the idea of Swift's coining it is most unlikely.

One often encounters the hypothesis that cats and even small dogs used to climb up onto the thatched roofs to sleep. And when heavy rains came, they would not be able to hold on to the wet thatch and fall to the ground; hence the idiom. This looks like a feeble exercise in folk etymology. How often would one have to watch a picture of multiple cats and dogs falling off a thatched roof to coin an idiom now in popular use? Several phrases combining *cat and dog* exist, and a few are old, but as far as I can judge, the order of the elements is usually *dog and cat*, as in *lead a dog-and-cat life*. Yet it rains cats and dogs, not dogs and cats.

I believe that the best clue to the origin of the idiom was furnished by N. E. Toke (*Notes and Queries*, 12th Series, vol. 4, 1918, pp. 328–29). He paid attention to a 1592 sentence from the *OED* (under *cat* 17): "Instead of thunderboltes shooteth nothing but dogboltes or catboltes" (G. Harvey). By the end of the sixteenth century, our phrase (in some form at least) must have been known. Toke adds: " ... 'dogbolts' and 'catbolts' are terms still employed in provincial dialect to denote, respectively, the iron bolts for securing a door or gate, and the bolts for fastening together pieces of timber." If Harvey's *catbolts* and *dogbolts* are not a pun on *thunderbolts*, one can imagine that people compared a shower (or better a hailstorm) to heavy instruments falling on their heads from the sky, with *thunderbolt* supplying a convenient model for the other two words. Characteristically, the fuller version of the idiom is *raining cats and dogs and pitchforks (with their points downward)*. Evidently, cats and dogs were thought to belong with sharp instruments rather than animals. If there is any truth in this reconstruction, the idiom sounded *raining catbolts, dogbolts, and pitchforks*; the second element *-bolts* was later left out, perhaps because the whole came out too bulky or as a joke (whose humor soon became incomprehensible).

Have we found an answer to our riddle? Perhaps. But in such matters, one can never be sure.

Pay Through the Nose

Pay through the nose sounds puzzling: either *pay* or *nose* or both seem to mean, in this phrase, something different from what we expect. The idiom has been current since the second half of the seventeenth century and was probably transparent to its contemporaries. It makes no sense to us, even though *pay* and *nose* still mean what they did four hundred years ago.

The Internet supplies those who look for the history of *pay through the nose* with four or five explanations from fairly recent books bearing the generic title *Phrase Origins*. All of them, regardless of their reliability, have a fatal flaw: they do not cite their sources. At best, they say "it is usually believed" or "according to legend" but never add where they found the legend, who wrote what they repeat, or even approximately where the gossip originated. Only dictionaries of quotations try to discover the authors of famous lines, and their efforts have been crowned with great success.

This, then, is what we can find. "If you were caught stealing in medieval times, they sliced a slit in your nose." Anywhere (or only in England?) in the Middle Ages at any time? "In medieval times, when the Jews were being bled for money, any objection by them to paying was greeted with a slitting of their noses." (The allusion to bleeding noses will recur below.) In this case, it was the Jews, rather than the Swedes of the Middle Ages (which, incidentally, lasted more than a thousand years). But wait! "Odin laid a tax of a penny a nose upon every Swede." However, Odin (or Othinn) was the greatest god of the Scandinavian pantheon (especially in its Old Icelandic version), and it is hard to understand what he could have done with such a tax, for he neither sold nor bought anything. In the next essay, about the origin of the idiom *it rains cats and dogs*, we will be informed by an imaginative author that Odin was surrounded by cats and dogs, which caused rain. Why should people who have never read Scandinavian myths pretend that they are familiar with them and have the temerity to flaunt their ignorance in print? Also, what payment has even the cruelest dictator ever obtained *through* the noses of his subjects?

"The Swedish poll tax was a nose tax." This is a variant of the preceding one, and, for a change, I think I can state where this "explanation" of the English idiom came from. An Icelandic-English Dictionary (i.e., the great *Old* Icelandic dictionary by Cleasby-Vigfusson) says the following in the entry *nef-gildi*: "'*a nose-tax*', *poll-tax* payable to the king. . . . This ancient 'nose-tax' was also imposed by the Norseman on conquered countries, and the name gave rise to strange legends; thus[,] king Thorsgisl, the Norse conqueror of Ireland (A.D. 830–845), is, by an Irish chronicler, said to have levied a tax of an ounce on each hearth, the penalty for defaulting being the loss of their nose. Prof. Munch . . . has traced the origin of this legend to the simple fact that the king imposed a '*nose-tax*' or *poll-tax* on the conquered Irish, just as Harold Fairhair afterwards did in Norway."

There is no mystery in the phrase *nose tax*. The rhetorical figure called synecdoche ("part for the whole," or *pars pro toto* in Latin) is common in just such situations. *Poll* means "head" (this, despite the difference in spelling, also happens to be the second element of *tadpole*, "toad head"), so that *poll tax* is a formation of the same type as *nose tax*. When we say *a hundred head of cattle* or *all hands aboard*, we don't mean that the heads or hands will be separated from the rest of the bodies. In medieval Scandinavia, *nose*, rather than *head*, was the synecdoche for "person." Consequently, the tax was levied on every "nose." Reference to Odin may have appeared from *Ynglinga saga*, the mythological part of Snorri Sturluson's *A History of the Kings of Norway*. (Snorri was a famous politician and a great writer.) In chapter 8 of that engrossing book, it is said that "in all Sweden people paid a tax to Odin, a penny for every nose." There, according to Snorri's design, Odin is represented as a king rather than a god.

The rest is now plain sailing. "A possible explanation for this [phrase] lies in the 'nose tax' levied upon the Irish by the Danes in the ninth century. Those who did not pay had their noses slit." "The most plausible [explanation] is perhaps that the Swedish poll-tax was once called a nose-tax." Cautious authors state that there is no evidence for the legend. It would be better to say that no evidence exists for the slitting of noses. Especially important is the fact that the English idiom that surfaced eight centuries after the Vikings' raids cannot possibly have such an old source.

Another hypothesis reminds us that, as early as the seventeenth century, *rhino* was slang for "money" and *rhinos* is Greek for "nose" (as seen in *rhinoceros*, literally "nose-horn"). "Noses bleed, and the man who is forced to pay is also 'bled.' Some elaborate word-play of this character must lie behind the phrase." Clever, but rather improbable, though the origin of the idiom in thieves' cant (or among university wits, who played with Greek words?) cannot be excluded. We sometimes hear that *pay through the nose* appeared as a variant of *lead by the nose* or as an alternation of *pay through the noose* (!), or is a direct translation from French. Since such an idiom does not exist in French, we needn't bother about the last etymology. Finally, the phrase *bored through the nose* "swindled" existed. This phrase (perhaps) evokes a picture of a medieval torture, but it provides no bridge to the outwardly transparent collocation *pay through the nose*.

An essay written only to declare surrender is a sad thing, but I stumbled on an explanation that, as far as I can judge, deserves being disinterred from the article bearing the title "Horse-Marines" (*Notes and Queries*, Series 9/II, 1898, p. 457). Its author is Richard Edgcumbe. "Then, again, 'Paying through the nose.' This was originally a common expression on board ship: 'Pay out the cable,' 'pay out handsomely.' The nose of a ship is, of course, the bow; its nostrils are the hawse holes on either side. Now, it does not seem very difficult (at all events, for a sailor) to associate extortionate disbursements with handsome payments—such, for instance, as paying out a chain cable (through the nose), especially when the order is conveyed in such a language as this, 'Pay out handsomely.' At all events, I can speak on this matter from personal experience as a midshipman. To my mind, 'paying through the nose' for anything has always been associated with the rattling of a 'payed out' chain cable, after the anchor has gripped the ground. Whatever the learned may say to the contrary, with me that impression will never fade. Now that the term 'paying through the nose' has reached the shore, it is natural that so obvious an origin should be lost. In conclusion, I ask to be forgiven for what may seem to be dogmatic in an old sea dog."

In my opinion, "the learned" should applaud Mr. Edgcumbe. His is the only reasonable conjecture I have been able to dig up.

God's Acre

Why was the churchyard (or graveyard) called *God's acre*? In 1913, a volume presented on the completion of George Lyman Kittredge's twenty-fifth year of teaching at Harvard University appeared in New York. One of the contributors to it was Professor J. A. Walz, a fellow philologist. Kittredge's name is known to many from the book *Words and their Ways in English Speech* by Greenough and Kittredge (at that time, George B. Geenough was a senior colleague, and his name stood first on the title page; but in any case, G precedes K in the English alphabet). Walz did exactly what should be done in such cases, and we follow the path of the research. He looked through multiple reference books, collected the publications on *God's acre* in *Notes and Queries*, "that unique meeting place of British ignorance and scholarship," as he called it, and summarized what he had found. I am saying this because many dictionaries of idioms offer explanations without telling the readers how they arrived at the conclusions, and here we view the process, which, in the acquisition of knowledge, is as valuable as the result.

The contributors to *Notes and Queries* discovered everything, including the earliest mention of the phrase in William Camden's *Remains Concerning Britain* (1605, published in 1617). Even Murray's *OED* could offer no antedating. They also dug up the relevant quotations from the New Testament. Several biblical texts, most pointedly one of the epistles, explain that the dead are "sown" and sleep awaiting resurrection. Finally, they, of course, asked the question about the originator of the phrase. At that time, in the 1850s and the 1870s, Henry Wadsworth Longfellow had numerous admirers on both sides of the Atlantic, and his early short lyric "God's-Acre" (1842) was known everywhere. Today, he seems to be nearly forgotten or looked down upon. Only his name has survived, and, in the United States, one occasionally dines at a restaurant with Longfellow in its name. In similar fashion, numerous towns in Italy have hotels called "Byron." Perhaps this is real immortality.

Be that as it may, even in Minneapolis, where I live and where there is Hiawatha Avenue, Nokomis Avenue, and a statue of Hiawatha carrying his bride over Minnehaha Falls, I have never met a single student who has read *The Song of Hiawatha* (to say nothing of Longfellow's short poems). But in Longfellow's lifetime, "God's-Acre" became an anthologized piece. It begins so: "I like that ancient Saxon phrase, which calls / The burial ground God's-Acre! It is just; / It consecrates each grave within its walls, / And breathes a benison o'er the sleeping dust." The poem goes on for three more stanzas before it reaches the conclusion: "With thy rude ploughshares, Death, turn up the sod, / And spread the furrow for the seed we sow; / This is the field and Acre of our God, / This is the place where human harvests grow."

What is "the ancient Saxon phrase" that Longfellow liked? It did not elude the discussants in *Notes and Queries* that German has the word *Gottesacker* "churchyard," while its English equivalent has not been attested. Let us not forget that the first volume of the *OED*, with the word *acre* in it, became available only in 1884. Some contributors to *Notes and Queries* missed the point when they said that German

Acker and English *acre* are related and believed that they had solved the problem. Of course, they are, but cognates don't have to mean the same. Thanks to the citations in the *OED* and the material supplied by Walz, we now know that, before Longfellow, *God's acre* occurred almost only in descriptions of Germany and with reference to the German idiom. The meaning of *almost* in the previous sentence will be made clear below. German *Acker* means "field" (like Latin *ager*). The "ancient Saxon phrase" did not exist (even in German, it appeared only in the sixteenth century), but thanks to Longfellow, *God's acre* is now part of the English vocabulary. How he came across it is not a secret.

Albert Matthews, an outstanding researcher of American English, provided some facts when Walz had asked him about *God's Acre*, the burial place in Cambridge, Massachusetts. It turned out that this name was current at the end of the seventeenth century. It is again met with in 1827. We can conclude that the equivalent of the German compound had some currency in Cambridge quite early. There is no way of ascertaining how it reached the East Coast, but reach it did, most probably via German speakers. As Matthews pointed out, Longfellow did not come to Cambridge before 1836. He loved the town (see his lyric "To the River Charles") and could not help hearing the name of the burial place in it. It struck him as poetic. He assumed that the name was very old, even ancient, and used it in his lyric. (Longfellow knew several languages, as, among other things, his translations from German, Italian, and Old English show.) Without it, *God's acre* (or *God's-acre*) would not have become a familiar phrase in English. However, as far as etymology is concerned, it remains a borrowing from German, and Longfellow knew it. The *Century Dictionary* quotes from his *Hyperion* (II. 9): "A green terrace or platform on which the church stands, and which in ancient times was the churchyard, or, as the Germans more devoutly say, God's-acre."

Rotten Row

Perhaps *Rotten Row* means what it says, namely, "rotten row," but more likely, this etymology is an illusion. The main difficulty in a search for the origin of *Rotten Row* is that streets bearing this name are numerous in the north of England and in Scotland. *Rotten Row* in Hyde Park goes back to the end of the eighteenth century, while the place name, distinct from the street name, occurs as early as 1561, and the variants of *Rotten Row* in Glasgow were known a hundred years earlier; thus, the fashionable bridle path in the capital could not be the model other towns emulated. The borrowing went in the opposite direction.

These are some of the derivations of *Rotten Row* in my database. (1) From Latin *Ratumena Porta*, allegedly called this in memory of some Ratumena, a charioteer who died at that gate in Ancient Rome. The accident was sad, but, as far as we are concerned, it can be dismissed without much regret. (2) From Latin *rota* "wheel" and "chariot." This guess has no advantage over the previous one. Latin place names are numerous in Britain, but they are old, while no record of *Rotten Row* has been traced to the Anglo-Saxon times. In Medieval Latin, *rota* also meant "road," but why should an undistinguished road have been given a bookish foreign name? (3) From the woolen stuff called *rateen*. The etymon of the English word is French, and in English, *rateen* turned up too late to be of use in the present context, but a Rateenrow seems to have been mentioned in 1437 in Bury St. Edmund's, which was the great cloth mart of the northeastern parts of the kingdom. (4) From the Old Germanic word *rot* "a file of soldiers" (compare German *Rotte*; many senses, including "pack; herd"; otherwise, a common military term). Although English *rat* "a file of soldiers" occurred regularly in the seventeenth century, it hardly has anything to do with *Rotten Row*. A similar derivation connects *Rotten Row* with the verb *rottaran* "to muster." I am not sure in which language this verb has been attested, but the famous William Camden (1551–1623), the author of this etymology, hardly invented it.

(5) A folk etymological "corruption" of French *Route du Rois* "King's Way" (an explanation one can find in numerous editions of Baedeker's guide to London); a similar Irish Gaelic etymon, with the transliteration *Rathad'n Righ*, has also been proposed. The streets called Rotten Row were, most certainly, not meant for royalty, while London's Rotten Row is relatively recent (see above). (6) From *Rother Row, rother*

being an old word for "cattle." No historical evidence shows that cattle were ever driven along any Rotten Row. Rother Street in Stratford-upon-Avon exists, and there is a family name Rother (the meaning is no longer understood, which is a blessing in disguise: compare the family name Heifer). One can see that Rother Street has not become Rotten Street. (7) From Old Icelandic *ruddr*, the past participle of a verb meaning "make a clearing" (its English cognate is *rid* in *get rid of*). Allegedly, *ruddr vegr* meant "a smoothed, paved way." The chance of any Rotten Row having once been a paved way, an analogue of the Anglo-Saxon *via strata*, is vanishingly small.

(8) From the name of someone who had a business in that area; the name was said to contain a German cognate of English *red*. This eponymous ancestor of Rotten Row, supposedly a purveyor of red herrings (!), is no more probable than the Roman charioteer. By contrast, some people derived *Rotten* directly from English *red*. (9) From Old English *rōt* (with a long vowel) "glad; bright; noble." Was Rotten Row named for its splendor? (10) From English *rattin* "undressed timber." This is a ghost word (it never existed). (11) From *Routine Row*, on account of the processions of the church passing in that direction.

A knowledgeable author summarized the case in 1867 so: "[These derivations] are all destitute of any substruction of historical evidence, and are all purely speculative or fanciful." Before I mention the only hypotheses that, in my opinion, deserve consideration, the following may perhaps be stated with some confidence. The Middle English name seems to have originated in the north. Alliteration and a shocking meaning contributed to its popularity. The vogue for *Rotten Row* makes it unnecessary to reconstruct the circumstances that led to the naming of each street called this. *Rotten Row* does not owe its origin to a local personal name or a local event.

Two etymologies sound more or less realistic. Streets were often infested with rats. In Scottish and northern English dialects, *rattan* and *rottan* mean "rat." *Rotten Row* emerges as *Rat Row*. Conversely, many streets, regardless of the presence of rats, were indeed rotten, with decayed houses on both sides (for instance, a place called Rotten Spot, near Sheffield, probably had some "rotten" structures in it), though the epithet *rotten* may at one time have referred to the surface good for the hooves. If that putative meaning had any currency in eighteenth-century London, *Rotten Row* in Hyde Park was a playful adoption of the widespread name, with reference to the quality of the road. *Route du Rois* would not have degenerated into *Rotten Row* so quickly under the influence of folk etymology. Hesitatingly, I would vote for the *rat* etymology.

14

Some of Our Greats

Walter W. Skeat

No one has been mentioned more often in these pages than Walter W. Skeat (1835–1912), and now that I have reached the end of the book, a few lines about that man may be not entirely out of place. In my library carrel, I keep several cartons full of paper clippings, the fruit of the loom that has been whirring incessantly for more than three decades devoted to English etymology: hundreds of short and long articles about lexicographers, with Skeat occupying a place of honor.

A self-educated man in everything that concerned the history of Germanic, he became the greatest expert in Old and Middle English and a brilliant etymologist. In England, only James A. H. Murray, the editor of the *Oxford English Dictionary* (*OED*), and Henry Sweet were his equals, and in Germany, only Eduard Sievers and Friedrich Kluge. Joseph Wright, the editor of the multivolume *English Dialect Dictionary*, was interested in many things outside English philology, but for Skeat, English remained the prime object of research all his life. Like most people who learned so much the hard way (i.e., on their own), he despised ignorance, especially when it hid behind pretense and pomposity. A professor (though not burdened with too much teaching, especially by modern standards) and a family man (yet in this area he could not compete with Murray, the father of a whole brood of children: Skeat had two sons and a daughter), he never flinched at the idea of writing an edifying or indignant letter to the editor for he was a born enlightener. His perennial target was the inability of his countrymen to understand that etymology is a science rather than mildly intelligent guesswork.

James Murray often asked the readers of popular journals (especially of *Notes and Queries*) to send him information on the words he was editing, and his letters used to end with this refrain: "But please send me facts, not guesses." Skeat offered a short "treatise" on this subject.

> As to "guesses," they differ greatly. It is quite one thing for a person to make them without any investigation and in defiance of all known phonetic and philological laws; and quite another thing to offer a suggestion for which it is worth after all available means of obtaining information have been exhausted. It is a curious thing that the worse a guess is the more obstinately it is maintained, the object being to hide ignorance by raising a cloud of dust. . . . The whole matter lies in a nutshell. If a man is entirely ignorant of botany or chemistry, he leaves those subjects alone. But if a man is entirely ignorant of the principles of philology (which has lately [1877] made enormous advances), he does not leave the subject alone, but considers his "opinions" as good as the most assured results of the most competent scholars. The knowledge of a language is often supposed to carry with it the knowledge of the laws of formation of the language. But this is not in the least the case. . . . My object has always been the same, viz., to protest against the usual state of things. In course of time the lesson will be learnt that there is really no glory to be got by making elementary blunders, or by suggesting ridiculous emendations even of Shakespeare. I cannot at all acquiesce in the notion that people who talk nonsense must never be reproved for it.

As an illustration of the principle that there is no glory to be got by making elementary blunders, I will quote Skeat's pronouncement on the word *bower* and on his opponent, a certain A. H.: "I submit that Old English should be learnt, like any other subject, by honest hard work, and the sense of old words ought not to be evolved from one's internal consciousness. . . . A. H. is merely showing us how little he has really studied the subject." The abrasive tone of Skeat's letters made many people wince: after all, no one likes being called an obstinate fool in public. Occasionally, the victims of his wrath tried to defend themselves, but very rarely did they know enough to be in a position to win the game on Skeat's field. More often than not, they hid behind what Skeat called a cloud of dust. Then he would strike back: "I do not understand what I have done to draw upon myself the ungenerous attack at the last reference. Even a professor is entitled to fair play, and I will now show that, in the opinion of impartial readers, he has not had it."

Miss Busk (i.e., Rachel Harriett Busk, a traveler and noted folklorist) was certainly not one of those ignoramuses whom Skeat loved to demolish, but the two did not see eye to eye on the origin of some words. Skeat: "I cannot feel that Miss Busk's account of me is quite accurate, and therefore beg leave to say a few 'last words.' It is not the case that I 'wince at a few knocks in return.' I have been attacked over and over again, and rather like it, if by such means we can get nearer to the truth. I have always accepted every correction that could be proved, and many such have been proved. . . . What I complain of is that any one should set himself up as correcting me when there is nothing to show that I am wrong; I cannot help feeling that it was merely my reputation that brought it upon me, and that it was not at all provoked by my combativeness." He said he would "retire" and stop writing letters. The editor of *Notes and Queries* begged him to reconsider, and the result was more letters and more sneers. Busk: "Prof. Skeat's lament is very pathetic. . . . When circumstances have put a person in possession of any department of knowledge, be it small or great, nothing can be more irritating than the pecking comments of self-constituted critics, who, whatever their attainments along other lines, are clearly not up to the work on which they yet presume to publish their judgment. But in the present instance, if, as the learned professor complains, a 'desire to correct him continually increases', is it not, perhaps, provoked by the tone in which he is rather fond of correcting others?" In parentheses, I may mention the fact that the style of British nineteenth-century reviewers was often unbelievably abrasive, especially because reviews were often anonymous. In *Notes and Queries*, all letters were signed, but frequently by pseudonyms: Alpha, Omega, Z. or for a change, *** (i.e., three asterisks).

Laurence Urdang (a noted lexicographer, editor, and author: 1927–2008) once brought out an article titled "The (Invariably) Right Reverend Walter W. Skeat" (*Verbatim*, Spring 1991; Skeat was indeed Reverend). His selection of quotes was similar to mine (we even share one), but I disagree most heartily with Urdang's calling Skeat an intellectual bully (though he does say at the beginning that Skeat was one of the greatest linguists of all time). Skeat was human and made mistakes and more than once "got into a serious hobble," but he was a Gulliver, and a host of the Lilliputians usually succeeds in tying each hair of a giant in such a way that he is unable to move his head. Urdang (or somebody else?) sent the article from *Verbatim* to Theodore Skeat, Walter W. Skeat's grandson, whose response appeared in the same journal five years later. It confirms some things we learn from Skeat's statements. For example, he dreamed of obscurity: "If I remain in health and strength a few years hence [1886; he, it will be remembered, died in 1912], and if such correspondents as waste my time by expecting me to answer questions which I either do not understand or which I have answered already many times only leave me alone, I should much like to rewrite the whole book [his etymological dictionary], as I do not see how else to reform it. The penny post is a hard task-master as well as a source of kindly help. What hours have I wasted in trying to meet demands! I do not think the modern system of *always expecting an answer* is at all fair, or even moral."

Alas, his dream of returning to obscurity did not come true. His grandson remembers: "he was constantly deluged with letters from complete strangers demanding to be told the etymology of various words, and I am not at all surprised that he should have shown irritation with those who had not even taken the elementary steps of consulting either his own dictionary or the *N.E.D.* [= *OED*]." After his death, his two sons "spent weeks tearing up old letters." I think I have read somewhere that they obeyed the wish of their father. Only a few letters survived: James A. H. Murray, on hearing of Skeat's death, recovered those he had sent him.

Let me finish with a few more lines from Skeat's pen. (Urdang also quotes part of this passage): "I do not set myself for a moment as a master of style, and I should advise no one to imitate any expression that I may use. I am merely a humble collector of facts, always endeavouring to find out authorities and quotations for the instruction of others. But I do not advise any one to ignore my authorities." Humble he was certainly not (humble and modest people, as we know, usually have a good reason for displaying those admirable qualities), but, like every true scholar, he realized the magnitude of the problems he was expected to solve and his inability to hew down a mountain before which he stood. Yet he hammered away bravely. Hail to the Chief!

Joseph Wright

Joseph Wright (1855–1930) was not an etymologist, but few articles on the origin of English words can do without consulting the *English Dialect Dictionary* he edited. This multivolume masterpiece contains thousands of local words whose existence reveals unsuspected and unexpected ties between the words all of us know and their "provincial" kin. Wright first attempted to offer tentative etymologies in his entries, but then, most wisely, gave up this practice. The descent of the words with which he dealt is often so obscure that guesses would have done the users only harm. Sometimes the source of a rural word is evidently French or Scandinavian, but in most cases no clue suggests itself.

Those who are in the habit of looking up word origins in our "thick" dictionaries or searching for them on the Internet may have noticed how often the etymological comments there run no further than "dialectal" or "slang," as though such references meant anything. English contains numerous words about whose origin nothing is or can be known because some of them came from the creative brain of an imaginative person now dead for centuries, or the coinage was triggered by a sound symbolic impulse or a joke (word creation and humor is a most promising topic). We are usually unable to reconstruct the impulses that resulted in the birth of a word, whether short-lived and geographically restricted or durable and used in several counties.

The life of Joseph Wright should serve as an inspiration to anyone who wants to understand the meaning of the phrase *self-made man*. A Yorkshire lad (born as the seventh son of a wool weaver), he became fully literate by the age of fifteen, ended up as an Oxford professor of comparative philology, and was the author of exemplary textbooks of Greek, Gothic, Old and Middle High German, and Old and Middle English. But his main achievement was the *English Dialect Dictionary* (it ends with a book-length supplement on English dialect grammar), a mammoth enterprise, which he, though not a rich man, partly financed, and which he considered to be his main contribution to linguistics.

He married his former student (Elizabeth Mary Lea, 1863–1958), who later co-authored his books on the history of English, though, according to her own statement, she was mainly responsible for collecting data. In 1932, that is, soon after her husband's death, she brought out a two-volume book titled *The Life of Joseph Wright*, 720 pages in all, supplied with a detailed index. Not only is this book valuable because it is based on the author's unique knowledge of the subject, but also because Elizabeth Wright (Lizzie, as those close to the family called her) quoted numerous documents and letters in it. Even the slightly hagiographic tone of the exposition does not spoil it. In her book *Rustic Speech and Folklore*, she also recounts their walks and scholarly pursuits in Yorkshire.

For Joseph Wright, Standard English was a foreign language, and, after a stroke, he tended to relapse more and more into the dialect of his childhood and youth. But even much earlier, his little son used to tease him when he heard his father pronounce a word like *Puck* with the vowel of *put*. Elizabeth Wright reported that the last word of her dying husband was *dictionary*. One need not concoct a pseudo-psychological story around this episode. Joseph Wright was not only aware of Elizabeth's compiling his biography but he also helped her do the work, and *dictionary* was his "last will and testament." His mind was unaffected by the pneumonia that carried him away, and he wanted to remind his wife that the production of the dictionary should be described as the defining event of his life.

Wright's career was brilliant, but his life was far from unclouded. The son and the daughter the couple had died in childhood, and the son's death was particularly tragic: purportedly, he was stung by an insect that had fed on poison, and blood poisoning killed him in a matter of hours. When he was born, his elder sister, also quite small at the time, called her brother "boy," and that is why he was known to everybody not as Willie but as Boy. The girl died of pneumonia several years later. The parents never overcame their grief, even though they continued to work with the same dedication. But, even to a linguist, living children are more meaningful than colorful vernaculars, let alone dead languages.

Elizabeth Wright did not mention an event that was significant in her husband's life. As a young man, he went to Heidelberg, studied there, learned German very well, and returned home. Back in England, he wrote the first ever grammar of an English dialect and was invited to teach at Oxford, where the main figure in linguistics was the great Max

Müller, a man universally admired at the peak of his career and universally mocked during the last years of his life and after his death. (Both verdicts were unjust.) Wright's position was that of a lecturer, but later he was promoted to deputy professor. Finally, Oxford instituted a chair of comparative philology.

At that time, advertisements for such positions were more rarely seen in England than a blue moon. There were two contenders: Joseph Wright and Henry Sweet, one of the founders of English historical linguistics. When Wright applied for deputy professorship, Sweet wrote a warm recommendation letter for him. Now in contention for the deputy professorship, they were rivals. The chair went to Wright. Sweet felt insulted and did not forgive the world for its treatment of him. As a man of ideas, he was far better qualified for the job than Wright. Yet the outcome had two beneficial consequences for scholarship: Sweet, in order to sustain himself, continued to produce his excellent books (published by Oxford University Press), while Wright might never have completed his dictionary without getting the position. To think of the choice Oxford had: Joseph Wright or Henry Sweet! Anyone in present-day academia may remember the last search in which he or she participated.

And now I would like to return to Skeat. Not everybody knows that we owe the existence of the English Dialect Society to the indefatigable Walter W. Skeat, who did a great lot of editing for it and participated in its meetings in different towns. His support for Wright's work was vital. Today, everybody extols Wright's dictionary, but, at the end of the nineteenth and the beginning of the twentieth century, no one was in a hurry to back it up with grants. At all times, people send good wishes much more readily than checks (cheques). The dictionary opens with the following dedication: "To the Rev. Professor W. W. Skeat, Litt.D. D.C.L., Founder and President of the English Dialect Society, Editor of 'Chaucer,' 'Piers Plowman,' and 'The Bruce,' the unwearied Worker in the varied Field of English Scholarship, to whose patient industry and contagious enthusiasm in connexion with the laborious task of accumulating dialect material the possibility of compiling an adequate Dictionary of English Dialects is mainly due." Skeat wrote in his testimonial: "After the work had . . . been at a standstill for at least a couple of years (if I remember rightly), I was so fortunate as to

discover in Dr. Wright the only man capable of undertaking the task."
And now a longer quotation from the biography: "In the autumn of
1899 Professor (now Sir) Israel Gollancz was raising money for a portrait of Professor Skeat, 'and *also* to found a University Prize—a Skeat
University Prize for English.' In a letter thanking Joseph Wright for 'a
generous subscription' he said, Nov. 27, 1899: 'S. has done so much for
English. Perhaps he never did a better thing than when he got you to
edit the Dialect Dictionary. He could not have imagined, however, that
it would be so glorious an achievement. God bless you for it!' " (p. 415).

The picture of Joseph Wright in his native Thackley graces the frontispiece of volume 1 of *The Life of Joseph Wright*. The best-known portrait of Skeat is, I think, the one for which Gollancz was raising money
in 1899.

The Word "Folklore" and Its Inventor
William John Thoms

William John Thoms (1802–1885) began his literary career as editor
of old tales and prose romances. He also investigated customs and
superstitions. Especially interesting are his studies of popular lore
in Shakespeare: elves, fairies, Puck, Queen Mab, and others. They
were published in the 1840s, the decade in which he met his star
hour. Special works on Thoms are extremely few, and the archival
documents pertaining to him remain untapped, but he related some
events of his life himself. It was not by chance that *California Folklore
Quarterly* printed an article about him (" 'Folklore': William John
Thoms" by Duncan Emrich, volume 5, 1946, pp. 355–74). (I could not
find a more recent publication on him.) A hundred years earlier, that is,
in 1846, a letter signed by Ambrose Merton appeared in the London-
based journal *The Athenæum*. Those who have leafed through its huge
folio volumes probably could not help wondering how the subscribers
managed to find their way through such an enormous mass of heter-
ogeneous materials. Yet that weekly had a devoted readership, and its
voice reached far.

The 1846 letter is available in two modern anthologies but, outside the professional circle of folklorists, hardly anyone has read it.

Therefore, I will quote its beginning and end. "Your pages have so often given evidence of the interest which you take in what we in England designate as Popular Antiquities, or Popular Literature (though by-the-by it is more a Lore than a literature, and would be most aptly described by a good Saxon compound, Folklore,—*the Lore of the People*)—that I am not without hopes of enlisting your aid in garnering the few ears which are remaining, scattered over that field from which our forefathers might have gathered a goodly crop. No one who has made the manners, customs, observances, superstitions, ballads, proverbs, etc., of the olden time his study, but must have arrived at two conclusions:—the first how much that is curious and interesting in those matters is now entirely lost—the second, how much may yet be rescued by timely exertion. . . . It is only honest that I should tell you I have long been contemplating a work upon our 'Folklore' (*under that title*, mind Messes. A, B, and C,—so do not try to forestall me);— and I am personally interested in the success of the experiment which I have, in this letter, albeit imperfectly, urged you to undertake." Not only did the editor of *The Athenaeum* welcome the letter: he opened a special rubric for "folk-lore," and "Ambrose Merton" (this was Thoms of course) became its editor.

The letter was followed by an injunction, part of which is so much to the point that it, too, must be reproduced here: "We have taken some time to weigh the suggestion of our correspondent—desirous to satisfy ourselves that any good of the kind which he proposes could be effected in such space as we are able to spare from the many other demands upon our columns; and have before our eyes the fear of that shower of trivial communication which a notice in conformity with his suggestion is likely to bring. We have finally decided that, if our antiquarian correspondents be earnest and well-informed and subject their communications to the condition of having something to communicate, we may . . . be the means of effecting some valuable salvage for the future historian of old customs and feelings. . . . With these views, however, we must announce to our future contributors under the above head, that their communications will be subjected to a careful sifting— both as regards value, authenticity, and novelty; and that they will save both themselves and us much unnecessary trouble if they will refrain from offering any facts and speculations which at once *need* recording and deserve it."

Thoms may have regretted the fact that he wrote his letter to *The Athenaeum* under a pseudonym because, a year later, in another letter to the same journal, he disclosed his identity. He more than once reminded his readers that it had been he who launched the word *folklore*. From time to time somebody would derive *folklore* from German or Danish. As long as he lived, Thoms kept refuting such unworthy rumors (he also suffered from the neglect of his Shakespeare scholarship); after his death others defended him.

The word found acceptance in both the English-speaking world and abroad. German, Austrian, and Swiss scholars eventually borrowed it with its original spelling (*folklore*), though the German for *folk* is *Volk*. By the end of the 1880s, *folklore* had become an accepted term in Scandinavia, as well as in the Romance- and Slavic-speaking countries. The British Folklore Society, which was also formed largely thanks to Thoms's efforts, adopted the title *Folk-Lore Record* for its journal (now it is called simply *Folklore*), and Thoms was elected the Society's director. In the introduction to the first volume, he noted, perhaps not without a touch of irony, that the word he had coined would make him better known than the rest of his professional activities.

As we have seen, the "Saxon" term *folklore* was applied to the vanishing "manners, customs, observances, superstitions, ballads, proverbs, etc." Thoms did not realize how ambiguous his agenda was. For more than 150 years, researchers have been arguing over whether the subject of folklore is only "survivals" (i.e., does modern folklore exist?); who are the "people," the "folk" to be approached; and whether folklore is the name of the treasures to be collected and described or of the science ("the lore") devoted to them.

Today, folklore is often understood as a study of verbal art, but not less often it passes off as a branch of cultural anthropology. In 1846, *folk* meant "peasantry," which excluded urban culture. One also spoke vaguely of common people, of storytellers nearly untouched by the advance of civilization, and of the working people in the "byeways of England" (the phrase, spelling and all, is from *The Gentleman's Magazine* for 1885). Railways were the main bugaboo of those who watched the rural landscape disappear under the wheels of the devil, the steam engine. Being run over by a train became a literary motif. (Both Dickens and Lev Tolstoy made use of it.)

In 1849, an event of great importance happened in Thoms's life: he began publishing his own weekly, which, after rejecting many titles and ignoring the warnings of some well-wishers, he decided, "on the advice of a learned lady," to call *Notes and Queries*. His old appeal to the readers to send ballads, tales, proverbs, descriptions of customs, and so forth brought many responses, and Thoms was loath to start a rival periodical for fear of undermining *The Athenæum*, but he received the editor's blessing. The new journal turned into a main forum for letters that Thoms had invited correspondents to send to *The Athenæum*. The rubric on "folk-lore" in both periodicals made the term familiar, and later two derivatives (*folklorist* and *folkloric*) emerged.

Before resigning as editor, Thoms told the story of his magazine in a series of short essays and published them in *Notes and Queries* for 1871 and 1872. In 1848, Dickens's novel *Dombey and Son* appeared. One of the novel's most endearing characters is the one-armed Captain Cuttle. Like so many other personages brought to life by Dickens, the good captain had a tag: he liked to repeat the maxim "When found, make a note of." Thoms used this catchphrase as a motto for his journal, and it was printed on the title page of each issue.

The magazine *Notes and Queries* is one of a kind. As must have become clear from this book, I owe a tremendous debt of gratitude to it because suggestions on word origins were (and still are) common in *Notes and Queries*, and I have nearly eight thousand of them in my etymological database. Many important words have been discussed only in its pages (e.g., see *henchman*, in Chapter 3). Some first-rate specialists, including the first editors of the *Oxford English Dictionary* (James A. H. Murray and Henry Bradley), asked questions and shared their thoughts in the pages of *Notes and Queries*. The great philologist Walter W. Skeat sent countless letters to the journal in which he offered and defended his etymologies, fought his opponents, and berated his countrymen for their ignorance and inborn inability to be like him. Joseph Wright, the editor of the great *English Dialect Dictionary*, and the now all but forgotten but astute polymath Frank Chance, who sometimes managed to bring down even Skeat a peg or two, sought no better exposure to their ideas.

Prime ministers, admirals, and important politicians were among the contributors, along with many a pushy whippersnapper who wanted to see their names in print and a host of self-effacing people with pseudonyms like *** and Zero. The periodical owed its allure to its omnivorous nature. John Thoms's venture was so successful that its regional and foreign cousins sprang up in many counties and abroad, from India to the United States. Some of them still exist, long after the illustrious *Athenæum* (1828–1921) brought out its last issue.

The man who invented the word *folklore* and founded *Notes and Queries* deserves to be remembered, and I am sorry that no one has written a book about him (see some information about his family in Mr. John Clinton's comment in the blog "Oxford Etymologist" for July 9, 2008). The reason may be that he was neither a professor nor a madman. Perfectly sane and of humble origin, he was survived by his wife and nine children.

Index

For the benefit of digital users, indexed terms that span two pages (e.g., 52–53) may, on occasion, appear on only one of those pages.

Danish, 243
Dante, 191–92
Davis, N. Darnell, 158–59
days of the week, 165
de [as infix], 187
declensions
  Gothic, 205
  Latin, 38–39, 60
  Old English, 207–8
DeMaria, Robert Jr., 228–29
De Morgan, A., 247
Dent, Joseph, 2
de Saussure, Ferdinand, 151–52
deterioration of meaning, 102
de Vries, Jan, 152, 216
Dickens, Charles, 31, 96–97, 277–78, 287–88, 319
dictionaries, 1, 40, 223
  Century Dictionary, 86, 267–68
  conflict between, 267–68
  English Dialect Dictionary, 313
  etymological, 66–67, 152
  Glossographia, 126–27
  Nathaniel Bailey's, 19–20
  Samuel Johnson's, 101
  of slang, 47, 81
  Urban Dictionary, 24
  Websters, 18–19
  See also Oxford English Dictionary
Diez, Friedrich Christian, 179–80
Digges, Leonard, 246
dildo, 248–51
dilly-dally, 250
dodge, 287–92
Drake, Daniel, 269–70, 271
dregs, 218–19
drinking songs, 32
dross, 218–19
drum, 283
dude, 4–5, 113–17
duet, 6
Dunn, Jacob Piatt, 272–73

Eaton, 50
Edgcumbe, Richard, 302–3
el [as suffix], 76–77
elves, 192–93

enantiosemy, 172
English
  American, 85, 255, 279
  history of, 3, 103–4
  Middle, 5
  Old, 5, 230
  relation to Celtic languages, 129–30
  word origins, 239
English Dialect Dictionary, 313
English Dialect Society, 315–16
erotic slang, 23
et [as suffix], 140–41
etymology
  bibliography of, 275
  politicization of, 267–68
  practice of, 180–81, 221, 228, 269–70, 289–90
  publishing, 162–63
Eurasia, 234
European common slang, 109
Everyman's Library, 2
exclamations, 150

fag, 46
fairies, 169–71, 198–99
fairy tales, 73
Falk, Hjalmar, 240–41
fanciful words, 86
Farrar, William M., 270
father, 30, 144–45
Fell, Christine, 259–60
finger, 141–46
Finley, John, 272–73
fist, 144
Flasdieck, Hermann M., 193, 194, 195
flowerbed, 215–16
folk etymology, 185, 213
folk rhymes, 9–10, 12
folklore, 93–94, 169–70, 273, 316–20
  British, 192–93, 195
  German, 73
  Scandinavian, 192–93, 195, 297
  urban, 294–95
  See also mythology
folklore, 316–20
fond, 102
Foote, Samuel, 39